THE POLITICAL ECONOMY OF NEW ZEALAND

Edited by Chris Rudd and Brian Roper

Auckland

OXFORD UNIVERSITY PRESS

Oxford Melbourne New York

OXFORD UNIVERSITY PRESS NEW ZEALAND

Oxford New York
Athens Auckland Bangkok Bombay
Calcutta Cape Town Dar es Salaam Delhi
Florence Hong Kong Istanbul Karachi
Kuala Lumpur Madras Madrid Melbourne
Mexico City Nairobi Paris Port Moresby
Singapore Taipei Tokyo Toronto

and associated companies in
Berlin Ibadan

OXFORD is a trade mark of Oxford University Press

ISBN 019 558331 0

Edited by Anna Rogers
Indexed by Simon Cauchi
Cover design by Anitra Blackford
Typeset by Egan-Reid Ltd
Printed through Bookpac Production Services, Singapore
Published by Oxford University Press,
540 Great South Road, Greenlane, PO Box 11-149,
Auckland, New Zealand

CONTENTS

Part III: The State

Introduction: New Zealand's Economy, Civil Society, and State During the Postwar Era

CHRIS RUDD AND BRIAN ROPER

The studies in this volume investigate the major changes in New Zealand's political economy that have taken place during the twentieth century, focusing in particular on the postwar era. New Zealand's history during this period can be divided into two distinct epochs. The first, from 1945 to 1973, was characterised by economic prosperity and, at least until the late 1960s, societal integration and political stability. The second, from 1974 to the 1990s, has been characterised by economic stagnation (the cyclical recovery of the mid-1990s must be placed in the context of the recessions that preceded and will follow it), societal conflict, and political instability. Fundamental changes in the economy and civil society including, among others, the collapse of the postwar long boom, the rise of business political activism, the upsurge of increasingly bitter class conflict, growing inequality in the distribution of income and wealth, increasing politicisation of gender and ethnic inequalities, and a shift in the prevailing economic orthodoxy from Keynesianism to neoclassicism, generated the paradigm shift in policy-making from social democratic Keynesianism to New Right neoclassicism that occurred during the 1980s.

Precisely because the state is not an isolated and free-floating ensemble of institutions that operate regardless of the structuration of, and conflicts within, civil society, it is vitally important to place the state firmly in the context of the economic system and civil society in which it is embedded. Consequently the paradigmatic shift in policy-making from social democratic Keynesianism to New Right neoclassicism that took place during the 1980s must be understood, at least in large part, as a product of structural crises and conflicts occurring outside the state itself. Further, in order to understand this fundamental shift in policy-making, and hence New Zealand's political history during the entire postwar era, it is necessary to identify and investigate closely interrelated changes in the economy, civil society, and polity that have occurred during the twentieth century. This has meant trying to locate the specific aspect of New Zealand's political economy being considered within its wider economic, social, and political context and also to provide an historical analysis that investigates changes in the area being considered over prolonged periods of time.

Placing issues of New Zealand's political economy in an historical perspective poses numerous problems. As the chapters clearly show, certain time periods are more crucial than others to the development of particular aspects of New Zealand's political economy. It must also be recognised that there are different theoretical approaches to interpreting these historical developments. Anyone familiar with events in New Zealand since the fourth Labour Government came to power in 1984 will be aware of the New Right or neoclassical critique of the previous government's attempt to manage the economy and of what should be done to correct the country's parlous state of economic affairs. Although none of the contributors adopts a New Right approach per se, a number do outline the New Right argument with regard to their own specific area of analysis. Roper, in the first chapter, compares the monetarist explanation of the collapse of the long boom and the mid-1990s recovery with the explanations put forward by Marxists and Keynesians. Bertram, in Chapter 3, spends some time discussing the demise of Keynesian macroeconomics during the 1970s and the rise of monetarist and New Classical approaches. Goldfinch, in his discussion of the Treasury, sets out in some detail the extent to which Treasury adopted a New Right approach in its various briefings to government. Given its strategic institutional location within the machinery of government, Treasury was critical in facilitating the paradigmatic shift from Keynesianism to neoclassicism—and this in spite of Treasury's portrayal of itself as a neutral, independent, and value-free adviser to the government.

In their discussion of trade unions, Bramble and Heal review the New Right or 'unitarist' interpretation of the role of unions, an interpretation that they reject but nevertheless acknowledge as underpinning industrial relations reform of the 1990s. Again, without subscribing to the point of view, Hyman in her chapter sets out the neoclassical arguments with respect to gender inequality in the labour market, forcefully rebutting this with a feminist account. In particular, Hyman points out that while economic restructuring has offered some possibilities for the advancement of women, its major impact has been to increase the employment of women in service sector work that has been overwhelmingly of a low-paid and low-skilled nature. In the field of education, Freeman-Moir notes the growing influence of New Right or neoliberal theory on educational thinking since the mid-1980s. Finally, in his historical study of the New Zealand welfare state, Rudd shows how New Right thinking informed the major changes to welfare policy under the fourth Labour and fourth National Governments.

At the other end of the ideological spectrum, a Marxist approach to New Zealand's political economy is central to a number of chapters. Again, Roper sets the framework for analysis with his Marxist explanation of New Zealand's economic stagnation after 1973. This is followed by Maitra's chapter, which seeks to locate contemporary economic developments in New Zealand within the three broad phases of the globalisation of capitalism, the first of which began with New Zealand's mid-nineteenth century colonisation. In Maitra's view, the economic deregulation and liberalisation of the 1980s onwards is the inevitable consequence of the globalisation of investment. The continuation of a 'large state' has become 'a hindrance to the accumulation of global capital' and this accounts for the pressure on New Zealand governments to reduce 'unproductive' welfare spending.

In his chapter on the origins and development of the class structure in New Zealand, Roper offers two contrasting interpretations, Weberian and Marxist. Both approaches consider that the empirical manifestations of socio-economic inequality are determined by underlying structural class relations, but whereas Weberians conceptualise these class relations in terms of market situation and power, Marxists conceptualise class relations in terms of exploitation. In actual fact, income and wealth inequalities have been growing since the economic reforms introduced by the fourth Labour Government and have continued under the following fourth National Government. Like Roper, Poata-Smith is concerned with the structural mechanisms of capitalist society. Poata-Smith, however, focuses on how these structural mechanisms have generated and entrenched the inequalities between Maori and Pakeha rather than between social classes in general. He shows how capitalist economic development in New Zealand has led to the systematic oppression of Maori, beginning with the expropriation of Maori land during the nineteenth century, the proletarianisation of Maori during the long boom, and, most recently, the disproportionate costs borne by the Maori community as a result of the economic restructuring of the 1980s and 1990s.

The analyses of Roper and Poata-Smith can be contrasted with those of the New Right, which would rather view income and ethnic inequalities as the result of work effort and individual initiative—even luck—rather than conclude that they are the result of the very nature of the capitalist mode of economic production. Mulgan, in his pluralist analysis of New Zealand democracy, also recognises the division of society into different social groups, with some groups systematically more influential than others in shaping government policy. Such inequalities do not, however, lead pluralists to propose, as Marxists do, a complete transformation of society. For pluralists, no one social division predominates and the existence of countervailing forces means that, although liberal democracy in New Zealand is far from an ideal form of democracy, it is the best that can be realistically hoped for. Mulgan also explores the possible impact that the introduction of the mixed member proportional (MMP) system will have on the democratic responsiveness of the New Zealand political system.

Bramble and Heal also base their analysis of unionism in New Zealand on the premise 'that there are two major classes in capitalist society—the capitalist and working classes—with the former constituting a ruling class on the basis of its effective control of the major forms of production'. In this, they reject the New Right view of industrial relations as a mutually beneficial exchange, freely entered into by employers and employees. As Bramble and Heal show, trade unions are severely handicapped when seeking to influence the direction of public policy. In the changed economic environment from the late 1970s onwards, and the anti-union legislation of the 1990s, unions were even further weakened. Business interests, on the other hand, were able to increase their influence over government action and this is illustrated by the two case studies analysed in the preceding chapter by Vowles and Roper.

The final chapter to adopt an explicit Marxist approach is the one by Freeman-Moir concerning education. Whereas some may think it unusual to have a chapter on education in a volume on political economy, as Freeman-Moir succinctly says, 'New Zealand education corresponds to the political economy of capitalist society'. This view may not be shared by those supporting the social democratic or liberal theory of education but it is, ironically, the view of the New Right, who call for a 'restructuring' of education (and all the inequalities in educational opportunities this will entail) to correspond to the restructuring of New Zealand's economy since the 1980s.

Until the 1970s, social democratic Keynesianism was the dominant paradigm for analysing macroeconomic developments in New Zealand and other liberal democratic states. It is not surprising, therefore, that the New Right were quick to place the blame for New Zealand's poor economic performance after 1974 at the feet of the Keynesians. This accusation, as Roper notes, is rejected by the 'PostKeynesians', who claim that Keynesian economic policies were poorly implemented—and that subsequent monetarist policies have only worsened the situation. Bertram, however, attempts in his chapter to demonstrate that Keynesian and neoclassical approaches are not necessarily incompatible. Although both approaches differ in their conceptions of the role of the state in economic management, a synthesis of the two approaches is possible; the proponents of such a view are referred to as 'Market Keynesians'. Vowles and Roper also show in their chapter that the theoretical claims of the various approaches overlap. Rather than try to resolve this by oversimplifying the theories, Vowles and Roper incorporate the various theories into a single model and then test the model's robustness against data derived from two case studies. They find that both neoMarxist and neopluralist perspectives offer plausible explanations of business influence on government policy making in New Zealand.

Finally, there are a number of chapters in this volume that focus on the state, although only the chapter by Walsh would possibly fall into the 'state-centred' approach identified in the literature. Walsh adopts an institutional view of the state's role in managing industrial relations in New Zealand from the 1890s to the 1990s. He shows how the state's industrial relations strategy changed over this period from one of enforcing arbitration to facilitating bargaining. Du Plessis is also concerned with 'the state', this time from the perspective of women and feminist theory. She points out that there is a certain ambivalence to the feminist relationship with the state. On the one hand, the state is as an institutional means to consolidate male privileges; on the other hand, it can be used to improve the lot of women. The welfare state is one such form of state intervention that some feminists view as helping to relieve women's oppression. But, as Rudd details in his historical overview of the development of the welfare state, the state's commitment to the provision of welfare has weakened considerably since the 1970s. After setting out various 'models of welfare', Rudd shows how the New Zealand state has, since the early 1980s, increasingly assumed a residual role in the provision of welfare and, at the same time, has promoted the idea of individual, family, and community responsibility for welfare provision. This will undoubtedly have adverse implications not just for women but for other social groups with weak economic bargaining power.

It can be seen, therefore, that there are many different approaches to the analysis of New Zealand's political economy. It was neither feasible nor desirable for the editors to ask the contributors to discuss and compare all approaches with respect to their particular area of research. Nor was it possible for all contributors to examine developments across the whole postwar period;

events in the 1980s and 1990s were often too central to the analysis to treat in the same way as events during the first three postwar decades. This apparent lack of scope or uniformity of coverage across the chapters is, in the editors' view, an accurate reflection of the complex and multidimensional nature of the topic. If there were one universal approach, or even just two polar opposites, the situation would be simpler—but then there would be much less need for a multidisciplinary volume such as this.

The organisation of the book is as follows. In Part I, the four chapters focus on the economy and economic policy-making. The widespread societal consequences of the economic developments covered in Part I are then discussed in Part II, that is the increases in social, gender, and ethnic inequalities and the shifting balance of power between organised business and organised labour. The final section of the book focuses on the role of the state with regard to education, industrial relations, women, welfare, and democracy.

CONTRIBUTORS

Geoff Bertram is a Senior Lecturer in Economics at Victoria University. He has published in the areas of economic development, the labour market, and state sector reform. His main research interests include energy and environmental economics.

Tom Bramble is a Senior Lecturer in Industrial Relations at the University of Queensland. He is currently researching Australian workplace trade unionism and enterprise bargaining, and is a member of a research team investigating the effects of organisational change on middle management in Australia and New Zealand.

Rosemary Du Plessis is a Senior Lecturer in Sociology at the University of Canterbury. She teaches courses relating to feminist sociology; gender, sexuality and personal narrative; life history analysis and body politics. She is joint editor of *Feminist Voices: Women's Studies Texts for Aotearoa/New Zealand* (1992).

John Freeman-Moir is a Senior Lecturer in the Education Department at the University of Canterbury where he teaches educational and social theory. His most recent publication is an edited collection on Marxism and education.

Shaun Goldfinch is a PhD candidate in the Centre for Public Policy at the University of Melbourne. He has a variety of research interests and has published work on judicial independence and the administration of the courts, small business networking, and public policy formation.

Sarah Heal is a Masters graduate of the Political Studies Department, University of Otago. Her research interests include industrial relations, social policy, and political economy.

Prue Hyman is an Associate Professor in Economics at Victoria University. Her main research area is women and the economy, with particular reference to labour force participation, equal pay, and income maintenance. She has published widely in these areas and is the author of *Women and Economics: A New Zealand Feminist Perspective* (1994).

Priyatosh Maitra is a former Associate Professor in the Economics Department at the University of Otago. His main research interests are in the field of development economics and the globalisation of capital. He is the author of numerous articles and books including *Globalisation and Capitalism in Third World Countries* (1996).

Richard Mulgan is a former Professor of Political Studies in the Universities of Otago and Auckland, currently teaching in the Public Policy Program, Australian National University. His books include *Democracy and Power in New Zealand* (1984 and 1989), *Maori, Pakeha and Democracy* (1989) and *Politics in New Zealand* (1994).

Brian Roper is a Lecturer in the Political Studies Department at the University of Otago. He is coeditor of *State and Economy in New Zealand* (1993). His main research interests are classical and contemporary Marxism, social inequality, political economy and New Zealand politics.

Juliet Roper is a Lecturer in the Department of Management Communication at the University of Waikato. Her main research interests are corporate and political communication. She is currently undertaking a DPhil., for which she is analysing the campaign strategies of the political parties contending the first MMP election.

Chris Rudd is a Senior Lecturer in Political Studies at the University of Otago. His major research interest is the welfare state. He is coeditor of *State and Economy in New Zealand* (1993) and has contributed chapters to *The Decent Society?* (1992) and *Electoral Behaviour in New Zealand* (1992).

Evan Te Ahu Poata-Smith (Te Rarawa and Ngati Kahu) is a PhD candidate in the Political Studies Department at the University of Otago. His main research interest is Maori nationalism. He has published work on Maori political activism and Maori education and inequality.

Jack Vowles is a Senior Lecturer in Political Science and Public Policy at the

University of Waikato. His research interests are in electoral behaviour and comparative public policy. He is coauthor of *Towards Consensus? The 1993 General Election in New Zealand and the Transition to Proportional Representation*; and a co-editor of *The Great Experiment: Labour Parties and Public Policy Transformation in Australia and New Zealand* (both 1995).

Pat Walsh is Associate Professor in Industrial Relations and Public Policy at Victoria University. His main research interests are state sector restructuring, industrial relations, and new developments in human resource management strategies. He is a coeditor of *Reshaping the State* (1991) and coauthor of *The Dynamics of New Zealand Industrial Relations* (1990) and *Public Management: the New Zealand Model* (1996).

PART I

THE ECONOMY

CHAPTER ONE

NEW ZEALAND'S POSTWAR ECONOMIC HISTORY

BRIAN ROPER

The world recession in 1974 marks a crucial turning point in New Zealand's economic history. It separates an epoch of unprecedented growth and prosperity from an epoch of stagnation, declining real incomes, and rising unemployment. Although there was a significant cyclical economic recovery during the mid-1990s, this has not altered the overall contrast in economic performance before and after 1974. This chapter discusses the differing interpretations of this contrast in economic performance by monetarists, Keynesians, and Marxists. It begins by describing in greater depth some central characteristics of New Zealand's economic performance during the postwar era, considers monetarist, Keynesian, and Marxist explanations of the collapse of the postwar long boom, and then discusses, very briefly, monetarist, Keynesian, and Marxist assessments of the mid-1990s economic recovery and the future trajectory of New Zealand's economic development.[1]

End of the Golden Weather: From Boom to Stagnation

Almost all commentators agree that 1974 marks a significant turning point in New Zealand's economic history. The long boom from 1945 to 1973 was characterised by sustained economic growth fuelled by historically high levels of profitability and productive investment, full employment, low inflation, rising real wages, and the absence of prolonged balance of payments problems owing to the historically favourable terms of trade. For much of the period from 1974 to 1991, the New Zealand economy suffered from economic stagnation, high inflation, declining profitability, insufficient and poorly allocated levels of productive investment, historically low terms of trade, recurrent balance of payments deficits, increasing public and private indebtedness, the cessation of real wage growth, the highest level of unemployment since the 1930s, and the most widespread and intense strike activity experienced since the 1951 waterfront dispute. As Table 1.1 shows, the contrast in economic performance is dramatic.

Table 1.1 New Zealand's postwar economic performance averages for years ending March

Period	Real GDP (1)	CPI Inflation (2)	Registered unemployment (3)	Current account (4)
1960–74	4.18%	4.77%	0.17%	−1.48%
1975–85	1.83%	13.42%	2.73%	−6.34%
1986–94	1.77%	6.30%	9.89%	−3.44%

1. Average annual percentage change
2. Average percentage change
3. Per cent of Estimated Labour Force
4. Per cent of Gross Domestic Product

Source: Dalziel and Lattimore (1996).

In Table 1.1 the period since 1974 has been divided into two subperiods for reasons to be explained in the following section. Note that, although growth was slightly higher and unemployment was much lower in 1974–85 compared with 1986–94, both indicators were considerably worse than in the earlier postwar period. Similarly, although inflation and balance of payments deficits were lower in 1986–94 than 1974–85, both indicators were again considerably worse than 1960–74. Consequently, Gould aptly refers to 'the end of the golden weather' in his account of New Zealand's postwar economic history (1982, p. 113). Indeed, the balmy days of economic prosperity and political stability during the 1950s and 1960s have been replaced by stormy turbulence during the 1970s, 1980s, and 1990s—that is to say, by prolonged economic stagnation, wild swings in the popularity of the major and minor political parties, and fundamental changes in the direction of economic and social policy formulation.

New Zealand has not been alone in experiencing economic stagnation and rising unemployment after 1973; this was an international phenomenon (see Armstrong et al., 1991). Consequently, it is important to recognise that the collapse of the long boom and the onset of a prolonged economic crisis in the mid-1970s in New Zealand parallel to a considerable extent, post-1973 trends that have characterised all the advanced capitalist societies.

Monetarist and Keynesian Explanations

The collapse of the long boom in the mid-1970s called for an explanation from economists and the government's economic advisers. Two broad perspectives can be identified in the resulting body of literature—monetarist and Keynesian—although there are significant differences of opinion within each of these camps. Before discussing the differences between the monetarist and Keynesian explanations, however, it should be emphasised that monetarists and Keynesians are in broad agreement that New Zealand's economic performance has been adversely affected by a number of external shocks that had a major impact on the economy during the 1970s and 1980s.

Declining terms of trade
First, whereas for much of the twentieth century New Zealand had virtually guaranteed access to the British market, this access became much more limited after Britain joined the European Economic Community (EEC) in 1973 (Dalziel and Clydesdale, 1991, pp. 13–16; Hawke, 1985, p. 209). Second, the combined impact of the 1973–74 oil shock and the collapse of the commodity price boom of the early 1970s on the New Zealand economy was dramatic, as import prices rose relative to export prices and the terms of trade (the ratio of the import price index to the export price index) fell (Gould, 1982, pp. 126–32). Indeed, Shirley et al. claim that the deterioration in economic performance from 1974 to 1984 can be explained largely by reference to the decline in the terms of trade during this period (1990, pp. 27–33). From 1945 to 1966 New Zealand's terms of trade fluctuated around an historically high level. Although the terms of trade fell dramatically late in 1966, this fall, which continued unabated until 1970, was offset by the strong recovery in the terms of trade from December 1971 to October 1973 in the context of a world commodity boom. But following the oil shock late in 1973, the terms of trade plunged: '. . . in eight of the nine years between 1975 and 1983 inclusive the terms of trade were at a lower level than in any year from 1950 to 1974, and the average for 1975 to 1983 was more than 23 per cent below the average for 1950 to 1974' (Gould, 1985, p. 43).

New Zealand is a very small advanced capitalist trading nation. On the one hand, it has traditionally depended on a narrow range of agricultural exports to alleviate the foreign currency constraint on the domestic economy; on the other hand, both oil and capital equipment, as well as intermediate inputs for the manufacturing sector, have to be imported. The specific problem for New Zealand is that, as Gould notes, 'there are very few countries, certainly among the high income economies, which have suffered a *combination* of the effect of the oil shock *plus* a chronically weakening market situation for major traditional exports' (1985, p. 43).

Expressed very simply, a sufficiently large decline in the terms of trade will generate a current account deficit and deflate the domestic economy by lowering aggregate demand. The government can respond either by borrowing to offset the deficit or it can allow the economy to deflate, with adverse consequences for output growth and employment. In light of this, it is hardly surprising that most explanatory accounts of New Zealand's economic stagnation after 1973, and government responses to it, have placed a great deal of weight on the negative impact of the decline in the terms of trade on the New Zealand economy. Because the terms of trade reflect the specific configuration of New Zealand's integration into the world economy, their historically low level in the 1970s and 1980s has led many to investigate the nature of New Zealand's relationship to the world economy (see Chapter 2). In this vein, Easton (1980), Gould (1982 and 1985) Hawke (1985) and Shirley et al. (1990), all place the emphasis on some aspect of this relationship in explaining the collapse of the long boom.

These explanations are problematic because they fail to show why the other advanced capitalist countries, which differ from New Zealand in that they do not have to depend on a narrow range of agricultural commodities to alleviate the foreign currency constraint, have nonetheless shared New Zealand's experience of an historical decline in growth rates after 1973 (Roper, 1991a, pp. 44–9). The comparative evidence strongly suggests that growth rates would have declined in New Zealand even if the terms of trade had not.

Although both monetarists and Keynesians accept that the decline in the terms of trade has adversely affected New Zealand's economic performance, they disagree fundamentally in their interpretations of New Zealand's economic history after 1973. Table 1.1 subdivided the post-1973 period into two subperiods: 1974–85 and 1986–94. Essentially, monetarists have argued that the Keynesian policies of the first period were disastrous and that the monetarist policies of the second period did not work as well as they should have because they were insufficiently monetarist. Keynesians, by contrast, have argued that the monetarist policies of the second period were disastrous and that the Keynesian policies of the Muldoon Government did not work as well as they should have because they were insufficiently Keynesian.

Monetarism

The Treasury's 1984 briefing papers to the incoming Labour Government presented a monetarist explanation of New Zealand's poor economic performance during the preceding decade (see Chapters 3–4). Treasury does acknowledge that the decline in the terms of trade and the deterioration of world economic performance during the second half of the 1970s and early 1980s had a negative impact on economic growth in New Zealand. It places most emphasis, however, on the inadequate policy responses of the third National Government from 1975 to 1984. Hence statements acknowledging the impact of changes in external circumstances are invariably followed by statements which suggest that government failed to respond in a manner that would enable the economy to adjust to these changed circumstances.

Treasury considers that the ultimate determinants of two crucially important macroeconomic phenomena—the comparative decline in New Zealand's per capita GDP during the postwar era and the deterioration in economic performance from 1974 to 1985—are located within the sphere of state economic management. If it is accepted that the basic causes of New Zealand's poor economic performance are so located, then an explanation of why the economy has performed poorly requires a clear identification of the major faults in economic management. In other words, Treasury considers that the monetarist critique of the broadly Keynesian policies adopted during the postwar era simultaneously explains New Zealand's comparative economic decline and the experience of economic stagnation, inflation, and rising unemployment experienced since 1974.

The critique of Keynesian macro- and microeconomic policy, the deficiencies of which Treasury identifies as the primary cause of the prolonged economic stagnation in New Zealand from 1974 to 1985, involves a number of basic propositions. As Dalziel (1991) has noted, Treasury considers the economy to be self-righting. If the economy failed to recover following the decline in the terms of trade during the 1970s, then this must have been caused by state interference with the market allocation of resources. Treasury claims that poor macroeconomic policies, of the kind applied by the National Government from 1975 to 1984, 'depress economic performance by generating one or more of spiralling inflation, escalating debt, balance of payments deficits, recurring foreign exchange crises, a heavy tax burden, insufficient savings and investment, increasing unemployment and lower standards of living' (Treasury, 1984, p. 115). The expansionary fiscal and monetary policy settings of the government failed to produce a sustained increase in the level of employment and output; they merely generated rising inflation, which seriously undermined economic growth.

This problem was compounded by the fixed nominal exchange rate which, in conjunction with inflationary fiscal and monetary policy, prevented the real exchange rate from adjusting to reduce the current account deficit. Finally, the National Government failed to develop and implement a coherent and integrated medium-term economic strategy. The *ad hoc*, inconsistent, and unbalanced nature of its economic management created uncertainty and inhibited investment.

These problems with macroeconomic policy were compounded at a micro level by 'the sclerosis that has built up through the regulation of many markets of the economy' (Treasury, 1984, p. 107). Thus other causes of poor economic performance from 1974 to 1985 included:

(i) overprotection of the economy, which led to a misallocation of resources away from internationally competitive export-oriented sectors;

(ii) excessive regulation of the financial sector and capital movements;

(iii) rigidities in the labour market ('excessively powerful' occupational trade unions, national awards, 'compulsory' unionism, and so forth), which prevented real wages from being sufficiently flexible downwards and sufficiently sensitive to changes in productivity and profitability at the enterprise level;

(iv) an excessively large and inefficient public sector;

(v) high marginal tax rates, which had a negative impact on savings, investment, productivity, employment, and output; and

(vi) excessive regulation of business in the areas of environmental protection, equality of opportunity, and consumer protection (see Treasury, 1984, 1987, 1990 and Chapter 4).

From Treasury's monetarist perspective, the broadly Keynesian policies of the postwar era had prevented the New Zealand economy from realising its full growth potential during the golden weather of the 1950s and 1960s and had exacerbated the difficulties encountered during the stormy turbulence of the 1970s. The combination of macro and micro policies adopted by the third National Government prevented the economy from adjusting to the exogenous shocks caused by rising oil prices and falling prices for agricultural exports. Consequently, the road to growth and prosperity in the medium term depended upon the government rejecting Keynesianism and adopting monetarism, which, in practical policy terms, centrally involved:

(i) a monetarist disinflationary macroeconomic strategy;

(ii) a comprehensive program of market liberalisation;

(iii) a fundamental redesign of the welfare state; and

(iv) industrial relations reform in order to establish a more 'flexible' labour market.

Keynesianism

Keynesian explanations of New Zealand's economic stagnation after 1973 have been provided by Boston (1984), Dalziel (1991), Easton (1980), Easton and Gerritsen (1996), Gould (1985), Kelsey (1995), Rosenberg (1986), Shirley et al. (1990), and Whitwell (1990).

Economic history

Those of a broadly Keynesian persuasion emphatically reject Treasury's interpretation of New Zealand's postwar economic history and its explanation of the collapse of the long boom. Although there may have been a significant comparative decline in per capita GDP during the 1950s and 1960s from the peak in 1953 when New Zealand was ranked third highest in the world, it must be remembered that, despite this comparative decline, the economy grew substantially in absolute and historical terms during this period. The comparative decline in per capita GDP during this period can be attributed to structural characteristics of the New Zealand economy and a relatively high population growth rate rather than to Keynesian policies of macro-economic stabilisation and infrastructural investment (Gould, 1985, p. 62). Conversely, New Zealand's economic performance from 1974 to 1985, although disastrous in historical terms, was less serious when viewed comparatively because all the major OECD (Organisation for Economic Cooperation and Development) economics experienced lower growth rates during the 1970s and early 1980s. From 1985 to 1992 New Zealand's economic performance was disastrous in both historical and comparative terms because the economy stagnated during the world economic recovery from 1983 to 1989.

Muldoon's poor economic management

Treasury argued that the *ad hoc* approach to economic management of Sir Robert Muldoon, Prime Minister and Finance Minister from 1975 to 1984, contributed significantly to New Zealand's poor economic performance and presented this largely as a failure of Keynesian demand-management strategies. Keynesian economists in New Zealand reject this view. Although the Muldoon Government did use fiscal policy in order to influence economic activity, it was far from being a paragon of Keynesian virtue. First, as Gould (1985) argues, fiscal policy cannot be assumed to be neutral with respect to (medium-term) growth and output just because fiscal deficits, economic stagnation, and rising unemployment coincided from 1975 to 1984. Such an assumption overlooks the fact that the internal fiscal deficit did not increase sufficiently to stimulate activity in the domestic economy during this period. It also ignores the extent to which the recovery in the United States economy during the 1980s was fuelled by the unstated Keynesianism of the Reagan administration (see Riddell, 1988; Smithin, 1990, pp. 154–5). Second, although Keynes argued for state investment in the economic infrastructure, this does not imply support for state investment that is misallocated. Extensive subsidies for agricultural production that inhibited the diversification of New Zealand's export base, and massive state investment in the Think Big energy projects, can both be criticised on these grounds. Conversely, state support for manufacturing exports was largely successful in stimulating export growth. This suggests that the Muldoon Government was guilty of misallocating resources, not that state investment or intervention is always doomed to failure. Third, the *ad hoc* and inconsistent nature of Muldoon's economic management can also be criticised from a Keynesian perspective. In short, the poor economic management of the third National Government damaged the economy, not because it was Keynesian, but because it combined an inconsistent and poorly designed macroeconomic strategy with a series of poorly conceived and misdirected microeconomic interventions.

Abandonment of commitment to full employment
Therborn's (1986) comparative research on unemployment in sixteen OECD countries shows that the five countries that maintained low rates of unemployment following the world recession in 1974–75 (Austria, Japan, Norway, Sweden, and Switzerland) had an institutionalised commitment to full employment. This involved

(i)   an explicit commitment to maintaining/achieving full employment;
(ii) the existence and use of countercyclical mechanisms and policies;
(iii) the existence and use of specific mechanisms to adjust supply and demand in the labour market to the goal of full employment;
(iv) a conscious decision not to use high unemployment as a means to secure other policy objectives (p. 23).

Clearly both Labour and National Governments from 1935 to 1975 maintained this kind of institutionalised commitment to full employment. Arguably this commitment was slowly but steadily abandoned after 1975 (Endres, 1984 and 1989).

Destructive impact of monetarism
The postKeynesian schools of thought place more emphasis on establishing the historical realism of economic theory than those who uncritically accept

the basic axioms and macroeconomic theorems of pre-Keynesian neo-classicism. Most important, postKeynesians reject the neoclassical vision of the equilibrating tendencies of market economies, in which there is assumed to be an underlying tendency towards self-regulating, general equilibrium, with full employment of resources, on the compelling grounds that economic history has repeatedly failed to bear out the realism of this assumption. Yet it is precisely this assumption that is central to the monetarist macroeconomic strategy which has been applied in New Zealand from 1984 onwards. It is assumed that if the government reduces inflation and maintains price level stability, balances the Budget, reduces taxation, slashes social spending, and liberalises regulatory control over markets, then the economy will spontaneously generate non-inflationary economic growth and lower unemployment in the medium term.

From a Keynesian perspective the monetarist economic strategy of the fourth Labour Government had a largely deleterious impact on the economy during the 1980s.

> The impact of these policies on the domestic economy is now patently evident. GDP in New Zealand (including the financial sector) expanded by 1.9 per cent between March 1985 and March 1989, while the population expanded by 2.1 per cent. If the financial sector is not included then GDP fell by 2.9 per cent. Meanwhile, the world economy expanded by approximately 13 per cent. . . . When compared with other countries, New Zealand's performance between 1985 and 1990 was dismal . . . and by 1988 New Zealand had emerged as the country with the worst employment outlook of all the OECD nations (Shirley et al., 1990, p. 40).

This situation deteriorated even further as the economy plunged into a deep recession from 1990 to 1991.

The fourth Labour Government's monetarist macroeconomic strategy was problematic in a number of respects. First, this strategy proved to be technically inoperable since the Reserve Bank was unable successfully to control the growth of the broad money supply (M3) in the context of a deregulated financial environment (Whitwell, 1992). This forced the bank to target interest rates and the exchange rate in order to reduce (price ration) the demand for credit. Second, because the Reserve Bank was forced to drive up interest rates and the exchange rate in order to contain the escalating inflation that emerged after the end of the wage and price freeze in 1984, the exposed productive sectors of the economy experienced a decline in profitability and curtailed their investment expenditure. This resulted in a dramatic contraction of manufacturing and agricultural output and employment. Third, because of price and wage inflexibility in product and labour markets, monetarist discipline in New Zealand impacted primarily on real output and employment. It was only, therefore, through this contraction of real economic activity that prices were affected. Finally, in keeping with the neoclassical assumption of a tendency towards general equilibrium, monetarists assume that the lower growth and higher unemployment generated by economic restructuring will be more than offset by higher growth rates in the medium term. This is an anathema to Keynesians, who subscribe to the view that 'the long period has no independent existence, being nothing but the growth out of a succession in short periods: "the long-run trend is but a slowly changing component of a chain of short period situations ... no independent entity"' (Harcourt, 1985, p. 129). Hence both Whitwell (1992) and Dalziel (1992) use the concept of hysteresis—policies that have major short-run effects on economic activity also affect the long-run outcomes—to criticise the monetarist 'disinflation' from 1984 to 1991.

The Marxist Explanation

Both monetarists and Keynesians consider that the causes of New Zealand's economic stagnation after 1973 can, at least for the most part, be located within the sphere of government economic management. Both consider that the economy is buffeted by external shocks (sudden rises in world oil prices, declines in the terms of trade, and so forth) but place greater emphasis in policy debates on the role played by government in managing the economy. Hence, roughly speaking, monetarist and Keynesian economists locate the independent variables within the sphere of state economic management and the dependent variables in the economy itself.

Marxists fundamentally reject this. Although they accept and support many of the Keynesian criticisms of monetarism, they reject the Keynesian view that the state can successfully manage the economy in order to maintain economic growth and full employment over the long term. This is because Marxists, for the most part, locate the independent variables in their models within the economy itself and the dependent variables within the sphere of the state. In other words, the process of capital accumulation is held to be internally contradictory and these contradictions generate recurrent crises. Regardless of the policy stance adopted by the state, the long-run tendencies of capitalist development eventually generate crises characterised, among other things, by economic stagnation and rising unemployment. From this perspective the basic causes of the post-1973 economic crisis in New Zealand are located within the economy itself—they are not considered to be exogenous (external shocks) nor to be located within the sphere of government.

The core of a Marxist explanation of the crisis rests on the basic theoretical hypothesis that the general level of profitability is most likely to be the primary underlying cause of New Zealand's economic crisis because profitability plays a large part in determining the overall level of productive investment, and hence the rate of economic growth, in the economy as a whole. In this way, the prolonged economic crisis in New Zealand is deemed by Bedggood (1980), Mason (1979a, 1979b), and Pearce (1986) to be a crisis of declining profitability and insufficient levels of investment. New Zealand's specific position within the world economy, and the consequent decline in the terms of trade, have compounded this crisis and are the major determinants of the *comparative* decline of the New Zealand economy.

The driving force of economic activity in capitalist society, given the competitive war that is waged on both commodity and capital markets, is the necessity to remain profitable. Profit in capitalist society is the principal, but not the only, phenomenal form assumed by surplus value. Surplus value represents the difference between the value of the necessary labour that workers perform in order to cover the costs of their own reproduction and the value of the surplus labour that is the labour performed in the labour process over and above this necessary labour. This surplus value is the historically specific form that surplus labour assumes in the capitalist mode of production. Capitalists can appropriate this surplus value by virtue of their exclusive ownership (in the sense of effective control) of the means of production.

The necessity to remain profitable drives individual capitalist firms to battle simultaneously on two fronts: first, in the labour process, against workers over the production of surplus value; and second, in the circulation process or sphere of market competition, against other capitalists over the realisation of surplus value in the form of profits through the sale of commodities (see Shaikh, 1983, p. 159). Battle on the first front essentially involves attempts to maximise managerial control over productive labour in conjunction with the mechanisation of production in order to increase the productivity of labour and hence the production of relative surplus value. Battle on the second front essentially involves the increased capitalisation of production in order to reduce unit production costs relative to competitors and thereby obtaining a larger market share (assuming that there is no deterioration in product quality). But, because this ability to lower cost-price is itself generally purchased at a cost, in the form of a higher level of capitalisation, 'the cheapening of commodities through mechanisation is inevitably bound up with a tendency for the actual profit rate to fall. . .' (Shaikh, 1980, p. 75). The recurrent battles of individual firms to maximise profits ultimately reduces the profitability of the system as whole.

The general rate of profit falls in this manner because, given the Marxian theory of surplus value, living labour is the ultimate source of all profit in the capitalist mode of production. The attempt to increase the production of relative surplus value through higher productivity, and to increase market share through lower unit costs, involves investment decisions that result in greater quantities of fixed and circulating constant capital per unit of output. When these investment decisions become generalised across the economy as a whole, it should be clear that, in the long term, the proportion of variable capital will decline relative to the constant capital employed in production. The ratio of constant to variable capital (c/v) thus rises in the long term. Since variable capital is the source of all new value, of surplus value, and, consequently, profit then, other things being equal, as the organic composition of capital (c/v) rises the general rate of profit ($s/(c+v)$) will fall (see Shaikh, 1987). The rate of profit is not, however, determined purely by changes in the organic composition of capital. It is codetermined by changes in the ratio of constant capital to variable capital (c/v) and by the ratio of variable capital to surplus value (s/v). Thus the basic Marxian theorem is that 'there is a tendency for the rate of profit to fall because the organic composition of capital has a tendency to rise faster than the rate of surplus value' (Chernomas, 1987, p. 1). This is an extremely condensed summary of what Marx considered to be 'the most important law of modern political economy' (1973, p. 748)—the law of the tendency of the rate of profit to fall (TRPF).

In terms of theory and methodology, it is no more difficult empirically to operationalise Marxian economic concepts than those of the neoclassical and Keynesian traditions. In principle, it would be possible to establish a set of Marxian national accounts in order to measure economic activity over time (Shaikh and Tonak, 1994). In reality, resource constraints mean that it is not possible empirically to operationalise Marxian categories in this way (Marxist scholars cannot afford to fund their own departments of statistics!). It is necessary, therefore, to adopt the alternative approach of adjusting orthodox economic data in order to approximate Marxian categories. This is a complex process that poses many problems for researchers, but basically it involves disaggregating national accounts data and then reaggregating it so that it approximates Marxian theoretical categories (see Shaikh and Tonak, 1994). Using this approach, the key Marxian value ratios have been empirically operationalised in studies of a number of advanced capitalist economies. In addition, Armstrong et al. have provided a survey of empirical trends in profitability for all the major OECD economies during the postwar era (1991, pp. 119–22, 248–54).

Such research has generated considerable debate but in general two empirical findings seem increasingly secure. First, rises in the technical composition of capital are *in fact* associated with rises in the value composition of capital in all the major advanced capitalist economies. This means that the most common objection to the Marxian TRPF theorem is empirically unfounded (see Shaikh and Tonak, 1994, pp. 152–202). Second, by both orthodox and Marxian measures, a general decline in profitability has emerged as a clear empirical trend during the postwar era. Consequently, the rising value composition of capital in the 1950s and 1960s is associated with a falling rate of profit. Therefore there is strong empirical support for the orthodox Marxian explanation of the economic slow-down that has characterised all the major OECD economies from 1974 to the present (allowing for periodical fluctuations associated with business cycles). In turn, this points to an important part of the explanation of New Zealand's economic difficulties after 1973: the world demand for raw materials and foodstuffs weakened as the growth rates of the largest OECD economies declined.

The decline in profitability is also evident in New Zealand's official statistics. The rate of return of business capital fell from an average of 16.2 per cent (1967–74) to 10.3 per cent (1975–84) before recovering substantially during the late 1980s to 15.3 per cent (1985–89) (OECD, 1990/91, p. 17). Crocombe et al. suggest that profitability in the agricultural sector declined significantly from 1960 to 1990 (1991, p. 47). This decline in profitability is also reflected in the results of the *Quarterly Survey of Business Opinion* conducted by the New Zealand Institute of Economic Research. In the period from the September quarter 1973 to the March quarter 1996, sustained experiences of improved profitability have been recorded only three times. Clearly, businesspeople have been aware of the general decline in profitability that has characterised the period after 1973 (see Roper, 1990a, pp. 42–4).

Official and Marxian measures of profitability differ in many important respects. Fortunately, the key Marxian value ratios have been empirically operationalised in Pearce's (1986) long-run study of the New Zealand economy. This was achieved through the detailed disaggregation of official statistical data on factory production in New Zealand from 1923 to 1970 in order to facilitate the systematic reaggregation of this data into Marxian categories. Although the study has a number of serious limitations, it nonetheless provides empirical support for the Marxist explanation of the post-1973 prolonged crisis. The study empirically traces the movement of the organic composition of capital, rate of surplus value, and rate of profit from 1923 to 1970. It shows that the key Marxian aggregates do in fact interrelate in a way that is consistent with the basic postulates of Marxian economic theory for a substantial period of New Zealand's economic history. The organic composition of capital rose during the postwar era, and this gradually undermined the rate of profit.

So what are the implications of this study for developing an explanation of the specific trajectory of New Zealand's economic development during the postwar era? First, it provides the basis for an explanation of the postwar long boom. A primary cause of the long boom was the large decline in the organic composition of capital from 1932 to 1945. This facilitated a large rise in the rate of profit from 9.3 per cent in 1932 to 21.2 per cent in 1943. So the historically low level of the organic composition in the early 1950s facilitated an historically high general rate of profit. Another significant cause of the long boom was the major increase in the rate of surplus value from 1938 to 1951. This further contributed to the high level of the general rate of profit. An explanation of the increase of the rate of surplus value is not possible here since that requires a detailed concrete historical investigation of the actual course of the class struggle waged during this period. Nonetheless, it seems likely that this increase was due to the government's control of wages and conditions during the war years. This wage control was particularly effective because of the incorporation of the higher levels of the trade union bureaucracy within the state apparatus (the Economic Stabilisation Commission). In this regard, Chapman observes that

> the worker's job was secure but with fixed wages, direction of labour, and pressure against strikes, there was no advantage to be had from the strong demand for labour. Meanwhile, businessmen and manufacturers had guaranteed markets, sure sales, a disciplined labour force with set wages and conditions, and price margins which provided uninterrupted profitability, capital growth, and resources for further investment (1981, p. 351).

The gains of the war years were then consolidated when the National Government, aided by the ambivalence of the Labour Party and the complicity of the leadership of the Federation of Labour (FOL), succeeded in defeating the most militant section of the New Zealand working class in the 1951 waterfront lockout.

The historically high level of the rate of profit, determined by the low level of the organic composition and the increased rate of surplus value, generated a wave of new investment in fixed capital. This increased the productivity of labour and facilitated a prolonged increase in the rate of economic growth. Once under way, the long boom was sustained by a technological revolution in the production of capital equipment.

This technological revolution simultaneously facilitated an increase in the rate of surplus value and a reduction in the value of fixed capital, particularly plant and machinery. In this way, the postwar technological revolution counteracted the tendency for the rate of profit to fall by inhibiting increases in the organic composition of capital associated with the widespread mechanisation and capitalisation of production, and also by ensuring that increases in labour productivity continued to exceed increases in real wages, thus facilitating sustainable increases in the rate of surplus value (Mandel, 1975, Ch. 6 and 1980, Ch. 2, 1995).

Other significant causes of the long boom were the reductions in the turnover time of capital—made possible by vast improvements in communications and transportation during the 1950s and 1960s, the impact of rapid expansion of the world economy on the New Zealand economy, historically high prices for New Zealand's agricultural exports, and sustained productivity increases in the agricultural sector. Finally, the Keynesian macroeconomic policy settings of the postwar era were significant, particularly government expenditure on state housing and public works combined with expansionary monetary policy and regulatory control of the financial sector, which helped to keep real interest rates low. Although Keynesian policies did not generate the long boom, they probably did help to sustain the high rates of economic growth attained during the 1950s and 1960s (Mason, 1979b).

The development of the long boom from 1945 to 1973 was internally contradictory: the very factors that produced an increase in the general rate of profit also tended to undermine the rate of profit in the long term. The organic composition rose throughout the 1950s and, to a lesser extent, the 1960s and this tended to undermine the rate of profit. A comparison of changes in the organic composition with changes in the rate of surplus value shows that, for most years during the long boom, the increases in the organic composition were counteracted by increases in the rate of surplus value. From the mid-1960s this started to change: the rate of surplus value levelled out and then began to fall with the major upsurge in class struggle that characterised the late 1960s and first half of the 1970s. Real wages increased dramatically during this period. Finally, during the postwar era labour was increasingly allocated towards occupations in the service sector, which are not productive of surplus value (Employment Working Group, 1989, Ch. 2). As Chernomas (1987) and Moseley (1985, 1991, pp. 123–50) show, this depresses the rate of profit because unproductive labour expended in circulation activities (wholesale and retail sectors, financial services, insurance, and real estate) and maintenance activities (police, judiciary, public service) is ultimately a drain on aggregate surplus value. Together, these developments created the necessary structural preconditions for the onset of the accumulation crisis in New Zealand after 1973.

In light of this analysis it should be clear that the wild upward and then downward swings in New Zealand's terms of trade in the early 1970s were in large part a reflection of the deeper causes of the world recessions in 1974 and 1977–78. Thus Mandel argues that the

> generalized recession of 1974-1975 was the product neither of bad luck nor of some 'freak accident' of the international capitalist economy (such as the rise in oil prices). It resulted from all the basic contradictions of the capitalist mode of production, which rose to the surface after being partially contained by the inflation of two decades of accelerated growth' (1980, p. 78).

The evidence available at this stage suggests that the general rate of profit, apart from significant cyclical upswings during the late 1980s and the mid-1990s, has not recovered to the high levels of the 1950s and 1960s for any prolonged period since the 1974 recession. Therefore, given the significance of profitability as a mechanism governing investment and the patently inadequate levels of investment for most of the period after 1973, economic stagnation and high unemployment have been determined largely by those factors that are responsible for the economy-wide rate of profit falling to historically low levels.

This account of economic stagnation in New Zealand places the emphasis on the *internal* contradictions of capital accumulation, which generate the long-term tendencies and recurrent crises of capitalist development. But from the time of European settlement in the mid-nineteenth century the New Zealand economy has been integrated, in a succession of different phases, into the capitalist world economy (see Chapter 2). Although the largest OECD economies all experienced a fall in growth rates and a rise in unemployment after 1973, none has experienced a decline as precipitous as New Zealand's. This suggests that the crisis in New Zealand is unique in important respects.

Marxists such as Bedggood (1980) and Steven (1985) have, in different ways, placed a great deal of emphasis on the fact that capitalist development in New Zealand proceeded on the basis of highly efficient primary production in the context of its traditional colonial specialisation in the international division of labour. But further research is required to identify clearly the major changes in the pattern of commodity trade and to determine the significance of the thorough internationalisation of New Zealand's capital markets for the domestic economy and polity. It is also necessary to determine more precisely to what extent New Zealand's relationship to the world economy and the current crisis can be understood in terms of the Marxian theory of differential ground rent (see Fine, 1989, pp. 90–110). This theory, when applied to New Zealand's economic development, suggests that there was a net inflow of surplus value into the economy owing to the comparatively high productivity of agricultural production in New Zealand. Once a plateau was reached in agricultural productivity and output growth during the mid-1960s, it seems likely that the flow of differential rent into the economy declined, thereby depressing the general rate of profit. Steven argues in this respect that economic stagnation after 1973 has ultimately been determined by 'the gradual whittling away of differential ground rent' (1985, p. 55).

In this section it has been argued that the Marxist explanation of the crisis is theoretically coherent and that it has considerable empirical support. But currently there is no empirical study that follows Shaikh and Tonak (1994) in using disaggregated national accounts data to trace fluctuations in the key Marxian value ratios for the postwar era. Until such a study is done, Marxist analyses of New Zealand's economic development during the postwar era will remain incomplete and, to a considerable degree, speculative.

Where is New Zealand Going?

Following a prolonged period of economic stagnation and rising unemployment from 1974 to 1991, and a contraction of the economy from 1985 to 1992, a strong cyclical recovery in economic activity took place from 1993 to 1996. Real GDP grew by 5.3 per cent in the year to March 1994 and by 6.1 per cent to March 1995 (Statistics New Zealand, 1996, p. 124). The steam started to run out of the recovery, with growth falling to 2.8 per cent for the quarter ending March 1996. The number registered as unemployed fell from 215 562 in 1992 to 143 582 in 1996 (Statistics New Zealand, 1996, p. 36). The official unemployment rate fell from 10.9 per cent in September 1992 to 6.1 per cent in March 1996. The consumer price index (CPI) increased by 1.4 per cent in 1993, 2.8 per cent in 1994, and 3 per cent in 1995. This is by no means the first cyclical recovery to have occurred since 1973—there was also a significant recovery from 1983 to 1984. If measured purely in terms of economic growth, however, the mid-1990s recovery is the strongest since 1973. In view of this, it is hardly surprising that monetarists, Keynesians, and Marxists have radically differing assessments of the mid-1990s economic recovery and the future trajectory of New Zealand's economic development.

The supporters of the monetarist macroeconomic strategy that has been implemented in New Zealand from 1984 onwards, including the Treasury, the Business Roundtable, the Reserve Bank, the OECD, and the parliamentary wings of the National and Labour parties, hailed the mid-1990s recovery as providing conclusive evidence that this strategy had succeeded in permanently reversing New Zealand's economic decline. At the height of the recovery, the Finance Minister confidently predicted in his 1994 Budget speech that it was realistic to expect 'continued growth of 3.5% a year from now until 2010' (Birch, p. 8). He reaffirmed his 'Government's commitment to policies that have proved a winning formula for sustainable economic growth and job creation' (*ibid.*). Keynesian and Marxist critics of these policies have adopted a much less sanguine interpretation of the recovery. As Kelsey observes:

> New Zealand spent almost seven years of the [post 1984] experiment in stagnation and recession… The average growth across OECD countries in the period 1985-92 was 20 percent. New Zealand's economy shrank by 1 percent over the same period. The OECD calculates that New Zealand's real GDP in 1992 was still about 5 percent below its 1985/86 level. Although real GDP grew by nearly 5 percent in 1993, with an even higher rate for 1994, OECD figures indicate that this recovery only brought GDP back in line with the long-term trend (1995, pp. 243–4).

Rather than constituting a turning point in New Zealand's economic history, the critics argue that the recovery of the mid-1990s will be followed by a cyclical slow-down and that it is far too early to suggest that the high growth rates of the recovery will be sustainable over the long term. Investment remains weak. 'By 1994 non-residential fixed investment as a proportion of GDP was 73 percent of its level a decade earlier' (Kelsey, 1995, pp. 252–3). Further, the available income statistics show clearly that the recovery has primarily benefited the top quintile of income earners, while the majority have actually experienced declines in real disposable income (see Chapter 5). Unemployment has remained at a much higher level than the average during the postwar long boom—even at the peak of the recovery. It is likely to rise as the economy slows down in the late 1990s. Finally, the recovery has not prevented the persistence of large balance of payment deficits.

Marxists deny that the mid-1990s recovery means that New Zealand's prolonged economic crisis has come to an end. According to the 'Falling Rate of Profit' school of Marxian crisis theory, capitalist crises are characterised by, among other things, a long-term reduction of profit and growth rates resulting in rising unemployment, with major fluctuations of these variables across the course of the business cycle. The difference between a long boom and a prolonged economic crisis is that, in the case of the former, the cyclical recoveries tend to be strong and prolonged, and the recessions brief and shallow, whereas during economic crises the reverse applies. Although the empirical data is insufficient to determine this with any precision, it seems likely that the state's attempts to restructure the economy since 1984 have successfully increased the rate of surplus value and to some extent have devalorised fixed capital in unprofitable sectors of the economy, thus raising the general rate of profit. This explains the recovery but it also highlights its fragility, given that there is no evidence that the high profits rates of the 1950s have been attained again in the 1990s. Hence, from this perspective, the most likely prognosis is the continuation of growth and unemployment rates over the long term in line with the post-1973 historical trend, that is, lower growth and higher unemployment than that experienced in New Zealand during the long boom from 1945 to 1973.

---

1 This chapter is an updated and revised version of Roper (1993b).

Guide to Readings

The most comprehensive monetarist account of New Zealand's postwar economic history, and, in particular, the poor economic performance since the mid-1970s, is to be found in the various Treasury briefing papers (1984, 1987, and 1990). Keynesian explanations have been provided by Easton (1980), Gould (1985), Rosenburg (1986), Shirley et al. (1990), Whitwell (1990), Dalziel (1991), and Easton and Gerritsen (1996). Also see Hawke (1985) and Gould (1982).

Any appreciation of the Marxist account of New Zealand's prolonged economic crisis requires some understanding of basic Marxist economics. For this, see Cole et al. (1990), Mandel (1968, 1969, 1975, 1980, and 1995), Shaikh (1980, 1983, and 1987), Chernomas (1987), Moseley (1985 and 1991) and Sweezy (1942). Shaikh and Tonak (1994) show how it is possible empirically to operationalise Marxian economic concepts. For the application of Marxian economics in varying degrees of sophistication to the New Zealand case, see Bedggood (1980), Mason (1979a and 1979b), Pearce (1986), and Roper (1990a).

Dalziel and Lattimore (1996) provide commentary and data on key indicators of macroeconomic performance in New Zealand for the period 1960–95.

CHAPTER TWO

THE GLOBALISATION OF CAPITALISM AND ECONOMIC TRANSITION IN NEW ZEALAND

PRIYATOSH MAITRA

The economist is concerned with the future as well as with the past; but it is from the past that he has to begin. It is the past that provides him with his facts, the facts that he uses to make generalisations; he then uses these generalisations as bases for predictions and for advice. . . (Hicks, p. 4).

In examining the causes of the end of sustained economic growth in postwar New Zealand, emphasis has been placed on the role of 'external shocks' and, in particular, on the world recessions of 1974 and 1977–78 (see Chapter 1). Although this emphasis correctly identifies the crucial link between New Zealand's domestic economy and the global economic environment, it is important to understand that such a link has been important for New Zealand's economic development since it was first colonised by Britain in the mid-nineteenth century. Furthermore, it is only by adopting a long-term historical framework that the dramatic changes in New Zealand's political economy since 1984 can be fully understood.

Whereas it may be thought that 'globalisation' is a relatively recent phenomenon, this is not the case. The term refers to the penetration—via the trade of goods and commodity capital, finance capital, and production—of Western capitalism into the rest of the world, originating with the Industrial Revolution in Britain during the nineteenth century. Its impact on New Zealand was first felt with British colonisation in the latter half of the nineteenth century. Since then, three phases or distinct periods of the globalisation of capitalism have been identified. The first, which dated from the mid-nineteenth century until the Depression of the 1930s, centrally involved the globalisation of capitalist production and trade in commodities. The second phase involved import substituting industrialisation (ISI), initially market oriented then state led. Then, since 1984, the economic nationalism of the import substituting phase has given way to the economic internationalism of the third phase, involving the deregulation of markets and the shift from import substitution to export substitution.

Each of these phases will be examined in turn with respect to New Zealand (Maitra, 1993, 1996a and 1996b; Le Heron and Pawson, 1996a). Before that, however, it is important to emphasise the dynamic link between these phases. This point is vital to understanding the process of globalisation and its implications for policy formulation. This dynamic linking of the phases explains why advanced capitalist economies of the 1990s cannot return to the state intervention stage of social welfarism of the earlier postwar period. To view globalisation only in terms of its effects ignores this crucial factor altogether.

Phase I: Internationalisation of Trade in Goods and Commodity Capital

New Zealand's economic growth in the late nineteenth century can largely be accounted for in terms of the needs of British industrial capitalism. Britain needed a supply of cheap food to keep domestic wages low and to help maintain a high rate of capital accumulation. Britain, with its expanding industrial economy absorbing a labour force once engaged in agriculture, together with its rapidly diversifying economic activities, including the service sector, could not provide sufficient labour and land to cultivate food and raw materials for industrial growth without this having an inflationary effect on prices. The four newly colonised countries—the USA, Canada, Australia, and New Zealand—with their small populations and abundant land were to provide the sources of cheap food that Britain required.

The importance of Britain to New Zealand's economic growth is reflected in the destination of New Zealand exports over the period 1860–1940. Britain's share of these exports grew from about 40 per cent in the 1860s to over 70 per cent in the 1870s and although there was a slight decline in the 1880s, it grew again to about 75–80 per cent and remained there until the Second World War (Hawke, 1985, p. 57). The exports from New Zealand consisted mainly of meat, tallow, butter, cheese, wool, and gold. The shares of wool and gold began to decline while those of dairy products showed an increasing trend over the period (Prichard, 1970, pp. 425–6). With the introduction of refrigerated shipping in the 1880s, New Zealand was able to export meat to Britain at a lower cost and meat subsequently became an important item of food consumption in Britain's industrialising economy.

New Zealand's link with Britain, however, had a major consequence for the indigenous population. Britain had surplus capital waiting to be invested at a profitable rate and advanced agricultural technology to be applied to land, which was then abundantly available in New Zealand. But this required a change from the communal ownership of land by Maori to a private ownership system dominated by the Pakeha. This was necessary to operate a capitalist mode of production and introduce capitalist agriculture. Capitalist production in agriculture in New Zealand was imposed from the outside; it did not develop from a feudal ownership system as was the case in Britain, Europe, or Japan. In New Zealand and other newly established colonies, tribal economics did not get the opportunity to develop into a feudal system of private land ownership, which might have acted as a costly and discouraging force to immigration. As it was, the British Crown dispossessed Maori of their lands in order to subsidise emigration from Britain at little cost to the British taxpayers (see Chapter 9).

The colonisation of New Zealand provided not only a source of cheap food for Britain but also a market for British products. Considering the size of the New Zealand population, the market may not at first sight have seemed very large, but in the context of the current technology and the relatively well-to-do population (because of the diffusion of income from expanding food exports produced on family farms), it became an attractive market to achieve economies of scale of production at a time of growing capital intensive industrial activities in Britain.

From the 1850s onwards, Britain began to supply New Zealand with finished (mostly consumption) manufactured goods, plus essential commodity capital to build infrastructure to facilitate export-import businesses and supply necessary skills (Hawke, 1985; Simkin, 1951). The modernisation of agriculture, and, in particular, the introduction of refrigerated shipping, led to a significant increase in exports. This in turn led to a rise in manufactures which, with the help of capital inflow from Britain, created markets for certain consumer goods regarded as suitable for import substitution. At this stage, however, import substitution was piecemeal and small scale. The increase in imports of capital and intermediate goods to produce finished consumer goods as import substitutes, together with the rise in domestic manufactures, indicated that the growth of industrial capitalism in New Zealand was an offshoot of British industrial growth. By the turn of the century, New Zealand's geographically isolated economy was becoming, through its international trade links with Britain, an integral part of the world economy.

This first stage of globalisation, during the period of New Zealand's colonisation, can be anlysed by drawing upon some of the key theoretical insights of the classical political economists. Classical economists of the nineteenth century advocated the use of trade based on the principle of comparative advantage as the instrument of achieving mutual growth and development of industrial and agricultural economies. This was seen as the only way to bring about a higher level of global output. In Marx's terms, this was the beginning of the realisation of the role of capitalism in developing productive forces to their fullest extent. The first phase, therefore, was crucial for the later expansion of capitalist production by developing markets for industrial and manufactured goods, stimulating the production of consumption goods, capital goods, and intermediate goods, helping the development of the agricultural export sector, and by building infrastructures —especially railways, ports, and telegraph and postal communications. The state's role in all this was largely restricted to the last mentioned function— helping to build infrastructures. This limited role was to change dramatically during the second phase of the globalisation of capitalism.

Phase II: Import Substituting Industrial Growth— Economic Nationalism

The first phase of globalisation had been marked by the international trade in goods and commodity capital that led, in the course of time, to the building of markets for these products in the importing countries as well as to the development of an infrastructure to facilitate trade and the expansion of markets. In this way, when markets of a particular finished consumer good proved economic enough to be a candidate for substitution by domestic production, *market-oriented* ISI began. Inputs, like capital goods, intermediate goods, and skills, came from Britain and later from other Western nations. These inputs were achieved through trade surpluses, loans, and by direct foreign investment. The late nineteenth and early twentieth centuries witnessed the inflow of foreign capital to help establish ISI in light consumer goods.

Foreign investment was an important source of funds to provide the necessary capital equipment, intermediate goods, and technological know-how to stimulate economic growth. As might be expected, Britain, as the leading capitalist country of the time, played a key role in foreign investment in New Zealand, illustrating once again how New Zealand's economic development was inextricably linked to the globalisation of capitalist production. The outflow of British capital, first to Western Europe and North America, and later to the rest of the world, indicates the extent of accumulation of capital resulting from domestic industrial growth, as well as from the growth of foreign trade. Foreign trade growth was much higher than Britain's domestic economic growth and this resulted in a massive accumulation of capital funds that needed to be reinvested. Investment in the limited British domestic market would have caused a glut of output and loss of profit. British investment therefore began to flow overseas and when New Zealand markets for finished consumer goods proved sufficiently economic to be candidates for substitution by domestic production, British and other foreign investment was attracted and market-oriented ISI began.

A market-oriented ISI and the accompanying development of a service sector needed skilled labour, a large part of which was supplied by immigration. Immigrants initially came mainly from Britain but later they included West Europeans. Between 1854 and 1913 the European population in New Zealand increased from just 33 000 to over 1 million (Mitchell and Deane, 1962, pp. 8–10). Although the transfer of labour accounted for a very small proportion of the British population, the 'exportation of the working class population which had become "surplus" to the requirements of British capital' was a crucial element in combating the declining economic growth and social discontent of Britain (see Chapter 9).

Government-initiated ISI

New Zealand enjoyed satisfactory periods of high economic growth during the first two decades of the twentieth century, helped in no small measure by the demand for New Zealand's agricultural exports generated by the First World War. Economic prosperity, which had begun in the mid-1890s, finally came to an end in the 1920s when a series of recessions and recoveries gave way, in 1930, to a Depression that was to last until 1935 (Brooking, 1992, pp. 230–2). The Depression saw unemployment reach about 12 per cent of the labour force, per capita real incomes fall by an average of somewhere between 10 and 20 per cent, and export prices decline by 45 per cent (Hawke, 1985, Ch. 7). Although the Depression was not particularly severe in comparative terms, it forged a coalition of small farmers and wage labourers, who brought to power New Zealand's first Labour Government. This government sought to 'manage' the crisis of capitalism through intervention and regulation of the domestic economy. The Depression was seen as a consequence of the failure of classical economics and New Zealand politicians, like their counterparts in a number of European countries, embraced a new economic orthodoxy, Keynesianism. The government adopted a range of Keynesian demand management policies, such as an extensive scheme of public works programs and a radical expansion of welfare and health benefits. Policies were also introduced to regulate trade and so protect New Zealand's economy from 'external shocks'. These policies included import licensing, exchange controls, guaranteed farm prices, and the use of semi-governmental marketing boards to control agricultural exports.

Until the 1930s, ISI policy remained market based. The volume of imports of a commodity indicated the viability of this substitution by domestic production. Under the first Labour Government, this type of ISI gave way to *government-initiated* ISI, which depends not on the market size but on the importance of the imports to the growth of productivity. The import substitutes consisted of diverse products from producer goods, such as chemicals, metal products, and machinery, to consumer goods ranging from electric light bulbs to bread, from steel drains to ballpoint pens, from car radiators to hair shampoo.

State-directed ISI towards the development of industrial capital and production was a policy of economic regulation that was to last until 1984. This strengthening of the domestic industrial sector was a strategy that can be termed *economic nationalism*. Import substitution through import controls, which had originated in response to the Depression of the 1930s, continued to be advocated in the 1950s and 1960s by New Zealand economists, most notably W.B. Sutch, in order to maintain full employment and to develop self-sufficiency in supplies of essential goods. Measures of economic protectionism were seen as indispensable in order to utilise capital and labour to their full capacity. The main arguments for continuing ISI were based on creating long-term employment opportunities via growth of industrial capitalist production so that the market deficiency of New Zealand's primary exports in the post-1945 period could be rectified and balance of payments and foreign debt problems resolved.

The growth of the manufacturing sector was the prime target, to attain a greater national autonomy and a less dependent economy, and to strengthen the industrial capitalist sector. The actual export of manufactures was not in itself an important target in the program for developing manufacturing in New Zealand. It did, however, become a by-product of the growth of manufacturing to meet the needs of economies of scale and of the national aspiration to be less dependent on the external supply of manufactures and service products. There was, therefore, a significant rise in the export of manufactured articles, and between 1966 and 1975 the nominal value of manufactured exports increased from $7.7 million to $169.2 million (Franklin, 1978, p. 221).

There were, however, critics of this policy of industrialisation via import substitution. It was argued that ISI diverted resources away from the traditional exports sectors. Farmers and some traders belonged to this group of critics, who argued against developing a manufacturing sector in a small economy such as New Zealand's. But economic nationalism had strong backing from both major political parties and the policy was continued of trying to make New Zealand less dependent on imports of essential goods (such as oil) and of helping to develop national talents and skills (and, as a consequence, deter a 'brain drain through emigration). Foreign industrialists also favoured the policy of ISI as it tended to lead to greater demand for their capital goods, which they could supply via foreign investment. In fact, the ISI policy led to a fairly rapid internationalisation of investment in New Zealand, although traditional links encouraged the inflow of British and Australian rather than American or other foreign capital. The flow of foreign capital into New Zealand became substantial during the last two years of the 1930s when the government had first imposed import controls. This inflow continued during the postwar period and, according to Deane (1970), more foreign manufacturing firms established themselves in New Zealand during the decade 1950–60 than in any other preceding comparable period. In the ten years before 1965, there was a concentration of foreign investment in basic producer goods industries and this reflected the attempt towards making New Zealand a self-sufficient economy. Although government policy actively encouraged domestic participation in industrial enterprises, foreign-owned companies (mainly Australian and British) remained just that; the local shareholdings that occurred tended to be in smaller firms (Deane, 1970, p. 24).

The promotion of manufacturing industries in New Zealand, and the associated increase in manufacturing exports, were seen not just as strategies for achieving economic independence. They were also viewed as contributing positively to New Zealand's economic growth. As Elkan put it,

> For New Zealand a policy of industrialisation under protection has been correct, in the sense that it has generated a national product (measured at world market prices) that has been higher both in total and per head of population, than the national product would have been under a free trade policy (Elkan, 1972, p. vi).

From the 1950s to the 1970s, state-directed ISI in New Zealand undoubtedly helped the growth of the country's infrastructure, and the development of the energy, capital, and manufacturing sectors. Changes in the distribution of the labour force were also facilitated, as foreign investment was attracted to the services sector. Foreign investment in the service sector accounted for over 30 per cent of all direct overseas investment in New

Zealand between 1962/63 and 1972/73 (Franklin, 1978, p. 233). Consequently there was an increase in employment in the service sector from 46 per cent in 1951 to 55 per cent in 1981. Agriculture's share of employment fell during the same period from 19 per cent to 11 per cent (Statistics New Zealand, 1951 and 1981). But the cost of protecting domestic industries and maintaining full employment was rising real wages and growing international trade deficits and foreign debts. When agricultural exports began to lose their importance in the international market, as developed countries' income elasticity of demand for agricultural products fell, New Zealand could no longer export enough to finance ISI. Even if the income elasticity of demand for New Zealand exports had remained the same and Britain had not entered the EEC, export incomes would not have been sufficient to maintain the current level of living standards, let alone raise them via increased productivity and fuller employment.

A crisis of capitalism was on the horizon when the wage proportion of GDP began to grow relative to the profit proportion. Whereas the annual rate of growth of company incomes fell from over 14 per cent in 1965 to just 1.5 per cent in 1975, the annual growth rate of wages and salaries increased fourfold (Franklin, pp. 110–11). This had an adverse affect on the profitability of investment, undermining the rate of capital accumulation.

Phase III: Export-Led Economic Growth—Economic Internationalism

The end of the long boom in the mid-1970s signalled the end of the second phase of the globalisation of capitalism. Although the Muldoon Government (1975–84) strove to pursue a policy of economic nationalism—exemplified in the 'Think Big' projects—a new phase of capitalism was emerging that would redefine the state's role in economic management.

Whereas the response to the Depression of the 1920s and 1930s was to call for 'more state', the response to the post-1973 economic slow-down was a demand for 'more market forces'. Whereas state protectionism and regulation had been seen as necessary for capitalist development in the 1950s and 1960s, it was now argued that only through the deregulation of investment capital, labour markets, and trade (via the removal of both subsidies and import restrictions) could further capitalist productive forces be released. This shift towards more market and less state intervention was the result of the crisis that capitalism faced after two decades of the state management of resources, which had achieved increased productivity, full employment, and mass affluence. In other words, the state's active role in fostering capitalist growth and strengthening the capitalist structure of the economy was now declared over. The monetarist or New Right policies that began to grow in influence from the mid-1970s can be characterised as a 'strategy for capital', that is, policy designed to raise the rate of capital accumulation. This is in contrast to the Keynesian policy emphasis on full employment and mass affluence during the 1950s and 1970s—the 'strategy for labour'.

In response to the economic crisis, the New Zealand Government adopted measures designed to change the nature of the relationship between the state and the economy. These steps involved scaling down the state's role in the provision of welfare, privatising state-owned enterprises, liberalising foreign trade, money, and factor markets. The process of market deregulation, selling state assets, and the reduction of state expenditure was begun under the fourth Labour Government (1984–90) and was continued by the fourth National Government (1990–96).

The focus of policy was now on *export substitution* rather than import substitution, on *economic internationalism* as opposed to economic nationalism. Export substitution is different from export promotion, which refers to the promotion of a country's conventional or traditional exports. In the case of New Zealand, this involved the promotion of the exports of meat, wool, dairy products, and the like. Export substitution involves the substitution of such traditional agricultural exports by non-traditional manufactured goods—mainly technology-intensive consumer durables such as electronic products—and new agricultural products. Export promotion involves the production of goods originally intended for domestic consumption, whereas export substitution production is divorced from domestic consumption so that a country produces in whatever area it has a comparative advantage, irrespective of whether the good is consumed locally. Export substitution in New Zealand has taken place in the manufacturing and service sectors, but especially in agriculture.

Agricultural diversification

From the 1950s until the 1970s, agricultural exports played an important role in economic nationalism in the sense that the aim was to earn sufficient foreign exchange to buy industrial inputs, so that external dependence on these inputs could be gradually reduced. With the restricted access to the British market after 1973, the emergence of other low-cost agricultural producers, and the increasing cost of imported raw materials and manufactured goods, New Zealand agriculture responded in two ways. First, the types of agricultural export products were diversified by the further processing of primary produce. This led to the relative decline in importance of traditional primary products such as wool and meat and an increase in semi-manufactured goods such as furs, leather, pulp and paper, textile yarns, and fabrics.

The economic internationalisation of the 1980s also led to the growing importance of horticulture, food processing, and floriculture. These activities are relatively labour intensive and their products have a relatively high income elasticity of demand in both the New Zealand economy and overseas. Also, with the deregulation of labour markets after 1984, there was an increasing supply of cheap labour to meet the expansion of the agro-food industry. The rise of corporates in apples (in contrast to small family capitals), the arrival of some international companies in kiwifruits (Chiquita's shareholding in Kiwi Harvest and the integration of the New Zealand kiwifruit system into the global fresh fruit and vegetable industries), the penetration of New Zealand Dairy Board into Australia, and the shift towards producer-based cooperative dominance in the meat sector, all illustrate the globalisation process in agriculture.

In the 1989 season the Apple and Pear Marketing Board undertook, on behalf of the newly established Kiwi Marketing Board (KMB), to market the total kiwifruit crop through its outlets. The board's purchase of the fruit crops from New Zealand growers was funded by multicurrency loans raised abroad. In the case of the KMB loan of $205 million, banks from Europe and Japan were among those involved. A year later, the KMB was reporting the penetration of the complex sales system for fresh fruit in Japan with a joint venture agreement giving access to convenience, speciality, and department stores (Britton et al., 1992, p. 25). The importance of fruit crops is seen in their export earnings for the 1994 season: $311 million in the case of kiwifruit; $461 million in the case of other fruits (Statistics New Zealand, 1995).

The second way in which agriculture responded to the change in the international economic environment was to seek new external markets for New Zealand's primary products, both processed and unprocessed. The changes in the destinations of New Zealand exports, both primary and non-primary, since the end of the long boom in the early 1970s has been remarkable. Whereas in the late 1960s nearly three-quarters of New Zealand exports were going to Britain, the USA and the EEC countries, by the mid-1990s, South and South-East Asia, closely followed by Australia, were the destinations for the bulk of New Zealand exports. Overall, Asia Pacific Economic Cooperation (APEC) countries took more than two-thirds of New Zealand exports (with Australia accounting for 20 per cent and Japan for 17 per cent).

The third phase of the globalisation of capitalism, therefore, has had a marked impact on New Zealand agriculture. It has also had an effect upon the financial sector, investment, service activities, employment patterns, and welfare. The remainder of this chapter will briefly examine each of these areas.

The financial sector

Until the 1980s, capital flows had been closely controlled by the government. The reform of the domestic foreign exchange market after 1984 was pivotal in promoting an increase in off-shore investment by New Zealand companies. The deregulation of financial sectors helped the rapid growth of the New Zealand financial infrastructure consistent with this third phase of the 'international integration of financial, trade and production networks' (Le Heron and Pawson, 1996a, p. 8). First, deregulation enabled the government to fund its deficit from the New Zealand money market. With unrestrained currency movement, the funds offered to the government in the New Zealand market were typically sourced offshore. There was an upsurge in private sector capital flows, including non-resident ownership of public debt. Second, the New Zealand equities market developed dramatically. Although this initially replaced the company debenture market that had been faced in the early 1980s with strict interest rate controls, the move to equity funds began to alter investor perception of the market. There was a side effect, however. A preoccupation with share investments saw the fall-off in capital expenditure, both replacement and additional, in every sector of the economy, with agriculture and manufacturing particularly hard hit. The heady growth of the New Zealand sharemarket in the mid-1980s culminated in its integration into the global network of stock exchanges.

Third, deregulation led to the financial sector becoming deeply involved in the overseas expansion of New Zealand companies. Domestic retail banks such as the Bank of New Zealand and local merchant banks and insurances companies such as Marac and New Zealand Insurance assisted with the overseas ambitions of their clients. In a similar fashion, Australian financial institutions started to operate in New Zealand on an expanded scale (Britton et al., 1992).

Investment

The technological changes associated with economic internationalism created unlimited opportunities for investment, particularly by making available abundant supplies of labour and human capital. The International Monetary Fund (IMF), the World Bank and the World Trade Organisation (WTO) have been entrusted with the task of creating opportunities for investment all over the world. They have been assisted in this task by the privatisations and restructuring of economies and the decline in state welfarism and trade union power that have occurred, to varying degrees, in all the advanced capitalist countries. This has created an enormous demand for money capital which can be combined with the cheaper labour and other productive resources released through the deregulatory policies.

A survey of foreign investment in New Zealand showed that, up to 1978, overseas companies accounted for 22 per cent of net output in all industries and 24 per cent in the manufacturing sector (Reserve Bank, 1979). A later analysis, based on Inland Revenue Department data, revealed that in 1984 foreign companies owned 35 per cent of the country's total productive assets. In 1983 they also earned 34 per cent of reported net profits of all companies and paid 38 per cent of total company taxes (*New Zealand Herald*, 17 December 1987). The Reserve Bank put the total level of foreign asset holdings at $6.7 billion in 1982 rising to $9.46 billion (35 per cent of the total) in 1984 (Ward, 1987). Share market capitalisation data for 1986 showed that foreign-owned companies, conservatively defined as those with 50 per cent or greater overseas shareholding, accounted for assets to the value of $20.76 billion or 24 per cent of the assets controlled by the country's largest 250 enterprises. By the mid-1990s, foreign shareholdings of the Top Forty publicly listed companies in New Zealand stood at 51 per cent (Le Heron, 1996, p. 34). The privatisation program of the fourth Labour Government and then the National Government also saw the overseas purchase of Telecom, New Zealand Rail, and Power New Zealand.

Service activities
Service sector employment has grown dramatically during the postwar era. Rapid technological changes making both production sectors—agriculture and industry—increasingly less dependent on quantity or unskilled labour and more on quality or skilled labour have initially stimulated the growth of the service sector in all developed capitalist countries. This sector covers a wide range of activities involving both highly skilled and unskilled workers: trade services (banking, finance, insurance, etc.); business services (legal, accounting, technical); community services (educational, medical, cultural); recreation services (cinema, television, theatre); communication and information (aviation, telecommunications, internet); and personal services (catering, hotels, cleaning).

With the internationalisation of investment from the 1950s to the 1970s, followed by that of production, the service sector has received an unprecedented boost, with international communications, information services, education and research absorbing the largest proportion of high-level human capital. Rapidly developing international communications have assumed such an important position in the globalisation of capitalism, that they can easily be likened to the iron and steel industry of the past, which was the backbone of Western industrialisation (Maitra, 1986).

An important aspect of the internationalisation of capitalism is the integration of markets across national boundaries via the operation of individual companies. The development and adoption of a new generation of transport and communications technologies allowed companies to administer and coordinate complex organisations, and to transfer products and money between countries easily, effectively, and relatively cheaply. The deregulatory measures of both the fourth Labour and fourth National Government stimulated the growth of producer services in New Zealand by removing restrictions on activities previously heavily regulated or disallowed by law. Such measures included the removal of entry barriers to allow other local or overseas companies to operate in previously restricted New Zealand markets. Foreigners were also permitted to become members of national exchanges (for example, stocks, bonds, futures, and commodities). These and other measures forced local producers from all sectors to compete internationally and stimulated the demand for producer services. By 1994, employment in the service sector had reached two-thirds of the workforce (Statistics New Zealand, 1994). The down side of this was that much of the increase in service employment was part-time, low paid and low skilled. There was also a gender and ethnic dimension to the phenomenon. Many of the low paid, part-time workers were women and many of the jobs created in the service sector were offset by redundancies in the manufacturing sector where Maori and Pacific Island employment is concentrated (Larner, 1996, pp. 97–101).

The ability to compete in overseas markets, whether by exporting direct foreign investment or as forms of non-equity investment such as franchising, depends on the quality of information available to management. That information can include:

(i) identifying the size and segmentation of potential markets, strength of competitors, distribution channels, credit facilities, commercial properties, and suitable merger and takeover vehicles;

(ii) developing strategies for marketing, advertising, and product specifications; and

(iii) collecting details of current and projected currency and interest rates, and details of commercial regulations at both the national and international levels.

All this has spawned a rapid increase in the number of local specialist firms offering these services and the diversification of service products offered by existing firms such as banks, accountants, and lawyers. There has also been the internationalisation of American, European, and Japanese producer service firms marketing their specific skills, reputations, and branded products, and the growth, within large international enterprises, of inhouse units to service their own needs. Whatever form they take, these developments have created a large number of new producer service jobs (Britton et al., 1992).

The growing importance of services in New Zealand is reflected in foreign exchange earnings achieved by tourism during the period 1987 to 1993, which were estimated to equal those from the meat and dairy industries (Le Heron, 1996, p. 28). Other service industries showing significant growth in the late 1980s and 1990s were international education (zero earnings in 1989, to an estimated $200 million for the 1995 academic year) and consultancy services ($80 million in 1992–93) (*ibid.*).

Employment patterns

Free market operations in the late twentieth century have created a demand for and a supply of low-income and self-employed occupations. Part-time employment in New Zealand between 1989 and 1994 increased by 16 per cent while full-time employment increased by just 2 per cent (Statistics New Zealand, 1994). Furthermore, although the increase in males working part-time outstripped the increase in numbers of female part-time workers, overall women constituted three-quarters of the part-time workforce. Part-time working has also been accompanied by increases in the numbers of New Zealanders working at home—an estimated 48 000 in 1986 (Loveridge and Scholffel, 1991, p. 5). Those working unpaid in family businesses increased by 64 per cent between 1989 and 1994, and those in self-employment by 14 per cent (Statistics New Zealand, 1994).

These changes in employment status were largely the result of the restructuring of the economy and market deregulation. This has not only forced the labour force to become more flexible, but has also challenged the idea of 'full employment' as it was understood in the 1950s and 1960s. Increasingly, the full employment of the long boom period is coming to be seen as 'historically specific, a product of economic and cultural arrangements that have been superseded' (Pawson, 1996, p. 118).

Part-time low-income employment also increased after the introduction of restructuring and privatisation policies. After 1987 only small businesses with up to five workers showed a steady increase in employment. Most of the overall decline in employment between 1987 and 1992 was from the group of firms with over 100 employees, which shed 93 733 full-time equivalent positions (*Otago Daily Times*, 1 December 1995). The figures showed that, although large businesses had a much higher survival rate, they survived at the expense of ~~making employees redundant, which in turn led to greater governmental~~ expenditure in the form of increased unemployment benefits.

The welfare state

The development of the third phase of capitalism has also, in the 1990s, produced an uneasy coexistence between capitalism and welfarism. The welfare state results in Budget deficits, leading to a rise in interest rates and inflation on the one hand and, on the other, high taxes and high wage costs, all of which affect the economy's competitiveness and reduces the resources available for investment. Also, welfare expenditure, by definition, implies social consumption and expenditure, not investment. As such, it acts as a great hindrance to capitalism's role of releasing productive forces. As a consequence, the New Zealand welfare state under the fourth Labour and National Governments was 'redesigned', making it less generous and less extensive. Eventually it will have to be dismantled if New Zealand is effectively to conduct its international trade and remain an active partner in the globalisation process of capitalism. A welfare state and capitalism in its present phase cannot coexist.

Lastly, capitalism no longer needs social welfarism to achieve and maintain full employment, to achieve an equilibrium between aggregate demand and aggregate supply as it did from the 1950s to the 1970s. Capitalism in the 1990s has a limitless world market at its disposal and therefore just a fraction of the domestic market and a tiny fraction (say, less than 5 per cent) of a world market of five billion people, will provide a bigger market than a costly fully employed economy.

Conclusion

In the postwar period, until the 1980s, increasing state intervention in economic reproduction and in the internationalisation of investment was the order of the day. Then the need for state intervention in the economy was declared over and the internationalisation of economic production was possible only by the *negation* of state intervention so that market mechanisms could operate unhindered. In the latest stage of globalisation of production, state intervention is being dismantled under the influence of such international organisations as the IMF, the World Bank and the WTO. These organisations have created and are creating unlimited potential for investment all over the world via policies of restructuring, privatisation, and deregulation (particularly of labour and money markets). This has led to the unlimited demand for money capital that can be met by increasing the rate of government Budget surplus. The continuation of a 'large state' has become the greatest hindrance to the accumulation of global capital via the globalisation of production. High levels of government expenditure, rates of taxation, and Budget deficits all squeeze the resources available for 'productive' capital investment—hence the pressure on New Zealand governments to reduce 'unproductive' welfare expenditure. This highlights the uneasy coexistence of social welfarism with capitalism during the third phase of the globalisation of capitalism.

At the third stage of capitalist development the negation of nation states is a necessary condition. Since capital does not remain a national entity, the role of the state as an agent of social reproduction has been transformed. The traditional concept of the nation state needs to be reevaluated (Bina and Yaghmanian, 1990, p. 93). The nation state does not evaporate but, in an increasingly transnational environment, national policies can no longer remain independent or immune from the imposing influence of global capital. A fundamental contradiction arises between the task of reproducing capitalist social relations domestically and the reproduction of counterparts within the global economy.

The state's role in the third phase of globalisation of investment and production has been more complex and contradictory than in the earlier phases. In the third phase, 'national' policies are determined from without and the nation itself has to promote the objective of the globalisation of capital under the influence of the international organisations already mentioned. During the ISI phase, national policies were motivated to organise industrial capitalism supported by global capital and such policies were internationalist, enhancing the globalisation of investment and production, and the accumulation of capital on a global scale. ISI fulfilled the dual task of developing industrial capitalism and satisfying economic nationalism. But setting up industrial production via ISI networks in many different parts of the world, with the help of international financial investment, was to promote further globalisation of production.

The last 150 years have seen the transition of New Zealand's economy from colonial dependency, to economic nationalism and, finally, to economic internationalism; from a reliance on unprocessed primary exports, to the output from protected domestic manufacturing industries, to the export of processed goods and services. Similarly, the state's role has changed in the way it has 'managed' capitalism and its 'crises'. State involvement in economic management was minimal until the 1930s when, in response to the Depression, the New Zealand Government became a major economic producer, consumer and regulator of economic activities, a role it maintained until the 1980s. Beginning with the fourth Labour Government, the New Zealand state then began to reduce public ownership of the means of production, cut back public employment, and remove a host of state regulations on the economy.

It should be noted, however, that the 'negation of the New Zealand state' does not mean that it is 'withering away'. What it means is that states are voluntarily constraining their powers in order to facilitate the expansion of world capitalism. It is also the case that reregulation of economic activity is occurring during the period following the end of the long boom. The economic crisis was managed by dismantling *domestic* regulations but, at the same time, bilateral, regional, and international regulations are emerging to take their place. In New Zealand's case, the Australia-New Zealand Closer Economic Relations Trade Agreement (CER), APEC, the General Agreement on Tariffs and Trade (GATT), and the WTO are all examples where the domestic government has actively tried to establish bilateral, regional, or global economic regulatory structures.

But whatever the nature of this reregulatory role of the New Zealand state, its main function now is to remove all hindrances towards international competitiveness. It is only in this way that the New Zealand state can help to raise the rate of capital accumulation. Lastly, capitalism in its present phase of globalisation of production creates a condition that ensures capitalism a much longer life by diluting class conflicts. In an economy where a low-income, self-employed labour market (mainly in petty redistributive activities) dominates, with a small proportion of high-level human capital earning high income in the organised production and service sectors, the possibility of class conflict hardly exists. Tiny units of self-employed in completely free market conditions, with nobody to blame for uncertain conditions, live with the hope that there might, as the free market promises, be a better tomorrow.

Guide to Readings

A good introductory text on the global political economy is provided by Law and Gill (1988) while Hettne (1995) focuses on global 'disorder' in the era after the Cold War. Globalisation is examined from various perspectives by Maitra (1993, 1996a, and 1996b), Pettman (1996), Le Heron (1993 and 1996), and Dicken (1992). Cantwell (1989) and Dunning (1981) may also be consulted to understand the process of globalisation of capitalist production in recent times.

On New Zealand's economic developments before 1945, see Simkin (1951) and Prichard (1970). A classic text on New Zealand's economic history from colonial times until the end of the 1970s is Hawke (1985). Elkan (1972) provides a sympathetic view of New Zealand's import substitution policies of the 1950s and 1960s while Deane (1970) offers a detailed account of foreign investment over the same period. The third phase of the globalisation of capitalism and its impact on New Zealand is covered in various chapters by Le Heron and Pawson (1996b).

CHAPTER THREE

MACROECONOMIC DEBATE AND ECONOMIC GROWTH IN POSTWAR NEW ZEALAND

GEOFF BERTRAM

This chapter focuses on some developments in macroeconomic thinking among New Zealand policy-makers during the 1980s and 1990s, with particular emphasis on the rising importance of, and changing approach to, supply side issues. After 1984 New Zealand followed rather closely an orthodox neoliberal blueprint for stabilisation and structural reform, now known as the 'Washington consensus' owing to its association with World Bank and IMF advice to developing countries (Edwards and Van Wijnbergen, 1989; Dornbusch, 1990; Taylor, 1993, 1996; Sachs, 1994). This blueprint prescribes a two-stage approach to reviving economic growth, beginning with disinflation and the elimination of government Budget deficits ('stabilisation') and then moving on to deregulation of the markets for goods, labour, and finance. In a nutshell, the neoliberal approach is to use government intervention to dampen down the demand side of the economy, while turning market forces loose on the supply side. This package stands in contrast to what is often called the 'Keynesian' approach, of sustaining the demand side while using government intervention to promote non-inflationary growth of the supply side.

Preliminaries

The great intellectual divide underlying most modern economic thinking is a philosophical one, between communitarian and individualist views of society. The communitarian view takes for granted the existence of social aggregates such as 'the community' and 'the state' as institutional artefacts, created by human activity but not reducible to any simple aggregation of individuals' abilities and wants. The social whole is not merely the sum of its parts, because human behaviour in the aggregate displays important features that are not reproduced (or, if apparent, are of secondary importance) in the economic behaviour of individuals. Collective behaviour differs from individual behaviour because interactions among individuals, and the dynamic feedback of ideas and emotions across the community of individuals, yield outcomes that would not result from atomistic, self-interested behaviour.

The strong individualist view, in contrast, asserts that collective order emerges from individualistic maximising behaviour, through the agency of markets: impersonal, disembodied mechanisms that need not take any institutional form. Because the community and the state have no existence separate from the individual existences of their members, moral authority lies with the individual. It follows that the concept of 'community' itself is suspect, and the state lacks moral authority except in so far as it performs functions explicitly delegated to it by, and directly serving the interests of, individual citizens.

Real-world economists are mostly to be found somewhere along a spectrum between these two polar positions. The attempt to strike a balance that is both ethically defensible and 'scientifically' illuminating accounts for most of the debates within economics, and particularly for the research program of the neoclassical paradigm. Neoclassical economics, using the individual as its basic unit, is built around rigorous analysis of the market mechanism and demonstration of its power to resolve hugely complex issues of social coordination and resource allocation. Inevitably, such rigorous analysis throws up anomalies—areas in which the market fails to yield the best conceivable outcome—raising the possibility that deliberate conscious human intervention may do better as a coordination mechanism. In these cases neoclassical economics necessarily introduces some human agency or institution established and organised to undertake such intervention. If the state had not existed, neoclassical economics would have had to invent it.

So a potentially quite wide-ranging role for the state arises out of the logic of the neoclassical program itself. The resulting model of the mixed economy (in practice the typical twentieth-century constitutional arrangement) is well founded on neoclassical principles. Along the way, neoclassical economics has had to wrestle hard with difficult concepts such as 'the social good', and with the question of whether there exist feasible forms of state institutions that will sustainably embody some identifiable 'public interest' without falling into the clutches of organised vested interests.

On the other side of the divide, Keynesian and related schools with communitarian foundations begin from the vision of a benevolent state, directed by public-spirited ministers and legislators and staffed by specialist experts, which engages directly with the great economic aggregates from which individual welfare is ultimately derived: gross domestic product, tax revenue and government spending, the public debt, the balance of payments, the inflation rate, the interest rate, the money supply, employment and unemployment, the general wage rate, the capital stock.

To understand how the policy instruments cause the aggregates to change in systematic ways, the Keynesian program was obliged to develop a set of stories about how individuals behave within the aggregate setting. The behaviour of households as consumers, of firms as investors, of banks as intermediaries; the processes by which prices are set in individual industries; the ways in which the structure and level of tax rates affect market behaviour; and a variety of other essentially microeconomic questions, all had to be addressed to carry macroeconomic analysis forward. From the 1930s on, therefore, Keynesian research steadily expanded into the investigation of individual behaviour.

The resulting overlap between Keynesian and neoclassical paradigms has increased over the past half-century, producing among economists a complex intellectual culture full of unresolved contradictions, but also of shared understandings. Keynesianism and neoclassicism relate to each other in a fluid world of shifting allegiances and continual papering over of cracks. Party labels continue to capture important nuances in economic thinking, but can distract attention from the convergence of views in areas where logic and research produce the same conclusions whichever end of the ideological spectrum provided the original motivation.

To sum up, in neoclassical economics the state is the last resort when the market fails, whereas in Keynesian economics the market is the garden that the state exists to tend. A harmonious vision of wild nature, complete with grasslands and jungles, predators and prey, underpins the neoclassical paradigm; whereas Keynesianism springs from the civilising urge to subdue the natural order to conscious human design. Most people are instinctively drawn to aspects of both visions.

The sea change in New Zealand economic policy that began in 1984 moved the country significantly along the spectrum from a communitarian to a more individualist approach, but both the concept and the power of the state survive. The concept has been redesigned and the power has been redeployed, to produce a state that is still 'activist', but in new ways. The pre-1984 New Zealand state tended to place restraints on individual economic behaviour in the name of the social good. The post-1984 state tends to restrain collective behaviour in the name of individual freedom. Along with this, the nature of the social institutions that government seeks to strengthen has changed. As one commentator on the government's published 'Strategic Results Areas' recently remarked, 'the goal of "building stronger communities" . . . set out in the Government strategy statement *Toward 2010* should be reworded as "building stronger markets" ' (Robinson, 1996, p. 4).

The State, Money, and the Labour Market

In terms of recent New Zealand policy-making, a good illustration of philosophical mix-and-match within New Right thinking is provided by the contrast between the fourth Labour Government's Reserve Bank Act 1989 and the fourth National Government's Employment Contracts Act (ECA) 1991. The first of these is informed by the platonic conception of the philosopher king. Power (over monetary policy) is vested in a virtuous individual (the Governor of the Reserve Bank, supported by his employees), who is then supposed to act with wisdom to keep the inflation rate below 2 per cent. The economy-wide inflation rate, a statistical artefact far removed from the everyday market activities of individuals, is measured and interpreted for the Governor by a select group of trained specialists. Popular attempts to understand the issue using the familiar CPI are sternly rebuked by this priesthood for confusing mere 'headline' inflation with the real thing. The goal of low inflation is unambiguously declared to be in the general public interest, regardless of the highly audible complaints of numerous individuals whose private interests the Reserve Bank routinely overrides in pursuit of its social goal. Here the monetarist (but not the individualist) macroeconomic vision rules.

The ECA is from a different stable entirely (see Deeks et al., 1994, Chs 3–6, 20). Here collectivist institutions and protections are stripped away, leaving individual workers and employers confronting one another in a deregulated marketplace, subject only to a general framework of law relating to individual circumstances. The driving vision is of the invisible hand of economic Nature, operating without interference. There is an underlying presumption that the level and structure of real wage rates emerging from an unregulated market have greater moral authority (that is, are closer to the social optimum) than the old system of collectively negotiated awards and explicit relativity comparisons, operated under the active eye of the state. That presumption, in turn, springs from individualist scepticism about the capabilities of the state itself, and active hostility to the collectivist assumptions that formed the founding principles of the union movement.

These two key pieces of legislation, with their contrasting presumptions about the role of the state, became packaged together in neoliberal thinking, and have therefore become a joint target in the minds of many critics of the New Right. The differences between them are, however, significant. The Reserve Bank Act deploys state power to restrain the demand side of the economy, under the banner of fighting inflation. The ECA turns the market loose on the supply side of the economy, under the banner of promoting economic growth. The Reserve Bank Act was produced by a Labour Government that still retained some corporatist elements in its approach to the supply side, whereas the Employment Contracts Act came from the National Government's most evangelical stage of neoliberal restructuring (Dalziel and Lattimore, 1996). In terms of the two-stage process envisaged by the Washington consensus, the fourth Labour Government carried through stabilisation, but left completion of the structural adjustment agenda to the following National Government.

The Faltering and Resurgence of Demand Side Keynesianism

Up to the 1980s, the long-standing battleground between Keynesian and neoclassical traditions of macroeconomic analysis was the demand side of the mixed economy. The central issue in demand side analysis is the quantity of output that an economy's firms can sell at any given price level—in other words, the size of the aggregate market for goods and services. (Supply side analysis, in contrast, is concerned with the profitability of each level of output, and hence the willingness of the economy's firms to meet various levels of aggregate demand.) The familiar Keynesian policy tools are demand side tools. An important element in understanding the strength of the ideological and political swing in New Zealand away from the communitarian position is the rise of supply side issues as problems of economic management. Since 1984, New Zealand's most dramatic and innovative policy changes have been focused on the ways in which economic activity is organised and regulated—the area referred to in economics as 'governance'. The following discussion traces some of the events and thinking that shifted New Zealand's economic policy focus from Keynesian demand side intervention to individualist supply side intervention, and notes the existence of opposing communitarian and individualist paradigms on the supply side that are not necessarily to be identified with the Keynesian and neoclassical schools.

In the 1960s and 1970s, many policy advisers and politicians oversold the ability of a simplified version of Keynesianism to confront real-world problems that were becoming increasingly complex and difficult. The Keynesian economics which was the target of sustained and effective attack throughout the 1970s was this drastically simplified, stripped-down version used by governments for practical policy-making.

This stripped-down version offered three central ideas. First, cyclical fluctuations in capitalist economies were attributed to tidal ebbs and flows in aggregate demand, which would carry ungoverned economies to full employment only at the high-tide points, and otherwise tended to result in underemployment of resources. Second, two key areas of government activity—fiscal policy, and the supply of money—provided direct leverage on aggregate effective demand, so that government possessed the means to offset the forces of recession and thus hold the economy close to full employment on a sustainable basis. Third, the full employment supply of goods and services was given by the economy's endowment of labour, capital, and technology, and could grow only as fast as that endowment expanded. Although government could influence this process at the margin, the dominant forces on the supply side were seen as exogenous and hence beyond the reach of government.

The Keynesian policy synthesis thus attributed to government the ability and the duty to manipulate aggregate demand to keep it as close as possible to aggregate supply, as the latter grew at its own pace. If government had any influence on economic growth, it was likely to be as a by-product of demand management rather than as a result of direct intervention in the productive side of the economy.

Demand side Keynesianism therefore viewed the supply side from the perspective that exogenously determined 'full employment' represented the upper limit on what demand management could hope to achieve. The supply side was also given a role in the generation of inflation, in a sense that can be captured by the metaphor of (demand side) waves breaking against a (supply side) shore. Where the shoreline consists of rocky cliffs, the breaking waves are forced up, throwing spray high in the air. Where the shore is a gently sloping beach, offering less resistance, there are fewer conflicting forces and hence less spray. The Phillips Curve provided a picture of the (supposedly geologically fixed) cliff against which demand side waves broke with an inflationary force that increased as the tide rose up a steepening slope.

When, all over the OECD, this cliff began to move in the 1970s, the mental world of demand side Keynesianism was thrown into confusion, although it took some time before the geological view of the Phillips Curve became completely untenable. The 1970s was a decade in which the Phillips Curve not only moved about, but did so in a way that was clearly the product of human economic behaviour, not just chance tectonic upheaval. The 1970s brought a series of highly visible supply side shocks to the Western economies.

Labour unrest, beginning in 1968, drove up wages; from 1973, oil producers drove up oil prices. Both the wage push and oil shocks put pressure on profitability, and hence on supply. Many developed economies experienced sharper economic fluctuations, and they were perceived to be coming from the supply side. The rationale for demand management was abruptly reversed. Far from keeping aggregate demand pressed up against a full employment cliff, demand management became a matter of pulling aggregate demand back in the face of advancing thickets of supply side vegetation. The stagflationary era had arrived.

The conception of the supply side as a living thing rather than a rock required a significant mental repositioning for many policy economists, and while this was under way the intellectual and political initiative was seized by monetarist and New Classical schools, whose policy influence was at its height during the 1980s. At the same time a new set of ideas from the individualist camp seized the commanding heights of policy on economic growth of the supply side.

Supply, Demand, and the Cycle

Looking back from the standpoint of the 1990s, statistical work on New Zealand's business cycle has confirmed overseas research that renders the fundamental premise of demand side Keynesianism—that the business cycle under capitalism is driven by demand fluctuations—true only for certain historical periods. The 1930s appears to have been a period when big economic swings were demand driven, and so the original Keynesian model was a product of its time. But from the Second World War through to the 1980s, evidence suggests that the ups and downs of capitalist economies, including New Zealand, were, to a considerable extent, supply driven. The main diagnostic indicators are the price level (reflected in the inflation rate) and the real wage. To understand the significance of these, a brief digression is necessary.

The simple Keynesian story of a demand-led cycle in a competitive economy runs as follows. As demand expands, so employment and output increase to match. Because output and employment depend on the profit maximising behaviour of firms across the economy, the story requires that the demand expansion causes some set of market changes which individual firms read as a signal that it is now profitable to hire more workers and increase output. Generally speaking, the usual signal of greater profitability is an increase in prices relative to costs. Across the economy as a whole, this would translate to a situation where the general price level rises relative to the two great aggregate variable costs—wages and the cost of imports. With the price level rising more rapidly than money wage rates, the real wage rate (measured as the cost to an employer of hiring another worker) should fall as the boom takes off. Two empirical predictions from this model of the business cycle are that price inflation should speed up during booms and slacken during recessions; and that the real wage rate should drop at the onset of a boom, and, conversely, should rise during the downswing into recession.

Under scrutiny, the statistical record shows the opposite for much of New Zealand's economic history during the past half-century. Price inflation has shown a tendency to slacken during booms and increase during recessions (Gobbi, 1994; O'Donovan; 1994; Buckle, 1995). The real wage rate, meantime, moved with the cycle, not against it, for most of the years since 1969 (Kim et al., 1994, Figure 4, p. 66). These facts are consistent with a number of possible alternative theories of the business cycle. They can fit, for example, into a model which assumes that the typical firm is not operating under perfect competition (Chapple, 1993, Part 2). They can be used to support the view that cycles are driven by supply rather than (or as well as) demand. They cannot, however, easily be squared with the widely accepted Keynesian model of 1960s vintage, nor with Keynes' own analysis of price and wage trends during the Depression in Britain (Wells, 1995, pp. 318–21).

The most common response to the experience of the 1970s, and to the evidence from statistical analysis, has been for economists to adopt a more eclectic view of the forces driving the business cycle, and hence of the policies required to confront it (if government is to intervene at all). Undergraduate economics textbooks now routinely teach students to think in terms of supply shocks as well as demand shocks buffeting the economy and pushing it away from its sustainable, low inflation, reasonably full employment path (for New Zealand, see, for example, Wooding, 1992, Ch. 8). The menu of conceivable instruments that might be used by government is correspondingly expanded, but the difficulty of diagnosing each cyclical episode as it unfolds (and hence knowing which instrument to choose) is greatly increased.

Taking the supply side seriously is now common ground among economists of all persuasions. Equally, the overreaction that led some in the 1980s to reject Keynesian insights altogether has faded with time. Since the mid-1980s in New Zealand, the business cycle seems again to be conforming to the Keynesian model of demand-led fluctuations, but another period of supply-driven business cycle behaviour could emerge at any time.

The New Classical Mirage

In terms of policy thinking, the 1970s breach in the international Keynesian consensus allowed the overreaction against Keynesianism a window of opportunity—and nowhere more than in New Zealand under Roger Douglas and Ruth Richardson. It would be unfair to suggest that more than a few New Zealand officials fully believed the New Classical story, in which government is powerless to affect the course of output and employment in any systematic way. It would, however, be fair to claim that advice to economic ministers during the mid-1980s was coloured by strong suggestions that disinflation could be carried through relatively painlessly (that is, without causing serious unemployment), provided the government's policy was clearly announced and fully credible. In a setting where beating inflation had moved to the top of the list of demand management objectives, government hastened to embrace the hope of a low-cost, politically acceptable, disinflation process.

Subsequent experience, in New Zealand as elsewhere, demonstrated that Keynesian macroeconomics could still accurately identify the likely weaknesses in a neoliberal stabilisation program. The recession of output and employment that began in New Zealand in the mid-1980s and continued until after the late 1991 relaxation of monetary policy matched Keynesian predictions and refuted the painless disinflation predictions of the oversimplified New Classical model. Studies of the expectations held by firms and households repeatedly demonstrated that the rational-expectations hypothesis, despite its usefulness as a theoretical benchmark, does not accurately represent real-world behaviour (Roseveare and Millar, 1988; Buckle, 1988; Buckle et al., 1990).

New Zealand, indeed, experienced in its own way the same empirical discrediting of extravagant neoliberal claims that took place during the 1980s in the USA (Krugman, 1994). In the USA, the large-scale economic experience of the decade validated Keynesian stories. Sharp monetary contraction at the beginning of the 1980s, driven by the Federal Reserve, succeeded in killing inflation only at the cost of a severe recession. Then Reagan's (accidentally) very expansionary fiscal stance in the middle of the decade led to rapid recovery and near full employment. Similarly in New Zealand, Roger Douglas' experiment in fiscal and monetary deflation with a floating exchange rate produced high unemployment, weak export performance, and zero growth—trends accentuated by the fourth National Government's sharp fiscal contraction of 1990–91, and reversed only as fiscal and monetary pressures were relaxed after 1991.

New Zealand policy discussions in the mid-1980s were marked by repeated claims about the neutrality of monetary policy in the short as well as the long run—a New Classical proposition that did not survive the decade. By the 1990s all policy-makers recognised that fiscal and monetary policy have real effects on the economy in the short run, and there was renewed interest in building up a systematic understanding of those effects in order to improve policy. Even the New Zealand Treasury had a macroeconomic model built for it (Econtech 1995; Powell 1995; Osborne and Wells 1995).

There was, therefore, a far greater degree of consensus among New Zealand economists in the mid-1990s than had been apparent a decade earlier. The white heat of the New Classical revolution had come and gone, and policy macroeconomics was moving back to the less glamorous but more serious business of analysing the empirical record and attempting to build models that captured its essential features. This meant not only a growing volume of high quality empirical work on the history of output, employment, and the business cycle in New Zealand over the past several decades, but also a welcome revival in the scope and quality of official statistics on the economy, after a period in the 1980s when statistics were regarded within government almost as the enemy of economic analysis.

The Rise of the Supply Side

The supply side of an economy is where production is organised, factors of production are hired, and prices are set. Until the 1970s most Keynesian and neoclassical thinking shared a simple vision of the supply side, encapsulated by the concept of the aggregate production function. An economy at each point in time has a certain endowment of productive resources and a particular level of technology, all of which are combined together by firms to produce output. Full employment output is reasonably well defined: as population, capital stock, and technology all advance through time, the economy's productive potential increases. The short-term cyclical fluctuations on which Keynesian macroeconomics focuses, and which have been the main area of debate between Keynesians and neoclassicals, smooth out in the long run into a growth path for the economy, which macro-economic theorists long tended to treat in a rather mechanistic fashion.

Mainstream macroeconomics until the 1980s was generally content with the 1950s 'Solow-Swan' model of economic growth, based upon the premises of perfect competition and static efficiency. In this model the central conclusion was that a capitalist economy would tend towards a steady state, in which output would grow at a rate dictated by population growth and techno-logical progress, neither of which could be controlled by government. Policy issues, therefore, did not arise. Neoclassical thinking in microeconomics, as noted earlier, had grappled throughout the twentieth century with the issue of how market failure in particular markets could arise, and whether government intervention in those particular markets could improve matters. But this research program was motivated by the quest for static efficiency, not aggregate growth. Only fringe disciplines such as development economics, whose practitioners were constantly challenged to find policies that would accelerate the growth of poor economies, maintained high-level theoretical debates over whether industrial protectionism, central planning, labour training and employment subsidies, financial sector development, and so on could make a difference to the aggregate supply side in terms of its rate of growth.

The Keynesian tradition shared this lack of a satisfactory growth story. The belief that government could usefully intervene through demand management produced a general presupposition in favour of intelligent government intervention. There was, therefore, some tendency for Keynesian-influenced economists to take a sympathetic view of arguments for infant industry protection, economic planning, and government investment in social overhead capital. None of these, however, was in the 'hard core' of the Keynesian program. The main growth-related conclusion from the Keynesian model was a negative one: if government allowed resources to lie idle through unemployment, the long-run growth of the economy would be retarded, relative to the full employment path, because investment opportunities would be allowed to slide by.

In short, macroeconomics about 1980 really had nothing systematic to say about the long-run growth of the supply side. The great USA debates over demand management, which spilled into New Zealand during the 1980s and provided most of the focus of popular interpretations of Rogernomics, were not aimed at growth issues. The same is true of the celebrated 'supply side' school of evangelistic USA tax-cutters, whose primary focus was on short-run improvements in static market efficiency and the government Budget. Yet it was in pursuit of an improvement in long-run growth performance that the most dramatic and lasting policy changes of the past fifteen years were made in New Zealand. The 'Keynesians versus neoclassicals' story fails to illuminate this.

Institutional Reform and Growth

In growth, as in most other areas of economic policy, New Zealand governments since 1984 have relied on imported neoliberal economic ideas, mainly through the medium of government officials (especially from Treasury), some academics, and business-funded lobby groups (Easton, 1988; and Chapter 4).

Key planks were deregulation of markets, removal of protection, corporatisation and privatisation of government activities, and financial liberalisation (especially the removal of controls on capital flows in and out of the economy).

As in the area of demand management, the general topography of the debates was provided by the individualist/communitarian divide. But the individualist victory was more total and sweeping on this front than in demand management, leaving communitarian and corporatist ideas on economic organisation relegated to the shadows and still marginalised in New Zealand political debate.

Internationally, it was a slow-down in the growth of the leading capitalist economies that brought the spotlight of mainstream economics onto issues of growth and productivity in the 1980s (Baumol et al., 1994). For three decades after the Second World War it had been easy to suppose that growth simply happened of its own volition, owing to steady technological progress embodied in the growing capital stock and measured by rising labour productivity. This, essentially, was the neoclassical vision. The experience of OECD economies in the 1970s was that labour productivity growth suddenly slowed down, and failed to pick up in the 1980s. Two other grand empirical generalisations forced themselves on the attention of governments and economists at the same time. The experience of the less developed economies showed them failing to close the gap on the rich countries, despite the increasing integration of world markets. East Asian exceptions simply proved the rule. And the performance of planned economies in the Soviet Union, Eastern Europe, and China faltered even more dramatically, leading to the abandonment of planning itself and a switch towards market economics.

In the economics literature, debates that had been relegated to fringe disciplines now moved to centre stage. Three were of particular significance. First was the debate in development economics over whether industrialisation of backward economies could be achieved more effectively through regulated or deregulated markets. Second was the discussion among economic historians about the long-run dynamics of capitalist economies. Third was the rising research program of institutional economics, with its focus on the importance of industrial organisation and 'governance' in explaining dynamic economic performance. On all three fronts, the individualist tradition in social science made great strides in the two decades after 1970, while the communitarian tradition was on the defensive.

To provide some context for the ideas in the New Zealand setting, some long-run growth data is worth looking at. Easton (1990a) assembles consistent GDP data from the First World War through to the establishment of the present System of National Accounts in 1977. Linking his series to the official series since then, the long-run path of actual and trend growth can be plotted for the period 1918–95 (see Figure 3.1).

Figure 3.1 New Zealand GDP and GDP per capita, log scale, 1918–95

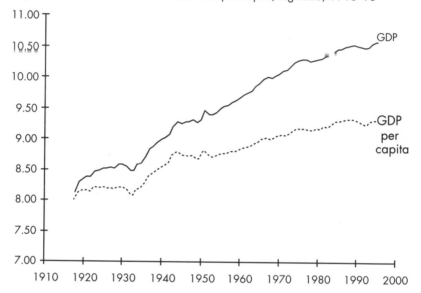

Three features stand out in Figure 3.1. The first is that the New Zealand economy for the half-century after the Korean War followed a smoother and less dramatic path than previously. Economic events in the first half of the twentieth century really were bigger, and hence probably easier to analyse and understand, than those in the second half. The Depression, the extraordinarily sustained boom following the election of the first Labour Government in 1935, and the bumpy postwar ride through to the early 1950s, all stand out. Then suddenly the picture becomes quieter, the trends more consistent, and the Holyoake slogan 'steady as she goes' sums up the postwar era.

The economic landmarks of recent history can certainly be discerned—the 1968 recession, the first oil shock, the late 1980s slow-down, and the 1990–91 recession are all there, as is the rapid recovery up to 1995—but in long-run historical context, these events are of secondary magnitude. The 1990–91 recession is the nearest approach to high drama in the post-1950 record.

Second, if one looks to history for clues as to how to make the New Zealand economy grow rapidly, the obvious starting point is the 1935–44 period when real per capita income registered an annual growth rate of over

7 per cent for a decade. That period was one of full-blooded government intervention, in an economy with unemployed resources where the Depression had produced a national ethos in favour of shared effort, and stimulated from 1939 by the Second World War (see Baker, 1965). The particular historical conjuncture which made possible that hugely successful period of national economic mobilisation was unique in the twentieth century, but Figures 3.1 and 3.2 show dramatically why Keynesian and social-democratic ideas on economic management came to have such high prestige in postwar New Zealand thinking. (They also illustrate why so few critics of 'Keynesianism', in New Zealand and elsewhere, have been willing to carry their arguments back before the 1950s.)

Figure 3.2 Annual growth rate of New Zealand real per capita GDP, 1920–95, expenditure basis, March years

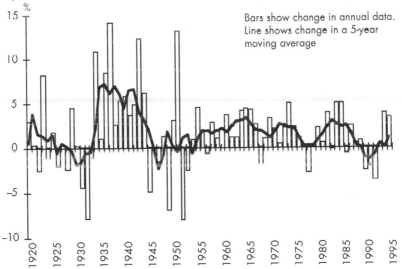

The third major feature of Figure 3.1 is that in terms of per-capita output (and hence average real individual incomes) the New Zealand economy's path over the four and a half decades since the Korean War was pretty steady up to 1990, and the recovery from Ruth Richardson's 1991 recession had only just brought the economy back on track again by 1995. The declining trend in the growth rate of total GDP after the 1960s, which is evident in the top line in Figure 3.1 and has been the subject of much commentary, was accompanied by a slow-down in population growth, and so is far less visible in the per capita GDP series, which is probably a better guide to how New Zealanders form their subjective perceptions of aggregate economic performance.

Figure 3.2 presents the Figure 3.1 data in terms of annual growth rates of per capita GDP. Some downward shift in average growth performance after the 1960s is discernible, owing mainly to the relative severity of the two most recent major downturns during the late 1970s and late 1980s-early 1990s. The 1992–95 growth rates, coming out of the latest recession, are seen to be consistent with long-run historical performance in the sense that they are in line with the rates of the mid-1960s, mid-1970s, and mid-1980s. Nothing comparable to the performance of the economy in the late 1930s is yet on the horizon. Meantime, in strong contrast to that postDepression decade when the first Labour Government's social policies dramatically improved the distribution of income, the past decade has been characterised by a radical shift towards income inequality and the re-emergence of mass poverty (see Chapter 5; Kelsey, 1995).

There are two stories on offer about what Figure 3.2 shows for the 1980s and 1990s. The official story runs as follows. From the late 1960s, the long-run growth performance of the New Zealand economy deteriorated as traditional export markets were lost and productivity growth slowed. Simple 'Keynesian' tools of demand management were powerless to deal with either of these problems, since world markets lie outside New Zealand control and productivity is a supply side, not a demand side, issue.

The old pattern of New Zealand economic growth was considered to have become unsustainable. In the mid-1980s, therefore, radical policy changes were introduced to shake up the supply side of the economy and restore sustainable growth. These policies imposed substantial economic sacrifices and took nearly a decade to pay off, but by the mid-1990s the economy's 'fundamentals' had been put right, with a strong fiscal position and flexible, efficiently functioning labour and goods markets. The prospects for sustainable growth were therefore good (OECD, 1993; Treasury, 1993, Ch. 3).

The alternative story is more cautious and less optimistic. It recognises that growth momentum slowed in the 1970s, and that economic shocks were becoming more severe compared with the golden era of stable growth from 1950 to 1968. It agrees also that the late 1980s and early 1990s were a period of radical policy innovations targeted mainly at the supply side, accompanied by contractionary demand management that ultimately subdued inflation at the cost of prolonged mass unemployment. The stabilisation process dragged New Zealand below its long-run trend growth and left the productive side of the economy weakened by a decade of low investment and the deskilling effects of long-term unemployment. Reliance on monetary policy to curb inflation squeezed profitability and confidence in the export sectors on which long-run growth depends. Economic insecurity and social dislocation increased sharply and the economy's infrastructure was allowed to run down. The cyclical upturn from the long recession has begun to take the pressure off, but growth rates since 1992 have remained comparable to those in previous cyclical upturns and there is not yet enough information to say whether the present performance can or will be sustained, especially given the recent weakening of the balance of payments current account (Bayliss, 1994).

The most careful and systematic scrutiny of the GDP growth and cycle data has been the recent work of Hall (1993, 1995, and 1996) and Kim et al. (1995). Hall emphasises the problems of trying to make strong claims about the economy's performance on the basis of short runs of data, and without taking account of the business cycle. Looking back to Figure 3.2, it is obvious that growth from 1991 to 1995 will look impressive if taken out of context, while growth from 1985 to 1995 was effectively nil in per capita terms. Several more years will have to elapse before it is possible to look back and measure the pay-off from New Zealand's stabilisation and re-structuring program, in terms of the economy's performance over a full cycle.

Bearing in mind Hall's strictures about the need to distinguish between cyclical swings and genuine long-run trends, it is instructive to take a carefully selected unrepresentative subset of the data in Figure 3.2, starting at 1965 and ending at 1981. Note that this involves taking a trend line from the peak of a boom to the trough of the sharp recession caused by the Muldoon Government's fiscal retrenchment of 1976.

The 1965–81 data explain the air of near panic over New Zealand's growth performance that came to pervade policy circles from 1979 on. The Muldoon Government's response was an eclectic mixture of demand side and supply side measures. To confront unfavourable external markets, the exchange rate was devalued between 1979 and 1982 on a crawling peg basis, and Closer Economic Relations (CER) with Australia was pushed ahead. To confront weak domestic investment and high oil prices, Think Big—a taxpayer-subsidised raft of major investment projects in energy-related industries—was introduced, and in 1983 monetary policy was loosened. The New Zealand economy responded in much the same way as the USA economy responded at about the same time to President Reagan's combination of a space defence program ('Star Wars'), tax cuts, and Federal Reserve monetary relaxation. By the mid-1980s economic growth was back to historically respectable levels and unemployment was falling.

As in the USA, this recovery was purchased at the price of a large fiscal deficit and rapidly rising government debt. In official and political circles there was widespread concern that the improved economic performance was unsustainable. Think Big projects were proving as grandiose, unproductive, and wasteful as Star Wars, while from the resurgent political New Right came urgent calls for a balanced Budget and a switch from incomes policy to monetary policy to contain inflation.

In 1984 the political cycle intervened, removing Muldoon in New Zealand but leaving Reagan intact in the USA. New Zealand abruptly changed policy tack, while Reagan stayed majestically on course. The USA proceeded to grow its way back to full employment while successfully bringing inflation down to comfortable levels in the second half of the 1980s, leaving the Budget deficit and government debt to another day. New Zealand opted for cold-turkey neoliberal stabilisation in pursuit of 'sustainability'.

So much of the neoliberal supply side package that followed was defined by contrast with the allegedly 'unsustainable' Muldoon approach, that serious debate on the sources of growth was effectively buried after the 1984 Economic Summit. The constantly chanted slogan 'there is no alternative' (TINA) sufficed to force through corporatisation and privatisation of government commercial activities, reform of the financial sector, removal of import protection, and the 1991 breaking of the union movement.

The main international influences on the supply side of Rogernomics are readily identifiable. From development economics came the deregulationist free trade ideas of Little (Little et al., 1970 and 1974), Lal (1983), Krueger (1978, 1981–83 and 1985), and the World Bank after Robert McNamara's departure (World Bank, 1987). From economic history came Mancur Olson's ideas on the rise and decline of nations, emphasising the 'sclerosis' of entrenched vested interests (Olson, 1982). From institutional economics came the ideas of Williamson (1970, 1975, and 1985), and Buchanan (1975), Buchanan and Tullock (1962), Buchanan et al. (1980) on the importance of governance incentives in keeping institutions honest. Combined, these added up to a formidable intellectual package which, in New Zealand during 1982–85, overwhelmed the corporatist wings of both the Labour and National parties and gave the Treasury a commanding intellectual lead among government departments, as a result of Treasury's practice of cycling its young recruits through top USA graduate schools and encouraging in-house reading and discussion of the new ideas (see Chapter 4).

The results of the institutional shock therapy to which many sectors of the New Zealand economy were subjected in the decade after 1984 cannot yet be fully evaluated, partly because many of the patients have only just regained consciousness and some remain on life-support systems. Two general observations do, however, seem justified. The first is that, outside the areas of education and health, there is ample evidence of sharp increases in firm specific productivity across considerable areas of the New Zealand economy—most spectacularly the privatised former state-owned enterprises such as railways and telecommunications. The second is that economywide productivity ('total factor productivity') rose at an historically low rate during the main phase of restructuring from 1985 to 1995, indicating that the sharp improvement in profitability for privatised enterprises resulted basically from mass lay-offs of workers (who then, unemployed, dragged down the economy's overall productivity performance). Preliminary indications of accelerated economywide productivity growth in the mid-1990s cannot yet be taken as evidence of a break with the long-run growth path followed by New Zealand since 1950.

New Zealand economic research is now, however, entering a period when the success or failure of the great restructuring will begin to emerge in the statistical record. The changes to the economy's structure and incentives have been as radical as those of the first Labour Government in the 1930s, albeit that the activism this time has involved more demolition than construction of the state's economic armoury. The New Zealand historical benchmark for a successful, sustainable growth boom is set by the achievements of import controls, state housing, war mobilisation, and the welfare state from 1935 to 1944. Even the strongest supporters of the recent changes generally set their sights lower than 7 per cent per capita growth sustained for a decade; but merely holding on to 2–3 per cent growth will probably leave nagging doubts over whether the sacrifice ratio has been acceptable.

Conclusion

Supply side dynamics—both long-run growth and short-run cycles—are at the heart of the 1990s research agenda of economists worldwide. The discussion in this chapter has served to locate the relevance of those debates to New Zealand policy-making, but only a sketchy outline of the theory and practice of neoliberal supply side policy intervention has been possible. Empirical evidence on the long-run success or failure of the post-1984 New Zealand reforms is not yet available, and discussion of the recently developed models of 'endogenous growth' and 'real business cycles' in the economics literature is a major task in its own right.

The new focus of economic thinking, however, will continue to flow through to policy in New Zealand and elsewhere. The production possibilities of the economy as a whole were for a long time treated in macroeconomic textbooks and thinking as physically given and not susceptible to change by social engineering. The result was a lifeless conception of the 'full employment' or 'natural rate' level of output, and a focus on the demand side as the arena of intervention by the state. The new models emphasise the importance of institutions and behaviour in determining total factor productivity, and thereby reopen old economic debates about the supply side role of the state.

Since 1984 a retreat from Keynesian demand management has enabled the state in New Zealand to reallocate its resources and attention into the institutional reform of markets and of the state apparatus itself. The first wave of this reform program has been strongly individualist and anti-statist in nature, a trend that is highlighted by comparison with the more corporatist approach of Australian reform up to the 1996 defeat of the Keating administration. As the discussion of the Employment Contracts Act and Reserve Bank Act above indicated, however, there is no necessary incompatibility between supply side deregulation and demand side management. Indeed, many New Zealand economists generally regarded as Keynesian in orientation were broadly supportive of the thrust of supply side reform; Easton (1985, 1997) has described these as 'Market Keynesians', who saw supply side modernisation as the proper counterpart to full employment policies.

It is not, therefore, helpful to try to schematise the supply side debates in terms of categories such as 'Keynesian' or 'neoclassical'. The division between individualist and communitarian thinking on the supply side takes a different, still evolving, form, and draws attention away from the arena of macroeconomics into the detailed microeconomic analysis of market organisation and the role of the state in imposing institutional structure onto economic behaviour.

Guide to Readings

The 'Washington consensus' on stabilisation and structural reform is set out in a large number of World Bank publications and clearly summarised in Dornbusch (1990). A leading figure in mounting a critique of the orthodox approach at international level has been Taylor (1993, 1996). The importation of USA economic thinking into New Zealand during the 1980s is documented in Bollard (1988), and the main microeconomic features of the New Zealand supply side reforms have been documented in a series of studies produced under the aegis of the New Zealand Institute of Economic Research, with an overview provided in Savage and Bollard (1990).

Discussion of the structural reforms from an economy-wide standpoint is provided by Dalziel and Lattimore (1996), and systematic quantitative comparisons of the performance of the New Zealand and Australian economies during New Zealand's restructuring decade 1984–94 are provided in Edwards and Holmes (1994). Two substantial critics of the New Zealand restructuring are Bayliss (1994) and Kelsey (1995). In contrast, OECD (1993) portrays New Zealand as a successful example of the orthodox package in action.

An historical study of New Zealand's long-run economic performance, which places the 1980s in context and focuses on issues of macroeconomic management during the reform years, is Easton (1996). His data on GDP trends since 1920 are in Easton (1990). The long-run GDP numbers are further refined and analysed in detail by Hall (1993, 1995, and 1997), currently the most systematic academic analyst of growth performance over the past two decades.

CHAPTER FOUR

TREASURY AND PUBLIC POLICY FORMATION

SHAUN GOLDFINCH

Constitutionally, elected politicians are responsible for making public policy decisions—public servants only advise. A growing body of literature has, however, recognised the power of bureaucrats in initiating, formulating, implementing and evaluating public policies. This can include determining what policy alternatives are available, excluding some issues from discussion and deciding what facts will settle questions (Aberbach and Rockman, 1988; Considine, 1994; Egeberg, 1995). In a similar vein, writers in New Zealand have noted the importance of bureaucrats, especially those working for the New Zealand Treasury and the Reserve Bank, in formulating and driving those economic and social changes known as Rogernomics that overtook New Zealand from the mid-1980s to the early 1990s (Easton, 1989a; 1990b; Jesson, 1989; Kelsey, 1995; Roper, 1991a). Treasury dominance of the public policy process in the small public policy community in Wellington, in the context of a unitary state with few checks on executive power, has also attracted considerable attention (Boston, 1989; Cocker, 1995).

This chapter identifies the basis of Treasury power in the policy process. In order, however, to assess Treasury's role in policy formation, it is necessary to consider the wider theoretical framework in which Treasury develops its advice. In the late 1970s and early 1980s Treasury gradually abandoned the social democratic Keynesian framework that had dominated in the postwar era. By 1984, Treasury was advocating a broad program of market liberalisation and macroeconomic disinflation that drew heavily on the analytical assumptions, ideological values, and policy prescriptions of schools of economic and social thought associated with the New Right. It is this close alignment with the theories and ideology of the New Right, and the functioning of neoclassical economics as a political ideology, that highlight the fallaciousness of Treasury's claim to be a 'non-political', 'rigorously neutral', and 'independent' adviser to the government (Treasury 1984, p. iii; 1986, p. 4; 1992, p. 2). Although it is no surprise that Treasury advice is pro-capitalist, the New Right neoclassical policies Treasury advocates present a picture of only one variant of capitalism. Furthermore, the power of Treasury in the policy process and peculiarities of policy-making in New Zealand limit the ability of alternative views of how the economy should be organised to be heard.[1] This exclusion of other views takes on added significance in the face of the far-reaching changes known as Rogernomics that were 'crashed through' in the face of considerable opposition, undermining the legitimacy of the political process.

Treasury Power Examined

Since before the Second World War Treasury has been acknowledged as the most powerful department within the policy community in New Zealand, with influence over almost all aspects of public policy (Boston and Cooper, 1989; Polaschek, 1958). This power derives from a number of sources. Most important, Treasury's role as financial controller requires it to report on all departmental submissions that have financial implications and gives it a key role in the Budget process. This includes providing advice on the state of the economy and on the impacts of fiscal policy, advising on specific revenue and expenditure decisions, including the votes of other departments, and preparing Budget documents (Boston, 1989; Fancy, 1993). The importance of this power in the Budget process is underlined by the use of Budgets to pass often large amounts of wide-ranging social and economic legislation (see Boston, 1993, pp. 126–31). This legislation sometimes raises funda mental questions of economic organisation and social policy, and may set the broader philosophical framework in which other public policy is made and evaluated. Because Budgets were traditionally prepared under secrecy, the ability of Parliament and others to debate Budget issues was constrained.

Treasury is able to establish a reputation for high-quality advice, expertise, and analytical strength, partly because of its comparatively large number of qualified policy and financial analysts. This, along with a socialisation and training process that produces an esprit de corps unique in the New Zealand public service, gives Treasury analysts a confidence and ability to press the well-established Treasury view in policy-making against competing perspect- ives. The Treasury view also permeates the public service through the appointment of Treasury officials to top posts in other departments. Treasury has sometimes had strong backing in Cabinet because of the high ranking of the Minister of Finance, as well as the support of the additional finance ministers (Boston, 1989, p. 77). This support can be extremely important if there are close ties between Treasury and the Minister of Finance, as was the case both when Roger Douglas and Ruth Richardson held the finance portfolio. Treasury has also seconded officials to the Leader of the Opposition since 1975 (Oliver, 1989). Finally, because of Treasury's strong ties with the business community, a government that consistently ignores Treasury advice risks losing business confidence (Goldfinch and Roper, 1993, p. 52). This loss of confidence was something Prime Minister Robert Muldoon experienced during the late 1970s and early 1980s.

Treasury's power has been strengthened by a number of changes to economic policy machinery in the postwar era, especially after 1984. Important developments in the immediate postwar era include the establishment of the Economic Stabilisation Commission in 1942, chaired by the Secretary to the Treasury and abolished in 1951; and the establishment in 1952 of the triple-tiered committee structure for economic policy-making (comprising the Cabinet Committee on Economic Policy, the Officials Committee on Economic Policy, and various working parties of officials), which remained in place, with significant changes, until its abolition in 1984.

The fourth Labour Government reorganised the Cabinet committee structure and in 1989 established the Treasury-serviced Cabinet Expenditure Review Committee (later the Expenditure Control Committee) (Boston, 1990; Galvin, 1985; Low, 1970; Moriaty, 1945; Schroff, 1993). For much of the postwar era there were frequent attempts to achieve some sort of consensus in policy-making, while significant power and research bases within other departments provided some limits to Treasury dominance (Galvin, 1991; Moriaty, 1956; Reserve Bank, 1960). During the fourth Labour Government, however, economic policy formation became increasingly centralised, with the Officials Coordination Committee and the Cabinet Policy Committee often being by-passed and policy being made by a small clique of officials and ministers. Consultation with interest groups or other departments was largely avoided, and with fiscal questions only Treasury and the tax authority were involved. Monetary policy was left largely to the Reserve Bank, with Treasury input when fiscal policy and monetary policy were to interact. Restructuring of the public sector also removed some potential rivals to Treasury influence (Boston, 1991b). Under the National Government after 1990, some formal consultative machinery, such as the Prime Minister's Enterprise Council and the Prime Ministerial Taskforce on Employment, was established.

Treasury During the Keynesian Era

In the 1950s and 1960s, Treasury, while seen by the standards of the time as having a slightly 'rightist' stance, operated within the dominant social democratic Keynesian framework, which saw an important role for the state in moderating 'over-violent ...competition' and in stimulating 'the economy in times of sluggishness' (Moriaty, 1956, p. 225). The demands of the interventionist state for greater sophistication in information gathering and provision of advice was probably a major factor in the growth of Treasury's research and operations sections and its evolution from an accounting-based organisation to one that, by the 1960s, was peopled largely by economists. Treasury officials were, however, at times critical of some of the economic policies followed (while still remaining within the Keynesian framework); they were wary of the import licensing schemes and the degree of import protection for domestic manufacturing, regarded the growth of some types of regulation with suspicion, and raised objections to some Think Big projects developed during Muldoon's National Government (Boston, 1992b, p. 201; Carpinter, 1979, p. 1, Morrison, 1987). The move away from the broadly Keynesian framework began in the late 1970s and early 1980s and, whatever the dynamics of this change, New Right neoclassicism was dominant in Treasury by the 1984 election and by the release of the postelection briefing papers, *Economic Management*.

New Right Neoclassicism and Treasury's Postelection Briefing Papers: The Herald of Free Enterprise

The term New Right refers to a broad neoliberal policy-oriented agenda that received most prominence under Thatcher and Reagan during the late 1970s and early 1980s (Gamble, 1988; Green, 1987). The term neoclassicism originally described what was orthodox economics from the time of the marginalist revolution of the late nineteenth century, until its supersession (or supplementation, depending on one's view of the Keynesian synthesis) to some extent by Keynesianism after the Second World War. Present neoclassicism is generally the term applied to what is, in many ways, a revival of this tradition; certain schools of orthodox neoclassical thought have largely rejected innovations of Keynes and Keynesian thinkers, and have attempted to rehabilitate (sometimes slightly modifying) theorems held by the early twentieth century neoclassicals (Clarke, 1988; Fine 1982, Ch. 6). Although the New Right can be seen largely as a product of neoclassical thought, all schools of neoclassical economics cannot necessarily be termed New Right; the use of the term neoclassical is complicated by the overlap between economists who accept some elements of Keynesian macroeconomics and others who may not hold totally orthodox positions. This being said, certain influential schools of economic thought such as the supply siders, the Chicago school, Public Choice and the New Classicals are normally seen as part of the New Right movement; most are also orthodox in the neoclassical tradition.

This section will look at the policy advice contained in four Treasury postelection briefing papers: the two volumes of *Economic Management* released in 1984; the two volumes of *Government Management* released in 1987; and postelection briefing papers released in 1990 and 1993. The first, *Economic Management,* prepared in a remarkable six weeks because of the ᵘʳᵍᵉⁿᶜʸ ᵇʳᵒᵘᵍʰᵗ ᵒⁿ ᵇʸ ᵗʰᵉ ᶜᵃˡˡⁱⁿᵍ ᵒᶠ ᵗʰᵉ ˢⁿᵃᵖ ᵉˡᵉᶜᵗⁱᵒⁿ, ᵖʳᵒᵛⁱᵈᵉᵈ ᵃ ᵇˡᵘᵉᵖʳⁱⁿᵗ of what were to be the Labour Government's economic policies for the next six years. All four papers show the influence of a range of New Right neoclassical theory and prescriptions, particularly the Chicago school, New Classical economics and Public Choice writings, while supply sider and Austrian economics and other New Right thinkers in the liberal and libertarian tradition are also influential.[2] Often these writings are borrowed almost verbatim and with questionable relevance to New Zealand's historical and social context. As documents, the briefing papers are notable for the detailed neoclassical explanation they give of New Zealand's economic malaise, and for the comprehensive and usually coherent set of remedies they offer. Their coverage extends from microeconomic issues to education and even Treaty of Waitangi issues.

A self-regulating economy

Neoclassical economics sees the economy as a self-regulating mechanism following natural laws (Dugger, 1989; Hosseini, 1990). These 'laws' can be discovered through a priori reasoning (as claimed by Austrian economics), but to a large extent reflect the history and development of economics from the late eighteenth century, when these basic laws were first developed and adopted (see Katouzian, 1980, Ch. 2). Critics of neoclassical economics note the continuing hold of core assumptions of neoclassical analysis despite the lack of empirical verification or even in the face of seemingly conclusive empirical falsification. Neoclassical economics, then, is essentially a deductive discipline, closer to mathematics than to more empirically based disciplines such as biology or a social science such as experimental psychology (see Bergmann, 1989; Rosenberg, 1992).

What does constitute the core assumptions of neoclassical economics is open to some dispute. According to Hahn, neoclassical economics attempts 'to locate explanations in the actions of individual agents' (that is, methodological individualism). In 'theorising about the agent [it looks] for some axioms of rationality' and it holds 'that some notion of equilibrium is required and that the study of equilibrium states is useful' (Hahn, 1984, pp. 1–2).

Methodological individualism, rationality, and the invisible hand

Neoclassical economics bases its study on units of the individual and the firm (treated as an individual). The individual is often elided with the household, with the household seen as having unitary wants and interests (little account is taken of labour or division/conflict within the household). Society and the economy are merely the aggregate of these individuals and firms—the sum of their individual actions, wants, and needs. Society and economy are not stratified by class or by legitimate interest groups, and class groupings or interest groups have no independent existence; instead, these are just collections of discrete individuals following their own interest (Hayek, 1979, pp. 90–7). These individuals are seen to be rational, where rationality takes an instrumental form which states that an agent will act selfishly (and largely asocially) to satisfy the set, stable preferences held by that agent, and will choose the best means of satisfying those preferences (Heap, 1989; Wolfson, 1994).

It is these rational optimisers contracting in the market that unconsciously and unintentionally bring about a 'spontaneous order' or 'catalaxy' in both the economic and social spheres (these are Hayek's usages; see Hayek, 1976, p. 73; 1979, pp. 90–7). This metaphorical invisible hand is formalised through Walrasian general equilibrium theory (Heap, 1989, pp. 42–3). The notion of general equilibrium is the belief that a set of prices is simultaneously determined in each market that allows all markets to clear; 'that everything depends on everything else'. This situation is Pareto optimal, which means that no one can be made better off by redistributing resources without anyone being made worse off. As commentators point out, although mathematically minded economists may be able to determine, under exceptionally strict conditions, that such a situation *can* logically exist, no one has adequately shown how such a situation would *come* to exist in reality, or that it has ever existed (Ormerod, 1994, pp. 71–91; Rosenberg, 1992, pp. 200–15). Despite this, general equilibrium analysis is central to neoclassical economics and underpins the belief that the economy is always tending towards full employment general equilibrium where all markets are cleared and all resources (including labour) are employed (Blaug, 1985, pp. 584–5; Rosenberg, 1992, Ch. 7). This is the case, of course, unless the economy is prevented from moving to such an equilibrium by 'market distortions', such as the stickiness of prices and wages or the interventions of government. The downward rigidity of wages is therefore the primary cause of unemployment. Equilibrium analysis also functions as a system of natural order for the economist; both society and the economy follow natural laws in reaching a harmonious state of order through the operation of self-interested individuals.

Although individuals following their own interest will lead to order, the pleading of interest groups, and the actions of government, tend to subvert this natural order of society and economy (Hayek, 1979, pp. 90–7).

The belief in a self-equilibrating economy peopled by atomistic rational individuals underpins Treasury policy advice. In places, Treasury adopts a rather extreme form of methodological individualism, where even families are broken down into their component individuals, and where families are themselves outcomes of instrumentally rational actions (that is, people belong to families because of self-interest) (Treasury, 1987, pp. 405–10). It is these individuals contracting in the market that will lead to a greater good for society as 'competition and markets can be seen as organisational arrangements that allow individuals to undertake mutually beneficial transactions while aligning the interests of the individual with those of society' (1987, p. 4 and p.16). Interest groups can use their influence to subvert this spontaneous order, and as such should be resisted (Treasury, 1984, p. 114). This belief that classes and interests have no legitimate claim to be heard has important policy implications. If the wishes of interest groups are debased to the expression of their selfish interests, which may have harmful society and economywide effects, they can safely be ignored by policy-makers.

Market liberalisation

In Chicago school theories, prices that agents transact in the market are generally assumed to be prices that clear the market and to be optimising prices for agents contracting in the market (Reder, 1982, p. 11). Markets behave as if they are perfectly competitive. Because of the assumption that market prices are optimal prices and will allocate resources of agents most efficiently, Chicago school policy prescriptions focus on allowing markets to achieve these 'correct prices' and permitting the unhindered operation of markets to generate allocative efficiency and the greater sum of welfare (Griffin, 1988–89, p. 74; Rayack, 1987, p. 54). The Chicago school therefore recommends a broad program of market liberalisation, including introducing markets where they have been replaced by other forms of allocation or where they have not existed. This includes the elimination of trade barriers, subsidies, and exchange controls; a reduction of consumer, labour, and environmental regulation; the deregulation of the financial sector; the curtailment of the influence of trade unions; and the privatisation of state enterprises and state services (Friedman and Friedman, 1980, pp. 189–227, 237–8; Griffin, 1988–89).

For Hayek and the Austrian school, the importance of the market resides in the scope it provides for innovation; it is a discovery procedure, a learning process bringing together the widely dispersed knowledge of many individuals, where this information can be simplified and coordinated by the price system. Central planning by government agency could not hope to acquire the broad knowledge carried by these individuals with their special skills, and because of factors of time and space, and so will be less efficient than the private market (Grassl, 1986, pp. 171–3; Hayek, 1982, pp. 67–75).

The Public Choice school applies the rational optimiser model of neoclassical economics to actors in government organisations; public servants and politicians are assumed consistently to pursue their own interests. Public servants seek better pay and conditions and attempt to increase their power and influence by expanding the resources held by their departments. They start to identify with the interest groups with whom they deal, acting in support of their wishes, against the greater good of society (that is, 'they are captured'), and they have no motivation to use resources efficiently because there is no market to discipline inefficiencies (Buchanan, 1988; Self, 1993, Chs. 2–3). Therefore government provision of services is 'inherently inferior to the market' (Buchanan and Tullock, 1984, p. 81). Followers of Public Choice claim that market failure has been overemphasised and the possibility of government failure all but ignored, so that even in the case of 'market failure' government intervention may be inappropriate (Green, 1987, p. 103).

Treasury policy advice is marked by an idealised view of the market that is characteristic of New Right neoclassical thought. Markets are held to be superior in terms of efficiency, the greater sum of welfare they generate, and the freedom they effect. Following Hayek, the market is also seen as a discovery process (Treasury, 1984, p. 297; 1987, pp. 15–16). Consequently, in 'many situations, provided markets are allowed to operate efficiently there is no superior alternative' (Treasury, 1987, pp. 3–33; 1984, p. 11). Accordingly, Treasury recommends a broad program of market liberalisation across all sectors of the economy. Inappropriate interventions in the interests of certain groups or sectors, such as subsidisation of industry, trade barriers, and restrictions of entry into the professions, as well as the regulation of the financial sector, are believed to have resulted in the protection of inefficient producers, distorted the efficient allocation of resources both within these sectors and over the entire economy, and led to an inflexible economy (1984, pp. 106–8; 1987, pp. 190–3, 239–90; 1990, p. 162; 1993, pp. 66–9). Trade unions and laws governing the operations of unions and the labour market (including incomes polices) have contributed to unemployment and low productivity growth by distorting the labour market (1984, pp. 239–47; 1987, pp. 270–9; 1990, Ch. 9). Other controls on the labour market, such as minimum wage laws, have hurt the people they are designed to help by pricing them out of the labour market (1984, p. 240; 1987, pp. 287–90; 1990, p. 156). Regulations have a large number of unforeseen costs, they may result in the coercive powers of government being stretched beyond their limits, and injustices that they are trying to correct (such as the violation of consumer rights) may be better dealt with by self-regulation (in the case of the professions), by competition in the market, by private contractual agreements, or through the law courts (1984, p. 297; 1987, pp. 27–9, 258–9; 1990, pp. 160 70). Accordingly, Treasury would prefer that 'regulation generally should not be used to restrict rights to enter into voluntary agreements' (1987, p. 256).

Rather ironically for a state sector policy body, Treasury is an enthusiastic advocate of the Public Choice critique of the public sector. Bureaucrats are seen by Treasury to follow their own interests in terms of extending their own power, salaries and conditions; there is no market to discipline their work and the work of their managers; they do not have incentives to conserve resources; they are open to capture by client groups; and the funding of government services creates a tax burden on the rest of the economy (1984, pp. 130–1; 1987, pp. 58, 41–8). Although market failure has been over-estimated, government failure has been all but ignored (1987, pp. 41–2; 44–7). Treasury recommends that social services be funded, where possible, by private insurance and provided by private firms, unless a case can be made for them not to be, and that state-owned businesses be privatised (1987, pp. 38–41; 1990, pp. 91–2).

Macroeconomic disinflation

The Chicago school advocates the abandonment of activist fiscal and monetary policy because, in a self-regulating economy that is moving towards equilibrium or is at equilibrium, a non-individually optimising government can only be ineffective or cause outcomes that are less than optimal (Reder, 1982, pp. 16–31). Fiscal spending and investment crowd out private investment and informational limitations of government and time lags in implementating policy mean that activist policy has unpredictable and destabilising effects. The Chicago school claims that there is a 'natural rate of unemployment'; although the government can, in the short run, trade off increased inflation for employment, in the long run (as workers react to the fall in their real wages and withdraw their labour) this is ineffective and the economy returns to its natural rate of unemployment at a higher rate of inflation (Blaug, 1985; Weeks, 1989, pp. 197–200). The New Classical school claims that activist policy is impotent even in the short run. As agents are assumed to hold rational expectations and so can effectively model the economy without systematic error, they will anticipate intended policy results and so react to any government policy, negating its impact on real economic activity (Hoover, 1988, part III; Ormerod, 1994, pp. 106–10).

Chicago School theorists believe that money is neutral; that is, in the long run changes in the supply of money have no impact on real variables such as income and output but may affect inflation. The increase in the money supply then, is the substantial reason for inflation and inflation is, in the long run, 'always and everywhere a monetary phenomenon' (Friedman and Friedman, 1980, p. 254). Some New Classicals see money as superneutral; even in the short run, increases in the money supply have no effect on real economic variables (Hoover, 1988, pp. 214–16). Both schools, however, have similar policy prescriptions. Although discretionary monetary policy is rejected, monetary policy has an important role in targeting inflation. Ideally, prices should be controlled by rule-based reductions in money supply growth. For the Chicago school, inflation is considered damaging because it distorts relative price signals and therefore the efficient operation of markets, leads to uncertainty, and erodes international price competitiveness (Whitwell, 1992, pp. 192–3). Any shocks to the economy caused by controlling inflation will be quickly overcome by the self-regulating economy, so that targeting inflation through the money supply will not have detrimental long-run effects on employment or outcome.

Treasury's macroeconomic policy advice is heavily derivative of Chicago and New Classical thought. The use of discretionary fiscal and monetary policy is rejected as only short-term benefits are seen to be gained for the cost of inflation in the long run. Also, private individuals anticipate changes in monetary and fiscal policy and react to them, negating their impact on real economic activity. Discretionary macroeconomic policy can also be subject to time lags and can create uncertainty in the economy. Expansionary fiscal policy is rejected because private investment is crowded out through high interest rates caused by funding the fiscal deficit, while at the same time funding fiscal deficits can generate inflation. Ultimately, unsustainable taxation and debt-servicing burdens are placed on the economy (Treasury 1984, pp. 108–10; 139–41; 1987, pp. 5–6, 231–2; 1990 pp. 72–3; 1993, pp. 93–4).

A distinctly monetarist explanation of inflation is adopted in the 1984 Treasury papers, where growth of the money supply is seen as 'the fundamental . . . source of inflationary pressure' (1984, p. 15). Later, although the language used may have softened somewhat, Treasury was still advocating the use of monetary aggregates 'as an indicator or even target of monetary policy' and recommending a move away from targeting the exchange rate (1990, p. 60; 1987, pp. 217–19, 221–2). Inflation is seen as undesirable because it 'tends to obscure the price signals which are fundamental to the working of a market economy' and leads to an erosion of international price competitiveness (Treasury 1984, p. 144).

The aim of monetary policy, then, is to combat inflation in the medium term; it is not to be used as an instrument to influence output (1984, pp. 141–7; 1987 pp. 209–10; 1990, p. 61). Because the discretionary use of fiscal policy is rejected, it should instead act purely in a supporting role for this disinflationary monetary policy (Whitwell, 1990, pp. 104–5). So the role for macroeconomic policy is focusing on eliminating fiscal deficits and moving towards (or maintaining) fiscal surplus, and attacking inflation through manipulation of the money supply (Treasury, 1984, pp. 141–7; 1987, pp. 209–10; 1990, pp. 45–6; 1993, pp. 89–99).

Supply side economics and the welfare state

Supply side economics focuses on the investment, savings, and work decisions of individuals and how these are affected by the spending and taxing decisions of government. Individuals are seen to be motivated primarily by monetary considerations. High marginal income tax rates are considered to provide a disincentive for workers to produce and save, as less take-home pay causes workers to substitute leisure for work and present consumption for savings (Garrison, 1990, p. 153). High corporate tax rates on profits lower the incentive for capitalists to invest as net returns will be lower, lower the profit available for reinvestment, and reduce savings available for investment. Welfare payments that are high relative to wages provide a disincentive to seek work (Rinder, 1984, pp. 17–38). Because reducing taxation will provide for greater productivity and increased investment, and therefore higher growth and incomes, as well as reducing the incentive for tax avoidance, then cutting taxes may actually increase the aggregate tax return (Roberts, 1988, p. 19).

For Friedman and the Chicago school, the welfare state creates dependency, decreases incentives to seek employment, contributes to higher tax rates and fiscal deficits, and creates a self-interested and inefficient bureaucracy. Benefits often accrue to the middle classes, rather than those in genuine need (Friedman and Friedman, 1980, pp. 119–20; Rayack, 1987, Ch. 8). If welfare is provided at all, it should be by direct income supplement such as a negative income tax rather than by direct provision of goods and services (Friedman and Friedman, 1980, pp. 119–20; Griffin, 1988/89, pp. 83–4).

The writers of the Treasury postelection briefing papers share some of the misgivings Friedman and supply siders have about the redistributive welfare state. High welfare payments are seen to reduce incentives for individuals to provide for themselves, to decrease their independence and dignity, and to discourage them from seeking employment (1984, Ch. 12; 1987, p. 170; 1990, Ch. 8; 1993, p. 83). The high marginal tax rates that are needed to support the welfare state and other government spending lead to disincentives for work effort and wealth creation, resulting in lower savings rates, and therefore funds available for investment, as well as lessening the incentives to invest by reducing net profitability (1990, pp. 46–7; 1993, p. 101). High tax rates also increase tax avoidance and evasion (1987, p. 37). Also, the cost of the welfare state is seen as unsustainable in a climate of low growth and adds to debt burdens for future generations (1984, p. 249; 1987, Ch. 3; 1990, pp. 99–100). Treasury claims that social services have been captured by the middle classes, have led to the creation of large and inefficient bureaucracies, and should be narrowly targeted on the basis of need through income redistribution rather than the direct provision of services (1984, Ch. 12; 1987, pp. 7–8, 173–83; 1990, pp. 103–4, 112–16). The possibility of using Friedman's negative income tax is also suggested (1984, p. 217).

A minimal state

Treasury writers see the state, ideally, as a minimal one existing substantially to protect private property. Their approach is similar to that of Nozick (1974), Hayek, and other writers in a liberal or libertarian tradition upon which neoclassical economics draws. Treasury sees individuals having basic rights: 'human rights' that 'express relationships between individuals with respect . . . to each other' and private property rights (Treasury, 1987, p. 13). From the first principle of enforceable rights, Treasury moves to the correct place and function of government, where enforcing these rights is 'perhaps the fundamental explanation for the existence of government' (p. 13). The role of government is to provide the legal, institutional and constitutional structure to maintain these rights, to provide limited income transfers, to protect the economy from internal or external threat, and then to stand back and 'let individuals . . . voluntarily transact between one another' in the marketplace to 'pursue their own well-being' (p. 124). Once fiscal balance is achieved, taxes are reduced and prices controlled, deregulated markets will 'spontaneously generate non-inflationary growth, balance of payments equilibrium, and higher employment in the medium term' (Goldfinch and Roper, 1993, p. 57). Inflation is to be controlled through the money supply, but even this is to be insulated from democratic control by placing it under the control of the Reserve Bank (Dalziel, 1993). The Fiscal Responsibility Act 1994 has further locked future governments into this 'fiscally responsible' path (Kelsey, 1995, p. 3).

Treasury: a Non-Political, Rigorously Neutral and Independent Adviser to the Government?

Treasury claims that it provides 'independent economic and financial advice and information to the Government' (Treasury, 1992, p. 2). Similarly, Roger Douglas introduced the 1984 briefing papers as a 'comprehensive, independent and professional assessment of the state of New Zealand's economy and of the many difficult policy issues which confront us all' (Treasury, 1984, p. iii). If it is true that Treasury officials are just technicians applying value-free scientific analysis to society and economy in order to generate the maximum efficiency and welfare for all, then Douglas and Callan are justified in claiming that Treasury can 'give advice based on the interests of the nation as a whole' (1987, p. 128). This is in marked contrast to the 'viewpoint of many others who seek the Government's ear, whose role it is to pursue the interests of particular sections or groups within the community' (Treasury, 1986, p. 4).

Claims that policy advice can be neutral, independent, and non-political are, however, fallacious. Such claims are also self-serving, and seek to deflect critics who might maintain that polices being advocated reflect the particular ideologies and value systems of the policy-makers. Few would now accept that it is possible for any social science, economics included, to be value-free (Bhaskar, 1989, Ch. 4; Grant and Nath, Ch. 1; Nelson, 1993). Indeed, neoclassical economics could be seen to function as a political ideology or philosophy. It defines the role of the state; the ideal human being (as an atomised optimiser), the role of the market and how social order is to be determined, and conditions how such things as power, race, gender, and social relations are to be discussed; that is, it eulogises a *particular type* of *laissez-faire* capitalism (see Rosenberg, 1992, Ch. 7; Mullard, 1992, Ch. 2). In any event, Treasury goes past the barest use of neoclassical techniques and adopts much of the ideology of the New Right, as the previous sections have shown.

Policy-making is an inherently political process (Aberbach and Rockman, 1988). Politics is more that just the clash of political parties; it is also sometimes an undignified struggle over resources, power, the access of particular interest groups or classes to influence, and the role of the state, among other things. All these are part and parcel of policy formation. There is no reason to believe Treasury officials would or can be any more 'neutral' than anyone else in such a political struggle. It is no surprise that policy-makers will act to maintain capitalism and that business has a privileged position when it comes to policy formation (Lindblom, 1977). This being said, Treasury officials are often drawn from the same classes that go to make up business executives and they may move back and forth from the private sector or into business-oriented think tanks (such as the Business Roundtable, which prescribes remarkably similar policies to Treasury). These ties with business may be further cemented by the social connections that are unavoidable in Wellington's small policy community. It is also the case that while those outside the business sector, such as unions and some interest groups, can be openly hostile to or even contemptuous of Treasury officials and their views, many business leaders, especially in the financial sector, are often strongly supportive of Treasury and its policy prescriptions. It is, of course, something else again to jump to a conclusion that Treasury is the tool of business. It is quite possible, however, that Treasury officials will bring their own interests and values to bear when formulating policy, especially if their actions are driven by the same optimising self-interest and if they are open to the same client capture they impute to other bureaucrats.

Limiting Treasury Power: A Corporatist Solution?

While the New Zealand economy in the 1990s appears to be performing reasonably well on a number of indicators, it may seem churlish to raise objections regarding Treasury's power in policy formation.[3] Possibly, despite the criticism of its policy advice and the ways this advice dominated policy formation, in the end Treasury has been vindicated. This, however, raises three issues. First, could a similar (or better) performance have been obtained using other policy measures and other types of economic analysis? Second, while New Right theory claims that insulating policy formation from interest groups and other élites improves policy outcomes, are there good grounds to believe that, in fact, better policy outcomes might be obtained by the interplay of different forces in policy formation? Third, and most important, whether or not one believes the changes were for the good, what are the implications for a democratic state when changes largely foreign to a nation's history and culture are imposed by a small élite of public servants and ministers, largely by 'crashing through', and in the face of wide-scale opposition?

At the beginning of the 1980s New Zealand seemed to be facing an economic crisis and growing globalisation of the world economy may have demanded some liberalisation of the economy (Easton and Gerritsen, 1996). But, despite claims of 'there is no alternative' (TINA) (James, 1992, pp. 190–6), and the certainty of tone in Treasury briefing documents, there is certainly no one path to economic success. First, the particular neoclassical policy response presented by Treasury is only one type of economic analysis in a field that is anything but unified. The neoclassical paradigm itself, plus the two major competing paradigms, Keynesianism and Marxism, include a host of occasionally overlapping and competing schools (see, for example, Cole et al., 1991). A wide variety of theoretical and research work, not strictly within any of these three paradigms, is carried out by institutional economists, economic geographers, and political economists of various shades. Second, there is a host of successful national economies that do not necessarily fit with the neoclassical model; such as the corporatist economies of Western Europe (Lijphart and Crepaz, 1991; Pontusson, 1991), the partly state-directed economies of the so-called Asian Tigers (Bell, 1995; Wade, 1990), the networked economies of the Third Italy, Baden-Wurttemburg, and Japan (Cooke and Morgan, 1993; Kumon and Rosovsky, 1992; Perry and Goldfinch, 1996), and the Australian 'hybrid of neo-liberalism and neo-corporatism' (Higgott, 1991, p. 15). That Treasury did not examine alternatives to its neoclassical framework, nor deal with the many and long-standing objections raised to neoclassical economics, makes their policy advice, at times, partial. Although it is difficult to say if alternative economic policy frameworks would have given similar or better results, if New Zealanders had been given a choice, it is possible that some would have preferred the type of economic policy that was less likely to lead to rapid growth of poverty and income disparity, breakdown of social cohesion, and attacks on union power through the Employment Contracts Act 1991, or that may have avoided the extended recession of the late 1980s and early 1990s.

The second point concerns the way policy is made. Public Choice literature and the beliefs of Treasury both provide rationales for the exclusion of 'vested interests' from policy formation. According to Douglas, structural reform must 'crash through' or 'crash' (Douglas, 1993, Ch. 10). There is, however, a respectable tradition of analysis in political science that looks at how better policy outcomes are generated exactly through the interplay of different forces and through negotiation and compromise (Lindblom, 1988). It is unlikely that Treasury and Roger Douglas were correct all the time, and it is quite possible that having to explain, justify, and compromise would have improved the quality of policy advice and outcomes. Also the 'blitzkrieg'-like way changes were imposed (Easton and Gerritson, 1996), especially considering the role of an unelected bureaucratic élite in advocating and introducing those changes, raises questions regarding the operation of democracy in New Zealand. New Zealanders have a strong belief in participatory democracy (Lamare and Vowles, 1995), but had little say in or notice of the changes imposed. The powerlessness that some may have felt was magnified by the reneging of both the Labour and National Governments on election promises and on party traditions (Mulgan, 1992). As Boston (1993) points out, such a 'crash through' strategy runs the risk of undermining the legitimacy of a political system. Although well short of violent revolution, the changes to the electoral system, and the partial eclipse of the Labour Party and the rise of new political forces such as the Alliance and New Zealand First, suggest that something close to a loss of legitimacy occurred in the early 1990s.

How, then, is the power of Treasury to be limited, and how are views other than Treasury's to be given a fair hearing in policy formation? If the Australian experience is anything to go by, it is unlikely that a mere division of Treasury would achieve this result. The Treasury-Ministry of Finance split in Australia in 1976, specifically to counter the Treasury, did not in fact lead to the new ministry espousing views much at variance with Treasury. Potential rivals in Wellington, such as the Department of the Prime Minister and Cabinet, do not now offer significantly different views from those that would be found in Treasury. An entirely new policy body would need considerable resources and ministerial support or be doomed to irrelevance. It may be that, given the small size of the public policy community, it would be difficult to justify two major competing economic policy bodies. Claims that bureaucracies should be made more representative by increasing the number of women or of minority groups (Hale and Kelly, 1989) may be a good idea for a number of reasons, but is of itself unlikely to limit Treasury power, especially given the effectiveness of the socialisation process for new groups in Treasury itself. It is also unlikely that mass action will significantly limit Treasury power, as Goldfinch and Roper (1993) claim. This is because policy formation is a process often dominated by élites, and the most immediate way to reduce the power of one élite (such as Treasury) is to increase the ability of counter-élites to balance this power.

So although institutional change to the machinery of government and broad opposition may be significant, more important change would be to the way policy is made. A policy-making framework that explicitly recognises the right of certain groups to be involved in policy formation and implementation, and coordinates and facilitates this involvement, such as is found in corporatist-type systems, may be the most effective way of ensuring that alternative views are heard. Real attempts at consensus building (rather than window dressing exercises such as the Economic Summit of 1984 in New Zealand), where interest groups are consulted and brought on board for policy changes, may ensure that policy developments obtain support and legitimacy. It may be that part of the solution already lies in the 1993 adoption of the mixed member proportional (MMP) electoral system. It is possible that Treasury power was partly a function of New Zealand's elective dictatorship (Mulgan, 1992) and that the advent of MMP will see a greater range of views being aired and a greater likelihood that such a corporatist-type model would be adopted.

---

1 It is not being suggested that Treasury was always the dominant actor in policy formation or that there were not other important factors and players in the adoption of Rogernomics. A large body of literature, however, suggests that, at least on some issues and a certain times, Treasury was the most significant actor formulating policy. Kelsey would go so far as to say 'Treasury was, without doubt, the driving force behind the structural adjustment programme' (1995, p. 50).

2 Other important influences that can be detected are Chicago school-related economics of property rights and contestability theory, agency theory, and transaction cost analysis.

3 It could be argued, however, that the short period of positive economic performance experienced in the mid-1990s is not enough to vindicate empirically the 'Treasury line', given the poor economic performance since 1984 (see Chapters 1 to 3).

Guide to Readings

There have been a number of articles and books written on the New Zealand reforms. A recent and accessible one is Kelsey (1995). Castles et al. (1996) puts the New Zealand experience into an international perspective by comparing it with changes in Australia. A number of chapters in Roper and Rudd (1993) examine reasons for the adoption of these reforms in New Zealand. For a survey of new right neoclassical thinking, see Reder (1982) on Chicago school economics, Hoover (1988) on new classical economics, and Self (1993) on public choice; for a general overview, see Green (1987). Rosenberg (1993) makes a challenging critique of the methodology of neoclassical economics. Mullard (1992) provides a useful study of economic policy-making. For a study of the role of bureaucrats in policy-making, see Aberbach and Rockman (1988) and for a critical study of policy-making in general, see Considine (1994).

PART II

CIVIL SOCIETY

CHAPTER FIVE

THE CHANGING CLASS
STRUCTURE

BRIAN ROPER

Inequality is a pervasive feature of New Zealand society. The existence of gender and ethnic inequality is widely recognised, both by those on the right, such as the Treasury (1987), and by those on the left (Kelsey, 1995). Such inequality is evident in the official statistics, has been carefully documented in numerous studies, and has been thoroughly discussed in the scholarly literature. In the universities, women's studies and Maori studies, along with other social scientific disciplines, address the issues arising from women's oppression and inequality between Maori and Pakeha. Although they remain largely ineffective in remedying inequality, equal employment opportunities (EEO) programs in the public and private sectors have been formally implemented and aim to eliminate discrimination based on gender and ethnicity. But writers in the liberal tradition have consistently dismissed the view that the existence of socio-economic inequality is evidence that class relations, interests, and struggles are central to the structuration of New Zealand society (Treasury, 1987; Mulgan, 1993).

Although it is understandable that those on the political right, such as the Treasury, the Business Roundtable, and the National Party, seek to deny that society is characterised by class inequality, many of those on the left have also failed explicitly to discuss class inequality and conflict. For example, the terms 'class' and 'class struggle' appear no more frequently in Kelsey's (1993, 1995) otherwise valuable critiques of Rogernomics than in the Treasury briefs upon which that program of reform was based. The feminist literature in New Zealand pays scant regard to the interconnections between gender and class—even Du Plessis (1993) seems reluctant to conceptualise socio-economic inequality explicitly in terms of class. And Awatere (1984), in her seminal text on Maori nationalism, fails to provide a systematic consideration of the class dimension to Maori subordination.

In opposition to this neglect of class, the central argument of this chapter is that New Zealand society is fundamentally stratified by class and that class inequality, class interests, and class struggle are central both to the overall organisation of this society and its polity. Class matters. Whether we are conscious of it or not, it shapes our lives in profound ways. The denial of the centrality of class to social structuration and politics is based much more on an acceptance of, or at least passive acquiescence to, the dominant liberal ideology that legitimates class inequality, than on sound intellectual reasoning.

The Reality of Class Inequality

Income and wealth have always been unequally distributed in New Zealand society, even during the long boom of the 1950s and 1960s when it was generally assumed that this was an egalitarian society free of class divisions (Gould, 1982, pp. 32–6; Easton, 1983, p. 188). There have, however, been significant historical shifts in the overall pattern of income distribution. In this regard, the postwar era can be divided into two distinct periods. The first period, from 1945 to 1974, was characterised by a small but significant decline in income inequality (Easton, 1983, p. 7). The second period, from 1975 to the late 1990s, has been characterised by a sharp rise in inequality with respect to the distribution of income and wealth.

Easton observes that although between 1951 and 1976 income became slightly more equally distributed, by 1976 it was clearly still distributed in a highly unequal manner. According to his review of the census data, in 1976 the richest decile earned 34.6 per cent of total income while the bottom five deciles earned only 7.7 per cent (1983, p. 188). The richest 20 per cent of the population earned 54.4 per cent of total income while the remaining 80 per cent earned just 45.8 per cent. In the late 1980s, the Income Distribution Group reported that the richest quintile earned 54.4 per cent of market income in 1981/82, 54.6 per cent in 1985/86 and 55.8 per cent in 1987/88 (Income Distribution Group, 1990). The poorest three quintiles earned just 16.7 per cent in 1981/82, 17.5 per cent in 1985/86, and 15.9 per cent in 1987/88. It must be remembered that these figures understate the actual income of the poorest quintile because, being non-wage earners, individuals without market income generally receive some kind of income support from the state (for example, welfare benefits and superannuation). But what they do highlight is the remarkable propensity of New Zealand's capitalist economy to distribute income in a highly unequal manner across the population as a whole.

There is now abundant evidence that the distribution of both market income (that is, income such as wages, salaries, rents and profits generated in the private sector) and disposable income (that is, gross income less tax payments) became increasingly unequally distributed following the collapse of the long boom in 1974 (Income Distribution Group, 1990, p. 25). The growth of inequality became particularly dramatic as successive Labour and National Governments implemented the policy agenda of the New Right from 1984 onwards. In this regard, Stocks et al. observe that 'market income—income prior to any government redistribution—became less equally distributed among households during the 1980s' (1991, p. 9). According to the Income Distribution Group, 'for individual employees in general, real incomes fell during the 1980s. Only for the top fifth of full-time employees did the purchasing power of their after-tax income increase over the decade' (1990, p. 14). Indeed, it is clear that the top quintile was the only section of New Zealand society to experience a significant rise in real household disposable income between 1980 and 1996.

Graph 5.1 Real disposable income indexes: full-time wage and salary earners. Base: year ended March 1981=1000

As Graph 5.1 shows, the richest decile gained a 13.5 per cent rise in real disposable income between 1980 and 1994 (Stephens et al., 1995, p. 105).[1] In particular, the richest quintile benefited most from the regressive taxation reforms of the fourth Labour Government: 'the degree of change in inequality at the top of the distribution in New Zealand after 1985–86 is . . . nothing short of remarkable' (Saunders, 1994, p. 108).[2] By contrast, between 1980 and 1992 the second richest quintile's real disposable income declined by 2.7 per cent, the middle quintile by 3.6 per cent, and both the second lowest and poorest quintiles by 6.4 per cent each (Department of Statistics, 1992, p. 26). Overall average real household disposable income for all groups was at the same level in March 1994 as it had been in March 1980 (Department of Statistics, 1994, p. 23). An investigation by the Rowntree Foundation found that income inequality in New Zealand had increased at a faster rate than any other OECD country during the 1980s (1995, p. 14). By 1994 *The Economist* ranked New Zealand as the third most unequal country in the OECD (5 November, p. 20).

Personal wealth is even more unequally distributed than income. This is clear from the available statistics, even though the collection of reliable wealth data is notoriously difficult, both for methodological reasons and because the wealthy tend to disguise the full extent of their wealth and income for taxation purposes (Income Distribution Group, 1990, Ch. 9). Easton's data shows that 'in 1966 about 20,000 people owned about one-fifth of the total wealth; and 100,000 owned half of it. Allowing for the smaller population, the situation in 1956 is not dissimilar. Thus there is a substantial concentration of wealth in few hands' (1983, p. 136). The available data suggests that wealth has become increasingly unequally distributed since the 1950s and 1960s. In a detailed empirical study of New Zealand's fifty largest companies, Roper (1990a, Ch. 3) shows that capital ownership became increasingly concentrated and centralised from 1974 to 1987 (see also, Britton et al., 1992, Ch. 3). The Income Distribution Group (1990, p. 102) study shows that in 1985/86 and 1987/88 assets in the form of houses and contents, motor vehicles, and financial assets were unequally distributed across income quintiles, the richest quintile holding most of the wealth. Anecdotal evidence, such as that provided by the *National Business Review*'s annual 'Rich List', suggests that these figures grossly underestimate the real concentration of wealth because so much of it is actually owned by a very small number of individuals and families. In 1995 the 117 families and individuals who made up the rich list between them controlled wealth of $6.088 billion *(National Business Review,* 21 July 1995). The wealth of the richest family—the Todd family—was 'conservatively valued at $1 billion' and the richest individual— Business Roundtable head Doug Myers—was estimated to be worth at least $275 million.

In short, the overwhelming weight of the available data suggests that, since the collapse of the long postwar boom in 1974, the real incomes of the bottom 60 per cent of the population have fallen, while the incomes and wealth of the richest 20 per cent have increased substantially. This experience is by no means unique to New Zealand. Saunders observes that there is 'increasing evidence for a range of [OECD] countries that the distribution of income has become more unequal since around the mid-1970s' (1994, p. 97). Gottschalk (1993) also shows that inequality grew substantially in Australia, Canada, France, Netherlands, Sweden, Britain and the USA during the 1970s and 1980s.

There is not space here to describe many other important empirical manifestations of class inequality, including the growth of poverty during the 1980s and 1990s, the rise of unemployment, the deterioration of the housing conditions of the poor, the restriction of working class 'life chances' for health, education, and travel, alienation in the workplace and in society, the prevalence of competition, accumulation, and material acquisitiveness, and the extent of industrial accidents and violence in capitalist societies. One point in particular, however, is worth emphasising. From 1968 to 1977 a major upsurge in class struggle took place that involved the highest levels of strike activity experienced in New Zealand's history (see Chapter 7 and Roper, 1990b). Throughout the 1980s strike activity remained at historically high levels. Only in the wake of the anti-union Employment Contracts Act did strike activity decline precipitously. This is highly significant for at least two reasons: first, because it shattered the postwar myth that New Zealand was becoming an egalitarian and classless society; and second, because it highlights the extent to which classes exist only in relation to other classes. Historically, classes are formed and constantly reshaped in the 'heat of battle'.

Theoretical Interpretations—Marx and Weber

Scholars writing within the liberal tradition, whether in economics, political science, philosophy, or history, acknowledge that socio-economic inequality exists in capitalist society but they tend to conceptualise this in terms of the gradational distribution of resources and rewards among discrete individuals in society. Indeed, the refusal to conceptualise socio-economic inequality in terms of distinctive social classes, with their own mutually antagonistic sets of social, economic, and political interests, is a general feature of liberal thought, being shared by scholars within the liberal tradition who have widely differing views on other issues (see, for example, Mulgan, 1993 and Treasury, 1987). The available data on socio-economic inequality, as presented in the official statistics, is organised very much on the basis of gradational categories. The focus is on inequalities as evident in income, wealth, occupation, and status differences between individuals and households. Gender, ethnicity, and age are commonly used to categorise socio-economic inequality; social class is not.

The hallmark of the gradationalist view of socio-economic inequality is that this inequality is categorised in terms of strata that are above or below each other, rather like the layers in a cake. Hence reference is typically made to high-, middle- and low-income earners each corresponding to specific socio-economic strata that are, in a sense, stacked on top of each other. Yet, as Callinicos (1987) points out, it is highly problematic to define social classes in terms of status, occupation, or income. Status is difficult because similar patterns of consumption may conceal different positions within overall relationships of power and privilege in society and it is inherently subjective because it rests on individual perceptions of relative social prestige. There is also no simple correspondence between occupation and class location because individuals working in very similar occupations may in fact belong to different social classes (for example, farmowners and farm labourers) and individuals working in very different occupations may actually belong to the same class (for example, clerical workers, supermarket checkout operators, and factory labourers). The official statistics tend to group occupations together into wider categories but as soon as this is done assumptions are being made, even if implicitly, about the relations between these various occupational groupings. Sociologists are generally highly critical of gradationalist approaches, not only because status, income, and occupation provide little more than a rough guide to a person's location in the class structure, but also because gradationalist approaches are patently unable to explain the historical formation of classes, the origins and prevalence of class conflict, or the trajectory of social change.

Within sociology, at least since the late 1960s, the Marxist and Weberian traditions have been the dominant approaches to conceptualising class inequality in capitalist society. Both of these traditions reject gradationalist conceptions of class in favour of a range of 'relational' approaches.

Marx's analysis of class

So far this chapter has established that socio-economic inequality is a pervasive feature of New Zealand society and that this is most commonly conceptualised in gradationalist terms. But the mere description of the extent and growth of socio-economic inequality cannot explain why capitalism has an historically unprecedented capacity to generate surplus product and to distribute this surplus in a highly unequal manner. Indeed, one of the historically unique characteristics of capitalism is that the way the system works tends to obscure the source of the surplus product, its appropriation by the dominant social class in capitalist society, and the highly complex processes through which the monetised forms of the surplus product (rent, interest, and profit) are distributed. Superficially, capitalist society appears to be composed of discrete individuals who are free and equal contracting parties in the labour market. This should sound familiar to anyone who has read the Employment Contracts Act 1991—it portrays the labour market as characterised by free and equal individuals entering into contracts that are of mutual benefit to both parties. The central point is that, despite the fact that capitalism has an historically unprecedented capacity to generate social surplus product, and despite the fact that it distributes it in a highly unequal manner, it is entirely unclear that this process involves exploitation.

Marx developed his theory of surplus value in order to 'uncover the secret of profit making', in other words, to uncover the process through which the workers produce a surplus product over and above their own needs for subsistence, which is appropriated by a dominant capitalist class. Hence the theory of surplus value is fundamental to Marx's analysis of class relations in capitalist society.

Despite the fact that there is an enormous social scientific literature on Marx, Marxism, and Marxist interpretations of class, Marx's class analysis is frequently misunderstood and/or misrepresented. Much of the misunderstanding of Marx's class analysis arises from a failure to grasp central features of his methodology. In particular, it is impossible to develop a sophisticated understanding of Marx's contribution to class analysis unless one clearly distinguishes between the materialist conception (or general theory) of history and Marx's critical analysis of the capitalist mode of production. The former involves the differentiation of the various societies, based on specific modes of production, which have appeared in human history (slavery, feudalism, capitalism, socialism). The analysis is consciously undertaken at a transhistorical and cross-cultural level and generates transhistorical concepts relating to, among other things, physical necessity and human needs, social relations governing material production, forces of production, dialectical determination within historical totalities, social classes, and state forms. By contrast, the critical analysis of the capitalist mode of production is historically specific—it centrally involves the historically specific analysis of production, distribution and exchange, exploitation, class relations, and state forms in capitalist societies. In sum, there are two stages in classical Marxist analyses of class inequality: the first establishes the specificity of a particular class in relation to the broad sweep of history; the second seeks to uncover the nature of class relations in a specifically capitalist society.

The materialist conception of history provides the conceptual apparatus required to identify and distinguish all the various social classes that have appeared in human history, for example, slaves and slave owners, serfs and lords, workers and capitalists. Societies based on slavery, feudalism, and capitalism all have distinctive relations of production and hence distinctive configurations of class relations. This is neatly encapsulated in Table 5.1.

Table 5.1 The ownership positions of immediate producers

Owns	Her/his own labour power	The means of production she/he uses
Slave	None	None
Serf	Some	Some
Proletarian	All	None
Independent producer	All	All

Source: Cohen, G. (1978), *Karl Marx's Theory of History: A Defence*, p. 65.

As this shows, each of the subordinate classes in slavery, feudalism, and capitalism have distinctive degrees of effective control both over their own labour power and over the means of production. Marx used the conceptual apparatus of the materialist conception of history to develop initial relational definitions of the major social classes in capitalist society. The working class is composed of individuals who do not effectively control the means of production and so are subject to a socio-economic compulsion to sell their labour power (the capacity to work) to a capitalist employer. In contrast, the capitalist class is composed of individuals who have no socio-economic compulsion to sell labour power (because they typically inherit sufficient wealth to survive without working) and who effectively control the means of production. The petite-bourgeoisie is composed of small businessowners who do not sell their labour power and who own their own means of production but who do not derive their income from exploiting the labour of workers.

Marx cautioned against the misinterpretation of the materialist conception of history as being a suprahistorical philosophical schema that can, in itself, make sense of history and society. Put somewhat oversimply, it is an heuristic guide for further research, a starting point for analysis. In other words, the materialist conception of history provides preliminary conceptual guidance for the systematic analyses of specific modes of production that Marx considered essential to uncover the real nature of class relations in capitalist societies.

As previously discussed, the production, appropriation, and distribution of surplus product in capitalist society are hidden and obscured by the appearance of freedom and equality in the sphere of circulation. In this sphere, labour power appears on the market as a commodity. Like any other commodity, labour power has both an exchange value and a use value. The exchange value of labour power is determined by the amount of socially necessary labour time that goes into its production. It is a measure of the historically determined level of subsistence of the working class. The use value of labour power is the actual work that is performed for the capitalist in the labour process.

So far, labour power appears to be like any other commodity that is freely exchanged on the market. Workers own and are formally free to dispense with their labour power as they see fit. But this apparent freedom and equality between buyer and seller is illusory. Unlike any other commodity, labour power in use is capable of producing value over and above its exchange value. Marx termed this surplus value, that is, the difference between the necessary labour the worker performs in order to cover the costs of his or her own reproduction and the surplus labour, which is the labour performed in the labour process over and above this necessary labour. This surplus value is the form that surplus product assumes in the capitalist mode of production and it is appropriated by the capitalist, who owns and effectively controls the means of production.

One of the most common misconceptions about Marx's class analysis is that he adhered to a simplistic dichotomous model of classes. Even an author as sympathetic to Marx as Callinicos falsely claims that 'Marx's model is a "dichotomous" one' (1987, p. 14). Actually, neither Marx nor any of the other classical Marxists adhered to dichotomous models of class as such. Rather they saw the processes of class formation, interests, and struggle in terms of bipolar relations of exploitation. Although this may seem a trivial point, it is fundamental. For it is the Marxian labour theory of value that provides a rich source for analysing the considerable complexities of class relations in capitalism, including the internal differentiation of the major social classes, the relative decline of the petite-bourgeoisie, the empirical identification of class interests, the ideological obfuscation of exploitation, and so forth. Put very crudely, surplus value assumes the phenomenal form of money that flows around the system and is appropriated in different ways by different sets of capitalists. Marx's economic theory enables us to identify both three major fractional divisions within the capitalist class (industrial, commercial, and financial capital) and the process through which a class of landowners can appropriate a share of the mass of surplus value produced elsewhere in the system. It is also consistent with this model to argue that managers on high salaries are in fact receiving, in a monetised form, a share of surplus value.

Marx's sensitivity to the complexity of class relations in capitalist society is greatly enhanced by his recognition that, in any concrete historical society, there are:

(i)   emerging classes, 'which are in the process of formation within a society based on a class system which is becoming "obsolete": this is the case with the rise of the bourgeoisie and "free" urban proletariat within feudalism' (Giddens, 1973, pp. 30–1);

(ii) declining classes constituted by 'a superseded set of relations of production that linger on within a new form of society—as is found in the capitalist societies of nineteenth century Europe, where the "feudal classes" remain of definite significance within the social structure' (*ibid.*);

(iii) 'quasi-class groupings', which share certain common economic interests but which are, for differing reasons specific to each, peripheral to the dominant set of class relationships (*ibid.*); and

(iv) fractions, subfractions and strata of classes.

Far from drawing a simplistic two-class 'map' of the class structures of the advanced capitalist societies that he observed during his lifetime, Marx identified not only the three major classes specific to capitalism—bourgeoisie, proletariat, and petite-bourgeoisie—but also the landowning aristocracy and rural peasantry that were residual feudal classes existing within, and being transformed by, capitalism. In his famous incomplete section on classes in the third volume of *Capital,* he also observes that 'the stratification of classes does not appear in its pure form' because 'middle and intermediate strata ... obliterate lines of demarcation' (Marx, 1894, p. 885).

Weber's analysis of class

The central focus of Weber's class analysis was on the distribution of power and 'the general process of rationalization entailed by the spread of the modern capitalist order' (Giddens, 1981, p. 46). Hence, in his most famous article on class inequality, Weber begins by explicitly conceptualising inequality in terms of the distribution of power within society. He defines power as 'the chance of a man or of a number of men to realise their own will in a communal action even against the resistance of others who are participating in the action' and considers that 'classes, status groups, and parties are phenomena of the distribution of power within a community' (1947a, p. 180). Weber accepts Marx's view that the emergence of capitalism rests on 'the propertied' acquiring a monopoly on the possibility of transferring property from the sphere of use as a fortune, to the sphere of 'capital goods', which means that the propertyless 'have nothing to offer but their services in native form or goods constituted in a form through their own labour . . . in order barely to subsist' (1947a, pp. 181–2). For this reason, Weber also accepts Marx's point that 'property' and 'lack of property' are '. . . the basic categories of all class situations' (*ibid.*).

Where Weber differs fundamentally from Marx is in arguing that 'within these categories, however, class situations are further differentiated: on the one hand, according to the kind of property that is useable for returns; and, on the other hand, according to the kind of services that can be offered in the market' (*ibid.*) For Weber,

> 'classes' are not communities; they merely represent possible, and frequent, bases for communal action. We may speak of a 'class' when (1) a number of people have in common a specific causal component of their life chances, in so far as (2) this component is represented exclusively by economic interests in the possession of goods and opportunities for income, and (3) is represented under the conditions of the commodity or labour markets (1947a, p. 181).

This is a crucial point because, although Marx recognises that the major social classes in capitalist society differ greatly internally, his analysis of surplus extraction enables him to argue that, despite the existence of sectional divisions and interests, there is an underlying clash of interests between capitalists and workers. Weber rejects this. Differences of interest within specific classes may be just as significant as differences between classes. Further, the internal differentiation of classes is much more complex than Marx is prepared to acknowledge. For example, whereas Marx identifies industrial, financial, and commercial fractions within the capitalist class, Weber argues that the class situations of the propertied can be differentiated by a wider range of forms of ownership, including domestic buildings, productive establishments, wholesale and retail outlets, agricultural land, the size of holdings, financial assets, control over others' labour, disposition over transferable monopolies of any kind, and so forth (*ibid.*).

One of the major problems with arguing that the labour market capacities of individuals determine their class situations is that this can lead to the absurd position that, since virtually every individual has a slightly different market capacity, there are as many classes in capitalist society as individuals participating in the labour market! In his historical writings Weber developed a conception of 'social class' that goes some way to avoiding this problem. He considered that 'a social class exists only when . . . class situations cluster together in such a way as to create a common nexus of social interchange between individuals' and these clusters of class situations 'are linked together by virtue of the fact that they involve common mobility chances, either within the career of individuals or across the generations' (cited by Giddens, 1981, p. 48).

On this basis, Weber identified four major social classes: the manual or 'blue collar' working class; a middle class composed of propertyless white collar workers; the petite-bourgeoisie, composed of small businessowners; and an upper class composed of 'those occupying a privileged position through property and education' (1947b, p. 42). These classes bring together individuals who share not only similar 'mobility chances' but also life chances, which are the rewards and advantages afforded by market capacity. They include income, wealth, perks, and superannuation, as well as less tangible benefits such as employment security, working conditions, and access to housing, health, culture, and education.

Weber's conceptualisation of class interests, therefore, differs fundamentally from that of Marx. For Weber

> the concept of 'class-interest' is an ambiguous one: even as an empirical concept it is ambiguous as soon as one understands by it something other than the factual direction of interests following with a certain probability from the class situation for a certain 'average' of those people subjected to the class situation (1947a, p. 183).

This approach to class rests on the empirical estimation of interests according to the specific market situation of the individual members of a social class. In contrast to Marx, analysis takes place at the level of market or exchange relations rather than relations of production. Weber rejects Marx's theory of exploitation and fails to develop a systematic theory of surplus extraction in capitalist society. Not surprisingly, Weber views class interests as being complex and extensively differentiated—to a much greater extent than Marx is prepared to acknowledge. In addition, Weber considered that political and cultural factors played an important role in the historical formation of class interests.

Historical Formation of Class Structure in New Zealand

Origins

Both Marxists (Bedggood, 1978 and 1980; Armstrong, 1980; Steven, 1989; Miles, 1984; Wilkes, 1990; Loomis, 1990) and Weberians (Pearson, 1990; Pearson and Thorns, 1983) have recognised that white settler colonialism, centrally involving the systematic appropriation of communally owned Maori land, was central to the process of establishing capitalist class relations in

New Zealand. Pearson (1990, p. 38) has drawn attention to the fact that the social organisation of a pre-capitalist indigenous society can have a profound impact on the kind of settler society that can be imposed upon it. In Maori society, 'land was the key resource in production and the whole organisation of Maori society was concerned with its protection and conservation' (Bedggood, 1980, p. 25). The land was communally 'owned' or, more accurately, some degree of control was exercised over it by specific tribes or iwi on the basis of traditional cultural ties. Further, 'the Maori tribes lived in relatively permanent settlements which aided military organisation and facilitated trade' (Pearson, 1990, p. 40). Economically, Maori society was based on agricultural production that was largely subsistence—enough was produced to meet community needs.

Maori society was not egalitarian, it was organised hierarchically, on the basis of, among other things, genealogy (whakapapa) and age. Elders who were descendants of rangatira, and were rangatira themselves, were ranked above other men of less chiefly descent and those who were younger. Although there was significant variation between iwi, men generally had higher social standing than women. But although Maori society may have been unequal, it was not stratified on the basis of class. As Bedggood observes, the 'chiefs acted not as a ruling class, but as representatives of the community to reproduce non-exploitative social relations. As such, the chiefs proved highly resistant to the "simple corruption" of the capitalist market and the Christian faith' (1980, p. 25). In other words, unlike class societies such as those based on slavery, feudalism, or capitalism, the agricultural production that underpinned Maori society involved neither the production of a surplus product sufficient to sustain a non-productive, exploitative, and politically dominant class, nor a set of state institutions apart from civil society.

The point is not to romanticise traditional Maori society but to stress the fact that it was a pre-capitalist society of the type described by Marx as 'primitive communism', that is, lacking clear class divisions. The fact that Maori society was organised with permanent settlements of iwi and hapu tied to particular areas of land, the long history of intertribal military conflict over the land, the high degree of military organisation of Maori society, and the hierarchical and acquisitive nature of this society, meant that it was better placed than many other pre-capitalist societies to resist colonisation. But this did not alter the fact that capitalism could be established in New Zealand only if Maori society in its traditional form was destroyed.

As Mandel (1975) and, more recently, McNally (1993) have pointed out, the historical pre-conditions of capitalist class relations include: the separation of the producers from effective control of the means of production, the monopolisation of effective control of the means of production by the capitalist class, and the commodification of labour power. In England, this took the form of the enclosure movement, in Aotearoa the expropriation of Maori land by white settlers. In both cases, land ownership became fully privatised and the pattern of ownership became sufficiently concentrated that the majority were subject to a socio-economic compulsion to sell their capacity to work to capitalist employers in order to make ends meet.

The emergent class structure

The class structure that emerged in the nineteenth century through the process of white settler colonialism varied significantly by region, but the dominant pattern of class formation was established in the southern colonies of Canterbury and Otago. Here European settlement came closest to implementing Wakefield's theory of 'systematic colonisation'. During the 1830s and 1840s British society was in a state of economic and social crisis. There was an extraordinarily high level of unemployment which, at the time, was viewed as a problem of surplus population. The first major upsurge of working class struggle took place in the form of the Chartist movement. Against this background, Wakefield proposed systematic colonisation as a solution to the crisis. As Sutch put it, Wakefield considered that 'colonization would help remove the fear of political disturbance and at the same time induce the common people to "bear their lot with patience". And, properly organized, colonization could find profitable employment for both labour and capital and at the same time reproduce the civilization of England' (1966, p. 7). The key to establishing the conditions for capitalist accumulation, and hence 'the civilisation of England', was ensuring that land would be of 'sufficient price' to ensure that wage labourers would not be able to buy land cheaply and become independent producers. This was essential because a capitalist economy cannot function without a pool of workers who are subject to a socio-economic compulsion to sell their labour power. At the same time, the 'sufficient price' was meant to prevent undue land aggregation by a few unscrupulous individuals.

In reality, capitalist class relations were established in Aotearoa, but not entirely in the manner that Wakefield had envisaged. In Canterbury and Otago the land was expropriated from Ngai Tahu in a number of highly suspect land deals, and then virtually monopolised by a small number of extremely wealthy landowners. Eldred-Grigg has referred to this fraction of the dominant capitalist class as constituting a 'landed gentry' and points out that

the wealth of the landed gentry was based . . . on two hundred or so estates. These estates, monopolising eight out of every ten acres of farmland in the province, produced the bulk of the export crops of wool and wheat, and were the biggest employers of labour. They also represented the largest capital investment in the province, some of them being valued at £300,000 and more. Most of them were owned by private families, who lived in the country or in Christchurch town houses, and whose fortunes had been founded for the most part by upper and upper-middle class Englishmen. These men, having brought substantial sums of money with them to the colony had simply gone on to multiply their assets (1982, p. 51).

Throughout the second half of the nineteenth century the dominant capitalist class in the emerging capitalist society was composed of large landowners, many of whom had substantial urban business interests, together with urban merchants, bankers, mine owners and, increasingly, manufacturers. As Eldred-Grigg accurately observes, 'merchants and wool kings were essentially one economic bloc' (1982, p. 52).

This class did not concern itself simply with preserving and expanding economic wealth—it also exerted political dominance. In this regard, 'by 1880, the Legislative Council was like a pastoralists' club—it had been founded as a Colonial House of Lords—and a sizeable proportion of the General Assembly, not to mention nineteenth century Ministries, were also pastoralists (or urban merchants and speculators with large investments in pastoralism)' (Olssen, 1977, p. 28). This political pre-eminence was buttressed by the pastoralists' growing control over the newspapers of the colony. Even where they initially failed to be profitable, as was the case with the Christchurch *Press*, the conservative papers were well funded, unlike more 'liberal' papers, and, predictably, the former eventually triumphed over the latter to become the major dailies in all of the main centres. Finally, the social and cultural reproduction of this class was ensured by the development of élite secondary schools modelled on the public schools of the mother country—Waitaki Boys, Christ's College, and so forth. Wakefield's scheme may not have been implemented in the manner that he had envisaged, but the dominant class did succeed in creating a 'little England' in the South Pacific, in the sense that they successfully transplanted capitalism to Aotearoa.

During the early decades of European settlement, the settler society appears to have had a reasonably fluid social structure, particularly in the northern colonies (Olssen, 1977, pp. 23–4). But by the 1870s and 1880s the major social classes associated with capitalism had emerged: a dominant capitalist class composed of large landowners, financiers, industrialists, and merchants; a rural farming petit-bourgeoisie composed of small landowners; an urban petite-bourgeoisie composed of small businessowners and professionals; and a working class composed of rural and urban waged workers.

The Contemporary Class Structure in New Zealand

Within sociology, there is broad agreement that those who exercise effective control over the productive resources of society—capital, labour, and land—constitute the dominant class in New Zealand society. There is also broad agreement that those who are self-employed and own their own small businesses constitute a distinctive 'old middle class' or petite-bourgeoisie. The real disagreement and debate between Weberians and Marxists, as well as between individuals within each camp, has centred on what has incontrovertibly been one of the major empirical trends in societal change during the twentieth century: the expansion of white collar employment relative to blue collar employment. This trend in occupational change has characterised all the advanced capitalist societies. The extent of this occupational change is clear from the official statistics. In 1951, over half of the total workforce was employed in the agriculture and manufacturing sectors. By 1994, two-thirds were employed in the services sector (Statistics New Zealand, 1951 and 1995).

The expansion of white collar employment has created difficulties for class analysts, regardless of their particular intellectual persuasion. On the one hand, the expansion of new white collar occupations, such as university teaching and computer programming, which are highly paid and give the employees a relatively high degree of autonomy, appears to undermine the Marxian prediction that the middle classes would decline in size relative to an expanding proletariat. And even if Marxists can successfully rebut this claim, it remains the case that some highly skilled and well-paid white collar occupations do not sit neatly within classical Marxist categories. On the other hand, although the expansion of white collar employment is consistent with Weber's prognosis concerning likely changes in the class structure, it has also created difficulties for Weberians. They have difficulty in explaining the evident proletarianisation of large areas of white collar employment, which frequently involves very routine operations, skill levels that are lower than those required in the skilled blue collar occupations, subjugation to strict managerial control, poor pay and conditions, and so forth. Weberians also have difficulty explaining the extensive unionisation and growing industrial militancy of white collar workers since 1968.

At first glance this debate may appear to be over relatively trivial questions of definition. Dig a little deeper and it becomes clear that the issues are of great importance. Ultimately, they give rise to fundamentally differing interpretations of the direction of societal development, the recent histories of the advanced capitalist societies, and different political programs for social change. The need for brevity and the extent of the literature rule out a comprehensive survey. In any case the debate has increasingly come to be dominated by two individuals—Antony Giddens (neoWeberian) and Erik Wright (neoMarxist)—who are arguably the most prominent and influential class theorists in the late twentieth century.

According to Giddens, classes emerge through related processes of mediate and proximate structuration. Mediate structuration refers to 'the factors which intervene between the existence of certain given market capacities and the formation of classes as identifiable social groupings, that is to say which operate as "overall" connecting links between the market on the one hand and structured systems of class relationships on the other' (1981, p. 107). The mediate structuration of class relationships is governed, above all, by the distribution of mobility chances pertaining within a given society: 'the structuration of classes is facilitated to the degree to which mobility closure exists in relation to any specified form of market capacity' (*ibid.*). There are three key sets of market capacity: (i) ownership of property in the means of production; (ii) possession of educational or technical qualifications; and (iii) possession of manual labour power. The mediate structuration of class relationships cannot provide a complete account of the emergence of classes. It is necessary to recognise that three, related, key sources of proximate structuration also play an important role: (i) division of labour within the enterprise; (ii) authority relationships within the enterprise; and (iii) distributive groupings. In so far as these sets of market capacity and sources of proximate structuration 'tend to be tied to closed patterns of inter- and intragenerational mobility, this yields the foundation of a basic three-class system in capitalist society: an "upper", "middle", and "lower" or "working class"' (*ibid.*).

Wright agrees with Giddens that classes may give rise to various forms of organisation, but a class is not, in itself, an organisation. Rather, classes are constituted by common positions within the social relations of production. This means that 'classes must always be understood in terms of their relationship to other classes' (1979, p. 21). Class relationships are contradictory in the sense that they are intrinsically antagonistic. This antagonism arises because class relations are simultaneously relations of exploitation, and this exploitation takes place within the sphere of production. For Wright (1979, p. 24), capitalist relations of production involve 'three interdependent dimensions or processes' pertaining to social relations of control over: (i) investment; (ii) physical means of production; and (iii) authority over labour power within the labour process. Because capitalists control investment, physical means of production, and exercise authority over labour power, and workers are excluded from such control, 'the fundamental class antagonism between workers and capitalists can be viewed as a polarization of each of these three processes' (1979, p. 25).

The essence of Wright's argument is that the three processes that comprise capitalist social relations of production do not always perfectly coincide and this 'is the key to ... understanding the class position of the social categories that are labelled "middle classes"'. In this regard, the new middle class is composed of social categories that occupy contradictory locations within the basic contradictory class relations of capitalist society. For ease of reference, Wright terms these social categories 'contradictory class locations'. There are three distinct clusters of such locations: (i) managers and supervisors, who occupy a contradictory location between the bourgeoisie and the proletariat; (ii) semi-autonomous employees, who retain relatively high levels of individual control over their immediate conditions of work; and (iii) small employers who occupy a contradictory location between the bourgeoisie and the petite-bourgeoisie. By modifying classical Marxist class analysis in this way, Wright is able to develop a rigorous conceptualisation of the new occupations that have emerged from the process of capitalist development during the twentieth century.

Somewhat surprisingly, given the healthy size of the discipline of sociology in New Zealand, the empirical research and literature on class inequality is sparse and the quality of the available literature is highly uneven. Pearson and Thorns (1983; 1986) provide the most sophisticated neoWeberian analysis of New Zealand's class structure during the postwar era, while Steven's (1978) remains the most sophisticated Marxist analysis. Bedggood (1980) provides a valuable analysis of the historical emergence of capitalist class relations during the nineteenth century, but his analysis of the changing class structure during the twentieth century fails completely to deal systematically with the available official statistical data. Wilkes (1990) attempts empirically to operationalise Wright's theoretical model through a New Zealand survey but generates results that can only be described as questionable at best.

While claiming to develop an approach which 'eschews fundamentalism of either a Marxian or Weberian character', Pearson and Thorns actually develop an analysis of New Zealand's class structure that clearly belongs within the Weberian tradition (1983, p. 3). In accord with Weber and contemporary neoWeberians such as Goldthorpe, Giddens, and Parkin, they emphasise that 'the combined effects ... of the labour and property markets and state allocation shapes the life chances of individuals and this determines their class location' (*ibid.*, p.14). In general, neoWeberians argue that the market capacities conferred by educational and technical qualifications, life chances, and class situations of white and blue collar workers are sufficiently divergent to warrant the conceptual drawing of a 'boundary line' between them. White collar workers form part of the new middle class because, relative to blue collar workers, they have greater employment security, ascending rather than declining income curves during their working lives, better promotion opportunities, are more likely to receive fringe benefits such as pension and sick-pay schemes, and because, as a result of the above, they have better access to housing finance and home ownership (see, for example, Giddens, 1973, p. 180). Hence, the class divide between white and blue collar workers becomes evident in urban residential segregation.

From this perspective, New Zealand census data can be interpreted as indicating the growth of a new middle class throughout the twentieth century. By 1976, 8.9 per cent of the workforce were members of the 'old middle class' composed of the higher professions, businesspeople and farmers, 41 per cent were members of a new middle class composed of the lower professions, salespeople, and white collar workers, and 49 per cent were working class (Pearson and Thorns, 1983, p. 52).

Steven (1978), and many other Marxists (Callinicos and Harman, 1987; Meiksins, 1986; Mandel, 1985; Miliband, 1989), reject this interpretation of occupation change and the growth of white collar employment during the twentieth century. For example, Callinicos observes that 'lumped together under the general heading of "white collar employees" is an extraordinarily heterogeneous collection of jobs—company executives, senior civil servants, school teachers, nurses, shorthand typists' and argues that, in reality, white collar employment 'embraces three distinctive class positions' (1987, pp. 15–16). First are the 'senior managers and supervisors who are effectively salaried members of the capitalist class'. Second, there are white collar employees, such as clerical and sales workers, who are clearly members of the working class. Third are those professional and administrative employees who occupy contradictory locations between the bourgeoisie and the proletariat and who collectively constitute the new middle class. The upshot of all this is that, in terms of exploitative capitalist relations of production, many of the occupations that neoWeberians consider to be middle class are in reality within the working class.

From a Marxist perspective, the expansion of white collar employment has centrally involved the occupational recomposition and expansion of the working class, rather than its decline relative to an expanding new middle class. Further, Marxists dispute that the overall class situations and life chances of white and blue collar workers diverge to the extent claimed by neoWeberians. Following the collapse of the postwar long boom in the mid-1970s, white and blue collar workers have faced very similar attempts by their employers to erode their pay, conditions of employment, and employment security. Steven's detailed Marxist analysis of New Zealand census data paints a very different picture of the contemporary class structure from that of Pearson and Thorns. In 1976, 10.4 per cent of the economically active population were members of the bourgeoisie, 11.6 per cent were in the middle class, 6.6 per cent were in the petite bourgeoisie, and 71.5 per cent were working class. The great strength of Steven's analysis is that, unlike Pearson and Thorns, he more accurately categorises low-waged white collar employees with minimal workplace control, particularly clerical and sales workers, within the working class.

Conclusion—The Centrality of Class

During the 1980s the idea that class was in decline became increasingly popular. According to this view, which was predominantly, but by no means exclusively, promulgated by neoWeberians, the working class was declining in size relative to an expanding new middle class of white collar employees. This view appeared to be corroborated by the international decline in industrial struggle during the 1980s. From the perspective of the late 1990s, these arguments now seem weak. First, most serious empirical research on white collar employment has highlighted the extent to which the majority of white collar workers are actually members of the working class. That is, white collar employment is extensively proletarianised. Second, a significant revival of class struggle has taken place during the 1990s, suggesting that the 1980s represented a conjunctural 'downturn' in working class struggle rather than its permanent cessation as a result of changes in the underlying class structure. Third, all the available data, both in New Zealand and internationally, suggests that, far from class inequality diminishing in the advanced capitalist societies, it is actually growing. Income and wealth have in fact become increasingly unequally distributed since the 1974 collapse of the postwar long boom. Fourth, the intimate connections between class and inequalities of gender and ethnicity have also become more obvious during the 1980s and 1990s. Maori and Pacific Islanders have borne the brunt of 'economic restructuring' since 1984, and women have been seriously disadvantaged by the fourth National Government's 'redesign' of the welfare state and its anti-union Employment Contracts Act. It is quite simply impossible to develop an adequate analysis of either women's oppression or inequality between Maori and Pakeha without seriously addressing the impact that class has on both these forms of inequality and domination. So far from disappearing, class remains central to the social structuration of the advanced capitalist societies.

---

1 Statistics New Zealand discontinued the Real Disposable Income series in the June quarter 1994.

2 The fourth Labour Government's tax changes had a significant impact on disposable income. 'When direct and indirect taxes are combined, the progressiveness of direct taxes tends to be balanced by the regressiveness of indirect taxes. In 1987/88, apart from the lowest decile, total tax incidence is much more nearly a constant proportion of household income' (Income Distribution Group, 1990, p. 41).

Guide to Readings

Callinicos and Harman (1987) provide an excellent short introduction to recent debates in class theory. One of the clearest introduction to the major theoretical interpretations of class from a neoMarxist position is that by Wright (1979). Giddens (1973) provides a representative statement of the neoWeberian position. On the theoretical implications of the growth of a 'new middle class', see Meiskins (1986), Mandel (1985), and Miliband (1989).

Bedggood (1980), Armstrong (1980), and Steven (1989) provide Marxist accounts of the class structure in New Zealand. For the Weberian perspective, see Pearson (1990) and Pearson and Thorns (1983). Eldred-Grigg (1982) and Olssen (1977) offer very readable historical accounts of the emergence of social classes in New Zealand.

Studies that contain empirical evidence of social inequality in New Zealand include Easton (1983), Income Distribution Group (1990), Stocks et al. (1991) and Stephens et al. (1995). For comparative data see Saunders (1994).

Chapter Six

Business and Politics During the Postwar Era

JACK VOWLES AND JULIET ROPER

Most advanced democracies have encountered economic difficulties since the 1970s, and perhaps few more so than New Zealand. Having accepted a highly regulated economy during the years of prosperity, in harder times New Zealand businesses began to demand liberalisation (Roper 1991a and 1991b). Interpretations of the subsequent events raise a key question: does business political activism shape a shift in government policy, or do state decision-makers independently perceive a need for change? Pluralist, Weberian, Marxist and rational choice theories provide different answers. Various narratives highlight the emergence of the New Zealand Business Roundtable as a focus of advocacy (Murray, 1989; Roper, 1990, 1991a, 1991b, 1992, and 1993a). Until the mid-1980s, New Zealand business organisations were not so prominent politically, and were viewed within a pluralist perspective as defending particular interests: Federated Farmers with respect to agriculture, the Manufacturers' Federation with respect to industry, and so on (Cleveland, 1972; Mulgan, 1989a).

This chapter examines business influence on some public policy changes. It argues that most theoretical approaches contain valuable insights, but it is premature to state that one or other is a superior analytical tool. Most of the theories incorporate claims made by others. Critiques of one theory by proponents of others are often based on unsympathetic constructions of their opponents' positions (Mulgan, 1992, p. 129). Defence of theory owes more to researchers' value preferences than to rigorous hypothesis testing. When efforts are made to identify key differences between the theories, it may be possible to generate refutable hypotheses to test their claims. This chapter elaborates a model incorporating a variety of theoretical insights and applies tentative alternative hypotheses to two New Zealand case studies.

Theoretical Approaches

Pluralism

Pluralism is essentially a normative theory. Empirically, it is more descriptive than explanatory. Pluralism values power shared among organised associations. The state is seen not as a simple unit but as a focus of competition within and between bureaucracies, political parties, and even within governments (Dahl, 1956; Polsby 1963). There is no singular power élite or policy-dominant capitalist class but, rather, a collection of plural élites.

Normatively, mid-twentieth century liberal democratic theory emphasised competitive democratic elections. But its theorists remembered the fragility of interwar democracies, and had learnt from political behaviour research that voters are ill-informed and imperfectly committed to liberal democratic values. Pluralism broadened democracy by describing how, between elections, bargains could be struck among plural élites. But there were also problems in the early pluralist notion of power, which was one-dimensional. It incorporated only direct influence between one actor and another, and excluded situations where potentially significant political issues remained submerged because of the political weaknesses of the unorganised (Bachrach and Baratz, 1970, Lukes, 1974).

Ironically, pluralism's empirical claims were rejected because the world did not conform to a pluralist ideal shared by many of its critics. Classical pluralism was transformed into neopluralism, which accepted that democracies contained inequalities, and that power was more complex than hitherto assumed. Neopluralists conceded that the resources and political influence of business organisations were more substantial than those of other organisations (Lindblom, 1977; Mulgan, 1989).

Marxism and neoMarxism

A major weakness of early pluralism was its tendency to reduce the state to another focus of political competition and thereby to ignore its formal and legal authority, not to mention its capacities. This was not an assumption that the state was neutral in class conflicts, as Marxists asserted. Rather, the state in general had no independent role at all, although parts of its bureaucracy and political leadership could engage in pluralist bargaining in the same way as interests outside the state.

Marxists were the first to address this problem effectively. They asked to what extent the democratic capitalist state could be relatively autonomous from social forces. One school postulated economic determination via the logic of capital, while another imported aspects of pluralism, postulating a democratic class struggle that could advance working class interests within and through the democratic state. Another debate focused on how the state's actions might be constrained or determined. An instrumentalist emphasis on élite socialisation and networks linking business and political élites was countered by claims that the capitalist state was inevitably obliged to promote capitalist accumulation, regardless of the composition of its political élite (see Carnoy, 1984).

Going beyond this debate, Claus Offe moved on to some common ground with neopluralism. For its survival, a state requires an economy with a tax base secure enough to provide revenues. Thus the democratic state promotes the private wealth accumulation that provides it with a tax base. This also underpins the economic growth that makes it possible to redistribute income to legitimate both the economic and political orders. Consequently, maintaining a stable form of democratic capitalism is problematic because of the system's contradictions. A democratic capitalist state will promote the interests of business, but will be less likely to do so in conditions of economic prosperity, and more likely to do so when the economy falters. In economic crisis, the legitimating or more pluralist side of democratic capitalism will be sidelined in order to enhance capitalist profits and promote investment (Offe, 1975, 1984, and 1985). Marxists and pluralists had converged, although not entirely, in acknowledging that the state was an actor, and that within the state there were individuals and institutions with particular interests to defend (Held, 1987, p. 212).

Another neoMarxist theory highlights the role of an ideology that becomes hegemonic because it is popularly accepted as 'common sense' (Gramsci, 1971; Hall, 1988). Once achieved, hegemony may only be temporary. It can face opposition from many parts of society. To survive, the hegemonic order must deal with opposition by concession or compromise. Under capitalism, this implies that business priorities are privileged but can be contested by a vigorous counter-ideology. Some concessions may be carefully chosen by the controlling élite to draw the teeth of anti-business forces and so strengthen public acceptance of the status quo, but others may amount to a real challenge.

Rational choice and neoliberalism

Pluralism came under even more devastating attack from rational choice theory. Olson demonstrated that collective action is problematic because of recruitment difficulties when the benefits obtained by associations are available to non-members (Olson, 1965). He deduced that the fewer the potential members, the lower would be the costs of organisation. This implicitly supported the contention of radicals that organisation of business was less problematic than that of other interests. Offe extended Olson's work, emphasising the advantages of business over labour, owing to two distinct logics of collective action (Offe, 1985, pp. 170–220).[1]

Another line of attack came when neoliberals identified democracy itself as a problem. Organised interests and voters were demanding more than states could provide without cost to economic productivity. Neoliberals sought to revert to a very 'thin' notion of democracy: simple electoral choice between competing political élites. They rejected democratic accountability between elections and pluralist interest accommodation. Proliferation of organised interests was said to make governments unwilling or unable to take economically optimal decisions (Olson, 1982). The malign influence of voters and organised interests was said to be associated with the growth of government and the overexpansion of welfare states. A consequent governmental fiscal 'overload' on the private sector was said to be responsible for slowing economic growth (Brittan, 1975; King, 1975). Robust empirical support for such propositions was lacking (Castles and Dowrick, 1990), but this was secondary to the associated normative attack on pluralism. Drawing on rational choice theories, neoliberals subsequently sought to reduce the political influence of voters and organisations that want to determine resource allocation by political bargaining. Neoliberal strategy is to 'roll back the state', reduce its interventions, and allow market forces to distribute resources with only residual provision for social assistance to those in extreme need.

Corporatism provided an alternative strategy to structure the influence of organised interests and, in economic crisis, to prevent 'overload'. Theoretically, corporatism has much in common with pluralism and can be most rigorously theorised within a rational choice framework. It focuses on the role of the state and the institutionalisation of organised interests within formal and informal decision-making processes. Offe identified what he called 'the attribution of public status' to interest groups as a 'structural' response to increasing demands on governments. Corporatist arrangements act as a filtering mechanism, allowing governments to advantage some groups at the expense of others less willing to cooperate. Corporatism obliges privileged groups to moderate their demands, and prevent their members and affiliates from engaging in tactics that might threaten the relationship with the state. Corporatist arrangements gave centrally organised union movements an insider status that enhanced their influence, but obliged them to discourage militancy and limit wage demands (Offe, 1985, pp. 221–57; cf Panitch, 1977).

State autonomy and state capacity

Neoliberals paradoxically seek to enhance state autonomy by reducing state intervention and therefore weaken public influence in decision-making by limiting state capacities. Recent Weberian theories identify varying state autonomies as explanations of policy outcomes. State capacity and state autonomy are conceptually distinct but closely linked (Skocpol, 1985; Cammack, 1989; Smith 1993, pp. 47–75). But state capacities were declining owing to greater international economic competition and the liberalisation of financial markets. Floating exchange rates reduced the states' capacity to make strategic currency devaluations. Debt incurred by earlier attempts to offset economic problems reduced the policy flexibility of states dependent on credit ratings from international financial institutions.

State capacity is not necessarily positively correlated with state autonomy. Governments that extensively regulate, subsidise, and redistribute resources can lack autonomy, because their interventions may lock decision-makers into formal and informal understandings with organised associations that have interests to defend. Such expansions of state capacity often required an initial area of state autonomy to make them possible. But once established, they encouraged defensive coalitions among those who benefited, and thus reduced future state autonomy. With economies in recession, governments can initially opt for fiscal deficit strategies less politically damaging in the short term but which, in the longer term, further reduce state autonomy.

For example, social democratic governments in states with large public sectors, strong trade union movements, and traditions of involvement by corporatist interests tend to rely on coalitions of voters who support such arrangements. Corporatist bargaining allows for a certain amount of flexibility, but within limits. Under pressure of economic change, social democratic governments in states with apparently high capacity can lack the political autonomy necessary to break away from particular public policy patterns. Both state capacity and state autonomy may be reduced by economic crisis, but in other circumstances a high state capacity may, paradoxically, reduce autonomy, particularly with respect to internal electoral and social influences (Schwartz, 1994; cf Neilson, 1995).

State autonomy theories also redirect attention to a recently neglected pluralist variable. For Marxists and neoMarxists, democracy is the victim of business influence, and a limited influence in its own right; for neoliberals, it is a constraint upon the plans of liberalising political élites. Yet the major agents of twentieth-century democracy, political parties, remain important actors in determining public policy outcomes, particularly if they are strong and have close ties with organised interests that are themselves embedded in class formations.

Developing and Testing a Model of Business Influence

The above theories provide valuable insights and identify salient variables, and can help to interpret the relations between business and the state. Empirically, in New Zealand as elsewhere, case studies can sustain pluralist hypotheses: for example, that governments will consult organised associations and that campaigns by such associations will influence government policies. During the 1960s, the Holyoake National Government had consulted a wide range of organised interests and larger businesses in order to create a National Development Plan (Roberts, 1969a and 1969b; cf Cleveland, 1972). The success of cause groups such as the Save Manapouri Campaign also fitted this pluralist perspective. But such examples do not mean that the pluralist approach was dominant.

Olson's rational choice approach draws attention to comparatively high industrial protection in New Zealand (Olson, 1983, pp. 132–6). It explains its existence as the result of successful rent seeking by unions and manufacturers, made possible by New Zealand's long experience of uninterrupted democratic government. Analysis of the highly regulated New Zealand economy between 1945 and 1984 is further assisted by a combination of corporatist, pluralist, and rational choice theory. Consistent with Olsonian analysis was the legal enactment of compulsory union membership in the private sector, which had increased union membership eightfold in the late 1930s; this is also strong evidence for a state autonomy explanation. A partnership had developed between the Labour Government elected in 1935 and the FOL, New Zealand's first effective central union organisation, the creation of which had been encouraged by the government itself. A quasi-corporatist relationship was underpinned more by state regulation of a centralised wage-setting process and informal élite-level links, than by formal bargaining (Vowles, 1992).

Also consistent with hypotheses from the collective action literature is the fact that business political organisation in New Zealand has developed as a response either to state intervention or to unionism (Wanna, 1989, p. 2). The formation of Federated Farmers in 1946 was a reaction to the corporatist relationship between the government and the unions (Chapman, 1962, p. 271). The development of the Employers' Federation was limited by the centralised wage-fixing process, through which employers' interests could be serviced by a relatively small organisation. Industrial militancy was contained by the FOL. If necessary, as in the 1951 waterfront dispute, there was resort to the heavy hand of the state, which had powers to deregister unions and terminate their existence (Roth, 1986). The high capacity of the postwar New Zealand state makes state-centred theories particularly useful in understanding this period. Destruction of the left wing of the union movement in 1951 ensured the survival of an, albeit informal, relationship between governmental and union élites and the retention of compulsory unionism (which employers also supported on grounds of industrial stability from the 1950s to the 1970s). It was only in the early 1970s, under pressure from the Manufacturers' Federation's threat to deal independently with industrial relations issues, that the Employers' Federation began to develop a more effective organisation.

State autonomy theory also emphasises the importance of party politics. Tightening electoral competition by the late 1960s reduced the policy autonomy of the National Government. By overruling the Arbitration Court's nil wage order in 1968, National continued to nurture the postwar policy consensus based on full employment, social welfare, and industrial peace. New initiatives in welfare policy followed, in an attempt to beat Labour on its own ground. Ties between the parties and economic interests in New Zealand also mean that an account of the relations between business and the state must include the nature and outcomes of party electoral competition (Vowles, 1992 and 1993). For example, despite the wishes of Finance Minister Roger Douglas and his supporters, it was impossible for the fourth Labour Government to legislate for radical labour market deregulation. That had to wait until National's election in 1990 (Walsh, 1989). As promised, and as a payback for strong union support at the 1984 election, in 1985 Labour had restored the private sector compulsory union membership the National Government had abolished two years earlier.

Surprisingly little has been written applying the dominant or hegemonic ideology thesis to the study of business influence in New Zealand. Certainly, the role of ideology has been documented, but not in terms of a drive for a new hegemonic order. There was a shift from Keynesian to monetarist neo-classicism in economics among business leaders and state officials, particularly in Treasury (Roper 1990a, 1990b, and 1992, pp. 19–20). Easton has similarly traced the importation of Chicago school economics into New Zealand. In terms of dominant ideology theory, Treasury made a case that pre-1984 economic policies were in crisis, and gained business élite support. This approach gained wider ascendancy among policy élites, but other than dubious inferences from the 1987 election result, there is little evidence that its popular acceptance assisted market liberalisation. Public agreement with key policy changes lagged behind their implementation (Vowles and Aimer, 1993; Vowles et al., 1995). Business influence on public policy was élite-driven and achieved without the need to secure substantial public agreement. Hegemony theory, however, may indicate that the drive towards a new ideological order was pushed too rapidly and failed to recognise opposing views and make concessions towards them.

Scepticism about business motives and popular commitment to what could be described as a previous social democratic hegemony may have limited business influence. For example, minimum wages for adult workers remained into the 1990s, despite arguments from business lobbyists. There are even more deep-seated moral and cultural constraints on business and state power that either limit agenda-setting options, or, if they become political issues, can be attacked by mobilising public opinion. This means that certain fiscally advantageous policy options, such as mercy killing of the disabled or the forcible sterilisation of beneficiaries, are excluded from debate (Mulgan, 1992, p. 140). Concern about business practices emerged in the aftermath of market liberalisation, as a reaction to some of its excesses. Despite initial resistance, Winston Peters, leader of the New Zealand First Party, eventually forced an unsympathetic government to establish a commission of inquiry into alleged tax evasion involving large New Zealand companies, which did not want such scrutiny.

Such general interpretations and the testing of specific hypotheses aid understanding, but a connected series of hypotheses may help to construct a more in-depth explanation of the specific process of policy change. Such a series is summarised below.

1. Both business influence and pressure for neoliberal policies will intensify as the economy moves towards crisis, and weaken if the economy moves toward prosperity (*neoMarxist*).
2. a) State perceptions of decline or crisis preceding or running parallel to business perceptions indicate *state autonomy*;
   b) if business perceptions and arguments precede state perceptions, then a more *neoMarxist and instrumentalist society-centred* explanation is appropriate.
3. Division within a set of actors will limit influence, unity will promote it (*pluralism, rational choice*).
4. The party in power will facilitate or limit particular policy decisions, depending on its support and mobilisation (*pluralism, state autonomy theory*).
5. The greater the extent of legal, regulatory, and constitutional state

powers, the more likely that change can be achieved in the teeth of opposition (*state autonomy*).

6. Business or non-business organised associations incorporated within state decision-making structures may be able to encourage, slow down, or even prevent policy changes (*pluralism, rational choice, state autonomy*).

7. The more voters are mobilised behind political parties with commitments to policy positions, the less likely that the preferences of political or business élites will prevail against public opinion and social values (*pluralism*).

Where particular theoretical claims overlap, hypothesis testing can do little to indicate the relative success of theories that make the same claims. But it can compare them against other theories that fail to generate the hypothesis in question. And whatever the implications for the theories involved, the process itself assists explanation. Hypotheses can also be combined in a model that deduces a causal order among relationships, as in Figure 6.1.

Figure 6.1 A model of business influence on regulative policy change

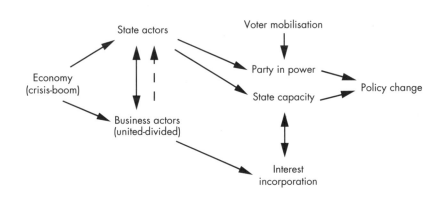

The model assumes that economic conditions begin the explanation of policy change in New Zealand. This is a claim borne out by Marxist economic analysis (Pearce, 1986) as well as other commentary. But the effects of economic conditions are mediated through the perceptions of state and business actors. At a further step, the combined effects of economic conditions and actor perceptions are mediated by possible constraints derived from pluralist and state autonomy theories. Within the model, it is possible to compare hypotheses which make opposed claims. An instrumentalist Marxist approach hypothesises that business perceptions of the economy will influence state perceptions, as implicitly argued by Roper (1992 and 1993a), and indicated by the broken line in Figure 6.1. A Weberian state autonomy hypothesis will claim a two-way causal relationship between business and state perceptions. It predicts that state actors will be influential even after business influence is taken into account.

Two case studies address key aspects of this model, and make up the remainder of this chapter.

Opening Up New Zealand's Economy

Business was politically weak in New Zealand from 1945 until the 1980s because state intervention divided the two most powerful business interests: farmers and manufacturers. The establishment of the regulated economy began with the first Labour Government. The introduction of import licensing in 1938, later assisted by the effects of the Second World War, had encouraged the development of manufacturing industries geared towards import substitution and had also generated the 'spectacular growth' of the Manufacturers' Federation (Rudman, 1974, p. 55). Farmers and manufacturers diverged on the key issue of import controls. New Zealand's heavily protected manufacturing industries made products for farmers to consume that cost more than similar goods sourced overseas, to the detriment of farming efficiency and profits.

Postwar import controls were justified by goals of industrial development and full employment (see Chapter 2). New Zealand farming had climatic advantages, was technologically advanced, and had a guaranteed British market. As one of the wealthiest countries in the world, and having escaped the effects of war, New Zealand was a favoured economy. Concerns about the efficiency of New Zealand farming were dismissed, even after 1949 by National Governments that had close links to the farming community. Fearful of adverse electoral reaction, National Governments that might otherwise have preferred a liberal economy allowed industrial protection to persist. Labour's return to power in 1957 confirmed the risks of any National policy strategy that might threaten full employment and welfare. Under Labour, there was a renewal of policies promoting import substitution and an increase in social expenditure.

From 1966 a long-term decline in New Zealand's terms of trade set in, and hit with a vengeance in 1974 (see Chapter 1). The Muldoon National Government elected in 1975 addressed those difficulties with state intervention, but this began to draw together a hitherto divided business sector. In 1974 the 'top tier' was established as informal confidential meetings took place between the leading officials of Federated Farmers, the Employers' Federation, the Manufacturers' Federation, the Chambers of Commerce, and the Retailers' Federation. These soon expanded into a regular formal meeting.

Muldoon engaged in strident populist rhetoric against interest groups. Ironically, his strategy belied the rhetoric. Economic difficulties in the 1970s led to challenges to the postwar compromises established through most of the OECD states. In New Zealand, the situation was made more extreme by the Muldoon Government's mode of resistance to the monetarist economic policies introduced by other governments. Full employment was maintained at the cost of inflation, with government-led investment in energy continuing to promote the import substitution model of previous decades, but at the cost of increasing public debt—a defensive social democratic strategy pursued by a nominally conservative government.

Meanwhile, opinion among both public and private sector élites was beginning to favour market liberalisation and a more anti-inflationary policy regime. With inflation moving beyond a tolerable range, by the early 1980s the government had run out of room for manoeuvre. Resisting thoroughgoing liberalisation, Muldoon imposed controls on wages, prices, and interest rates. Business support for his government ebbed. The development of greater business unity was not only a reaction against intensified state intervention. It was also a product of new government policies in response to the changing economic situation. Postwar business disunity had fed on the conflict of interest between import substituting manufacturers and export market dependent farmers. A shift toward a more open economy had long been promoted by Federated Farmers and opposed by the Manufacturers' Federation.

Import controls had emerged to address the chronic external dependence of the New Zealand economy. The goals were retention of a high employment level and relatively high wages, and to keep control over the balance of payments between imports and exports. By the late 1950s the rationale was to encourage infant industries protected behind trade barriers until they developed sufficient strength to become internationally competitive. By the 1970s, increasing protectionism in international agriculture, coupled with Britain's entry into the EEC, indicated the need to diversify New Zealand's exports into manufacturing and other value-added goods. The initial policy instrument chosen was subsidies or export incentives.

The new strategy of CER, a process of liberalising trade with Australia, was designed gradually to open up the New Zealand market to competition.

Resisted by some manufacturers, CER was embraced by other firms that could see advantages. The government encouraged and promoted pro-CER sentiments within the Manufacturers' Federation by keeping in close contact with its leaders and officials, and by negotiating concessions allowing specific sectors more time than originally suggested to adapt to the new policies (Thakur and Gold, 1983). The next step was to secure agreement on progressively replacing quantitative import licensing controls by tariffs. This was secured by unprecedented summit meetings between the Manufacturers' Federation executive, its director-general, and four Cabinet ministers and key officials. Short-term concessions secured agreement for longer-term change. The agreement was then endorsed at the Manufacturers' Federation conference in 1983, and the scene was set for the opening up of the economy over the next decade (Vowles, 1992, p. 351, Roper 1992, p. 8).

Abandonment of this long-established policy pattern was achieved before the election of the Labour Government in 1984. In opposition, Labour had agreed to the change, muting the possibility of voter opposition. The policy shift was initiated from within the government bureaucracy, in tandem with business opinion, but not necessarily in direct response to greater business activism. Within government, key officials and departments such as the Treasury saw a need to deal with an emerging 'fiscal crisis' by means of liberalisation. Their initial open economy strategy went against the current of many other policies of the Muldoon administration. For that reason, the initial Australasian focus was chosen to provoke little opposition while encouraging more sustainable outward-looking economic activities. Business opinion played a part, but government élites largely drove the process, supporting pro-CER elements within the Manufacturers' Federation. By the mid-1980s, the political foundations of the conflict of interest between manufacturers and farmers were eroding. Where state autonomy had been constrained by an institutionalised policy pattern favouring manufacturing import substitution, the government was able to employ the high capacity of the New Zealand state (Palmer, 1979) to begin to change those policies.

Such evidence indicates support for Weberian state autonomy, but supplemented by neoMarxist political economy. The major policy changes of the 1980s and 1990s, the shift toward an open economy, and labour market deregulation were contingent on initiatives within the state. The shift toward the open economy required a state-driven strategy to encourage the constituency for change within the Manufacturers' Federation. The historic shift in policy that took place from 1979 onwards can best be interpreted in Offe's terms as a reaction by state officials to what they perceived as a threat to the economic viability and tax base of the state, as a result of inappropriate economic policies that had run their course. Many of the leading advocates of change were American-educated economists with public sector careers in the late 1970s and early 1980s (Easton, 1994). Consistent with both neoMarxist and neoliberal political economy, changes in the economic situation put pressure on state actors to adopt a new strategy. Consistent with neoWeberian theories, the timing of the change was shaped by contingent and autonomous developments in both electoral and bureaucratic politics. Full flowering of liberalisation had to wait for the election of a new government in an atmosphere of apparent economic crisis.

The Business Roundtable and Takeovers Legislation

A changing political economy threw New Zealand business into flux. After the 1960s, a more varied and liberalised financial market emerged. From the 1970s, business ownership, traditionally characterised by small firms producing for the internal market, became more concentrated and a larger number of bigger firms emerged with more outward-looking and diverse interests (Jesson, 1987; Roper, 1990a). Within the established business organisations, larger firms found their voices outweighed, in the sense that they were outnumbered by smaller firms who favoured continued protectionism (Wanna, 1989, p. 5). Informally in 1976, and formally in 1980, they formed the New Zealand Business Roundtable, made up of the chief executives of most of New Zealand's largest companies. Membership, however, is by invitation. Not all large firms are represented.

The Roundtable was modelled on its American counterpart to represent large business interests in New Zealand. Its clout increased in 1986 when it appointed a former Treasury official, Roger Kerr, to a new post as executive director. The Roundtable established itself as a major policy advocate, making an impressive number of widely circulated major submissions to government. Its strategy of energetic promotion of market liberalisation post- rather than pre-dated the beginnings of the process, and remained consistent with the Chicago school economic theories that earlier informed key actors in Treasury (see Chapter 4; Easton, 1988). In its submissions, and as a general principle, the Roundtable saw itself as an advocate for the efficiency and prosperity of the New Zealand economy in general, not for the particular economic interests of its members (Roper, 1992, p. 18).

The deregulatory policies of the fourth Labour Government and the subsequent National Government were introduced, together with a policy of internationalisation of the New Zealand economy. International investment in New Zealand increased in the form of takeovers of New

Zealand-owned companies (Haworth, 1992). Reliance on foreign investment to promote economic growth intensifies the economic constraints on government. Policies to promote social goals in response to public opinion may discourage future investors and lead existing investors to move elsewhere. Neoliberalism reduces state autonomy in relation to the international marketplace, even as it enhances state autonomy from organised interests and voters by ceasing to intervene in the internal economy.

Changing ownership of New Zealand companies since the early 1980s made takeovers legislation a matter of keen debate, initiated by the Securities Commission in 1983. It saw a lack of competition in the market for corporate control and argued that shares of potential target companies were undervalued because the stock market was failing accurately to value companies with relatively high asset values. Consequently, New Zealand companies were vulnerable to corporate raiding for asset stripping. The case for legislation also rests on the ethical premise that all shareholders should be treated equally, and should be protected against stockmarket losses resulting from unscrupulous corporate activity (see Farrar, 1993).

The model presented above predicts that social values expressed through public opinion will take a political form. As a reaction to market liberalisation, by the 1990s new parties had indeed appeared—the Alliance and New Zealand First—opposed to many business-driven policies. By the mid-1990s the public reputation of large businesses was much diminished when compared with the heady years of 1986 and 1987. The morals and ethics of formerly admired business leaders were being called into question. Within the business community itself different views began to emerge.

Proposals for takeovers legislation were countered by the Reserve Bank and Treasury, who argued, in line with the Chicago school view, that takeovers promote a more efficient market because they constitute a value-creating activity (Easton 1988). In a climate of fiscal crisis, the Securities Commission could not convince a government already committed to deregulation of the financial markets, but the sharemarket crash in 1987 generated a better reception for its takeover law reform proposals. The commission was asked to speed up the completion of the report, which was produced in October 1988.

In 1991 the call for takeover law reform resulted in a Takeovers Bill, and the appointment of a Takeovers Advisory Committee. Submissions were called for by the committee both before and after the publication of a draft Takeovers Code. Reactions to the draft were strongly divided. The Business Roundtable was undoubtedly the main publicly visible force behind the opposition to takeovers legislation. Treasury officials expressed their own opposition in their confidential advice to the Minister of Finance.[2] Following the Chicago school analysis initially applied by Treasury, the Roundtable continued to use its resources to sponsor academic research and to import expert advocates for its views. Both the Roundtable and Treasury saw takeovers legislation as a key test of continued government support for neoliberalism.

Opponents of the code objected strongly to the provision for equal treatment of all shareholders, with no premium paid for controlling parcels of shares. They also objected to a mandatory bid threshold, whereby anyone purchasing more than 20 per cent of the voting rights in a listed company must make a full or partial offer for the remaining shares, and to pauses and publicity rules that would require bidders to give prior notice to a target company of their intention to make a takeover offer. They argued that takeovers create wealth for the nation as a whole, as well as for shareholders, including those who do not receive a premium for their shares. In the long run, and in general, they claimed, small shareholders do well out of takeovers. Takeovers legislation makes takeovers more difficult, and so protects underperforming managers.

Most of the submissions in support of the code, including those of the Securities Commission, the Institute of Directors, and one from the secretary of a major New Zealand corporation, Fletcher Challenge, expressed a moral concern for the rights and protection of minor shareholders which, it was said, were jeopardised without regulation. They also argued that the enforcement of a code of ethics would encourage greater investment and so increase New Zealand's economic growth rate. They made their case in the context of persisting cynicism about the ethics of major sharemarket players among small New Zealand investors.

Supporters of the code pointed out that the New Zealand sharemarket was unusual in that over 70 per cent of listed companies were controlled by one major shareholder and over 80 per cent of listed companies had one shareholder holding at least 20 per cent of the shares. Consequently, control of these companies could be transferred without any involvement by minority shareholders. The Takeovers Code would be against the interests of large investors such as overseas interests and Business Roundtable members because they would lose the premium that would otherwise be paid for their controlling parcel of shares.

The key supporters of the code cited documented evidence of the experience of specific New Zealand companies. Many were celebrated cases, such as the asset stripping of London Pacific Ltd, in which a Singaporean businessman stripped the company of more than $30 million by acquiring

Equiticorp's 70 per cent share holding, using London Pacific's cash to fund the purchase. Further investments were made, causing the collapse of the company and leaving the shares of 7000 minority shareholders worthless. At least seven highly publicised cases between 1986 and 1991 could be cited as cause for concern (McKenzie, 1993, pp. 121–4).

The central conflict between the supporters and the opponents of takeovers legislation was based on contending empirical claims. Because of the uncertain state of the empirical research, there was scope for considerable disagreement. If takeovers generated wealth and legislation would inhibit takeovers, then it could be argued that legislation would not be required. If, on the other hand, a code of ethics imposed by legislation would result in enhanced confidence in the sharemarket and, therefore, greater investment, then legislation would be desirable. The most comprehensive evidence appeared to indicate that takeovers in general benefited all shareholders. The number of unpalatable cases could be used, however, to indicate an unacceptable situation that might deter investors.

Whether the proposed code would inhibit takeovers also remained at issue. The British code, very similar to that proposed for New Zealand, was not preventing very substantial takeover activity during the mid-1990s. Another issue not pursued in the debate was whether the stockmarket is an efficient and effective allocative and monitoring instrument in the first place. Some authorities argued that firms which were continually at auction have incentives to seek short term stock price advantages at the expense of more productive long-run investment policy (Porter, 1992; cf Franks and Meyer, 1990).

Because the empirical evidence could be deployed to support either side, the greater energy, resources, and persistence by those opposed to the code gave them an advantage. A feature of the Roundtable's lobbying efforts is the use of sponsored academic research. A key tool in this area has been the Centre for Independent Studies which, from the start, has had very close ties with the Roundtable (Jesson, 1992; Venables, 1988). The group's primary submission to the committee was a report that it had commissioned. It also submitted an extensive evaluation of the code from an American professor and then had that evaluation endorsed by yet another American academic. The Roundtable report was extensively referenced and relied heavily on a study carried out by Pound and Zeckhauser (1988) and published by the Centre for Independent Studies.

There was organisational association among many of those who opposed the draft Takeovers Code, usually through membership of the Business Roundtable, or of the Centre for Independent Studies (Roper 1995). Of the nine submissions that specifically opposed the code, only two did not refer directly or indirectly to the Pound and Zeckhauser work, which was said to be 'undoubtedly reflecting mainstream informed expert professional opinion' (see the university academics' submission, p. 2, in Roper, 1995).[3] While claiming to rest their arguments on 'empirical evidence', the opponents of the takeovers legislation argued from the authority of their academic experts (Roper, 1995). Unable to mobilise such expertise to the same extent, supporters of the code limited the effectiveness of their arguments, which were otherwise at least as tenable as those of their opponents.

The debate wound up with agreement on a voluntary code to be enforced by the New Zealand Stock Exchange, requiring companies to assent to one of three procedures to regulating takeovers. Of these, one was minimalist, and directed almost entirely against insider trading, but the most rigorous largely followed the principles of the Takeover Code. Fletcher Challenge adopted the most rigorous version, against the preferences of its chief executive and Roundtable member, Ron Trotter. Those representing larger New Zealand shareholders would have preferred a less demanding code, whereas overseas and smaller New Zealand investors were in favour of the maximum option (Holm, 1995, p. 35).

As of late 1995, it was clear that compromise had been achieved. Both ethical and economic considerations had entered into the calculus. With a healthy economic growth path since 1991, there was more scope for ethical arguments promoted by the Ministry of Justice, but the greater clout of the Treasury, and its minister within Cabinet, almost certainly told against support for a systematic code. Covered only in the business pages and in the business press, the issue was of no public interest, nor was it a matter of debate between the political parties. Probably because of the complexity of the issues involved, neither the Alliance or New Zealand First mobilised public opinion on the issue. Consequently, the Roundtable-based mobilisation of intellectual resources, coupled with the close ideological rapport between key actors in the New Zealand Business Roundtable, the Reserve Bank, and Treasury, was able to win the day, albeit at the price of some compromise.

Business Influence in Context

In terms of hypothesis testing, an historical overview of business and politics in New Zealand, coupled with two illustrative examples, only scratches the surface. The determinants of policy outcomes are almost invariably multiple and complex, and in different contexts variables are likely to have different effects. Further progress in analysing business influence on market liberalisation is likely to be made by comparing different national experiences. Both case studies, consistent with neoMarxist and neoliberal theory, confirm that the state of the economy sets the scene for policy change, in the case of the open economy because of an obvious need for structural reform, and in that of takeovers legislation in a climate where economic recovery made it possible to consider both ethical concerns and economic efficiency.

Although, ultimately, economic influences may oblige a government to bend to necessity, that decision can be postponed, thus influencing the depth of the ultimate crisis and the consequent responses. New Zealand's response was delayed, and came after a shift in ideology and strategy, largely among state officials, and a critical election result. Business opinion largely ran in parallel and did not emerge strongly in support of liberalisation until relatively late. After all, the National Party, the natural ally of business, was in charge, and business criticism of National took time to emerge, intensifying from about 1982 onwards. After 1986, the New Zealand Business Roundtable promoted an established policy trend and so its advocacy fell on fertile ground. Business, hitherto divided against itself, had to rely on the mobilisation of state capacity to remove the interventions that had limited its political influence since the late 1930s. Once market liberalisation was under way, powerful interconnected élites, made up of politicians, senior public officials, and businesspeople, sought to drive the process further. But with the economic recovery of the 1990s, new tensions may well emerge between the larger overseas-oriented corporate sector and a wider community of investors for whom New Zealand is a place to live as well as a source of dividends and capital gains.

1 For an interpretation of the development of organised interests in New Zealand drawing on these insights, see Vowles, 1992 and 1993.

2 An examination of Treasury documents addressed to the Minister of Finance and released under the Official Information Act revealed Treasury's insistent opposition to the Takeovers Bill, their objections being very much in line with those of the New Zealand Business Roundtable.

3 Brian Easton (1988) raises the issue, albeit in a related but separate context, of whether the Chicago school view (which underpins the Pound and Zeckhauser work referred to here) can, in fact, be claimed to represent the mainstream of contemporary economic analysis (p. 75).

Guide to Readings

A good introduction to the international literature on organised interests and politics is Smith (1993). Vowles (1992 and 1993) generally describes and analyses organised economic interests in New Zealand in the late 1980s and early 1990s. Deeks and Perry (1992) provide a useful series of case studies. Wanna (1989) gives an account of the centralisation of the organisation of business interests in New Zealand that occurred to facilitate and increase the input of those organisations into government policy formation. His description of the close links between members of the public and private sectors are supported by, for example, Deeks (1992) and Jesson (1992). The latter gives a useful account of the movement of Treasury personnel into the private sector, which has strengthened the personal networks between government and business. Further means of influence in government policy formation are put forward by Gandy (1992) in his discussion of the sponsorship of information that supports a particular viewpoint. Easton (1988) provides an illuminating account of the influence of Chicago school economics on Treasury and New Zealand Business Roundtable officials. Roper (1990, 1991a, 1991b, 1992, and 1993a) outlines a Marxist interpretation. Thakur and Gold (1983) provide the classic account of the CER negotiation process.

CHAPTER SEVEN

TRADE UNIONS

TOM BRAMBLE WITH SARAH HEAL

With 362 000 members in 1995, trade unions are the single most significant mass institution in New Zealand society. They remain, therefore, the best organisations to give voice to workers' industrial and political concerns at workplace and national levels. This chapter considers the continued relevance of trade unions and their strengths and limitations, both theoretically and in practice. The chapter starts with a theoretical discussion of the role of unions as organising institutions and of union officials as bargaining agents who are both part of the labour movement but also separate from the working class. The second section turns to the practice of New Zealand unionism since 1945. Particular attention is paid to the political strategies pursued by employers and union officials, culminating in an analysis of the industrial and political paralysis that has gripped the leadership of the Council of Trade Unions (CTU) since its foundation in 1987.

The Politics of Unionism

Broadly, there are three major interpretations of the role of unions—the unitarist, the pluralist, and the radical or Marxist. The unitarist perspective, which has become increasingly prevalent since the enactment of the Employment Contracts Act, suggests that the interests of employers and employees are one and the same and that unions, as 'third parties', interfere in the natural order of business life. Both workers and bosses benefit from thriving businesses, the former with job security and higher wages, the latter with profits and the ability to invest in further growth (Brook, 1990).

To the extent that unions gain a foothold, blame can be attached to one of two culprits—poor managers or agitators. By communicating badly, managers can unwittingly give employees the wrong message and 'upsets' may result. This is all the more likely if malevolent individuals, the 'agitators', are at work. Such agitators use a combination of misinformation, deceit, hard work, and charisma to sour relations between employees and employers, thereby creating the conditions for union growth.

Unitarists see the 'labour market' as constituting mutually beneficial exchanges between employers and employees, in which both exercise 'freedom of choice'. Workers should be free to decide how and under what conditions to sell their labour power and whether to join unions or to engage unions as their bargaining agents. Relations between workers and employers, as freely trading individuals, should be governed not by statute law but by the law of contract, a case most influentially put by Epstein (1984). The resulting 'freedom of contract' therefore enables employers and employees to deal with each other as equals in the pursuit of their common goals. Such was the blueprint for industrial relations set down by the New Zealand Business Roundtable (1987) and New Zealand Employers' Federation (1987).

Although some writers from this tradition claim that they care for the interests of unions (suggesting that their only concern is to improve their effectiveness), the kernel of the unitarist view is strongly anti-union. The underlying unitarist view is that unions and conflict are essentially illegitimate, dysfunctional, or a sign of an underlying pathology in what is essentially a harmonious relationship between employer and employees.

The unitarist view has been strongly criticised over the decades. Although the labour contract appears to be entered into freely by two independent actors, worker and employer, there is an acute imbalance in power between the two parties that is either not recognised, or is consciously hidden, by the unitarist approach. There are various manifestations of this imbalance, which have their origins both in the employment relationship itself and in the state and the judiciary. The key factor is that, for the workers, the freedom of the labour market is the freedom to work or to live in poverty. Workers cannot, for any length of time, hoard their labour power waiting for the price to rise or for their bargaining opponent to give way. Employers, by contrast, usually have reserves of capital to fall back on. Workers cannot usually afford to call upon the services of legal advisers to advise them on how best to gain leverage in bargaining. And, in the case of disputes with their opponents, workers cannot usually rely on assistance from the courts or agents of law enforcement who respect rights pertaining to property rather than the right to a job and a decent livelihood. Individual workers, therefore, face their employers as supplicants, not as equals, negating any genuine freedom in the contract between the two parties.

The second major approach to unionism is the pluralist or institutionalist. This starts from the premise that society is divided into a series of interest groups that are in a constant state of tense cooperation. Tension, because interest groups are formed by individuals with their own needs coming together to advance their interests collectively in opposition to other social groupings. Cooperation, because ultimately society has to function collectively, and interest groups, while fighting to improve their own situation, must acquiesce to the greater needs of unity against external threat or internal implosion.

In the field of industrial relations, pluralists view conflict as being endemic within the system, as wage earners, through their trade unions, try to increase wages, reduce hours, or otherwise improve their lot in the face of opposition from employers, who have a vested interest in enhancing profits and managerial prerogatives. Battles over 'shares of the pie' result. Pluralists therefore regard trade unions as legitimate, and industrial conflict as merely the expression of competition between parties of roughly equal strength. They emphasise, however, that conflict should not be taken too far, for otherwise the economy will suffer. So pluralists urge the state to step in and establish a framework whereby union affairs and industrial conflict can be managed. The key task for the pluralist approach is how best to manage conflict through mechanisms such as collective bargaining, conciliation and arbitration, works councils, wages boards, and the like. This is where the connection between pluralism as a political philosophy and social democracy as a governmental practice is most apparent.

The problem with the pluralist analysis is its insistence that the various parties have roughly equivalent power, a notion that cannot be sustained in practice. Some of the same criticisms of the unitarist analysis also apply to the pluralist: although workers are undoubtedly stronger when banded together in unions, they still face capital from a position of weakness because they have little control over the major economic decisions taken by business and the government. By encouraging unions to be restrained in their demands, the pluralists overlook this basic difference in power. Furthermore, the more uncertain the economic environment, the more the pluralist analysis comes to resemble the unitarist because, at its core, it also accepts that the interests of labour and capital are the same. In conditions of business hardship, the space for workers to put their own demands on business is reduced drastically by the insistence of both unitarists and pluralists that unions be 'reasonable'.

The final interpretation of unionism, and the one that will be adopted in this chapter, is the radical or Marxist view, which denies that society is organised on the basis either of the invisible hand or of a plethora of roughly equally balanced interest groups. Rather, it starts from the premise that there are two major classes in capitalist society—the capitalist and working classes—with the former constituting a ruling class on the basis of its effective control of the major forms of production. It further argues that the two classes have mutually antagonistic interests, and that the tension between them is not of a type that can forever be contained by institutional forms.

Within this broad arena, trade unions come into being partially to redress the underlying structural power imbalance between employers and workers. But rather than seeing unions simply as one of several interest groups, Marxists set the workplace into its broader socio-political context and argue that unions are basic combat institutions of a class, providing a means whereby workers begin to organise and act independently, as a class, to combat capitalist exploitation. Whereas pluralists are concerned with channelling conflict into safe procedures, and warn against a tendency by unions to go 'too far', Marxists celebrate workers' struggle against employers, at the same time lamenting that union struggle on its own does not go far enough. Marxists argue that unions are, by their very nature, profoundly contradictory institutions, part of capitalism but also containing within themselves the potential for its supersession. Unions negotiate the terms on which labour power is exploited, rather than seeking to end exploitation. They organise workers by trade, occupation, industry, or region, not on a classwide basis. Trade union consciousness is, therefore, usually limited to advancing the interests of particular sections of the class, and trade union action never leads spontaneously to revolutionary challenges to the capitalist order as a whole.

The Role of Union Officials

The fact that unions are essentially self-limiting capitalist institutions has a profound effect on the behaviour of trade union officials. Collective agreements or awards are a form of 'industrial legality' and represent a gain for the working class because they reduce the arbitrariness of capital (Gramsci, 1920, p. 93). But, by the same token, the legality and formalisation of collective bargaining can be used by trade union officials as a platform from which to promote their own interests, against those of the rank and file membership.

The American union movement affords the clearest case of the alienation of union officials from the members that they represent. Mills described the American labour leader as 'a business entrepreneur in the important and specialised business of contracting a supply of trained labour' (1948, p. 6). Although New Zealand unions have never been so marked by corruption as their American counterparts, the difference is only one of degree. All senior union officials in New Zealand tend to defend their unions in ways that emphasise their own expertise rather than mass mobilisation. They seek to insulate themselves from pressure from below, fearful of losing their jobs, which, compared with the membership at large, entitle them to a privileged existence in terms of income, working conditions, social prestige, and opportunities for social advancement. Most important, conservative industrial tactics are encouraged by employers and governments who promote moderation in union aims and methods. System-breaking demands are replaced by those that can be met without jeopardising union-employer relations. As a result, union officials become firm defenders of the established system of bargaining, and compromise comes to be seen as a desirable end in itself. The union official therefore becomes, in Mills' famous phrase, 'the manager of discontent' (Mills, 1948, pp. 8–9).

This approach to trade union officials (what has been called the 'rank and filist perspective') can be defended against three common criticisms. One objection is that it oversimplifies internal processes and that, in practice, there is no such thing as a united rank and file union membership with common interests counterposed to those of full-time officials. Divisions between members may be just as significant as those between members and their full-time representatives. Although it is true, however, that the membership of most unions is fractured along a number of lines, the logic of even the most basic industrial action is to promote unity in practice. Innumerable historical examples indicate this phenomenon. For example, those unions that established barriers to entry on the basis of sex or race in their early days now appear to have abolished these obstacles. There are no longer any separate tailoresses' and tailors' unions, for example. The trend is also indicated in the struggles of workers of both sexes and from a host of different national and racial backgrounds. For example, the industrial campaigns in the meatworks in the 1960s and 1970s threw together Pakeha, Maori and Pacific Islanders. Such is the multinational and multiracial nature of most contemporary working classes that all modern strikes, if they are to succeed, require workers to set aside their prejudices and to work together in order to forge a common fighting organisation. In the course of industrial campaigns, a collective consciousness emerges that gives real meaning to the term 'rank and file'.

A second criticism of the rank and filist perspective is that union officials are prevented from becoming a conservative and unrepresentative stratum because they must respond to membership sentiment. If they do not respond, they stand the chance of being turned out of office and replaced by those who are more in tune with membership wishes. It is certainly true that there are such limits to the conservatism of trade union officials. Precisely because trade unions themselves are contradictory institutions, trade union officials 'perform a dual role, both shackling their members to the system and bringing home limited benefits within it' (Anderson, 1967, p. 277). Faced with pressure from below, they may seek to repress the threat in order to preserve the status quo in form and substance, or they may attempt to accommodate to it, to change the form of relations within the union and between the union and employers, in order to preserve the substance of leadership dominance. This may involve taking a more militant stance towards management and adopting measures designed to coopt those within the union promoting a more aggressive industrial strategy.

But the fact that full-time officials are forced to respond to pressure from below does not remove the pressure from capital and state. Caught between these powerful social forces, the official tends to vacillate for, as Hyman argues, 'his task is to sustain a delicate balance between grievance and satisfaction, between activism and quiescence' (1971, p. 37). Officials play an inherently conservative role for the reasons already outlined, but such conservatism is mediated by the relative pressure from bargaining partners and rank and file members. Their conservatism is therefore contingent and historically determined.

The final criticism of the rank and filist perspective appears the most damaging. There is no evidence from surveys that full-time officials incline to conservatism and an emphasis on procedure at the expense of industrial action, or that rank and file members can be regarded as more militant or more prepared to endorse bold industrial action than their leaders (Kelly, 1988, p. 178). But this is to misinterpret the argument, which is not that officials are always conservative, rank and file members always militant. Rather, it is suggested that the conditions of existence of both groups do have a strong impact on their consciousness and thereby on their activity, so that, in periods of sharp conflict, the actions of workers and those of full-time officials can diverge quite dramatically from their attitudes as revealed in surveys. Hence there is the phenomenon of union members who vote for the National Party being more prepared to engage in militant industrial action than Labour or Alliance union officials.

In order to understand why this can occur, it is important to consider the volatile nature of working class consciousness and the factors that shape it. Gramsci has provided the most useful theoretical approach for understanding the complex nature of working class consciousness. He argues that the worker's

theoretical consciousness can indeed be historically in opposition to his activity. One might almost say that he has two theoretical consciousnesses (or one contradictory consciousness): one which is implicit in his activity and which in reality unites him with all his fellow workers in the practical transformation of the real world; and one, superficially explicit or verbal, which he has inherited from the past and uncritically absorbed (Gramsci, 1971, p. 333).

To paraphrase: the more abstract and distant the issue under consideration, the more that workers' attitudes, as revealed in surveys, are influenced by the 'commonsense' ideas of society at large. The explicit consciousness of most workers may therefore be quite conservative, for such 'commonsense' ideas invariably support existing social relations. By contrast, the more concrete and personal the issue, and the more it bears upon their immediate relations with their fellow workers, the more likely workers are to respond to opinion pollsters on the basis of their own life and work experience. The answers that workers give in such circumstances are more indicative of their implicit consciousness, and often stand quite at odds with accepted social mores.

Many unionised workers with experience of industrial action share a common frame of reference whose elements form a basic class consciousness. These include: the need for workers to stick together, an antipathy to the boss and those who would break strikes, a suspicion of the role of police on picket lines, and an understanding that workers can protect what they have (or improve on it) only by being prepared to fight. Such notions are especially likely to come to the fore in periods of collective industrial action, when workers are engaged in what Gramsci called 'the practical transformation of the real world' (1971, p. 333). Only by recognising the contradictory elements of working class consciousness can one explain why trade unionists questioned in surveys say that they think unions in general are too powerful or too ready to strike, but that this is not the case with their own union.

Industrial action by trade unionists has a powerful effect in stimulating workers' consciousness of the identity and power of their class. The struggle of rank and file union members tends to break from the legal channels sanctioned by full-time officials, not least because members have no material attachment to the formal procedures of industrial relations. Once mobilised and conscious of the issues at stake, rank and file union members can rapidly be driven into industrial action that goes well beyond what their full-time officials are willing to sanction. Sharp swings of membership sentiment can occur very quickly, from docility and acquiescence to aggression and confidence and back again; it is in the fluidity of their ideas that members stand in contrast to full-time officials.

The consciousness of full-time union officials is not subject to the same major fluctuations. In contrast to rank and file workers, such officials, even those dedicated to advancing working class interests, have no collective interest in breaking established union-management relations, since they depend on these for their very existence. The power of full-time officials rests, in the last instance, on their specialised role as negotiators over the terms on which labour is exploited. In the event of a strike, full-time officials are forced to consider what effect this action has on the distribution of power within their union. Does it threaten the bargaining relationship with the employers and the officials' role in it, or does it strengthen it? This factor helps explain their industrial timidity at critical moments. In this sense, the differing positions of rank and file members and full-time union officials, with respect to capital and state, give the former an intrinsic tendency to shatter industrial routinism and the latter a tendency to reinforce it.

Thus far, the argument has been couched at a relatively abstract level. What follows uses the Marxist framework developed to this point to shed light on developments in New Zealand unionism since 1945.

The Domination of Labourism and Arbitration, 1945–66

In order to understand the specific nature of New Zealand trade unionism as it stood in 1945 and how it evolved over the following decades, it is critical to establish its relationship with the state and the Labour Party. The political agenda of the Labour Party has always been reformism, not revolution. Reformist politics can be understood as a theory and practice that 'create defensive barriers against the naked exploitation of capitalism but at the same time accept the possibility of social change within the existing framework of capitalist society rather than seeking through revolutionary means to overthrow it' (Darlington, 1994, p. 14).

The formation and electoral success of the Labour Party in the early part of the century consolidated a particular form of capitalist class rule in New Zealand based on the incorporation of trade union officials into the political process, rather than their exclusion from it. This has discouraged radical demands and actions that might jeopardise Labour's electoral chances. The close connections between the Labour Party and leading trade unions officials were evident with the formation of the Federation of Labour (FOL) in 1937, as a result of pressure from the Savage Government. Labour, in turn, amended its rules, giving the unions large block votes in party conferences, and this allowed the party leaders more control over fractious conferences because it concentrated decision-making in a few hands. In the period during and immediately after the Second World War, FOL leaders were involved in government affairs to an unprecedented degree, culminating in their involvement in the tripartite Economic Stabilisation Commission and the appointment of the FOL president to the position of Minister of National Service, later Minister of Labour. In return, the higher levels of the union bureaucracy gave unstinting support to wage control and work intensification arising out of the war effort. As Olssen comments, 'the Federation thus became a means of disciplining the labour force on the government's behalf' (1986a, p. 24).

Even after the fall of the Labour Government in 1949, and the advent of more than two decades of almost uninterrupted conservative rule, the state interventionist agenda made a place for the union officialdom. State mechanisms were established to minimise explicit class antagonisms and these, in turn, were underpinned by full employment and economic growth (Wilkes, 1993, p. 200). Critical to the role of the union officialdom was the arbitration system that affected the internal politics of New Zealand trade unions in a variety of ways. According to Walsh,

> This system offered a glittering array of benefits to participating unions: for registered unions the state guaranteed their coverage rights against potential rivals, obliged employers to negotiate with them, gave easy access to compulsory arbitration by state tribunals, ensured the application of resulting awards to all workers in the occupation or industry concerned and accepted a responsibility to enforce the award upon all employers. From 1936 the state also guaranteed membership and thus revenues for registered unions (1991, p. 1; see also Chapter 11).

Membership in the private sector grew strongly under state protection and by 1945, there were 282 000 members of registered and state sector unions, representing 59.6 per cent of the workforce. Table 7.1 indicates that growth continued at a steady pace throughout the two postwar decades as membership increased to just under 450 000 members.

Table 7.1

Year	Private sector union membership	Public sector union membership	Total trade union membership	Trade union density	Working days lost
1945	229 103	53345	282448	59.63	66 629
1946	247 498				30 393
1947	260 739				102 725
1948	271 100				93 464
1949	275 977				218 172
1950	275 779	58713	334492	56.95	271 475
1951	272 957				1 157 390
1952	283 496				28 123
1953	290 149				19 291

Continued

Table 7.1 Continued

Year	Private sector trade unions	Public sector trade unions	Total trade union membership	Trade union density	Working days lost
1954	299 254				20 474
1955	304 520	69 186	373 463	56.51	52 043
1956	307 031				23 870
1957	317 137				28 186
1958	324 438				18 788
1959	327 405				29 831
1960	332 362	82 191	414 553	54.71	35 683
1961	324 747				38 185
1962	332 801				93 157
1963	334 128				54 490
1964	346 857				66 834
1965	353 105	95 132	448 237	50.94	21 814
1966	362 760				99 095
1967	366 884				139 490
1968	364 872				130 267
1969	366 523				138 675
1970	378 465	115 019	493 484	50.63	277 348
1971	386 275				162 563
1972	394 748				140 672
1973	427 692				271 706
1974	436 623				183 688
1975	454 991	150 000	604 991	55.64	214 632
1976	464 453	160 000	624 453		488 441
1977	473 432				436 808
1978	486 533				380 605
1979	506 963				381 896
1980	516 297				373 496
1981	519 705				388 086
1982	527 797				330 028
1983	527 545				371 774
1984	485 484				424 921
1985	490 206	192 800	683 006	43.5	756 432
1986	489 763				1 329 054
1987					366 300
1988					381 700
1989	486 483	162 342	649 875	44.7	193 300
1990			610 265		330 900
1991			603 118	41.5	99 032
1992			428 160	28.8	113 742
1993			409 112	26.8	23 770
1994			375 906	23.4	38 300
1995			362 200	21.7	53 352

Sources: Roth (1973 and 1978); Brosnan et al. (1990); Harbridge and Hince (1992); Crawford, Harbridge and Hince (1996).

State protection did not come without strings, however, and unions had to accept an extensive range of statutory restrictions on their structure and activities. The outcome was that unions were, for the most part, 'arbitrationist' in character, created by the system and dependent for their existence upon the protections it offered' (Walsh, 1991a, p. 1). Such unions tended to be small, covered poorly organised workers, and had precious little in the way of workplace representation. State-sponsored compulsory unionism led to union officials becoming lazy for, as Peetz and others comment, 'unions had been able to demand fees from a captive membership and had thus been under no obligation to perform' (1993, p. 266). Employers, as well as conservative union leaders, were keen supporters of compulsory unionism, because it gave a power base to conservative leaders of industrially passive unions. It also allowed governments to break more militant unions by deregistering them and establishing tame unions in their place (Roth, 1973, p. 80).

There was also, however, a minority of unions, chiefly industrial unions in the export industry sectors (waterside workers, seafarers, miners, freezing workers) and also drivers, who were opposed to the wage-fixing elements of the Arbitration Court and made advances in wages and conditions through industrial action. While the arbitrationist unions looked to the protection afforded by the arbitration system, the unions who mobilised preferred to rely on their strategic location, high levels of membership solidarity and commitment, and effective leadership (Brosnan et al., 1990, p. 99). Such unions had a better developed workplace structure of delegates and stewards and chafed against the industrially passive politics of the arbitrationist unions.

For a large part of this century, therefore, New Zealand unions have been divided in their approach and general philosophy, and these tensions came to a head in two historical periods: with the rise of the Red Federation of Labour in the years before the First World War (Olssen, 1986b), and in the postwar industrial upsurge that culminated in the formation of the Trade Union Congress (TUC) and the 1951 waterfront lockout (Barnes, 1987; Roth, 1986). On both occasions the pro-arbitration union leaders sided with the conservative government and employers to crush the threat posed by the anti-arbitrationist unions, in the process killing off the Red Feds in 1913 and the TUC in 1951. As a result of their victory in 1951, the leaders of the arbitrationist unions were able to consolidate their domination in the FOL and used this control to rewrite the federation's constitution, thereby making the executive more remote from rank and file control (Roth, 1973, pp. 137–8). This, in turn, led to a fifteen-year period of industrial quiescence within the New Zealand labour movement (see Table 7.1). Although, as may be seen from Table 7.1, union membership grew significantly in this period, actual coverage ('union density') fell from nearly 60 per cent of the workforce in 1945 to just over 50 per cent twenty years later.

The Working Class Upturn, 1966–77

In line with many other Western countries, the New Zealand labour movement began to stir again in the mid- to late 1960s (see Table 7.1). The major factor responsible for this was a desire by New Zealand workers to improve their living standards, in circumstances of labour shortages, alongside a long-term decline in the wages share of national income (Roper, 1990b). Increasing union pressure was demonstrated by the rise of over-award payments from 0 per cent of award rates in 1947 to 30 per cent in 1965 (Roth, 1970, p. 47). Then in 1968, when the Arbitration Court made a nil general wage order (the benchmark against which all increases in award wages were determined), this led to a collapse in union confidence in the court and a decision by the leaders of all major unions to engage in direct action to win pay rises through collective bargaining. Rank and file union militancy now came to the fore, most obviously among public sector workers, such as public servants, nurses, postal workers, and teachers. The overall effect was an explosion in strike activity from just under 22 000 working days lost in 1965 to 277 000 by 1970, peaking at nearly 500 000 in 1976. The strike wave was characterised by a sharp increase in the number of strikes—145 stoppages in 1966, 313 in 1971, and 562 in 1977—and an increase in the average number of workers involved in each strike. Approximately 12 per cent of the entire New Zealand workforce took some form of industrial action in 1969–70, and this figure was topped by the 19 per cent who took action in 1976, the highest levels of working class participation in strike activity for the entire twentieth century until this point (see Deeks et al., 1994, p. 374).

The union offensive led to strong gains in membership. Union coverage rose to 55.6 per cent by 1975, as total private and public sector membership increased sharply from 450 000 to more than 600 000 (Table 7.1). Compositional trends that had been gathering pace in the union movement over the postwar decades now accelerated, with the result that public sector unionism increased by more than 50 per cent, alongside rapid growth in the manufacturing and distribution industries (Roth, 1973, p. 162) (Table 7.1). At the same time, the traditional strongholds of militant unionism, the railway workers, the seamen, and the mine workers, were losing ground as their industries were restructured and further mechanised.

Government and employers took a variety of sometimes quite contradictory steps to push back the working class offensive. The general position of the Employers' Federation was to continue the policies that had served them well in previous years—centralised wage bargaining and the continuation of compulsory unionism (Roper, 1990b). This, however, became increasingly untenable. The election of the Muldoon Government in 1975 and his attempted imposition of an austerity drive and a twelve-month wage freeze, did not halt the industrial push but, rather, inspired a wave of protest action, resulting in a tactical government retreat on the wage freeze in 1976–77.

The failure of Muldoon's wage freeze led to a crisis of confidence within employer ranks by the late 1970s. Statutory wage controls of the type experimented with throughout the decade had either failed to rein in industrial action or had been actively broken by the unions. Nor had collective bargaining worked—indeed, it had generated wages breakouts of an uncontrolled nature. The failure of Muldoon's interventionist style of government, most particularly his second attempt at a wages freeze in 1982–84, led to employer desertion of the National cause and a turn to Labour and the politics of Rogernomics.

The Ruling-Class Counter-Offensive, 1984–95

The factors behind, and the content of, the ruling class offensive against New Zealand's working class under the stewardship of the fourth Labour Government have been described extensively elsewhere (Roper, 1993a). Of most importance for this chapter is the fact that at the heart of the neoliberal market-driven orthodoxy of the fourth Labour Government, lay the notion that high levels of welfare benefits and strong trade unions were to blame for the problems faced by New Zealand capitalism, a belief also held firmly within the ranks of the successor fourth National Government.

Under both governments, organised labour was dealt several damaging blows. The emergence of mass unemployment, deregulation, and the impact of competition all hit the traditional bastions of militant unionism hard. In the core areas of mining and transport, Labour Government policy hastened a process that had been under way for some years. The meatworkers' union, the major surviving base of militant blue collar unionism, was devastated during the 1970s and 1980s by mechanisation, the export of live sheep, and a deliberate strategy by the major companies to move away from large works in the cities to smaller satellite works in small towns and country areas. Likewise, public sector unionism was hard hit under the impact of Labour's State-Owned Enterprises Act 1986, which facilitated the corporatisation and sell-off of all major state-owned commercial operations.

The result was a decline of union membership for the first time since the Depression of the 1930s. After peaking in 1981 at 520 000, registered (private sector) membership declined thereafter, while state sector union membership peaked in 1985 at nearly 193 000 and then fell precipitously by 1989 to 162 000 (see Table 7.1).

The ruling class offensive against unionism was met first by a slow recovery in industrial action in the early 1980s, a sharp explosion in 1985–86, and then a collapse that developed into a rout by the early 1990s (Table 7.1). The increase in the strike rate in the early to mid-1980s in New Zealand runs counter to the trend in most other Western nations at this time, but, despite the impressive burst of activity, the underlying characteristic was one of retreat (Roper, 1990b). There was a steady decline in the number of industrial disputes, falling back from 562 in 1977 to 291 in 1981, and 215 in 1986, and the number of workers involved in the 1986 strike peak was actually half that of 1976. The wave of industrial conflict in 1985–86 evident in Table 7.1 was due not to an outbreak of aggressive strikes in a wide variety of workplaces and industries, a feature of the 1960s, but to an employer offensive. Disputes over redundancy payments became common and in some sectors lockouts became significant (Henning, 1995, p. 90). The bitterness of these disputes is indicated from the lengthening of the average dispute, from a typical two to three days in the previous years, to thirteen days in 1986.

The retreat of the labour movement and a pressing need to drive productivity up and costs down more quickly than before led to a shift of sentiment within employer ranks towards a deregulationist agenda. Key elements of the new agenda were voluntary unionism, enterprise bargaining, pay increases to be based on company 'capacity to pay' rather than on relativities or the cost of living, the removal of 'restrictive work practices', the introduction of youth rates, the elimination of national awards, the introduction of anti-strike legislation, and the reduction of non-wage costs of employment (such as sick pay, maternity leave, and accident compensation levies) (*The Employer*, April 1986, pp. 1–4).

Legislation introduced by Labour, and then by the National Government, realised many of these goals. The Labour Relations Act 1987 was the first significant step in undermining the framework of national awards. The legislation restored compulsory unionism, but it also prohibited unions from seeking access to enterprise bargaining (second-tier agreements) while still maintaining award coverage for the affected workers. Although relatively few unions deserted the award system (Harbridge and McCaw, 1991), this provision clearly encouraged a process of union and award fragmentation as stronger groups of workers were encouraged to opt out of awards, leaving their defence in the hands of weaker unions and non-union workers. The fourth Labour Government thereby paved the way for the ultimate abolition of awards by its successor. The State Sector Act 1988 further undermined unions by scrapping job tenure in the public sector and reducing other long-established conditions of employment.

The Employment Contracts Act (ECA) 1991 represented the complete enactment of the agenda of the New Zealand Business Roundtable, with devastating results for organised labour. Organising on the job was made immensely more difficult as employers now had the right to refuse to negotiate with an employee's chosen bargaining agent, to use lockouts to force concessions, and to replace striking workers with blacklegs (Douglas, 1993a). Union membership fell sharply as a result, from 600 000 to 362 000 between May 1991, when the act took effect, and December 1995. Union coverage therefore fell back—from 41 per cent of the workforce to 22 per cent (Harbridge et al., 1995) (see Table 7.1). Entire unions, such as the Clerical Workers' Union, collapsed, while membership fell by 50–75 per cent in the agriculture, construction, and wholesale and retail industries in the act's first three years. Union decline has been most evident in the private sector, with state sector membership declining by 'only' 13 per cent, half the rate of decline across the labour movement at large (Harbridge et al., 1995). This difference is at least partly due to the fact that a portion of workers in private sector unions were reluctant conscripts before 1991, that is, they were members only because of closed shop arrangements, which were absent in the public sector.

The ruling class offensive of the 1980s and 1990s met with two responses within the union movement: organisational restructuring and, much more significantly, a new political strategy.

Organisational restructuring

At the peak level, the decline of blue collar and the rise of white collar unionism through the 1970s and 1980s eventually led to pressure for unity between the FOL, comprising private sector workers, and the Combined State Sector Unions (CSSU), with an exclusively public sector membership. The result, the CTU, with 530 000 affiliated members, was formed in 1987, on the fiftieth anniversary of the foundation of the FOL, and took over responsibility for developing general union policies and providing overall leadership to the labour movement. The CTU picked up some unions that had not been members of either federation but also lost some of those which had been members of the FOL in the past, chiefly in the transport and maritime unions but also electricians and timber workers.

The CTU and the fourth Labour Government were keen proponents of union amalgamation, the former proposing in its key 1989 document,

Strategies for Change, that the union movement be restructured around fourteen key industry unions (Council of Trade Unions, 1989). As a result of the provision in the Labour Relations Act 1987 requiring unions to have at least 1000 members, the number of unions halved from 223 to 112 between 1986 and 1989. The ECA, by strangling union finances, further encouraged this trend, and the number of unions slipped by the end of 1994 to eighty-two. By this time, only ten unions had more than 10 000 members, but these ten covered 70 per cent of total union membership.

A further organisational trend has been the evident attempt by some unions to shift their focus away from the centralised structures typical of the arbitrationist days, to a decentralised structure capable of dealing with the requirements of local bargaining and contract negotiations. With the shift of wage determination away from arbitration or multiemployer industry bargaining to enterprise level bargaining in the 1970s and 1980s, the lack of workplace structures in some unions had become a liability, and the ECA simply further highlighted this fact. According to Peetz et al.,

> This change in bargaining level has required a far greater degree of participation and responsibility by branch officials and workplace delegates than had previously been the case. It has required a much greater emphasis on direct bargaining with individual employers and a closer, more responsive relationship between union officials and their membership ... In many instances the function of bargaining has had to pass from paid officials to local delegates (1993, p. 268).

As will be seen, however, this drive towards 'closer, more responsive relationships' between officials and members is limited by the overall political agenda of the CTU.

The adoption of strategic unionism

A key feature of CTU strategy in the final years of the fourth Labour Government was its adoption of the 'strategic unionism' model first pursued by the Australian Council of Trade Unions (ACTU) across the Tasman. The ACTU had been in close partnership with the Australian Labor Government since the signing of the Prices and Income Accord in 1983. The Accord philosophy embodied what became known, by the late 1980s, as strategic unionism, which involved a commitment by unions to forsake workplace industrial action in return for access to political power in the national capital. The purpose of the latter was to lobby government to improve working class living standards through job creation and expanded welfare, superan-nuation, and pensions. A critical argument behind strategic unionism was that unions had to move away from arguing over the distribution of the proceeds of production to intervening in the process of production itself and, at the national level, in economic policy processes that ultimately determined employment opportunities for union members. This required unions to take responsibility for increasing productivity and cutting wage costs.

Consequently, Australian unions agreed in the 1980s to cooperate in massive industrial restructuring of core industries, in return for their involvement in consultation with employers and government representatives over the shape of industrial relations, industry, and economic policy. Australian union strategy was developed along these lines in the seminal 1987 document, *Australia Reconstructed*, which paved the way for the transition away from an award system to enterprise bargaining.

Key to the implementation of ACTU strategy was reciprocity, that is, agreement by the Australian Government and major employers to include union leaders in the policy process. In terms of many of its original goals as regards living standards and social equity, the Accord failed the interests of Australian unionists, but in terms of the process it was a partial success—there was extensive consultation by the government with the peak union body, and union-busting was the exception, rather than the rule, as an employer strategy. This laid the basis for the outstanding longevity of the Accord process throughout the period of the Hawke and Keating Labor Governments.

In New Zealand, the CTU sought to pursue a similar strategy. It promoted what it called a 'third way' between the rival capitalist strategies of unbridled free markets and Muldoonite centralism, 'shifting bargaining away from occupation and towards enterprise and industry, changing work methods, negotiating around improvements to productivity, and recognising the need for modern, internationally competitive production systems' (Council of Trade Unions, 1991, p. 23). The Engineers' Union went furthest in attempting to implement such a strategy and sold itself to employers as being 'responsible' and amenable to major changes in established working methods and reductions to conditions of employment.

Unlike the ACTU, however, the CTU had little success in pursuing a corporatist strategy. Influenced by the Business Roundtable and Treasury, the fourth Labour Government refused to consult with the union leadership in any significant economic policy decisions (Bray and Walsh, 1995). In effect, the CTU leadership had nothing to sell that the government and employers did not feel they could take by virtue of the industrial climate and their perception of the CTU's inability to discipline its affiliates.

The failure of CTU strategy was best illustrated by the débâcle over a proposed Compact with the Labour Government, a document that provided for union endorsement of wage restraint in return for a commitment by the government to involve the CTU more closely in developing its macroeconomic policies (Council of Trade Unions, 1988a). The CTU leadership kept discussions within a tight-knit group of senior officials and politicians and expended extensive resources on promoting the case for the Compact within the wider union movement. All of its endeavours were in vain, however, as the Compact was ultimately scuppered by government and employer indifference, and its successor, the Agreement for Growth, signed in April 1990, was a much more limited document, representing merely the CTU leadership's preparedness to accept further wage cuts under a re-elected Labour Government, in return for a government commitment to involve the CTU in economic planning. The defeat of Labour in 1990 ensured that this agreement was never tested.

At the same time as the CTU was facing continued rebuffs by the Labour Government, working class dissatisfaction with the government was growing. Dannin has pointed to the crux of the CTU's problem.

> The CTU's formal and institutional alliance with Labour left it unable to criticise Labour when it privatised government agencies and deregulated industries. In turn, by failing to keep faith with its membership and by failing to promote their interests within their party, the CTU became estranged from its membership and allies and thus weakened. A large number of the public looked to the CTU for leadership and heard nothing (1995, p. 39).

The exclusion of the CTU from decision-making processes in Wellington was replicated at workplace level by an anti-union offensive by employers. Although a small number of employers gave some formal recognition to union involvement in workplace reform initiatives, they were clearly in the minority. Only the Engineers' Union appears to have sustained continuing relationships with a minority of large employers such as Fisher and Paykel. But the assistance offered by the union at such workplaces calls into question the continuing independence of the union itself. Furthermore, the urgency of restructuring meant that even these efforts were easily overridden. The Fortex meatworks in Dunedin, for example, was a model of workplace reform but was closed down by its owners as a cost-cutting measure in the early 1990s.

The Battle over the ECA

The failure of New Zealand's labour leaders to defend working class living standards and even the basis of unionism itself was most evident in its strategy in the battle over the Employment Contracts Bill between its tabling in late 1990 and its enactment in May 1991. At the time of its enactment, the bill was widely opposed and the National Government itself was extremely unpopular after only six months in office. The key task for the CTU was to mobilise public opposition to the bill in a fashion that would damage the government politically. Central to this was the organisation of a general strike among all unionists. Such an action could have forced the government to back down and, perhaps paradoxically, was the only approach that would attract solid support from the largest number of workers. That a general strike would have hurt National's business backers is evident. But economic uncertainty and an aggressive employer mentality meant that any strategy based on partial actions, involving only small groups of workers, was bound to fail as workers stayed at work fearing victimisation.

The willingness of the majority of workers to participate in a general strike is clear from events as they unfolded in the first four months of 1991. Public servants, engineers, teachers, nurses and health workers, seafarers, harbour workers, steelworkers, railway workers, shop assistants, cleaners, caretakers, and security guards all took action, ranging from stopworks to strikes against the bill. Marches and rallies took place in the capital and all major regional centres. It has been estimated that participation in such action involved between 300 000 and 500 000 New Zealanders, with 50 000 working days lost in strike action in the first week of April 1991 (Dannin, 1995, p. 83). According to Roper, there was not 'a single instance amongst the major unions of workers failing to endorse, and by very large majorities, strike action where they were balloted' (1995, p. 270).

The missing element in the whole campaign was leadership, as workers had neither the confidence nor the networks to organise a general strike from below. Central coordination by the established union leadership was needed, but the CTU leadership failed in this task. The CTU strategy was effectively limited to organising a massive publicity campaign that highlighted the drawbacks of the bill. This was certainly effective in raising awareness of its dangers, but what action workers were to take in response was left completely unspecified (Dannin, 1995, pp. 76-81). Enamoured of strategic unionism and convinced of a need to move away from 'old-fashioned' forms of union action (most notably strikes), the CTU leadership actively sought to demoralise those pressing for a general strike, and at a Special Affiliates Conference in April 1991, the majority of union officials present voted against a national general strike, preferring to endorse a strategy of organising a public petition to protest at government actions and mounting regional campaigns, with each region deciding for itself the appropriate action. Faced by the most aggressive onslaught by capital and the state for a full century, the CTU leadership continued to believe that it was facing merely a minor upset in a basically harmonious relationship. The leadership's failure to lead caused a collapse of morale within the union ranks. Although other groups sought to fill the vacuum caused by the CTU's desertion from the field of battle, they were too small, lacked industrial clout or, in some cases, were consciously marginalised by the CTU leadership, leaving the way clear for the bill's progress into law (Dannin, 1995, pp. 74–8).

The failure of the CTU's political strategy in the late 1980s and early 1990s had an impact on the organisational structure of the union movement. In 1993, a left-wing rival peak federation, the Trade Union Federation (TUF), centred on the Manufacturing and Construction Workers' Union, was formed as a result of dissatisfaction with the CTU and its failure to resist attacks by the National Government. By 1995, however, the TUF had made little ground in attracting individual unions to its ranks, with twelve affiliated unions and coverage of 23 000 workers, in comparison with the CTU which remained the dominant union federation with twenty-seven member unions and 300 000 members. Outside both federations were forty-three non-aligned unions with 56 000 members.

Conclusions

The experience of New Zealand unions since 1945 supports the notion that trade union officials represent a conservative layer within the union movement. Indeed, a recurring theme of New Zealand's union history is one of former militant union leaders first being tamed by, and then becoming active supporters of, the industrial and political establishment. During the 1930s and 1940s, figures such as Bob Semple, Tim Armstrong, Paddy Webb, Jim Roberts, Angus McLagan, Ken Baxter, and Fintan Patrick Walsh, who were in the first wave of industrial militancy in the early years of the century, all rejected their pasts and became committed to wartime mobilisation, work intensification, and the drastic curtailment of union rights and living standards in their capacities as Ministers of Labour or leading figures in the FOL. Many even pressed for the continuation of restrictions after war's end. In New Zealand's Red Purge of 1946–52, these former militants campaigned actively for the smashing of renegade unions, such as the carpenters and waterside workers. In more recent times Tom Skinner, FOL president in the 1960s and 1970s, was knighted for his services, and Ken Douglas, formerly a militant unionist in the Wellington drivers' union, has sought solace in the CTU's utopian 'third way'.

The understanding by New Zealand employers and governments that such union leaders could be trusted lay behind their decision to incorporate them into the management of industrial relations matters. The postwar settlement was shattered, however, by the working class offensive of the late 1960s. A sea change in employer opinion, forged in the adverse economic circumstances of the 1970s and 1980s, then led to the final destruction of the postwar settlement, with the decision to marginalise and then dismantle the entire apparatus of unionism in the latter period. The failure of New Zealand's union leaders to fend off the ruling class offensive means that the bitterness widely prevalent among workers, both union and non-union, over the effects of the decade-long New Right offensive, finds no outlets. The demoralisation and pessimism abroad among union leaders, obsessed by their chase for 'a quality economy in a quality society' (Council of Trade Unions, 1993, p. 3), prevents them from campaigning for a fair share of the benefits of the economic recovery of the mid-1990s, let alone mounting a major assault on the government. Union recovery will occur in New Zealand only when workers are able to break through this blanket of pessimism, and this will require a combination of industrial action and a political revival of the left, the two factors that lay behind advances made in the 1960s.

Guide to Readings

For the original exposition of the unitarist pluralist radical typology, see Fox (1973). For the unitarist perspective in New Zealand, see Brook (1989 and 1990) and the New Zealand Employers' Federation (1990). These arguments are echoed by other writers such as Coddington (1993). Dannin (1992 and 1996) has exposed the flimsy basis of these works.

The classic literature on trade union officials is summarised in Hyman (1971) and Kelly (1988). Challenges to the notion that union officials constitute a conservative force in the labour movement are to be found in Hyman (1979), Zeitlin (1989a and 1989b), and Heery and Kelly (1994). Their arguments have been critically evaluated in Bramble (1993).

On New Zealand unionism, see Olssen and Richardson (1986), Olssen (1986a), and Roth (1973). Roper (1990b) and Boston (1984) summarise union strategies from the late 1960s to the early 1980s, while Bray and Walsh (1992 and 1995) trace the strategies of the Australian and New Zealand union movements during the 1980s. Literature on the ALP-ACTU Accord includes Singleton (1990) and Ewer et al. (1991). The shift to strategic unionism, evident in two key Council of Trade Union (CTU) documents (1988b and 1989), is set out in Campbell and Kirk (1983) and Harvey (1992). For the CTU's own assessment of its strategy, see CTU (1991 and 1993) and Douglas (1991, 1993a, and 1993b). Dannin (1995) and Heal (1995) provide critical accounts of CTU strategy between 1987 and 1994.

Plowman and Street (1993), Roper (1993a), Kelsey (1995), and Murray (1996) provide studies of the power of the New Zealand Business Roundtable. Employer analyses of the fourth Labour Government's industrial relations legislation, are found in the New Zealand Business Roundtable (1987) and New Zealand Employers' Federation (1987). Walsh (1989), Dannin (1992), and Deeks et al. (1994) offer academic accounts of this legislation. The policies of the New Zealand Employers' Federation towards New Zealand's unions are recorded in its magazine, *The Employer*.

Douglas (1993a) and Dannin (1995) have provided useful analyses of some of the problems facing unions under the Employment Contracts Act (ECA), while Anderson (in press) has followed the effect of recent Employment Court decisions.

CHAPTER EIGHT

GENDER INEQUALITY IN PAID EMPLOYMENT

PRUE HYMAN

Feminist analyses of inequalities in paid employment between women and men vary widely, although all would see gender as a major structural variable in organising society, and gender roles as constraining women's choices. Liberal feminists focus on the elimination of unnecessary barriers to women's progress in economic and social systems. By contrast, socialist feminist and other more radical analyses see gender inequalities and patriarchy as being linked with class, ethnic, and other structural power differences, which shore up capitalism and require more change than simply equal opportunity for women. Most feminists, however, would agree that both neoclassical economics and a range of political economy alternatives, including Marxism, have, until recently, neglected the gender power dimension. None of these schools, therefore, has analysed adequately the constraints on women (and to some extent, men) arising from the division of labour by gender in paid and unpaid work, gender bias in the definition and construction of skill, and other gender power dimensions in employment.

This chapter begins by looking at how neoclassical economic theory tries to account for gender inequality and discrimination in the labour market. This is followed by an overview of feminist criticisms of the neoclassical interpretation. The chapter then moves on to a detailed analysis of female labour market participation, job segregation, and equal pay and opportunity in New Zealand. Finally, the impact of labour market deregulation during the 1980s and 1990s is examined, with respect to women's paid and unpaid work.

Gender Inequality and Discrimination in the Labour Market: Neoclassical and Feminist Explanations

Since the 1970s, governments would claim to be committed to equality for women, and most could point to specific anti-discrimination policies, education and training initiatives, and other measures to support their claims. This, however, needs to be seen in the context of many of the policies discussed below, which in fact impede such equality. Further, general economic policies, including fiscal, monetary, labour, industry, government sector, and international trade policies, have far more impact on the economic and social status of most women than specific policies aimed to improve that status. The impact of equal opportunity policies, for example, may be significant alongside a favourable economic situation and policy climate, but can be negligible if rising joblessness and reduced union and employee bargaining power.

To explain gender differences in the labour market, including occupational segregation and segmentation, it is important to consider different views on what constitutes inequality and discrimination. Neoclassical economic theory, for example, would deny that inequality of outcomes implies discrimination, stressing differences in choices and acquisition of human capital, specialisation within households dictated by comparative advantage, and market processes. In contrast, institutional accounts stress the roles of segmented labour markets, the overcrowding of women into a limited range of occupations, and employer monopoly power. Many feminists will add that trade unions have, in the past, colluded with employers to limit women's opportunities.

Equality for women in the labour market has proved elusive, both conceptually and factually. Justified both in terms of efficient use of all human resources, and on the basis of equity, equal opportunity can hardly be opposed in principle by any school of thought. But mandatory provisions, programs incurring costs, or going beyond the dismantling of barriers towards affirmative action are more controversial. Equal pay for work of equal value, discussed below, is even more controversial with little agreement on what actually constitutes discrimination. One clear principle, however, is that discrimination does not have to be deliberate or perpetrated through prejudice, even though it may be. It is simply the unfairness of the process or outcome that defines discrimination, although what counts as unfair is disputable. One helpful distinction is between wage discrimination and other forms that may operate in the labour market. To the neoclassical economist, wage discrimination occurs only when workers of equal productivity to an employer are paid unequally. Of course, this begs the questions of assessing productivity and skill mentioned earlier. Non-wage labour market discrimination can occur with unequal access to jobs, training, promotion, and any other human capital enhancing factors.

Another useful distinction is between direct and indirect discrimination by gender, race, or other factors. The former is simply a wage or non-wage difference in treatment based on the classifying variable, even if it is less straightforward to prove when denied. The latter may be more difficult to detect, arising when a practice that is not needed for efficient operation in a job occurs and has a differentially adverse effect on a particular group. For example, requiring educational qualifications not really needed in a position, rather than assessing whether an applicant has the relevant skills, can indirectly discriminate against Maori or women.

There is a large econometrically based literature, especially in the United States, that attempts to determine what proportion of the gender earnings gap is due to differences in human capital endowments and what proportion to difference in returns to those endowments. In other words, do women receive lower pay because they bring to the job lower levels of education, skill, and work experience—or because discrimination causes women to be rewarded less for the same skill? Some empirical studies argue that more of the gap is attributable to lower returns afforded to women than to their lower endowments (Buchele and Aldrich, 1985). These lower returns are found whether women are in male- or female-dominated occupations, implying a degree of pay discrimination.

Earnings function studies do not, of course, yield unchallengeable answers to the extent even of direct wage discrimination, let alone overall discrimination. Some neoclassical economists believe that the human capital measures, such as years of education and experience, are too crude to pick up all the productivity differences. In addition, they argue that occupational crowding and industry or enterprise differences in ability to pay may mean that lower returns for women to human capital variables are not necessarily discriminatory.

For pay equity advocates, the wage discrimination found in earning functions studies are minimal estimates of overall discrimination, possibly picking up the direct wage discrimination but not the lack of equal opportunity. A New Zealand study that attempted to explain pay differences by human capital variables covered 751 employees in the executive/clerical permanent staff of Treasury and Internal Affairs at March 1984, for whom data on pay levels, educational qualifications, and years of experience were available (Sutton, 1985). Average earnings for women in the study were three-quarters of the equivalent figure for men, with about one-third of the gap due to the women's lower average level of qualifications, one-third to differences in years of experience, and one-third unexplained and therefore due to discrimination or other factors not measured in the study.

In neoclassical analysis, different wages between different occupations and industries arise from variation in supply and demand curves. On the demand side, higher levels of skill, training, experience, and responsibility are the human capital factors that should increase the productivity of types of labour and hence increase its demand and wage rate. The upsurge in female labour force participation means that women are, on average, younger and have less training and fewer years of experience than men in the labour force, which is one factor in women's lower average wages. There is also a need to recoup the costs of training through increased wages. Attributes of jobs other than salaries are also relevant to the labour supply at any level. According to the neoclassical viewpoint, 'the advantages of employment include not only the pay and any perquisites or amenities that go with it, but the prestige in which it is held and the satisfactions of working in it. If an occupation is disagreeable or held in low esteem, its pay must be higher to compensate for this' (Rees, 1979, p. 155).

Feminists and other critics of the neoclassical approach have many doubts about these *stories* and their application to the gender pay gap. A new trend among some economists is to acknowledge that much of the theory is rhetoric and simply an attempt to persuade (McCloskey, 1985; see Strassman, 1993 for a feminist interpretation). Do high prestige occupations, which easily attract recruits, really pay less than those involving comparable training but lower prestige, particularly when the numbers entering many professions are controlled by professional associations, universities, and governments? It is also assumed in Rees' (1979) analysis of occupational differentials, that skill is an objectively measured variable, something that was questioned earlier.

There are also doubts about the whole basis of the orthodox demand for labour and marginal productivity theory. Whether the marginal productivity of labour can be measured is doubtful (Thurow, 1975). Teamwork, the dependence of every type of worker on the work of others, the other inputs that are held constant in the analysis, and the quality of management are among factors that blur the picture. Further, marginal productivity can be seen as one of the neoclassical economists' circular tricks. Analytically, the wage rate must reflect the value to the employer of the extra amount produced (in perfect competition at least). Only the wage is observed, however, and so it is presumed simply to reflect the marginal product. This can persuade people that there is an objectivity to the wage determination process. In service industries there is even less chance of determining the value of output. In the labour market, employers need to find ways of ensuring that they receive the work input for which they are paying. Hence attempts to assess individual or team performance are growing, but they are often crude and subjective, with many of the output measures open to question.

There are also monopoly elements on both sides of most labour markets. Collective bargaining can result in more powerful trade unions or employer groups gaining outcomes that favour their interests. Overall, few labour markets operate along lines of perfect competition with a large number of buyers and sellers, none of which are strong enough to dictate the terms of exchange. Institutional factors, horizontal and vertical occupational segregation, and discrimination in the assessment of skill, rather than the simple operation of supply and demand factors, may thus be major determinants of the earnings gap. Hence those advocating equal pay for work of equal value do so on the grounds that markets, in the absence of interventions, are unlikely to produce equitable outcomes. It can also be argued that efficiency requires some equality of rates of return with human capital acquisition, to avoid distortion of career choice decisions by both women and men.

The main arguments of opponents of equal value policies are the desirability of pure market valuation and the subjectivity of other processes, including job evaluation. They also suggest excessive costs and employment losses arising from interventions. Such fears were also raised before the Equal Pay Act 1972 was passed and in similar overseas initiatives. Empirical results show these fears to be exaggerated. The evidence does not support such substitution during the New Zealand equal pay implementation period, when full-time employment of females grew by 19 per cent, as against 8 per cent for males. Only in a few female-dominated industries, such as textiles, was there some evidence of slower employment growth than might otherwise have occurred. The Australian evidence is similar.

Finally, many feminist critiques of neoclassical economics consider that it uses circular reasoning in several spheres, not just with respect to marginal productivity. By taking preferences as given and joint for the household, it can reinforce and justify the status quo. If men earn more on average than women, specialisation of roles emerges appropriately from rational household decision-making, with women doing more of the unpaid work. In turn, this expectation can justify less education and training for women, which will perpetuate their lower average earnings. For feminist analysis, therefore, too much is taken as given in the conventional explanations, including the realities of discrimination and gender occupational segregation, and women's responsibility for child rearing (MacDonald, 1981).

Women and the Labour Market—Extent and Nature of Participation and Rewards

Participation in paid employment

The major source of both greater economic independence, at least for some groups of women, and opportunities for fulfilment beyond home and community activities, has been improved access to a variety of areas in the paid labour force. Women were 17 per cent of the labour force at the beginning of the century, with a slow increase to 25 per cent by 1945 and an acceleration in the participation rate from the early 1960s. Fluctuations around the rising trend occurred in the Depression of the 1930s and as a result of the Second World War. Women were drawn into many areas of the labour force to replace men and then dropped out by choice and/or pressure as servicemen returned. As a result, the 1945 rate of participation was not reached again until 1961. In 1991 women were 36 per cent of the full-time (thirty hours or more a week) labour force and almost half of the total labour force. A short-term reversal in the proportion of the female working age cohort participating in the labour force occurred with the increase in unemployment of the late 1980s, even though those officially unemployed are counted in the labour force. This arises from the discouragement effect of poor labour market prospects, which can lead to women ceasing actively to seek work. This is particularly the case with some attitudes and policies that still see women as more marginal in the labour force, to be used as a reserve army of labour.

The long-term rising trend in participation arises from both demand and supply factors. Increased demand for goods and services, and therefore labour, in the 1950s and 1960s required growth in the labour force, which men alone could not meet. Much of the demand was in areas of female specialisation. On the supply side, technological change affecting both the market and household sectors, reduced average family size, increasing education levels and changes in social attitudes, became linked with economic necessity and personal preferences to increase the female labour force pool. Married women became overwhelmingly the largest section of the female labour force. Economic necessity and the consumption ethic encouraged by advertising made two incomes essential or desirable for many families. The participation rate for married women was only 7.7 per cent in 1945 and had increased to 58.8 per cent by 1994, with the share of married women in the total female labour force increasing from 23 to 63 per cent (Statistics New Zealand, 1951–91, 1993, and various years for statistics not otherwise attributed).

Much of the long-term increase in women's employment has been in part-time work, with a five-fold increase in numbers employed under thirty hours per week between 1961 and 1981, as against a doubling in total employment. Hence, although only 15 per cent of the female labour force was part-time in 1961, this had risen to 36 per cent in 1994. In 1991, women comprised 76 per cent of part-time workers. The increasing proportion of part-time work in the early years reflected married women's entry into the labour force, given their lack of options because of family commitments. Since the mid-1980s, however, part-time employment has also grown from the demand side, owing to a slack labour market, with men's part-time work also growing quickly. Between 1980 and 1987, part-time jobs grew by 41.7 per cent but full-time jobs by only 5.6 per cent. Between 1989 and 1994, male and female part time employment each grew by about 20 000, with men's share of the total growing from 22.5 per cent to 26 per cent and the percentage of males working part-time from 7.3 per cent to 9.6 per cent.

While part-time work suits many married women, given the current division of unpaid labour, the numbers wanting to work longer hours has risen sharply, three-fold between 1987 and 1992 for all part-time workers. By 1993, 28 per cent of women working part-time wanted more hours, with 20 per cent wanting to work full-time; two-thirds of those wanting more hours were women. Further, focus group discussions among part-time workers found widespread dissatisfaction about conditions of work, particularly since the passage in 1991 of the Employment Contracts Act (ECA). Removal of penal rates and overtime, meaningless contracts with wages and hours cut and changed overnight without prior warning or consent, anti-social hours of work, lack of career prospects, and poor treatment by management were all the subject of complaint, with juvenalisation, casualisation, and intensification common in the retail trades (Davidson and Bray, 1994).

There are conceptual and measurement problems in trying to determine the extent of women's unemployment, absolutely and relatively to men. Census, registration, and the official Household Labour Force Survey statistics give different pictures, with a past tendency for women to underreport and fail to register, in the latter case partly because, for heterosexual couples, eligibility is based on both incomes. A tighter labour market, the New Zealand Employment Service's entry into the part-time job market, and the need to register to be eligible for some training and job schemes are among factors that have increased female registration. But disguised unemployment, in the form of discouraged and underemployed workers, is likely to be higher for women. The official unemployment rate for women and men in June 1986 was 4.7 per cent and 3.7 per cent respectively; in June 1993 it was 9.1 per cent and 10.6 per cent; and in June 1995 the respective figures were 6.4 per cent as against 6 per cent. Maori and Pacific Island unemployment rates were much higher, with teenage Maori women having rates as high as 40 per cent in some surveys.

What jobs do women do? Horizontal and vertical segregation
Technological and social change led to an increasing range of work being available to women, with domestic work reducing from over one-third of women's jobs to its near disappearance as a live-in occupation during and after the Second World War. An increased range of opportunities gradually became available for women as access to higher levels of education improved. Some occupations, including clerical work and keyboarding, became feminised. Such feminisation was usually accompanied by a lowering of status, with the occupations becoming deskilled. The trades defined as skilled were even slower to admit women through the apprenticeship system. As the pool of single females contracted, barriers to married women entering the labour force decreased. Marriage bars vanished and access to higher level positions gradually improved.

There is some evidence that women are moving into male-dominated occupations and that this is reducing the horizontal segregation of the labour force. As many as 697 occupations out of a total of 1071 were 80 per cent or more male in 1971. These occupations employed only 3.5 per cent of female employees, but by 1986 this had increased to 11.7 per cent (Van Mourik et al., 1989). By 1991, women represented 22.2 per cent of general practitioners, compared with just 6.4 per cent in 1971 (see Table 8.1). Similar increases occurred with accountants and lawyers, but many areas, including the more scientific-based training professions such as architects and engineers, were less receptive. In 1986 two-thirds of women still worked in the 16.5 per cent of occupations that were 60 per cent or more female, while some areas, such as construction, machinery, and transport, still remain almost entirely male provinces.

Segmentation, therefore, remains a key issue in women's position in the labour market. New Zealand is developing a dual labour market with well-paid secure jobs with good promotion prospects in the primary labour market and poorly paid marginal jobs, from which there is little or no chance of advancement, in the secondary market. Female-dominated jobs are dispro-portionately represented in the secondary labour market. This phenomenon

Table 8.1 Women in selected male-dominated professions [1] 1971-91

	Per cent female				
	1971	1976	1981	1986	1991
Physical scientists [2]	5.3	6.0	7.1	11.8	14.0
Life scientists [2]	12.3	12.2	16.9	19.4	22.3
Architects	1.1	1.8	3.9	5.8	8.1
Civil engineers		0.2	0.5	1.2	2.0
General practitioners	6.4	9.8	12.2	17.4	22.2
Hospital doctors	13.6	16.2	23.6	28.4	34.8
Dentists	1.7	1.6	6.2	7.6	16.0
Veterinarians	2.9	4.2	8.9	15.6	20.4
Pharmacists	13.7	17.2	23.3	30.1	41.2
Systems analysts	5.2	10.1	15.9	26.8	27.2
Economists	2.9	9.5	11.7	20.3	22.5
Accountants	3.6	7.2	10.5	21.3	30.2
Lawyers	1.8	4.5	9.2	15.8	23.4
University professors/lecturers	13.0	13.3	15.7	20.7	26.1
School principals	9.3	8.2	14.6	20.3	31.7
Ministers of religion	3.8	6.7	8.9	12.5	16.7
Females as percentage of labour force [3]	29.8	32.0	34.2	38.5	40.6

[1] Selected professions in which males represented 85 per cent or more of employed persons in 1971. Includes only those employed 20 or more hours per week.
[2] Excludes technicians.
[3] Includes persons employed for 20 or more hours per week or unemployed and actively seeking work.

Sources: *Census of Population and Dwellings*, 1971–91.

is considerably more pronounced for Maori and Pacific Island women than for other ethnic groups.

The extent of occupational segregation is sometimes underestimated by studying the labour force at too broad a level of aggregation. Indices of segregation calculate the proportion of the male (or female) workforce who would have to change occupations to produce similar male/female proportions in each occupation, as in the total workforce. These are invariably greater, indicating greater segregation, when calculated at a more detailed occupational level. In 1991, within the broadest occupational definition, around 40 per cent would have to have changed occupation; the figure was 53 per cent at the intermediate level; and in 1986, with occupations classified more narrowly, the figure was 65 per cent. A disquieting fact was that overall levels of occupational segregation were higher for younger women than for the whole female labour force and were declining only very slowly, particularly when standardised for different rates of growth of occupations (Gwartney-Gibbs, 1988; Van Mourik et al., 1989). So the overall picture on occupational segregation is complex. Even in some female-dominated areas, men are disproportionately represented at high levels; this is happening more as men move into such occupations as nursing. Vertical segregation, with women underrepresented in top jobs, remains an issue, even though such jobs as school principal (up from 9.3 per cent female in 1971 to 31.7 per cent in 1991) show a reasonable rate of change.

Discussing the still very low representation of women in top management in New Zealand, Bev James and Kay Saville-Smith (1992) point out that, at middle management level, women are predominantly in the less powerful support divisions. Three main reasons are advanced for this under-representation. First there is the organisational culture's reinforcement of gender typing, with differential access to mentoring and resources. Second, women's socialisation, education, and training channel them into areas seen as less appropriate for top management. Finally, there is women's ongoing greater responsibility for family life. Women at the top may, therefore, be isolated both at work and at home, since single or childless women have more chance of reaching such positions.

There is an extensive literature advising women on how to act to become senior managers, enjoining them to value themselves sufficiently and to learn how to persuade others to do the same. Such advice places on an individual plane the general feminist arguments for valuing work that is traditionally done by females, and is an understandable response in an age of performance appraisal and individual settling of contracts at quite low levels of management and technical/professional work. On the one hand, this advice can be seen positively from a feminist viewpoint. But the associated individualist analysis paradoxically exists side by side with the postFordist emphasis on teamwork, which fits the philosophy and style of many women. It is also less concerned than the many feminist arguments with criticising the overall system of rewards.

Equal pay and opportunity

Equal pay for equal work requires that women doing the same work (sometimes extended to highly similar work) as men should receive the same pay. Worldwide, in the nineteenth and early twentieth centuries men were paid more than most women doing the same jobs. Occupational segregation by gender also kept women's average pay low, with areas of women's work defined as unskilled, whatever their content. For example, dexterity and the ability to undertake repetitive accurate work were seen as natural to women. They were not rewarded in the same way as the demands of men's jobs, such as heavy lifting.

Equal pay for work of equal value is a broader concept. It suggests that work assessed as requiring similar overall levels of skill, responsibility, effort, and working conditions (in total, not necessarily on each component separately) should be paid equally. The case is based on the argument that characteristics of female- (and minority ethnic-) dominated work are undervalued by the market or in negotiations, as explained in the dexterity example. Historic differentials are therefore challenged in terms of gender and ethnic bias. Generally, it is argued that skill definition and assessment is very largely a social construct, with the skills involved in many jobs undervalued or ignored. There is a large literature on skill analysis that supports this view (Cockburn, 1983; Hill and Novitz, 1985; Wood, 1985). Opponents argue that there is no real or objective measure of value or skills, distinct from the market value level of pay.

Despite an earlier commitment to equal pay, the first Labour Government in the wake of the 1930s Depression supported the family wage concept, which allowed higher wages for men, irrespective of whether individual men or women actually had dependants. The family wage principle had been regularly enunciated by the Arbitration Court, which did not set a minimum wage for women until 1936, at 47 per cent of the male rate. A new campaign led by the Public Service Association in the 1950s finally resulted in public sector equal pay legislation in 1960. It took a further decade, and a commission of inquiry, before the Equal Pay Act, extending the principle to the private sector, was passed in 1972, and fully implemented by 1977. It should be noted that early support for equal pay legislation was often more on the basis of protecting men's jobs by preventing the employment of women than with any principles of equity in mind—it was seen as an alternative or supplementary strategy to employing women in segregated work at a lower wage.

Average female factory wages were only half those of males as late as 1967–68. For nominal weekly award wage rates across the economy, the ratio had reached 70.2 per cent by then, with equal pay already legislated for in the public sector. No figures are available on actual wages paid until 1973, when the female-male ratio for ordinary time hourly earnings was 72.1 per cent. Weekly earnings show wider gaps, with women predominating in part-time work and having less access to overtime (see Table 8.2). The ordinary time hourly earnings ratio narrowed to 78.5 per cent during the equal pay implementation period and has crept up to 80–81 per cent since then. When annual incomes are considered, the gaps are even wider. Non-Maori women reported an average of only $9309 from employment in the year ending March 1992, less than half of the $19 877 for non-Maori men. Maori incomes were much lower, with the corresponding figures $5959 for women and $10 511 for men.

Low-level policing of the Equal Pay Act, based mainly on complaints, and use of discriminatory job titles may have contributed to evasion of its provisions. Placement of individuals on pay scales, access to promotion,

Table 8.2 Average earnings of women in New Zealand as per cent of male earnings

| | Ordinary time earnings | | Weekly earnings including overtime | |
	Hourly	Weekly [a]	Gross [b]	Total [a]
October 1973	72.1	69.2	57.8	na
October 1975	76.4	73.8	60.9	na
October 1977	78.5	76.2	63.2	71.1
May 1980	78.2	75.0	62.3	70.4
May 1983	78.0	76.1	66	71.9
May 1985	78.0	75.1	na	70.2
May 1988	79.5	76.1	na	72.2
May 1990	81.0	77.6	na	72.2
May 1993	81.4	77.1	na	74.1
May 1995	80.9	76.3	na	73.1

[a] In calculating these figures two part-time workers are counted as one full-time equivalent worker: divisor is number of full-time equivalent workers.
[b] In calculating this figure the divisor is the number of workers irrespective of whether full or part-time.

Sources: *Labour and Employment Gazette* and *Key Statistics,* various issues.

and the allocation of above-award payments in a gender unbiased manner are even harder to enforce. A further problem arises in the area of female-dominated work, where comparisons are difficult to make. These ongoing concerns and the gap between male and female pay narrowing less than had been expected led the Clerical Workers' Union to take a case to the Arbitration Court in February 1986. Jurisdiction was effectively declined, which reinforced pressure for new legislation. The government then commissioned an Equal Pay study which led, finally, to the passing of the Employment Equity Act 1990, which covered both equal opportunity and pay equity/ equal pay for work of equal value (for discussion of this period see Wilson, 1992.) The act was repealed later in the year by the incoming fourth National Government, which was committed to minimal intervention in the labour market by third parties, preferring to leave decisions to employers and employees.

One legacy of the act was expertise in attempting to build gender neutral remuneration systems; the Gender at Work scheme, for example, proved a useful resource (Burns and Coleman, 1991). There were also a few successes along pay equity lines. For instance, midwives had gained parity with doctors in fees for normal births, thanks largely to the Labour Party leader Helen Clark's commitment to equal pay for work of equal value. The midwives succeeded in retaining this parity against an attempt by the medical profession to reverse it.

With the repeal of the Employment Equity Act, the Equal Pay Act continues to govern this area. Its efficacy in the new industrial relations environment is doubtful. Enforcement is not well suited to a climate of individual and small collective contracts, even though contracts are formally covered by the legislation. Many people do not know the salaries of their colleagues, so cannot assess if they are receiving equal pay. Only collective contracts covering twenty or more employees now have to be registered. Discrimination in individual cases is much harder to establish than separate rates in an award. Most such cases previously taken to the Arbitration Court were unsuccessful, with very wide interpretation of the clause allowing a rate of remuneration 'that is special to that employee by reason of special qualifications, experience, or other qualities possessed by that employee' (Section 2.2).

Harbridge's contract database shows a higher weighted average increase for men (0.37 per cent) compared with women (0.14 per cent) in the first eighteen months of the ECA's operation, with more equal increases thereafter (Harbridge, 1993b). Further, women were less likely to have contracts that attracted overtime or penal rates for inconvenient working hours or weekend days. Only in an area less directly related to take-home pay, that of leave, were female-dominated contracts slightly better than men's, with more providing a fourth week of annual leave and/or better than minimum sick leave (Hammond and Harbridge, 1993).

The effect that horizontal occupational and industrial segregation has on pay levels overall, and particularly in female-dominated areas, is less easy to document unequivocally than the phenomenon itself (see Hawke, 1991, for a discussion of the statistical complexities). There is, however, considerable evidence that female-dominated industries and occupations in New Zealand are low-paid both for females and, to a lesser extent, for the males in those industries or occupations. The importance of historical relativities and occupational segregation to the earnings gap is pointed out by Iverson (1987). Clearly vertical segregation, with the low levels of female representation in managerial and other senior positions, also contributes substantially to the pay gap.

Equal employment opportunity programs remain mandatory in the state sector for women, Maori, Pacific Island, and other ethnic minorities, and for people with disabilities. The State Services Commission's EEO unit continues to monitor progress. The private sector, led by the New Zealand Employers' Federation, must rely on exhortation and arguments about efficiency. A low-budget EEO Trust encourages the removal of barriers to equality and uses awards and literature to encourage good practice. Although discrimination in employment and other matters on the basis of gender and ethnicity is illegal under human rights legislation, it is hard to police through complaints. Some successes have been achieved, however, towards equality for women workers in areas including firefighting, freezing works, and aircraft cabin crew. Disability, age, health status, family status, and sexual orientation were among grounds for discrimination added to the human rights legislation in 1993, although the government exempted itself until 1999.

The Impact of Deregulation on Women's Paid and Unpaid Work

The official New Zealand report to the United Nations Beijing Conference in 1995 gave the impression that New Zealand was making unimpeded steady progress towards equality for women in the labour force and elsewhere, and that there were only a few barriers left to break down (Ministry of Women's Affairs, 1994). The reader of this report would find little about the increased inequality, the benefit cuts, and the extra burdens placed on New Zealand women to prop up the social welfare, health, and education systems. Absent was any mention of the women picking up the pieces of the extra caring work, of the women who had no choice but to feed their families from food banks, or of the women working to ensure that there was food in those banks. Missing, too, was any comment on how hard it was to combine paid work and part benefits, and the struggles of those on the domestic purposes benefit (DPB).

Although this chapter focuses on paid work, gender inequality in that context can only be fully understood against the imbalance of responsibilities for unpaid household and caring work, where women continue to have the major role. A slow shift is taking place in New Zealand. Some households are sharing more equally in this work. There has been an increase in sole fathers, up from 13 per cent to 16 per cent of all the sole parents between 1986 and 1991 (Department of Social Welfare, 1993), and in some households the woman's career comes first. The big picture, however, is unchanged. Most women with dependants carry a double burden when in paid work, which makes achieving equality in the labour market beyond reach as long as commitment is equated with single-minded devotion to very long hours at work. The desirability and the need for structures that encourage this unbalanced devotion to paid work can, of course, be questioned, both generally and in terms of their effects on women, and on men.

Another link between paid and unpaid work that disproportionately affects women is the structuring of tax systems, family support, and childcare in such a way that both sole parents and second-income earners in low-paid two-income households may have little incentive to enter paid work or to increase their hours of work. The poverty trap problems posed by high effective marginal tax rates, low levels of exempt income, and rapid abatement have long been recognised. The solutions are not easy, since less rapid abatement would result in reduced benefits still being paid at income levels comparable with those of many in full-time low-paid work, which is often seen as politically unacceptable. There was some amelioration of this problem with the increase, from July 1996, of $30 in the amount of weekly earnings allowed before abatement of benefits. For those on the DPB or invalid benefits who were seen as unable immediately to move to full-time paid work, the lower abatement rate of 30 per cent applied up to other income of $180 per week, so a sole parent with that level of earnings would be $46 per week better off than before. This change did not apply to unemployment benefits, the Minister of Finance commented that, for this group, it would be unfair to allow those combining part-time work and a part benefit to be better off than full-time workers on low wages (*Dominion*, 20 February 1996).

How far these changes will improve the situation is a matter for later assessment. Lack of access to affordable child care is still a major issue for many women, and there is also a need for workplaces to be family friendly so that paid and unpaid work can be better combined. Adequate access to training and skills development, with assistance particularly on return to the workplace, is another ongoing concern. Some initiatives are being taken, for example with pilot programs for sole parents attempting to return to paid work, but the consultations undertaken in conjunction with the Employment Taskforce indicated that this remains a critical area for women (Prime Ministerial Task Force on Employment, 1994).

For many New Zealand women, the economic deregulation and restructuring of the last decade has accentuated these problems. With a retreating welfare state and increased unemployment, inequalities have widened, and burdens on families, nuclear and extended, and on whanau, communities, and voluntary organisations, have increased. Women, responsible for most of the caring work and for balancing the household budget, take most of the direct and indirect strain of these additional demands. This further accentuates the impacts of the welfare expenditure cuts and the labour market deregulation that occurred under the fourth Labour and National Governments between 1984 and 1996. Poverty has increased among low-income families, particularly in Maori and Pacific Island communities, and this has meant that women have had to be in paid work even more than before. Yet there are still occasional signs of women being used as a reserve army of labour; the withdrawal of married women is still suggested when jobs are short. At such times, renewed emphasis is put on the desirability of full-time mothering in a child's early years for partnered women—but not for women without partners, who would have to be paid a benefit. Simultaneously, the ideology of the nuclear family is reasserted, together with the desirability of children being brought up by both parents (Mannion, 1993, p. 21). Feminist arguments that unpaid work should be valued are coopted to try to establish that some families would be better off if the earners of lower second incomes (usually women) were at home, where they would be more 'productive' (Infometrics, 1991; see Hyman, 1994, for a critique).

In the labour market, deregulation at a time of high unemployment shifted the balance of bargaining power away from employees and unions towards employers, with negative effects on wages and conditions of the lower paid. Here, as elsewhere, deregulation is oblivious to discrimination and to the systemic differences in opportunities, resources, power, and choice that operate against ethnic minorities, women, and lower socio-economic groups. With protection swept away, extensive restructuring in search of efficiency caused redundancies in both the private and public sectors. Unemployment replaced hidden underemployment, which went with earlier low levels of productivity.

These labour market changes were accompanied by industrial relations decentralisation, which accelerated following the passage of the ECA. The Minister of Women's Affairs claimed that this legislation, together with enterprise bargaining, 'has done more towards providing equity for working women than any other development for a long time' (*Dominion*, 1 January 1992). Her comments provoked strong reaction from female trade unionists and from the Labour Party. Helen Clark drew attention to the 10 per cent drop in women's overtime earnings, to the overrepresentation of women in the low-paid section of the workforce, which had been adversely affected by the ECA, and to attacks on wages and conditions in female-dominated occupations (*Dominion*, 1 January 1992).

The claim that a deregulated labour market and bargaining at enterprise level benefit women is highly dubious (Novitz and Jaber, 1990; Hyman, 1991). In terms of numbers employed and unemployed, women fared slightly less badly than men over the period of substantial job loss. This, however, is because of women's overrepresentation in the part-time, casualised, and low-wage sections of the labour market, and in service industries and occupations that came under fewer employment pressures. The impact of deregulation on those in the casualised secondary sector was strongly negative (Harbridge, 1993b; Sayers, 1991). An example comes from a 1993 survey of 962 women members of the Service Workers' Union. This found that 40 per cent had suffered a household income decline in the previous two years (Harbridge, 1993c). Thirty per cent had lower take home pay, 47 per cent the same, and only 20 per cent higher than two years earlier, with a large part of this small increase coming from longer hours, which were reported by 15 per cent of respondents. With as many as 32 per cent reporting higher basic pay than before, the lower incidence of higher take-home pay was largely the result of the abolition or reduction of overtime, penal, or weekend rates.

Nevertheless, it is too simple to claim that all elements of deregulation and the other major economic and social changes of the last ten years in New Zealand are regarded negatively by all or most feminists. Some saw the shake-up as necessary and the apparent economic recovery of the mid-1990s as evidence of its success. And some Maori women saw possibilities, within the approaches to devolution, decentralisation of decision-making, and separation of funder and provider in health and education, of greater autonomy and control of funding and decision-making for appropriate Maori providers, whether iwi or purpose-built bodies.

The ECA's intention to enhance labour market flexibility was claimed by government ministers and the New Zealand Business Roundtable, among others, as potentially to the advantage of employees in general, and women in particular. Such flexibility, however, was mainly at the behest of and for the benefit of employers. Only the small proportion of women with extremely scarce skills were able to bargain for any flexibility gains of their own. Even for those few women in senior management, individual contract negotiations possibly allowed gender biases, with men having better access to networks and information. Several respondents to a survey of ten such women 'expressed relief that their contracts were the "same as" men despite the fact that within their fields they might be "better than" men' (Tremaine and McGregor, 1994, p. 6). The authors point out the irony that these women were 'grateful for equivalence, a hallmark of collective agreements, when the stated purpose of the Act provides for difference and individuality' (*ibid.*). The authors went on to argue that this reflected past gender inequalities and their psychological impact on women, with even top women undervaluing themselves.

For the majority of women in lower-paid jobs, neither the environment created by the ECA nor the earlier one were conducive to equality. Previously, relativities discriminating against female-dominated work were often perpetuated in wage negotiations between largely male union and employer representatives. In theory, deregulation could reduce differentials and benefit women. It can be argued, however, that the definitions and measurement of skill, human capital, and productivity are imbued with discrimination against female dominated areas. Hence, outcomes are likely to depend as much on social and negotiating power considerations as they did before.

Future Prospects

For the growing proportion of workers who are poorly paid, part-time, casualised, and/or homeworkers, among whom women are overrepresented, an adequate minimum floor of conditions may be crucial, although hard to enforce. The contracting out of large areas of work has eroded the distinction between employee and self-employed. Only employees, on contracts of service, are covered by most labour legislation. Those on contracts for service have no such protections, so there is an incentive for employers to transfer work to this group. Several such trends are eroding the simple picture of a labour force with one person, one job, and instead producing a kaleidoscope where individuals may need several sources of work to survive, moving in and out of a number of them in a comparatively short time. The picture of the labour force produced by surveys based on old definitions is therefore becoming increasingly misleading.

Rising weekly hours of work for some people, and imposed reduced hours for others, means that overemployment and underemployment coexist, producing an unbalanced situation with some obvious solutions in terms of better sharing of all paid and unpaid work. Overemployment is partly a phenomenon of those high up in hierarchies, but is also relevant for those who, to make ends meet, are forced to take on low-paid work while, at the same time, looking after a number of dependants. For the latter group, higher basic pay or state support is needed. For the former group, 'family friendly' workplaces would attack overemployment as unnecessary, undesirable, unfair to dependants and partners, and discriminatory against those groups unable or unwilling to avoid unpaid caring commitments. Such policies should include improved domestic and (preferably, partly paid) parental leave, as well as a major boost to child care funding and facilities. This could allow paid and unpaid work to be combined more easily, by men as well as women, thus reducing the double burden effect on women. But trends in the 1990s do not induce much optimism that such policies will come about. Major economic, social, and attitudinal changes are needed before such improvement in the quality of life can be expected.

Guide to Readings

A comprehensive survey of trends in women's labour force participation, focusing on differences by age, ethnicity, and other factors is Davies (1993), while issues for women regarding part-time work are well covered in Davidson and Bray (1994). Factual material and assessments of women's position in the labour market are contained in Statistics New Zealand (1993) and National Advisory Council on the Employment of Women (1990). For quantitative treatment and discussion of horizontal occupational segregation by gender, see Gwartney-Gibbs (1988) and Van Mourik et al. (1989). On equal employment opportunity, see Commission for Employment Equity (1990) for an assessment of progress in New Zealand at that date. For varying perspectives on equal employment opportunity see all the articles in Sayers and Tremaine (1994) and some of those in Briar et al. (1992) and Olsson (1992), which also cover other aspects of women in paid and unpaid work.

For factual material and an assessment of equal pay in New Zealand up to 1987, see Urban Research Associates et al. (1987) and, for a discussion of the situation after the ECA, see Hyman (1993). An assessment of the arguments of proponents and opponents of equal pay for work of equal value is contained in Hyman (1994), while strong views against any intervention in this and other labour market areas can be found in New Zealand Business Roundtable (1988 and 1990) and Brook (1990). For a favourable view of intervention, see Du Plessis Novitz and Jaber (1990). Orthodox and alternative, including feminist, accounts of gender differences in the labour market are well covered, with Australian examples, in Mumford (1989), while standard treatments can be found in any labour economics text, such as Rees (1979). The impacts of the ECA on women in the labour market are discussed in Hammond and Harbridge (1993) and Sayers (1991 and 1993). Wage determinants, industrial relations issues, and equity concerns are discussed well in Deeks et al. (1994).

CHAPTER NINE

THE POLITICAL ECONOMY OF INEQUALITY BETWEEN MAORI AND PAKEHA

EVAN TE AHU POATA-SMITH

Liberal and nationalist theories of Maori oppression have dominated the official discourses on social inequality in Aotearoa. These dominant explanations for the inequality that exists between Maori and Pakeha are problematic in significant respects because they tend to ignore the wider structural mechanisms of capitalist society that have generated and entrenched Maori inequality. This chapter will first provide a brief overview of the empirical pattern of Maori inequality, focusing in depth on the inequality that exists between Maori and Pakeha in paid employment. It is not enough, however, to provide purely descriptive accounts of Maori inequality. Rather, it is crucial to reveal the underlying structural causes of Maori inequality. One of the basic weakness of studies between collectivities that differ physically or culturally has been the causal predominance they give to those differences. With this in mind, the second section of the chapter explores the dominant explanations of Maori inequality in New Zealand society. It then presents an historically informed account of capitalist development in Aotearoa, which locates Maori inequality within its wider economic, social, and political context. The fourth section of the chapter provides a brief analysis of the political response by Maori to racism and oppression since the late 1960s.

Patterns of Maori Inequality

Caution is required when interpreting the statistical profile of Maori in New Zealand society. Definitions and categories are subject to change from census to census and from one official survey to the next. Furthermore, the actual data collected is not available for all groups over time. Although the broad parameters of Maori and Pakeha employment patterns are well documented, there are problems, for example, in analysing the profile of the Maori population, not least because the statistical definition of who is categorised as 'Maori' has changed considerably. In addition, changing occupational classifications have complicated statistical comparisons of Maori participation in the labour force. Despite these difficulties, the overall empirical pattern of Maori inequality in paid employment is well established.

The labour force

Maori participation in the New Zealand labour force is one key indicator of the inequality that exists between Maori and Pakeha. Labour force participation usually refers specifically to those who are actively engaged in the workforce according to the Labour Department and/or census definitions. In this section, the labour force includes members of the working-age population who are classified as 'employed' or 'unemployed', as defined by the Household Labour Force Survey.

The Maori labour force more then doubled in size between 1961 and 1987 from 47 818 to 100 600. The 1991 census revealed that there were 153 258 Maori in the labour force, of whom 116 208 were in employment and 37 050 were unemployed and seeking work (Statistics New Zealand, 1991). The labour force participation rate for Maori males was 66.4 per cent, while the participation rate for Maori females was 46.9 per cent. Although the gap between women and men has narrowed, the full-time employment rates of both Pakeha and Maori males have been consistently higher than those of their female counterparts. Both Pakeha and Maori women are, however, more likely to be in part-time employment. Indeed, at the 1991 census, the part-time Maori labour force, with 26 856 persons, represented 17.5 per cent of the total Maori labour force. Maori females comprised 68.6 per cent of the part-time Maori labour force.

The rates of unemployment for Maori, both male and female, have consistently been much higher than for their Pakeha counterparts (see Graphs 9.1 and 9.2). The average unemployment rate for Maori for the year ended March 1995 was 19.4 per cent, nearly three and a half times the unemployment rate for Pakeha (5.6 per cent). Of particular note is the high proportion of long-term unemployment and unemployment among Maori women and youth.

Occupational distribution

Between the 1936 and 1966 censuses, the proportion of Maori who were classified under the category 'Craftsmen, production process workers and

Graph 9.1 Unemployment rates for New Zealand Maori and Pakeha

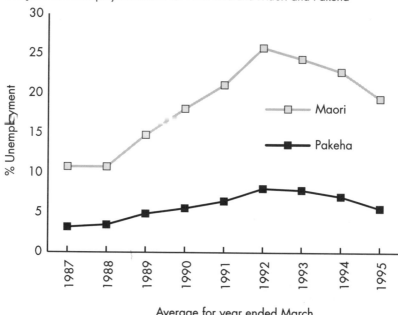

Average for year ended March

Sources: Statistics New Zealand (1994), *Labour Market Statistics;*
Statistics New Zealand (1995), *Household Labour Force Survey,* December Quarter.

Graph 9.2 Unemployment rates for New Zealand Maori and Pakeha by gender

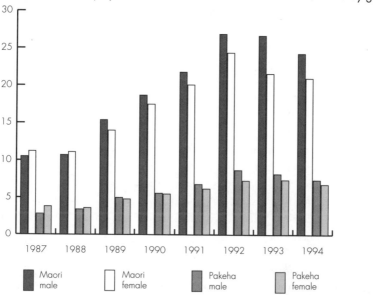

Source: Statistics New Zealand (1994), *Labour Market Statistics.*

labourers' increased from 37 to 50 per cent. By the mid-1970s, just under 60 per cent of the employed Maori population was engaged in manual labour in manufacturing, mining, transport, and construction. Maori men and women continue to be underrepresented in the 'professional', 'legislators', 'administrators' and 'managers' occupational categories and overrepresented in the 'production', 'transport equipment operating', and 'labouring' occupations. At the 1991 census, over two-thirds of Maori men in the labour force (compared with 50.2 per cent of Pakeha men) were categorised as being employed in the occupations (by major group) of 'agricultural and fishery workers', 'trades workers', 'plant and machine operators and assemblers', and 'elementary' occupations. Similarly, Maori women are more likely than those women classified in the New Zealand European ethnic group to work in these occupational categories (Statistics New Zealand, 1991).

Income
The income of Maori men and women is, on average, less than that of their non-Maori counterparts. Maori aged fifteen years and over received a total annual median income of $11 001 at the 1991 census. For Maori men, a median income of $12 958 was received, while the median income for Maori women was $10 024 per year. The majority (76.4 per cent) of all Maori aged fifteen and over received a total annual income of $20 000 or less, while for Maori women this proportion increased to 85.2 per cent. Whereas a total income of more than $40 000 was received by 5.4 per cent of Maori men, only 1.1 per cent of Maori women achieved this income.

In the year ended March 1994, nearly two-thirds of Maori received weekly individual income from wages and salaries of under $500, compared with just over half their Pakeha counterparts. The proportion of Pakeha receiving $1000 a week or more from wages and salaries was double the rate for Maori.

The relative position of Maori in the labour force, and in particular their occupational distribution and participation rates, have crucial implications for the levels of income that can be accrued and therefore the ability to accumulate wealth. Furthermore, the overrepresentation of Maori in the low-paid, predominantly blue collar working class occupations, and their relatively high levels of unemployment, have a major bearing on the capacity of Maori to participate equally with Pakeha in society at large. Low income is directly linked to inadequate housing and reduced disposable income for food and fuel, which, in turn, is linked to poor nutrition and cold and/or damp environments (Te Puni Kokiri, 1993, p. 39). Children raised in such environments have double the risk of infant mortality and a greatly increased risk of death from infectious diseases or accidents. Other problems associated with low income include chronic ear infections, anaemia, iron deficiencies, dental caries, learning disabilities, poor school performance, and an increased suicide rate. In addition to this, international research confirms that the unemployed have higher levels of physical and mental ill-health than the employed.

The inequality between Maori and Pakeha in the labour force is only one of a number of indicators that reveal the extent of Maori material deprivation in New Zealand society. Numerous studies confirm that Maori continue to experience: poor educational outcomes, ill-health, and thus lower life expectancy; high rates of imprisonment; low rates of home ownership; and high rates of state dependency (Ministry of Education, 1995; Spoonley, 1993; pp. 23–4; Te Puni Kokiri, 1992 and 1993). These patterns of Maori inequality are well established in the literature, but the theoretical explanations for them are far more contentious.

Racism and Maori Inequality

Historically, the official explanations for Maori inequality have placed the onus for Maori material deprivation in capitalist society on Maori themselves. Such accounts have fostered the ideas that certain 'inadequacies' of Maori social structures, cultural values, and language codes have prevented Maori from taking their place as equals with Pakeha in a complex modern society. This blatant ethnocentrism reinforced over 100 years of official state policies that sought to 'assimilate' Maori into a developing capitalist society dominated by Eurocentric values.

In the 1990s, dominant anti-racist explanations for Maori inequality tend to focus on the discriminatory practices of the state that prevent Maori from gaining equal access to the social and economic resources of society (Walker, 1990). This approach places the onus for racism on individual Pakeha. Pakeha racism is conceived of primarily as a matter of attitudes. In this context, the problem is that Pakeha are prejudiced against Maori. The solution, therefore, lies in educating Pakeha out of their prejudices. This diagnosis is implicit in decolonisation forums, cultural safety programs, and Treaty of Waitangi workshops. For Maori, the solution lies in educational systems that reflect their cultural values and priorities (Poata-Smith, 1996a). Such an analysis implies a program of remedial action that is strictly confined to the institutions of society, rather than focusing on the underlying structures of capitalist society which, it will be argued, have generated and entrenched Maori inequality.

'Race', racism and colonisation

Racism describes the ideological belief that people can be classified into 'races' and that this can explain other forms of social variation (Miles, 1989). Obviously, any anti-racist strategy presupposes an analysis of the nature of racism and the origins of Maori inequality in Aotearoa.

The ideology of 'race' emerged with the global expansion of capitalism in order to justify the exploitative relationship between indigenous peoples and colonists (Callinicos, 1992, p. 7). In the context of the colonisation of Aotearoa, racism provided the ideological justification for the denial of the equal rights to the indigenous people, 'rights' that were alleged to be synonymous with capitalist expansion. The classification of people into 'racial' groups therefore provided the justification for the domination of the 'new' world by Western Imperialism. Pseudo-scientific and social-Darwinist accounts of human evolution provided the intellectual rationale for the 'removal' of culturally and phenotypically distinct groups who proved an obstacle to the global expansion and reproduction of capitalism. The destruction of the territorial and cultural integrity of indigenous populations, by expropriating and commodifying their lands and human resources, was justified as part of the 'natural' evolutionary process that demonstrated the inherent superiority of the colonising 'races' and the 'inferiority' of others (Spoonley, 1993, p. 2).

The concept of 'race', which derived from nineteenth-century doctrines of racial typology, consisted of a number of fundamental propositions.

(i) the physical appearance and behaviour of individuals was an expression of a discrete biological type which was permanent;

(ii) cultural variation was determined by differences in biological type;

(iii) biological variation was the origin of conflict between both individuals and nations;

(iv) 'races' were endowed such that some were inherently superior to others;

(v) the idea of natural selection was combined with this typology to conclude with the idea of the survival of the fittest (that is social Darwinism) (Miles, 1989, p. 13).

The development of the biological and genetic sciences destroyed the validity of 'race' as a natural biological phenomenon. Although the ideas of 'race' and 'race relations' are historically specific and scientifically indefensible, many people continue to believe, and to act as if they believe, that the world's population is divided into a number of discrete, biologically distinguishable 'races' (Pearson and Thorns, 1983, p. 191). Thus the concept of 'race' remains an important feature of 'commonsense' views of Maori inequality.

Reification of 'race'

Theories that place the causal emphasis for the inequality between Maori and Pakeha on the incompatibility of the underlying values of the two 'races' are fundamentally problematic because they are based upon the reification of an ideological notion (Miles and Spoonley, 1985, p. 13). Simply employing a scientifically discredited notion in the analysis of Maori oppression leads to an explanation that implies biological determinism and that implicitly (and often explicitly) endorses 'commonsense' views of the characteristics of specific 'racial' groups (Miles, 1993, p. 47).

Although most would reject the conception of 'race' in its explicit racist form, the 'race relations' approach to Maori inequality can unintentionally reproduce racist ideology by insisting that 'race' is a social construct that has real effects in the social world. Ward, for example, examines Maori inequality and subjugation explicitly in terms of the attitudes and underlying values that developed within the wider context of 'race relations' in New Zealand (Ward, 1974, p. viii). The existence of 'race relations' obviously implies that 'races' actually have social relations with one another. By definition, then, 'races' must actually exist. Through such a process, the category of 'race' is given an objective status which obscures the fact that 'racial' differences are socially constructed.

Although certain populations may attribute social significance to particular patterns of phenotypical difference, these real biological differences do not, in themselves, have any determinancy. It is the selective perception and subsequent action of individuals and groups that lead to determinate outcomes (Miles, 1989).

From 'race' to 'ethnicity'

Although the doctrine that humankind can be divided into a typology of discrete 'races' is no longer respectable in a scientific sense, the events of the twentieth century have meant that biological racism, at least in its overt form, has become politically and morally disreputable. This has evoked a gradual shift in the way intergroup relations were analysed, with the emphasis moving from biology to 'culture' and from 'race' to 'ethnicity' (Callinicos, 1992, p. 17). This shift primarily reflected the influential growth in national liberation struggles against Western imperialism, together with the inter-national emergence of new social movements in the West from the late 1960s (Spoonley, 1993, p. 36). These movements represented a fundamental rejection of the old notions of biological determinism in favour of more liberating ideologies.

In Aotearoa, such explanations for Maori inequality were strongly influenced by the development of contemporary nationalist strategies for Maori liberation (see Walker, 1984, 1987, and 1990). These 'ethnic' or 'cultural' explanations for Maori inequality involve a clear acknowledgment of the social construction of 'race': the fact that real phenotypical difference has social 'effects' only when some social significance is attributed to that difference. Such approaches emphasise not the biological superiority of some 'races' to others, but the 'cultural' differences between 'ethnic' groups. In this way, differing cultural values are used to explain the totality of belief and behaviour of individuals who belong to a particular 'ethnic group'. Such 'cultural' or 'ethnic' explanations for Maori inequality tend to assume that identities are primordial, that they originate in the unknowable past, and that they are relatively unchanging. In this way, ' "Ethnicity" or "culture" is conceived as a fate from which those it embraces cannot escape. Although acknowledged as a product of (usually caricatured) history, it is no longer amenable to further change by human action: it has become effectively part of nature' (Callinicos, 1992, p. 17).

Those familiar with the derogatory ways in which the concept of 'human nature' has been used to justify women's oppression will not be surprised to note that just such a concept has also underpinned what some have referred to as the 'new racism' (Spoonley, 1993; Gordon and Klug, 1986). With its rhetoric of cultural difference, and usually an underlying tacit appeal to racist attitudes, modern racism promotes the idea that it is 'natural' for similar people to group together and be suspicious or even antagonistic towards other groups. Such an instinct, it is argued, is innate and permanent. The implication, of course, is that racist oppression is a universal feature of human development and, as such, cannot be eradicated. Such arguments about the permanence of particular forms of human behaviour are extremely spurious. Indeed, a substantial amount of anthropological and cross-cultural evidence confirms, first, that what is considered 'natural' behaviour for human beings changes radically throughout history (Segal, 1987, p. 10) and, second, that individuals and/or collectivities 'manipulate' their ethnic identities to fit different social situations (see Barth, 1969; Cohen, 1974; Hechter, 1975 and 1987; Hechter and Levi, 1979; Kendis and Kendis, 1976; Lyman and Douglas, 1973; Smith, 1981 and 1986).

The fact that the underlying values, attitudes, and cultural phenomena underpinning 'ethnic' groups are not fixed or primordial has important implications for the study of 'ethnic' conflict: it means that identifying as Maori or Pakeha is socially constructed and so historically contingent. But, most important, the implication is that attitudes and values associated as 'natural' or permanent today are just as likely to be amenable to further change.

Abstraction of cultural difference

Because the central object of analysis is cultural difference, 'ethnic' and 'cultural' approaches to conflicts between collectivities that do differ culturally are limited because they tend to analyse only the *perception* of difference. At one level this can lead to a simple cataloguing of cultural differences; at another it analyses the interaction between culturally distinct groups without referring to the material context in which these relationships develop.

There are many such accounts of New Zealand history that conceptualise the underlying values and cultural attitudes of Maori and Pakeha in isolation from their material context. Walker sees the colonisation of Aotearoa primarily as 'a historic process predicated on *assumptions* of racial, religious, cultural and technological superiority' (Walker, 1990, p. 8, emphasis added). Ballara attempts to explain Maori oppression by tracing the 'permutations of Eurocentric racial prejudice in New Zealand society', and studying the effects of these attitudes in the community (Ballara, 1986, p. 6). In this way the continued oppression of Maori is a result of racist Pakeha attitudes that have become 'institutionalised' within society as a whole. The organisational policies and practices of the state operate in the interests of Pakeha in the struggle against Maori for control over social, economic, and cultural resources because 'Pakeha values and assumptions underlie all procedures and practices' (Nairn and Nairn, 1981, p. 117).

This concept of 'institutional racism' refers to the different ways in which groups are treated by institutions. As Pearson rightly points out, however, the political vigour of the term is not matched by its conceptual clarity (Pearson 1990, p. 12). This is because, '[a]ll that is necessary for institutional racism to be said to exist is to show that whatever the intent, disadvantage is the result' (Spoonley, 1993, pp. 21–2). Thus institutional racism tends to be defined by its consequences (Pearson, 1990; Williams, 1985). This means that institutional racism may provide a useful description of the disadvantage experienced by a particular ethnic group, but it does not *explain* that inequality.

In this way, the evidence of Maori inequality, in terms of health or educational performance, for example, leads to an examination of the cultural practices, values, and expectations of the institutions concerned, without adequately explaining the society in which they operate. Walker, for instance, structures his account of Maori-Pakeha relations explicitly on this basis (Walker, 1990). Although he acknowledges a structural dimension to Maori subordination, he tends to focus exclusively on the institutional and policy level in isolation from the underlying structural mechanisms of capitalist society in which the state functions.

The prejudice and ethnocentrism that have characterised official state policies from the time of colonisation certainly reveal the extent to which racism has evolved as a pervasive feature of New Zealand society. Such a 'narrow' focus on cultural values, however, fosters the impression that the unchanging attitudes and prejudices of Pakeha, in and of themselves, are the source of Maori oppression. This is fundamentally problematic because attitudes and values have only limited influence. Moreover, the basis of racism is found not in the attitudes and values attributed to phenotypical or cultural difference, but in the economic, political, and ideological conditions and context that allow such attribution of meaning to take place. This necessitates going beyond a cataloguing of people's *perception* of difference to investigate the material basis for the reproduction of ideological relation.[1]

Because Maori oppression cannot be discussed and resolved solely by reference to the characteristics of Maori themselves, any analysis of Maori inequality must look at the structures or social formation within which Maori are incorporated (Miles and Spoonley, 1985, p. 8). Indeed, one of the significant omissions of 'cultural' explanations for Maori inequality concerns the analysis of New Zealand as a capitalist society with a system of production organised on the basis of profitable capital accumulation. It should not be surprising, then, that the state has appropriated those Maori resources, both economic and socio-cultural, in ways that reproduce capitalist social relations and further economic development. Although this is a mediated, contested, and often contradictory process, it is important to note that the state's role in what is often called 'race relations' involves producing a labour force with ideas, values, and practices that are consistent with, and accept, existing capitalist power relations (Barber, 1989; Miles and Spoonley, 1985, p. 11). In performing this role, the state is 'independent' of any direct or systematic control by the capitalist class. In a capitalist society, however, the state is fiscally dependent on the taxation of incomes generated by the process of private capital accumulation. This means that the state is structurally dependent on the continuing profitability and expansion of capital accumulation, although these structural constraints are historically contingent (Goldfinch and Roper, 1993, p. 69; Roper, 1993b, p. 22).

Clearly, capitalist accumulation, class inequality and conflict, and the pro-capitalist bias of state policy formulation have had a major impact on the relationship between the state and Maori. It is, therefore, important to look beyond the visible evidence of official legislation and state institutions to uncover the social forces that have shaped Maori and Pakeha relations.

White Settler Colonialism and the Political Economy of Labour Migration

Essential in explaining the emergence and present state of Maori inequality in capitalist society are the processes of white settler colonialism and labour migration (see Miles, 1984, 1989, and 1993; Miles and Spoonley, 1985; Pearson, 1984 and 1990; Spoonley, 1993). These are two distinct, though interlocking, processes. The first concerns the colonial land grab that dispossessed Maori; the second concerns the Maori labour migration, recruitment, and settlement necessary to provide a workforce for an emerging capitalist society.

It is important to place the white settlement of Aotearoa within its historical context as part of a global process of capitalist expansionism based on destroying the territorial and cultural integrity of the indigenous populations by taking and exploiting their lands and human resources. As Marx noted in regard to the process of capitalist development, '[i]n actual history, it is a notorious fact that conquest, enslavement, robbery, murder, in short, force, plays the greatest part' (Marx, 1976, p. 874).

The Age of Revolution

In European history, the period between 1789 and 1848 was characterised by tremendous social, economic, and political upheaval. The political turbulence created in the wake of the Industrial Revolution and the French Revolution had enormous implications for the social and economic relations that were to emerge in the European colonies around the world. This period is significant in the study of the political economy of Maori inequality because it corresponds with the transition from the first phase of contact, which saw the establishment of commercial relations between European traders and iwi, to the relentless process of land alienation that underpinned the systematic colonisation of Aotearoa.

This colonisation took place at a time when British capitalism was reeling from prolonged economic depression and declining prosperity. The cyclic bouts of capitalist crises had entrenched serious economic and social inequality which, in turn, had generated growing working class discontent (Hobsbawm, 1975). In the wake of the widespread working class rebellion that rocked Europe from the 1830s, there was the very real possibility of revolutionary upheaval in Britain itself. Indeed, the widespread working class resentment found its political expression in the Chartist movement, which flourished throughout England, Scotland, and Wales from 1838 to

1850. For the first time in British history, the ruling class came face to face with a mass working class movement when there was no known means of reviving economic prosperity.

Throughout the late eighteenth century, imperialist ventures based on the establishment of extractive colonies that supplied Britain with cheap raw materials and export markets were used to combat declining economic growth and social discontent (see Chapter 2). But official British enterprises in South Africa, Australia, Canada, India, and the West Indies had proven extremely costly. The British state was under such severe financial constraint it could no longer afford to become embroiled in another official colonial venture that required increased taxation of the British ruling class. This, in part, explains why the official British policy towards New Zealand until the late 1830s was characterised by a general reluctance to intervene formally (Adams, 1977, p. 52). Indeed, for the British state, it was far more preferable to see British interests advanced through non-official agents, such as traders, missionaries, and explorers, who moved beyond the empire's frontiers at their own risk and at no expense to the British Government (Orange, 1987, p. 8).

Exporting the working class population that had become 'surplus' to the requirements of British capital gradually emerged as the solution to the economic crisis. Emigration on the desired scale, however, required some form of subsidy, a subsidy that the British ruling class could not afford (Steven, 1989, p. 23).

But the systematic colonisation of Aotearoa was premised on the discovery that, if the British Crown sold land in the colonies to prospective settlers, subsidised emigration would be possible without any cost to the British tax-paying class. This is precisely why the complete control over all Maori land transactions formed such an integral part of Colonial Office plans to acquire sovereignty over New Zealand. Indeed, the annexation of Aotearoa was an attractive proposition only in so far as a land fund would allow the colonial administration to become financially self-sufficient, while any surplus capital would be used to finance further British emigration. The fact that the exclusive right of pre-emption over Maori land was such a major feature of the Treaty of Waitangi is testament to the significance of annexation for the British.

In order to entice immigrants from Britain in the first place, Aotearoa had to offer the material conditions necessary for the rapid accumulation of capital. The most distinctive economic characteristic was high-quality land that required few resources to produce profit. Acquiring this land proved the driving force behind settler society (Steven, 1989, p. 26), and this, in turn, involved the systematic expropriation of Maori land.

Primitive Accumulation

The capitalist mode of production differs historically from other modes of production in terms of the essential social relations that constitute it. Unlike other forms of society, capitalist society is defined by the unique and antagonistic relationship between the 'owners of money, means of production, means of subsistence', on the one hand, and the 'owners' of labour power on the other. The critical factor in the establishment of these social relations of production in Aotearoa was the existence of the means of production (including labour power) in commodity form.

Although the capitalist's monopoly of property and of access to the means of production is a necessary pre-condition for the production of surplus value, because it prevents the working class from producing its own livelihood in an independent way, it is only the labour power of living labour that actually produces additional value, including surplus value (Mandel, 1976, p. 33). The 'secret' of surplus value, the essential feature of capitalism, therefore lies in the existence of labour power as a commodity (Fine, 1975, p. 41; McNally, 1993, p. 7). In Aotearoa, the systematic commodification of labour power required separating a growing proportion of the Maori population from the land, which had for centuries provided them with an adequate subsistence, thereby giving them no alternative but to sell their labour power for a wage. This process was not unique to Aotearoa; the development of capitalism throughout Europe involved '. . . the historical process of divorcing the producer from the means of production' (Marx, 1976, pp. 874–5).

As with the process of capitalist development on a global scale, the emergence of a propertyless class of Maori wage labourers was not gradual or harmonious, but involved brutal dispossession, violence, and destruction (McNally, 1993, pp. 6–7). Aotearoa, however, contained a Maori population that was relatively large and sufficiently organised militarily to provide powerful resistance to the commodification of Maori land. Because the British state was unwilling to meet the costs required to oppose this resistance with military forces, the Treaty of Waitangi provided an inexpensive means of ensuring that Maori would not obstruct the annexation of land, at least not until there were enough settlers to threaten Maori military dominance (Steven, 1989, p. 26).

The discovery of pastoral wealth, which yielded greater profits than the moderate incomes earned by producing foodstuffs, was a turning point in the relations between Maori and the settlers. Profitable pastoralism required huge land-holdings and their acquisition at not too great a cost. The insatiable drive for greater profits manifested itself in the rampant expropriation of Maori land that took place from 1840 to 1870. The fierce and sustained fighting of the New Zealand Wars showed the depth of iwi resistance to this expansion (Walker, 1990; Belich, 1986). This opposition by Maori gave the state the opportunity to confiscate further Maori land to satisfy the requirements of an expanding pastoral industry. On the pretence of pacifying 'rebellion', the colonial state took, by force, millions of acres of Maori land that was so central for capitalist development (Bedggood, 1978, p. 287).

State legislation that aimed decisively to 'free up' Maori land, such as the Suppression of Rebellion Act 1863, the New Zealand Settlement Act 1863, and the Native Reserves Act 1864, resulted in the transfer of millions of acres of fertile farmland into the hands of large landowners. With the removal of British imperial support and the move to self-government, more subtle and less expensive measures had to be found to expropriate the remaining Maori land. In particular, the Native Land Act 1865 prepared the way by individualising the ownership titles of communally held Maori land.

In 1876 the provincial system of government was abolished. Maori were disenfranchised politically in the development of a centralised state and a national administrative infrastructure suitable for capitalist expansion. The territorial and regional separation of the Maori population contributed to the maintenance of traditional elements of Maori society that remained relatively insulated from the developing settler institutions. Together with the exclusion of the vast majority of Maori from orthodox political processes, this relative isolation allowed state and foreign investment to develop a national economic infrastructure without formidable opposition.

The transition from large-scale farming towards relatively small family farm production, the urban processing of the rural product, and the emergence of a manufacturing sector resulted in the erosion of state control by the landed oligarchy (Wilkes, 1993, p. 196). From 1890, the state sought freer land policies and even developed strategies for breaking up the large estates. The Native Land Validation Act 1892, the West Coast Settlement Reserves Act 1892, the Native Land Purchase and Acquisition Act 1893, and the Advances to Settlers Act 1894 were among the more overt measures introduced to hasten the process of Maori land alienation. By the turn of the century, most Maori were relegated to a precarious existence on the edge of a rapidly expanding capitalist society dominated by a Pakeha ruling class and state (Pearson, 1984, p. 209).

For the first part of the twentieth century the process of land alienation continued unabated. Maori land holdings were reduced further from 7 137 025 acres in 1911 to 4 787 686 acres in 1920. By the late 1930s,

Maori retained less than one-sixth of the land.[2] Because most of the remaining land was unsuitable for development, iwi no longer possessed the acreage to feed themselves. Although Maori continued to have only a marginal relationship with the capitalist mode of production, this relationship was becoming more important for the Maori economy. As the pace of land alienation increased, so did the Maori reliance on seasonal labour to supplement their declining resource base. Many Maori increasingly became a source of cheap and exploitable labour, primarily in the agricultural sector.

The world recession of the early 1930s had an enormous impact on New Zealand's economy, which was dominated by agricultural capital. The crisis of profitability, characterised, among other things, by low levels of foreign and domestic investment, decimated the employment base in the agricultural sector. This had a disproportionate impact on the overwhelmingly rural Maori population. As a casual, reserve army of labour, Maori agricultural labourers were among the first to be laid off. Indeed, it is estimated that Maori made up some 40 per cent of the unemployed, with three-quarters of adult Maori men registered as unemployed by 1933 (King, 1992, p. 293).

Proletarianisation

Whereas the first phase of establishing capitalism in Aotearoa involved the destruction of the subsistence economy and the partial exclusion of Maori from the developing capitalist society, the second phase saw the systematic incorporation of Maori into an emerging working class. This was because the development of capitalist production in Aotearoa necessitated the geographical concentration of the means of production and hence the process of proletarianisation (Miles and Spoonley, 1985, p. 15).

The long boom

In most advanced capitalist countries, the period 1945 to 1973 was one of sustained economic growth coupled with a gradual rise in the standards of living. In Aotearoa, the long boom was a product of historically high levels of profitability and productive investment, accompanied by full employment, low inflation, rising real wages, and the absence of prolonged balance of payment difficulties owing to favourable terms of trade (see Chapter 1). From 1945, there was a significant expansion of the manufacturing sector, which generated an absolute and relative increase in the size of the working class. The prolonged period of economic expansion further accelerated the centralisation of industrial production in the larger cities, particularly the greater region of Auckland.

The compulsion for Maori to sell their labour power for a wage (induced by the destruction of the traditional economy) combined with the demand for labour from the expanding manufacturing sector to cause a massive rural to urban migration of Maori. This exodus was reinforced by acute Maori overpopulation (with limited economic and natural resources) and high rural unemployment (Butterworth, 1967, p. 19). The process of proletarianisation was rapid. In 1926, 8 per cent of the total Maori population were located in the 'defined urban areas'.[3] By 1966 the figure had risen to 41.1 per cent.

Contemporary Maori Nationalism and the Economic Crisis

In the mid-1970s the long boom that had fuelled the rapid labour migration collapsed, as a result of steadily worsening conditions of economic decline and fiscal instability. These, in turn, were brought on by the inherent tendency in capitalist systems for the general rate of profit to fall, which inhibits investment and undermines profitable capital accumulation. This economic crisis generated the politicisation of ethnic and gender inequalities, and an upsurge in class struggle. From the mid-1970s, governments struggled to manage the deepening economic and political crisis. In particular, the political turbulence created in the wake of a dramatic increase in Maori protest and discontent forced governments to respond to the overwhelming evidence of racism and Maori inequality that characterised New Zealand society.

Such struggles embraced a considerable variety of political strategies, campaigns, and participants (see Greenland, 1984; Poata-Smith, 1996b; Sharp, 1990). Put simply, from the late 1960s Maori activists tended to reject strategies that relied entirely on orthodox political processes to reform the worst excesses of racism and Maori inequality. The activists believed that the only basis for Maori liberation was a fundamental transformation of the system, which was both racist and capitalist. This approach coexisted with the Brown power philosophies of the more militant wing of Nga Tamatoa, which urged Maori to unite, to recognise their common history, and to build a new sense of solidarity and community.

This nationalist influence faded as more conservative middle class elements came to dominate the movement and this development was reflected in the proliferation of strategies that emphasised constitutional change through electoral politics and the systematic reform of existing institutions. Such strategies rested on the expectation that the state would make significant concessions to Maori. But the failure of the third Labour Government (1972–75) to stem the tide of land alienation and secure Maori rights led frustrated activists to look at more direct tactics that challenged the state. As a consequence, the third National Government (1975–84) had to respond to a dual crisis of economic decline and a crisis of political legitimation created in the wake of the Maori land rights movement. National fumbled through the 1975 land march on Parliament, the occupations of Bastion Point and Raglan, and the regular protests at Waitangi, with a mixture of coercive state force and legal measures.

The restructuring of New Zealand economy after the mid-1970s saw the financial fraction of capital grow dramatically relative to the industrial and commercial fractions (Roper, 1991b). This had dramatic implications for the employment prospects of working class Maori, who were overrepresented in the manufacturing sector. It forced the third National Government to respond to the economic crisis, which had such a disproportionate impact on employment prospects in Maori communities, with an inconsistent set of policies based on Keynesian forms of economic management which, in turn, generated a fiscal crisis of the state. Amid a deepening economic and political crisis, the fourth Labour Government (1984–90) embarked on an economic restructuring program to restore levels of profitability in the New Zealand economy in order to encourage investment and growth by promoting those conditions most conducive to profitable capital accumulation. Labour's restructuring was underpinned by a theoretical agenda based almost exclusively on the analytical assumptions, ideological values, and policy prescriptions of the schools of economic thought associated with the New Right.

The fourth Labour Government attempted to appease the rising level of Maori protest in two major ways. The first involved extending the jurisdiction of the Waitangi Tribunal retrospectively to 1840 and the second involved adopting the policy of 'biculturalism', which was based on the selective incorporation of Maori cultural symbolism within the institutions of the state (Barber, 1989). As Maori demands became more strident, a contradiction emerged between Labour's economic program and the treaty settlement policy (Kelsey, 1990 and 1993). This attempt to appease Maori discontent was made easier by a qualitative change in the direction of the Maori protest movement itself, with the proliferation of 'identity politics'. In the absence of mass struggles against oppression, owing to the international decline of the working class movement and the rise of the New Right, many of the assumptions of identity politics were reflected, in New Zealand, in an emphasis on cultural identity as *the* determining factor in Maori oppression. The inherent traits of Pakeha were seen as the basic causes of an oppressive and unequal society, while the traditional and egalitarian virtues of the Maori community were critical to changing this situation. Such a 'cultural' explanation for Maori inequality was easily accommodated by the state because, unlike the demands of the earlier movement, cultural nationalism did not represent a fundamental threat to the underlying social relations of capitalism.[4]

Although the policies of biculturalism represented an advance for middle class Maori professionals with the expansion of employment opportunities in the state apparatus, the emphasis on identity alone as the determining factor in Maori oppression has been counter-productive for working class Maori whanau, as successive governments have shifted the costs of the economic crisis on to the weakest sections of the community. The restructuring of the economy has been a disaster for working class Maori and Pakeha, women, welfare beneficiaries, and users of public health and education, who have had to face increased poverty, falling real incomes, mass unemployment, deteriorating employment conditions and job security, social welfare cuts, and user charges for education and health services. Because most Maori whanau are within the working class, Maori have borne the brunt of the economic restructuring (Te Puni Kokiri, 1992). Indeed, in the two years between March 1987 and March 1989, one-fifth of the Maori working-age population was made redundant (Te Puni Kokiri, 1993, p. 41).

The upsurge in Maori protest and anger in the wake of the fourth National Government's attempt to evoke a full and final settlement of treaty grievances, following secret negotiations with tribal executive and corporate warriors, has generated intense anger and resentment at the lack of real options available to ordinary Maori within the system.

Conclusion

The empirical pattern of the inequality that exists between Maori and Pakeha in the labour force is well established. It is only one of many indicators that confirm Maori oppression as a pervasive feature of New Zealand society. Maori consciousness of this exploitative situation has heightened since the early 1970s, fuelling a new determination to effect change. Maori nationalist strategies for change are, however, contradictory, covering the political spectrum from Maori capitalism (in both individual and tribal forms) and cultural nationalism to Maori separatism and radicalism.

Liberal accounts of Maori inequality tend to focus on the discriminatory practices of the state and the values of individual Pakeha, which prevent Maori from gaining equal access to the resources of society. Such accounts ignore the underlying structures of capitalist society that have generated and entrenched Maori inequality. Even the emphasis of Maori nationalists on the Maori community as the central agent of the struggle against racism and Maori inequality conceals the structural inequalities in wider capitalist society that continually work against the objectives of even the most egalitarian of cultural strategies.

The systematic expropriation of Maori land was not an historical accident undertaken by morally destitute settlers. Nor was the subsequent economic, cultural, and political subjugation of the majority of the Maori population an inevitable expression of the exploitative qualities of the Pakeha. Rather, the violent process of primitive accumulation, which separated the mass of the Maori population from any direct access to the means of production, was an essential pre-condition for the commodification of labour power, the critical feature of capitalist development in Aotearoa.

The brutal destruction of the traditional Maori economy, and the creation of a propertyless class of Maori wage labourers with no direct access to the means of making a livelihood, are the key factors in placing the majority of Maori whanau in the working class, therefore affecting their levels of income, occupational distribution, educational attainment, health, unemployment, and housing. This essential feature of capitalist development has not been subject to appraisal at the official level.

The centrality of the commodification of labour power to capitalist development in Aotearoa has important implications for contemporary political practice. It means that ending Maori inequality and achieving meaningful tino rangatiratanga for the vast majority of Maori, while maintaining capitalism, is ultimately contradictory. Terminating both requires a revolutionary transformation of the existing system of capitalist exploitation which, in turn, is dependent on solidarity between Maori and non-Maori members of the working class.

---

1 I employ the concept of ideology to refer to the processes by which meaning is produced, challenged, reproduced, and transformed. This is based on Gramsci's notion that ideology does not simply reflect economic relations in a deterministic or instrumental way (see Gramsci, 1971, p. 407). In this way ideologies have their own conditions of existence and reproduction, although these are not independent of material forces. Ideas are not simply the instrumental expression of class interests but form a 'backdrop' against which class conflict takes place. Thus, in the course of struggle, classes will appropriate those themes and ideas that give expression and advance their material (class) interests. This means that ideologies are not static or permanent forms; rather, their content and object are dynamic and subject to change.

2 Over three-quarters of a million acres of the land remaining in Maori hands was leased to Pakeha, with a further three-quarters of a million deemed unsuitable for development.

3 According to the 1926, 1936, 1945, 1951, 1956, 1961, and 1966 censuses, the eighteen

'defined urban areas' are: Whangarei, Auckland, Hamilton, Tauranga, Rotorua, Gisborne, Napier, Hastings, New Plymouth, Wanganui, Palmerston North, Hutt, Wellington, Nelson, Christchurch, Timaru, Dunedin, and Invercargill.

4 For a critique of cultural nationalism and identity politics as a strategy for Maori liberation see Poata-Smith, 1996b.

Guide to Readings

For an analysis of the status of the concept of 'race' and the sociology of 'race' and 'ethnic' relations, see Miles (1989 and 1993). For an alternative view, see Pearson (1990). For general surveys on the political economy of labour migration and the relationship between capital, labour and racism, see Miles (1982). In relation to the political economy of Maori Inequality, see Miles (1984), Miles and Spoonley (1985), Spoonley (1993), and Pearson (1984 and 1990). Steven (1989) provides one of the best accounts of the historical relationship between Maori land and the social forces shaping capitalist development in Aotearoa. For a more general survey of capitalist development and the creation of an 'unfree' labour force, see McNally (1993). Pearson (1984 and 1990) and Pearson and Thorns (1983) explore the empirical patterns of ethnic inequality in the New Zealand labour force and the existence of Maori disadvantage in wider society.

PART III

THE STATE

Chapter Ten

FROM ARBITRATION TO BARGAINING: CHANGING STATE STRATEGIES IN INDUSTRIAL RELATIONS

PAT WALSH

The Employment Contracts Act (ECA) 1991 constituted one of the most significant shifts in New Zealand's industrial relations strategy from an arbitration to a bargaining model. Arbitration and bargaining entail quite different institutional structures and operating procedures. Arbitration regulates industrial relations through state agencies, political exchange, and politically determined and judicially interpreted rules; bargaining operates through an economic exchange based on market power, including organisational capacity. An arbitration model emphasises uniformity, industrial harmony, continuity in relationships, and equity in outcomes; a bargaining model emphasises diversity, conflict, dynamic relationships, and outcomes concerned with efficiency rather than equity. These are ideal models. No system corresponds in a pure form to either the arbitration or bargaining model; it is a matter of emphasis and inclination. Market resources will always be important in an arbitration system, while politically determined and judicially interpreted rules will always play a role in a bargaining system. No bargaining system will tolerate endemic conflict in the interests of flexibility and change; no arbitration system will tolerate extreme rigidity. No market system is totally indifferent to equity concerns and no arbitration system can ignore efficiency issues. Any industrial relations system combines aspects of arbitration and bargaining. The key issue is how the mix is organised and which organising principles predominate.

The New Zealand state chose arbitration in the 1890s. Although arbitration predominated from then on, it never operated in isolation from bargaining. The tension between the two, and the shifting and conflicting strategies of those who favoured one model over the other, were crucial to the development of industrial relations in New Zealand. For seventy-five years or more, with the notable and temporary exception of the Depression in the 1930s, the state consistently chose arbitration as its preferred industrial relations strategy and was able to force that choice upon unions and employers. Overall, the arbitration system prospered, despite support from other groups—sometimes unions, sometimes employers—for a shift to a bargaining system. But by the 1990s, the state had made a different choice: it opted decisively for a bargaining model and discarded what was left of the arbitration system. This chapter looks at why the state favoured arbitration over bargaining for so long, the response of unions and employers to this, and why, in the 1990s, the state switched to a bargaining model.

Theories of the State and Industrial Relations

It is frequently observed that the state is poorly theorised in the discipline of industrial relations (Giles, 1989; Keller, 1990; Adams, 1992). Giles (1989, pp. 124–30) has suggested three reasons for this. One is the multidisciplinary rather than interdisciplinary nature of industrial relations. This encourages a range of different, specific, discipline-based analyses of the state, making it difficult to achieve any theoretical synthesis. The second reason is the pragmatic, policy-oriented nature of mainstream industrial relations. Researchers tend to ask specific, often narrow-range questions about particular policies and to neglect wider issues about the overall role of the state. Third, and most significantly, the orthodox definition of industrial relations tends to focus not on the determinants of state policies and actions, but on their impact on variables of central interest to industrial relations researchers, such as trade union structure, employer strategy, collective bargaining, and industrial action.

This chapter adopts an institutional view of the state. Institutional theories assign an active role to the state (March and Olsen, 1984; Hall, 1986; Krasner, 1988). They build upon state-centred theories of policy-making, but take a more limited view of state capacities and autonomy. As Skocpol puts it,

> In this perspective, states matter not simply because of the goal-oriented activities of state officials. They matter because their organisational configurations along with their overall patterns of activity, affect political culture, encourage some kinds of group formation and collective political actions (but not others), and make possible the raising of certain political issues (but not others) (1985, p. 21).

Although broadly accepting this premise, an institutional approach qualifies it by locating the state in the centre of a complex web of institutional relations and looking for the constraints thus imposed on state capacities and autonomy.

Political and economic constraints bear upon the state's development of its industrial relations strategies. The operation of a capitalist economy gives rise to conflict between different economic classes. Conflict between workers and capital is, of course, tempered by a degree of common interests, often over specific issues—most obviously the survival of particular industries or firms. But, in general terms, the pursuit by workers and employers of their conflicting interests presents the state with a distinctive set of policy problems. The state does not play the role of a neutral umpire. The state's own interests, and the relationships that develop in a capitalist political economy, give capital a significant structural advantage over labour in the pursuit of favourable state policies. States in capitalist societies share, to varying degrees, responsibility for the efficient management of the capitalist economy. Failure in this task jeopardises the government's electoral prospects and, usually more immediately as tax revenues decline, its ability to finance its activities. The requirement to pay more attention to the needs and interests of employers applies not only to elected politicians but also to key state agencies, who develop a close relationship with business in the ordinary performance of their responsibilities. Moreover, workers and their organisations cannot normally match the resources that business organisations are able to mobilise in the pursuit of their policy interests.

This is not to say that labour is without some measure of countervailing power in its relationship with the state.[1] Workers can mobilise industrial and political resources to mitigate what Lindblom aptly calls 'the privileged position of business' (1977, p. 5). Industrially, workers can organise collectively in trade unions and seek to influence state policies by a range of industrial activities. Politically, workers can form, join, or actively support political parties or interest groups seeking to advance their interests. But neither industrial nor political activity itself is a guarantor of success. Policy-making forums are difficult to penetrate and dominant actors have interests vested in existing policies. Yet electoral factors can exercise some restraint upon governments in capitalist democracies. In New Zealand, the high electoral relevance of industrial relations and a concern for social stability have led, at times, to significant changes in the state's industrial relations policies, not all of them unfavourable to workers (Brosnan et al., 1990).

Just as the conflict between labour and capital, and the particular form it takes in each society, shape the state's industrial relations policies, so, too, those policies and the structures they establish shape the continuing relationship between labour and capital. The institutional structure established by the state not only brings union and employer organisations into existence, but its rules and procedures define their interests and shape the strategies they follow and how they relate to each other and to the state (Holt, 1986; Walsh and Fougere, 1987). This process captures well the role played by the New Zealand state in industrial relations. Explaining that role requires an understanding of the nature and development of the arbitration system, established by the Industrial Conciliation and Arbitration Act 1894.[2]

State Strategies and Industrial Relations in New Zealand

The state's choice of the arbitration system to govern industrial relations was bound up in the intersection of economic and political considerations in the 1890s. Unionisation and industrial conflict had grown swiftly in the 1880s. The great maritime strike of 1890 had brought a crushing defeat for unions. Employers took advantage of their industrial superiority to reverse union gains. The farming wing of the Liberal alliance wanted industrial stability for the emerging export-based economy and their craft union wing wanted protection for unions (Holt, 1986). Unions had previously opposed compulsory arbitration as likely to lead to union dependence on the arbitral process at the expense of autonomous collective organisation (Richardson, 1981). Industrial unions continued to oppose it for these reasons, but they carried little weight with the Liberal Government. The opposition of urban employers, who saw, rightly, that arbitration would give unions the basis they needed to restore their gravely weakened organisation, was equally ineffectual. The Liberals had already begun to expand greatly the role of the state in the society and economy. For them, further regulation of the employment relationship, following on from the Factories Act 1891, was consistent with this wider strategy.

The introduction of the system established a third set of state structures in industrial relations to operate alongside the government and the Department of Labour. The most important institution was the Court of Arbitration and its various successors, most recently the Employment Court established by the ECA. (The ECA set up the Employment Tribunal to mediate and adjudicate on contracts and the Employment Court to hear appeals against tribunal decisions and to adjudicate on breaches of the legislation.) In the state sector, similar specialist institutions were established in the 1940s. Although they were established to secure the government's industrial relations interests, arbitral tribunals became, instead, a constraint on government action. At times, their role and interests differed from those of the government. So, built into the very structure of the state, was the potential for conflict among state agencies over the state's industrial relations strategy. The courts must be analysed as political organisations (Brosnan et al., 1990, pp. 159–77). Their role, decisions, and even their existence have been continuing matters of political controversy. The courts have had to retain the confidence and support of key constituents, or at least a dominant coalition of them. But the courts cannot secure their support at any price. Their decisions have always had to take account of their statutory obligations and criteria, precedents set in the past, the industrial balance, and the need to satisfy the Court of Appeal. The 1990s have seen a strong attack on the Employment Court by the New Zealand Business Roundtable and the Employers' Federation.

The various courts have played two roles: as a national tribunal determining wages and other conditions of employment, and as an adjudicator in disputes over the employment relationship. In the private sector, the first role dated from 1894 until the 1960s. From then on, the parties had no confidence in the arbitral court as a wage-fixing body. The second role began in the 1970s and continues under the ECA. It falls into two categories: disputes over the interpretation or enforcement of the terms of an employment contract, and personal grievances, which are claims of unfair treatment, usually on an individual basis. If they are not settled at an earlier stage, these disputes culminate in compulsory arbitration by the court. It is important not to overlook the court's contemporary transformation into a tribunal with mandatory powers of contract interpretation and enforcement.

The importance of equity to the arbitration system was evident in the court's wage-fixing policies, which moderated the impact of market factors. The court, bound by its act to make decisions 'in equity and good conscience', gradually adopted the living wage concept (Woods, 1963) and accepted the principle that pay rates should move broadly in line with increases in the cost of living. The court also opted for a hierarchy of occupational wage relativities, which became the governing consideration in wage-fixing. The court's wage policies were patriarchal in character—from the beginning it gave men higher rates than women, and based male rates on the assumption that a non-earning wife and children were dependent on them. Brosnan and Wilson (1989) observe that the combined impact of these policies was to make marriage the primary option for economic support for women.[3] Gould has remarked that, of all the advanced capitalist countries, 'New Zealand had kept its women most rigidly bound to house and children' (1982, p. 93). Those women who were able to work, however, benefited from the relatively egalitarian wage structure of the arbitration system. Despite lower rates of pay for the same work and gendered skill assessments, the male/female pay gap was lower in New Zealand than in many other countries (Brosnan and Wilson, 1989, p. 7). Key features of the arbitration system, especially blanket coverage of awards and their enforceability, also benefited Maori and Pacific Island workers. Neither suffered lower rates of pay for the same job as women had done. The chief source of their labour market disadvantage lay in their patterns of occupational segregation, in the state's educational, training, and immigration policies, and in employer prejudice and discrimination, rather than in the arbitration system itself (Brosnan and Wilson, 1989, p. 20).

Governments, the second key state structure in industrial relations, have typically pursued strategies intended to reconcile the maintenance of their electoral coalition with what they consider to be acceptable macroeconomic outcomes. The arbitration system offered industrial order, wage and other outcomes that were, generally, consistent with economic stability, and some measure of social equity. Above all, it absolved governments of responsibility in an area of great potential political difficulty. As a result, governments, whatever their ideology, were predisposed to support the arbitration system and the policies of its arbitral tribunals. But governments also appreciated the coercive capacity of the system in periods of industrial crisis, especially in 1912–13 and 1951.

There have been exceptions to this general pattern of government support. In bad times, governments of the right have opposed the system, and in particular the court's policies, and have responded to pressure from their electoral coalition to restrict the influence of the system and to expose industrial relations to market forces. Government support for the system declined considerably from the 1980s onwards. The system had operated as the labour market and social policy companion to a general structure of economic protection in which domestic producers were able to pass wage costs on to consumers without great difficulty. So long as economic protection endured, so, too, did support for arbitration from governments and employers producing for the domestic economy. Conversely, farmers and other employers producing for the international market tended to oppose the system as a key mechanism in transferring surplus generated by exporters in the international market to employers and workers in the domestic sector (Walsh and Fougere, 1987). As economic protection was dismantled, and competitive pressures grew throughout the economy, Labour and National Governments moved to dismantle the arbitration system.

The Department of Labour, a third state structure involved in industrial relations, was generally inclined towards the maintenance of the arbitration system. Departmental officials became committed to the system, not just as a source of jobs for its staff and as a major component of its jurisdiction, but as a means of ensuring a balance between efficiency and equity concerns and delivering industrial stability. The department consistently pointed out to governments the longer-term economic and political risks of jettisoning the system for temporary advantage or to placate those clamouring for the use of sanctions as revenge for unlawful industrial action. Until the 1990s, successive governments heeded this advice; the National Government, elected in 1990, did not (Walsh and Ryan, 1993).

Trade unions have been divided in their attitudes towards the arbitration system, although it provided them with a remarkable range of protections. It granted registered unions monopoly coverage rights, thus protecting them against potential rivals; it obliged employers to negotiate with registered unions in conciliation councils and provided compulsory arbitration by state tribunals in the event of unsuccessful negotiations; the state ensured the application of resulting awards to all workers in the occupation or industry concerned ('blanket coverage') and saw that awards were enforced on all employers. From 1936 the state also guaranteed the membership, and thus the revenues, for registered unions. In exchange, unions accepted extensive restrictions upon their structure and activities. They were prohibited from extending their coverage beyond the occupation or industry originally designated, without the approval of the Court of Arbitration, which was rarely forthcoming; national unions were prohibited until 1936; unions were subject to legislative limitations upon the membership fees they could charge; they were confined to representing their members on 'industrial matters', which were themselves defined narrowly by the court; and, until 1964, unions were prohibited from undertaking any educational or welfare activities for their members.

Many unions were formed precisely to take advantage of the statutory protections offered by the legislation (Holt, 1986). These unions became dependent clients of the arbitration system, lacking effective organisational capacity of their own. They remained small regional organisations, of limited financial resources, restricted to representing their members on a narrow range of issues within the confines permitted by the procedures of conciliation and arbitration. These unions, typically craft and occupational in their coverage, became strong supporters of the arbitration system. By contrast, industrial unions favoured a bargaining system that would allow them to exploit their own organisational capacity, their strategic market position, and the solidarity of their members. The division between the supporters and opponents of arbitration and bargaining bedevilled the trade union movement throughout the twentieth century. By dividing, and therefore weakening, the union movement, arbitration operated effectively as a state strategy of control in industrial relations.

Employers were forced to form organisations to represent their industrial interests and to work within the structure of the arbitration system. If employers tried to operate outside it, workers could secure a binding award from the court. Employers, however, soon came to appreciate the benefits of industrial order offered by the system, and the removal of wages from competition, and, except where labour market conditions were firmly in their favour, they generally supported the system, except during the Depression of the 1930s. During the 1960s and 1970s, they called repeatedly for the restoration of the system and observance of its rules and procedures. But their attitudes changed again in the 1980s, when labour market conditions were decisively against unions and workers. Employers became opponents of the arbitration system and pressed successfully for the ECA.

The Cycles of Arbitration

Rise and fall, 1894–1968

Union and employer attitudes towards the arbitration system in this period were shaped by different groups' varying assessments of how well they would have fared in a more market-oriented system. The pro-arbitration craft and occupational unions gave only lukewarm support to the industrial unions in their challenge to the system in 1912–13 (Olssen, 1988), and the two remained divided both ideologically and organisationally. Employers remained opposed to arbitration from its introduction until the first great confrontation over the system in 1912–13. Faced with the prospect of bargaining directly with strong unions supported by a loyal and militant membership, employers discovered previously unsuspected merits in the system, and sought shelter in the stability and order it could provide. Although farmers resented the system's protections for unions, they also found merit in its capacity to control rebellious unions in 1912–13, and became strong supporters. Government support for the arbitration system lasted as long as employers and farmers formed a powerful coalition in its support. By the late 1920s, however, employers and farmers were pressing for the government to eliminate compulsory arbitration, which it did in 1932, to allow them to take advantage of the market factors in their favour.

As in the 1890s, a political strategy was the salvation of the pro-arbitration unions. They worked to elect the first Labour Government and persuaded it, over the opposition of the industrial unions, to restore compulsory arbitration and to introduce compulsory union membership. Labour also put enormous pressure upon the warring factions of the union movement to join together in the new Federation of Labour (FOL). The timing of the FOL's formation was crucial to its long-term role. Newly established pro-arbitration unions combined with old to form a dominant alliance within the FOL whose unwavering support for arbitration shaped the direction of the union movement for the next three decades or more. After the Second World War, when the call came again from the industrial unions, this time led by the watersiders, to abolish arbitration, the pro-arbitration majority were able to isolate the insurgents. The latter left the FOL and formed the Trade Union Congress (TUC). They were destroyed in 1951, as the Red Federation of Labour had been forty years earlier, in a great confrontation with the state, in which the FOL stood aside and left the industrial unions to their fate (Bassett, 1972). Once again, state policies created a supportive coalition among the union movement. The state built the system in such a way as to vest union interests in its survival.

During the 1960s, arbitration was undermined, not by a direct industrial or political challenge, but by the gradual unfolding of events embedded, on the one hand in wider economic developments, and, on the other hand, in the operation of the system itself. Labour scarcity, changing patterns of industrialisation, new workplace technologies, and managerial preference for negotiating their own agreements all contributed to the development of a network of direct bargaining outside the arbitration system. This set wages and conditions of employment superior to those in the award that would otherwise have applied. Although these agreements still covered only a minority of workplaces and workers, they jeopardised the jurisdiction of the arbitration system, while the advances made in direct bargaining became targets for unions to aim at in award negotiations (Walsh, 1984).

For much of the 1960s, the government came under pressure from employers and farmers, angry at rising levels of industrial conflict, who argued that the only way for the government to restore the arbitration system was to prosecute unlawful strikers. The National Government resisted this pressure, although it allowed itself to become a direct participant in trying to settle industrial disputes. It did put an end to state-enforced compulsory union membership but continued to allow unions and employers to agree to include a compulsory membership clause in their awards and agreements and virtually all did so. The government was swayed by advice from the Department of Labour which continued to support the system but conceded the need for change. Officials saw second-tier bargaining as offering a degree of much needed flexibility, while also maintaining a minimum set of wages and conditions through awards. They opposed prosecuting strikers as ineffective in the short term and, in the long term, counter-productive. National continued to accept this advice that any major change to the arbitration system was unnecessary and unwise. Suitably amended to take account of specific labour market conditions, the system could continue to fulfil its historical mission of equity and stability. From 1968, that position became steadily less defensible.

Searching for new solutions, 1968–84

The pressures on the Arbitration Court's role came to a head in 1968 when the court, guided by its obligation to have regard to economic stability, refused to award a general wage order. The nil order shattered what faith the unions still had in the court and the arbitration system. To forestall impending industrial chaos, the FOL and the Employers' Federation made a joint application to the court, where the worker and employer representatives joined forces to outvote the judge of the court, and issue a 5 per cent wage increase. The Minister of Finance, Robert Muldoon, dubbed this 'the unholy alliance' (Walsh, 1994). But the unholy alliance could not endure. The loss of the court's authority meant that there was no institutional mechanism to control the wage-fixing process, and in particular to coordinate the structure of occupational wage differentials. Instead, this was left to market power and organisational capacity, which amounted to a recipe for disorder between 1968 and 1971. Working days lost rose to levels unprecedented since 1951, as one relativity-based claim succeeded another. Beginning in 1971, successive governments controlled wage-fixing by statutory incomes policies, but also sought to recreate the court in the guise of a series of tribunals, charged with the responsibility of managing those policies (Boston, 1984; Walsh, 1984). In 1977 the National Government lifted its controls over wage bargaining, but with the proviso that it retained the right to intervene in particular wage settlements it considered too high. The Arbitration Court did not recover its former wage-fixing role, but the occupational wage relativities it had entrenched retained their predominance. Over the next few years, the first main award settled in each wage round set the pattern, with little variation for subsequent settlements. For the government, it became vital to influence the lead settlement, and negotiations were accompanied by anxious efforts to achieve this, including threats that the government would invoke its claimed power to nullify particular wage settlements it considered too high. This created an atmosphere of uncertainty and unpredictability, culminating in major conflicts, including a general strike, between the unions and the government during 1979–80 (Roper, 1992). It was evident that this approach provided no lasting policy solution and, in 1980, the National Government agreed to tripartite discussions to seek a consensus on industrial relations reform. But, apprehensive about the inflationary impact of wage settlements under the existing regime, and encouraged by rising unemployment, in June 1982 it imposed a wage and price freeze that lasted until 1984.

Deregulating industrial relations, 1984–92

Between 1984 and 1990, Labour implemented a radical program of economic deregulation. But the legacy of traditional union-party links meant that Labour did not deregulate the labour market to the same extent as other markets (Walsh, 1989). Labour's approach to industrial relations sought to balance efficiency and equity concerns. Efficiency concerns drove its re-structuring of state sector industrial relations, including corporatisation and privatisation (Walsh, 1991b; Walsh and Wetzel, 1993). Efficiency concerns were also paramount in Labour's most important policy change in the private sector—the abolition of compulsory arbitration in 1984. Labour expected that voluntary arbitration would lead to the collapse of the large occupational awards and threaten the viability of the arbitrationist unions. This would lead to different bargaining structures—industry awards or, in larger companies, enterprise agreements—with conditions of employment tailored to the specific needs of the bargaining parties. Efficiency concerns were also decisive in the inclusion, in the Labour Relations Act 1987, of a provision for unions to cite individual companies out of award coverage and negotiate separate enterprise agreements with them. It was also expected that unions would come under pressure from members in larger and more profitable firms to do this, meaning that awards would gradually become residual documents covering the industrially weaker and economically depressed sectors of the economy. Labour's equity concerns, however, led it to retain union registration, and thus monopoly membership and bargaining rights, blanket award coverage, provision for compulsory union membership, and compulsory arbitration in the Labour Court for disputes of rights and personal grievances.

Labour looked for the development of unions that were larger, better resourced, more democratic and membership-driven, more innovative, and more self-reliant. The most important of these measures were the introduction of paid educational leave and the creation of the Trade Union Educational Authority (TUEA) and the introduction of a minimum membership requirement of 1000 for registered unions. This was designed to rationalise union structures and also to forestall the development of enterprise unionism. Accompanying these measures was a major change in the role of the state in industrial disputes. The government changed from being almost the mediator of first resort to being almost completely uninvolved in settling even major disputes in sensitive public services.

Employer organisations hoped that these changes were the possible precursor of a more decisive shift to a more decentralised bargaining structure. They were, therefore, alarmed by Labour's attempts to negotiate a corporatist arrangement with the CTU. Inspired by the model of the Australian Accord, the Compact and then the Growth Agreement offered a return to a more centralised wage bargaining system in which unions exchanged uniform and restrained wage settlements for policy influence in other areas. Employers refused to have anything to do with the Compact, which was predictably unsuccessful, and were not invited to participate in the Growth Agreement, although they benefited from the low wage path it established (Harvey, 1992). Enterprise bargaining in the private sector declined precipitously under Labour and the award system was greatly strengthened. This was unexpected and unintended. Unions by and large chose not to negotiate separate agreements with firms; instead, they pulled their members back into award coverage in order to protect their awards. This became a major catalyst for employer pressure for more radical policy change to encourage new bargaining structures. Other state policies, both those of the Labour Government and those of its industrial relations agencies, mediators, and the Labour Court, fuelled the pressure for change. Labour Court decisions on personal grievances, especially those that widened employment security, angered key business groups.

The policy debate widened to fundamental questions about the role of the state in industrial relations. For the first time since 1894, whether to retain what remained of the arbitration system, including the Labour Court itself, was an active policy issue. The new debate was grounded in significant structural changes in the economy, but it took place in a framework set by state policies. The abolition of compulsory arbitration turned attention to the continuation of the other basic features of the arbitration system. Labour's non-interventionist posture towards disputes helped to create the sense that important aspects of the employment relationship could operate independently of the state. Also, apparent government efforts to recentralise aspects of the wage-fixing system just as decentralising trends were emerging, encouraged business to redouble its efforts to achieve radical change.

The ECA: the Bargaining Model Ascendant

These efforts met with success following the election of the National Government in 1990 and the enactment of the ECA (Anderson, 1991;

Boxall, 1991; Hince and Vranken, 1991; Walsh, 1992). The act signalled the ascendancy of the bargaining model over arbitration. It stripped away what remained of the arbitration system in the determination of representation and bargaining rights and the negotiation of employment conditions. The system of trade union registration, monopoly membership and bargaining rights for registered unions, blanket award coverage, and the right to negotiate compulsory union membership were all eliminated. The act separated union membership from representation. Workers were free to decide who, if anyone, would negotiate on their behalf and unions must seek individual bargaining authorisation from their members. Employers could veto who had access to the workplace to seek representation authority but, once this authority was given, the authorised representative could have access at any reasonable time to discuss contract negotiations. The focus of the new system moved from the collective to the individual and from multiemployer awards and agreements to enterprise bargaining. The act encouraged the latter by prohibiting any industrial action to force an employer to become a joint party to a collective contract.

The act provided for two forms of employment contract—collective and individual. When a collective contract expires, employees previously covered by it are deemed to be employed on an individual contract, with the same conditions as the expired collective contract. The act permits strikes and lockouts, but only in support of the negotiation of a new or an expired collective contract. Any form of industrial action while a collective contract is in force is unlawful and no industrial action may be taken in connection with an individual employment contract or as noted above in pursuit of a multiemployer contract. The act sets more stringent conditions as a justification for intervention by the Employment Court to set aside any terms of an employment contract than for other types of contracts (Hughes, 1991, pp. 181–2). In accepting the argument in favour of a contractual basis to employment relationships, the fourth National Government deliberately decided to exclude important remedies for exploitation available to parties to other contracts.

The radical achievement of the ECA was to overturn a system of collective representation and negotiation that had endured for almost a century. The state, however, remained decisively involved in the process of contract enforcement, in the mediation and arbitration of disputes and personal grievances. Indeed, the jurisdiction of the specialist state industrial relations agencies was enormously expanded by the fourth National Government. Under the Labour Relations Act, the Labour Court's jurisdiction included only workers covered by registered awards and collective agreements—about

60 per cent of the workforce. But under the ECA, the jurisdiction of the newly established Employment Tribunal (which replaced the Mediation Service) and Employment Court was extended to all employment contracts, including individual contracts. All employment contracts must contain effective procedures to settle personal grievances and disputes, culminating, if necessary, in arbitration by the Employment Tribunal or the Employment Court. For the first time, all employees in New Zealand were to have access to compulsory state arbitration to resolve any dispute that arose in connection with their employment relationship. By any standard, this was a remarkable extension of the role of the state in industrial relations.

The National Government's response to concerns about the danger of exploitation under the act was to provide a 'minimum code of employment'— a range of minimum employment conditions enjoyed by all employees delivered through other legislation (Brosnan and Rea, 1991). No employment contract could provide conditions inferior to these, although it was, of course, possible to improve on them.

How should this radical realignment in the state's industrial relations strategy be assessed? Space does not permit a detailed evaluation of the shift from an arbitration to a bargaining model, but it is possible to make some general observations about its most important consequences and their significance. Although it is not easy to disentangle the social and economic effects of the ECA itself from the impact of other policies, it is possible to identify the consequences for industrial relations institutions and procedures. The most important of these has been a greatly diminished role for trade unions and collective bargaining. In that respect, the chief objectives of the ECA were met. Trade union membership fell precipitously. Union membership was 41.5 per cent of the labour force at the time of the act's introduction. By December 1995, it had fallen to 21.7 per cent (Crawford, Harbridge, and Hince, 1996, p. 2).

The only good news for unions was that they still dominated the collective bargaining arena. Although some expected that the act would lead to the emergence of rival bargaining agents, in 1996 unions still represented the vast majority of workers covered by collective contracts (Department of Labour, 1996, p. 1). Unions were, however, unable to maintain the previous high levels of collective bargaining. Collective contracts, unlike awards, are not published and, in the absence of a comprehensive workplace survey, it is difficult to be precise about the level of collective bargaining coverage. Harbridge concluded, however, that collective bargaining coverage fell from 49 per cent of the total employed workforce in 1990 to 29 per cent in 1993 (Harbridge, 1994, p. 42). The major change to collective bargaining was the abandonment of the multiemployer bargaining that typified the arbitration system for almost a century. In the Department of Labour's data base, 98 per cent of contracts are single-employer contracts (Department of Labour, 1996, p. 1).

Unions struggle in the environment created by the ECA. They negotiate many times more contracts on behalf of fewer members and with fewer resources. And they do so, in many cases, with employers who are emboldened by the new legislative regime and by the depressed labour market of the mid-1990s to seek harsh changes to employment conditions. Some unions have adopted new organising models that give them some prospect of adapting successfully (Oxenbridge, 1996). Others failed completely, most notably the Communication and Energy Workers' Union, which collapsed and was dissolved. Industrial activity, one barometer of union vitality, fell substantially from its level during the 1970s and 1980s, although it should be noted that those years saw unprecedented levels of industrial conflict in New Zealand as all parties struggled to adapt to the breakdown of the arbitration system. The levels of industrial conflict for 1991–94 were on a par with those for the 1952–69 period (Deeks et al., 1994, p. 374; Statistics New Zealand, 1996, p. 38).

A major policy objective of the ECA was a more efficient and more flexible labour market. The evidence, up to the mid-1990s, suggested mixed outcomes. Productivity fell during the 1990s from an average of 2.2 per cent growth per annum between 1984 and 1990 to 0.4 per cent growth per annum from 1990 to 1994 (Rasmussen et al., 1995). It is clear that, under the act, traditional wage relativities were broken and there was much wider dispersion of wage settlements (Harbridge, 1994, pp. 14–15). There was no doubt that labour market flexibility, interpreted as downward pressure on wages and living standards, had already grown in the 1980s. Wage increases negotiated in awards and agreements under the Labour Relations Act 1987 had already fallen behind the rate of price increases, and this continued after 1991 (Harbridge, 1994, pp. 11–12). Similarly, real disposable income for all groups fell substantially following the election of the fourth Labour Government in 1984 (Income Distribution Group, 1990). Real wages continued to fall during the 1990s while income inequality and absolute poverty levels rose (Rowntree Foundation, 1995; Stephens et al., 1995; Chapter 5).

The impact of the ECA on women is difficult to assess. Hammond and Harbridge (1993) argue that women have fared worse than men, but Ryan, on the basis of her analysis of the 1993 employee survey, concluded that gender had been a less important explanatory factor than location in the labour market (Ryan, 1994, p. 21; see also Chapter 8). She placed more weight upon labour force casualisation than on gender. There has not been any assessment of the effect of the act itself on Maori and Pacific Islanders, but, as expected, their poverty levels remain much higher than those of Pakeha (Stephens, Waldegrave, and Frater, 1995). There was much emphasis, before the ECA, on the need to eliminate a range of 'restrictive practices' but there have not been major changes in collective contracts with regard to standard hours and days of work or the existence of penal and overtime rates of pay (Harbridge, 1994, pp. 27–32). A December 1995 survey by the New Zealand Institute for Economic Research did find, however, that 85 per cent of employers had reduced or frozen overtime rates since 1991 and 83 per cent had reduced or frozen penal rates (New Zealand Institute for Economic Research, 1995).

One of the most contentious areas since 1991 has been the role of the specialist industrial relations institutions. The Business Roundtable and the Employers' Federation have called for the abolition of the Employment Court. In their view, the court, like its predecessor, the Labour Court, has given workers an unreasonable degree of job protection. They claim that the court has set 'almost impossible standards' for employers to meet in its requirements for procedural fairness, that compensation levels are too high, and that the court is too quick to reinstate sacked workers (Kerr, 1993a and 1993b). These claims are an extraordinary distortion. Studies of the Labour Court show that it established ordinary standards of natural justice, it very infrequently reinstated a sacked worker, its compensation levels for a wrongly sacked worker were very low (average $7500), and in only about half the cases where it found the dismissal unjustified did it order reimbursement (Boon, 1992a and 1992b; Thomson, 1992). Nonetheless, it is true that both the Labour and Employment Courts refused to condone any shift towards making the dismissal and replacement of workers easier in a depressed labour market and insisted that employers meet both procedural and substantive standards for dismissal. Equally, in cases dealing with representation and negotiation rights, after an initial series of decisions that placed major obstacles in the way of unions, the Employment Court has, since 1991, issued a number of decisions that provided some measure of support for effective union organisation and activity (Harbridge and Kiely, 1995). The government's intent in the ECA was clearly to deprive trade unions of an effective basis for organisation. The Employment Court's view appeared to be that the wording of the act did not achieve that. This points, again, to the potential capacity for differences between key state structures in industrial relations.

Conclusion

The strength and durability of the arbitration system lay in its ability to serve the interests of different governments for a remarkably long period. The system was always subject to pressures for change or even abolition. But it showed its resilience and its capacity to serve the interests of key constituents. Its rules and procedures empowered some and weakened others, and, by and large, those it empowered, including governments, were able to secure its continued existence, despite ever present opposition. Other than in the highly depressed labour market conditions of the 1930s, governments of whatever ideological disposition or electoral coalition had always seen it as in their interests to maintain statutory regulation of the bargaining process. The justification for this had always been that it contributed to industrial stability and social equity and was not inconsistent with economic efficiency. The state's commitment to this position weakened during the fourth Labour Government (1984–90); it was abandoned by the fourth National Government (1990–96). Mass unemployment would ensure industrial stability more expeditiously than statutory regulation of representation and negotiation while social equity was not a government policy objective (Boston, 1992a; Stephens, 1992). The state's new industrial relations strategy was grounded in the wider policy mix of economic deregulation and welfare state deconstruction. The arbitration system had been, equally, an instrument of social and economic policy. It had served social equity goals as well as playing its part in the management of a system of economic protection. A radical redirection of social and economic policy necessitated corresponding changes in wage-fixing and industrial relations.

Above all, the government had decided that retention of the existing system was incompatible with the pursuit of labour market flexibility and international competitiveness as the keys to economic growth. The government's mind was closed to the active debate about the degree of labour market flexibility in New Zealand (New Zealand Planning Council, 1986; Savage, 1989; McAndrew and Hursthouse, 1991; Harbridge, 1990). This debate tended to conclude that the New Zealand labour market was more flexible than in many similar OECD countries, and much more so than many critics conceded. National, however, accepted the analysis of the Business Roundtable and the Employers' Federation that statutory regulation of contract negotiation was a major impediment to economic efficiency. But National resisted heavy pressure from the Roundtable and Treasury to eliminate the role of state agencies in the mediation and arbitration of disputes and personal grievances. The institutional key to this was the Department of Labour, whose traditional analysis of the need for the state to meet equity concerns by providing accessible arbitral institutions, again carried the day (Walsh and Ryan, 1993). National was motivated by a basic notion of fairness and a fear that a completely unregulated labour market would lead to unrestrained exploitation. It could not but be anxious about the electoral implications of the issue.

The state's new industrial relations strategy reflects important changes in the structure and operation of the economy and corresponding shifts in economic and political power. Politically, the ECA confirmed the weakness of the union movement and the left generally, and it consolidates that weakness for the future. The ascendancy of the bargaining model grew out of the increasing diversity of the newly deregulated economy and the alleged inadequacies of the uniform labour market fix applied by the arbitration system. This emphasis on diversity of circumstance and flexibility of response reflects a shift from the classic values of arbitration to those of bargaining. The uniformity of occupational awards gives way to the diversity of enterprise agreements; the emphasis on stability and harmony yields to an acceptance that market power will settle matters; the continuity of long-established wage relativities is replaced by decisions reflecting labour market advantage, enterprise needs, and organisational capacity; and arbitration's concern for social equity is subordinated to a focus on the efficient operation of particular firms. Since the 1890s, the New Zealand state had accepted a considerable measure of responsibility for what happened to its citizens in their employment relationship; the 1990s saw a significant retreat from that position. By any standard, this was a radical shift in the state's industrial relations strategy and in the state's relationship with civil society and its citizens.

---

1 For a Marxist view of this, see Chapter 7.

2 This chapter focuses on the private sector industrial relations system. Space does not permit consideration of the state sector system, which, until 1988, operated according to different rules and with different institutions. Much of the analysis here is, however, broadly applicable to the state sector system (Walsh, 1991).

3 It also underpinned the 'male wage earners' welfare state' (see Chapter 14).

Guide to Readings

The classic study of the initial development of the state's industrial relations role is Holt (1986). A useful complement to Holt's book are the papers from the Labour History symposium published in the *New Zealand Journal of Industrial Relations*

(1987), where a number of labour historians review Holt's analysis. Castles (1985) argues that both countries constructed a wage-earners' welfare state in which the arbitration system served as a substitute for the development of a European or Scandinavian welfare state. Comparative analysis of Australia and New Zealand is beginning to grow, and a collection edited by Bray and Howarth (1993) examines the impact of the Labour governments of the 1980s on industrial relations in both countries. Brosnan, Smith, and Walsh (1990) offer a useful complement to the account presented here, which focuses more on the electoral and bureaucratic dimensions of the role of the state. Boston (1984) offers a comprehensive account of the decade of direct state intervention in the wage-fixing process. Harvey (1992) assesses the short-lived re-emergence of incomes policies in the late-1980s.

There have been many attempts to analyse the changes wrought by the fourth Labour Government. Deeks (1990) remains the most thoughtful assessment of the 1980s. The ECA has spawned a wealth of studies, many of which are included in the references to this chapter. The best continuing source is the *New Zealand Journal of Industrial Relations*. A number of contributors assess the early impact of the ECA in Harbridge (ed.) (1993a). Harbridge and Hince have continued to document the impact of the act on collective bargaining and union membership and their papers appear regularly in the *New Zealand Journal of Industrial Relations* or are available in working paper form from the Industrial Relations Centre at Victoria University of Wellington. Wilson and Enright (1994) offer an interesting assessment of equity issues. The state's role as employer poses a distinctive set of issues which are not analysed in the chapter in the present volume. The best overall assessments are in Boston et al. (eds) (1991) and Boston et al. (1996).

CHAPTER ELEVEN

STATE AND EDUCATION ACROSS HALF A CENTURY

JOHN FREEMAN-MOIR

Education is a recurring focal point for modern hopes and fears. This follows from the central role played by education in the social reproduction of capitalist democracies. Maintaining the myriad and interwoven cycles of investment, management, production, and consumption characteristic of capitalist society, not to mention class domination, requires a vast range of relevant skills, attitudes, and appropriate motivations. Collectively, these human characteristics are called labour power or the capacity to make, do, and be useful. Because the principal objective of capitalism is to make profit and expand investment under conditions of market-imposed competition, it is relatively easy to understand why the formation of labour power is organised, and constantly reorganised, in terms of the demands of the system. Although much of the work in capitalist society requires only low levels of training, irrespective of the fact that educational apologists for capitalism frequently exaggerate the required levels of skill, nevertheless, education cannot be left to chance or tradition.

Ever restless, modern capitalism constantly changes and uproots the conditions of social life. This dynamic is reflected more or less permanently in concerns about the appropriateness of educational objectives, curricula, and teaching methods. Given the fact that education is a fundamental social force, it is also, on occasions, mistakenly thought to be the cause and the remedy of social problems, even of the prolonged crisis of profitability that began in the early 1970s. The central argument of this chapter is that New Zealand education corresponds to the political economy of capitalist society.

Education and State Within Capitalist Limits

It is useful to begin by distinguishing three theoretical perspectives on the role that educational institutions play within capitalist society. For most of the period covered by this chapter, social democracy or liberal educational theory has been dominant. This approach emphasises the capacity of the state to democratise society and, specifically, to make education an avenue for equal opportunity in life. All this is to be achieved by free access to publicly funded schools. Despite its undoubted idealism, and its hard-won historical roots in the struggles of the labour movement, the social democratic position on education and society has proved vulnerable to capitalist attack. This is because social democracy operated within the logic of the capitalist economy. For two decades after the Second World War capitalism could afford to support social democracy, and it did so on the basis of an accord that guaranteed productivity, profits, and social spending on health, education, and welfare.

From about the mid-1980s, New Right or neoliberal theory has informed the greater part of educational thinking, especially as it has been taken up in relation to policy development. Neoliberal theory argues that education is best understood in terms of market relations. This means that education needs to be freed from the inefficiencies of state intervention. Schooling, in this theory, is concerned with preparing individuals for an internationally competitive economic world.

The third, or Marxian, perspective on educational theory, while supporting the view that education should be a means of democratic opportunity in society, emphasises the state's failure to achieve equality, because it is bounded and shaped by the demands of the capitalist economy. This chapter relies on this insight to analyse the meaning of education.

Educationally, the state is that set of more or less permanent relationships centred on sustaining the conditions of capitalist production, specifically as these conditions relate to the development and delivery of labour power into the labour market. In this view, it is important to draw a distinction between day-to-day government and the state. Political parties compete for the favours of electors and particular governments come and go. By focusing on the particularities of government or regime, most contemporary policy analysis simply misses or underestimates the limits imposed on education by a hierarchical, undemocratic, class-dominated state. Furthermore, it is uncritically supposed that, if social democrats are elected to government, then capitalism with a human face will evolve. History runs against this proposition. Governments lie in the shadow of the state, and the state, in turn, lies in the shadow of capitalist imperative.

No other educational theory has registered so firmly the impossibility of realising the goals of equality and liberation within a capitalist order, as has the theory of reproductive correspondence. And this is especially so for an audience raised on the democratic potential of liberal education. The theory was originally developed by Bowles and Gintis (1976), who argued that 'The educational system, basically, neither adds to nor subtracts from the degree of inequality and repression originating in the economic sphere. Rather, it reproduces and legitimates a preexisting pattern in the process of training and stratifying the work force' (p. 275). The main point of the correspondence thesis is that, over the long term, education is a social force that tends to harmonise with the requirements of economic activity. This thesis does not require, for its scientific integrity, that there be a seamlessly fitting structural correspondence at every point. The key word is 'tend'. It is unnecessary to treat the correspondence theory as requiring a perfect structural integration of education and the social relations of production.

Correspondence theory is, then, to be understood as a relationship of demonstrable causation over time, a context in which to understand the meaning of education. What social democratic or liberal critics typically dismissed as a 'crude piece of Marxist theory' was, instead, a bold attempt to establish an explanatory framework for understanding the causes and effects operating in the domain of capitalist education. As such, the correspondence theory makes intelligible the effects of a wide range of causal events as well as the counter-tendencies and contradictions that are more or less permanently in evidence. This theory attempts to explain education by setting it within an appropriate materialist framework, in a way more recently elaborated, for example, by Fisk (1989, Part One).

Countering the theory of correspondence is a version of liberal pluralism, sometimes known as the theory of relative autonomy. This argues that the state and education can, given appropriate policies and socially democratic administrations, be relatively free from capitalist domination. If the main point of those who adopt this thesis is that correspondence is not a one-to-one functional relation between education and the organisation of production, then this view is perfectly consistent with a materialist conception of history. This is not, however, the principal reason behind the apparent attractiveness of the relative autonomy thesis. The theory's main thrust is effectively to free educational theory from the explanatory strictures of an historical materialist framework. Relative autonomy was attractive to liberal educational theorists because it provided a way to insulate the core of the liberal program, while giving some credence to a powerful critique that linked education to the limiting demands of capitalist production. Relative autonomy, then, effectively protects the liberal theory of education from the full critical implications of the correspondence thesis.

In essence, the correspondence theory answers the objective requirement that capitalism be transformed. It does so by demonstrating the limits of capitalism in relation to demands for equality of opportunity, the democratic control of production, and the demise of social hierarchies. Bowles and Gintis draw this conclusion in the last chapter of *Schooling in Capitalist America*, where they discuss the possibility that a participatory socialist democracy could solve the problems posed by the relationship between education and capitalism. Because the theory of correspondence identifies the outer limits of capitalist education it poses the future unambiguously as an option. Bowles spells this out in a later essay: 'To discuss the egalitarian or growth functions of education . . . in the absence of rebellion against the capitalist order is worse than ideal speculation. It is to offer a false promise, an ideological palliative which seeks to buy time for capitalism' (cited in Sharp, 1988, p. 206).

Left liberals and social democrats have seldom had more than a heavily qualified interest in moving beyond the limits of capitalist correspondence. As the mainstream of recent educational theory, liberalism has established the parameters for much of the ensuing academic and political debate. Correspondence theory claims that overall theoretical explanation is necessary if we are to understand education as a process of capitalist reproduction. On the other hand, the logic of relative autonomy-type theories is more conducive to forms of social and political explanation that support fragmentation. Pulling back from capitalism as the framework of explanation, encourages forms of institutional and policy analysis that are, for instance, state-centred (that is, the state understood as government/regime) and essentially unlocated structurally in relation to the power sources that define the limits of capitalist society. The capitalist nature of education, the state, work, technology, and so on, becomes steadily more obscured by dominant approaches to policy analysis and educational theory.

Without a clear view of capitalism, it is impossible to see alternatives other than those that fit within the ambit of capitalist political economy. During a period of recession, conservative neoliberal state policy has weakened the idea of challenging capitalism. Moving beyond it now seems illusory to many. Irrespective of what is practically possible, however, the limits imposed by capitalism are ever present. This means that the problem of what to do is made more difficult but not irrelevant, as postmodernists, among others, seem to imagine.

Education as Social Freedom and Economic Engagement

In response to campaigns of class struggle for welfare, equality, civil rights, and decent working conditions, education under democratic capitalism has taken on a dual meaning for its citizens. On the one hand, education is linked to social freedom; on the other hand, it has come to mean and promise economic engagement. New Zealand is no exception to this observation. After the election of the first Labour Government in 1935, education came increasingly to be regarded as a key feature of a state concerned with the welfare of all its citizens. Freedom and engagement were understood in a particular way that has already been referred to as 'the liberal theory of education'. After the election of the fourth Labour Government in 1905, education came increasingly to be regarded as a key feature of a state principally concerned with reconfiguring the economy. Again, freedom and engagement were at the heart of the matter but, in response to new demands from capital, their relative alignment was given a different ideological spin. Universal freedoms and access to social goods began to give away to freedom defined as individual responsibility and full care for those who could pay. Economic engagement under social democracy was defined as 'a fair day's work for a fair day's pay' and, more recently, as 'equal pay for work of equal value'. Since 1984, the economic engagement of citizens has largely been stripped of any potential for collective force, and this tendency was decisively reinforced in 1991 with the introduction of the Employment Contracts Act (ECA). This act resulted in a highly variable situation where fairness across levels of pay and conditions of work is no longer considered relevant by employers and the government.

For most educationists and social scientists, the 'golden age' of the welfare state, up to the 1970s, and the subsequent restructuring of the welfare state since 1984, are radically discontinuous periods; hence such phrases as 'leap into the dark', 'the New Right revolution', 'rolling back the state, 'the retreat of the state', and 'new territory'. Much has changed in daily life but this in no way contradicts this chapter's claim that the state displays certain crucial functions that are continuous across long periods of time. At a fundamental level, looking at New Zealand education in a way that emphasises discontinuity is one-sided because it too casually glosses over the essential connections between capitalism and education, across the long duration of capitalist development. The same is true for the development of welfare policy in general (see Chapter 13).

These connections centre on supplying the economy with labour power that is adequately trained and disciplined in relation to skill, attitude, and motivation. This means attending to the problem of how relevant the education system is to the requirements of the economy in such matters as skill, attitude, openness to change, technological development, economic competition and the degree of job-specific ability versus flexibility, mobility, and the ability to work in a team. During the expansionary period of the long boom (1945–73), solutions to these issues were found, while at the same time providing a significant degree of social democratic advance for the great mass of people through educational opportunity. During a period of uncertain profitability and recession, since the mid-1970s, the easier solutions of the social democratic era could not so easily be sustained. The capitalist system required new solutions. Since 1984 one major thrust of policy has been a concerted attack on what were formerly taken to be the educational opportunities funded by the welfare state.

Irrespective of whether we are speaking of a period of expansion or of recession, the state must continue to act as if it were finding an answer to this question: 'how can students be fitted into capitalist work structures and the wider political economy?' The balance of class forces can shift and, since the late 1970s, it has moved quite decisively against the working class. But the emphasis in this chapter on continuity of connection over discontinuity reminds us that the wider imperative of capitalist investment, production, and distribution provides the framework within which particular educational solutions are worked out. Naturally enough, the particularities of educational opportunity and outcome can feel quite discontinuous, especially to those who have lived in New Zealand for four or five decades.

The duration pointed to above is best understood as a long wave of capitalist expansion and recession, lasting about fifty years (Mandel, 1995). Instead of making capitalist development the appropriate framework of analysis, what happens in the educational world is portrayed as the outcome of conflicts and struggles solely within the state itself; for example, as conflicts between Treasury and teachers, or teachers and parents, or the government and parents. From this angle, the state is described as a 'site of struggle'. To be precise, the traumas of the state are the reverberations of difficulties posed by trying to sustain profitability in a society which, historically, has also extended educational and health opportunities to the population as a whole. That being said, there is no doubt that there have been, and are, many struggles within the state, many of which remain unresolved.

There is now an extensive literature that discusses administrative restructuring and school reform (see, for example, Dale, 1994; Grace, 1990; Codd, Harker, and Nash, 1990; Gordon and Codd, 1991). Little is to be gained from adding to this literature so the remainder of this chapter will confine itself to assessing the overall meaning of educational freedom and engagement, and showing how this might be understood within the socioeconomic context of capitalist development.

Education and State in New Zealand Across Sixty Years

Contrary to prevailing views in contemporary social theory, this chapter argues that it is the social scientist's task to analyse the essential structures of capitalism and to show how these relate to historical development and education. Only after this fundamental analysis is successfully completed can sense be made of the day-to-day detail that confronts the individual. Without a framework of explanation, the significance and causal efficacy of the details are lost. The structure and framework of capitalist development gives point to particular causes in the social life of education.

The postwar generation increasingly acted on the belief that it had access to opportunities that were denied to its parents. The obstacles for the previous generation were obvious enough: a deep economic recession from the late 1920s, followed by fascism and a Second World War that was even more encompassing than the First. Scrounging for work and fighting a war were the two main courses that had been offered to postwar parents in what they called, ironically enough, 'the university of life'. This brutal socialisation of attitude and outlook made them forever cautious, even those who were to achieve considerable material success. Life was uncertain but peace, paid work, education for the children, health care, the house, the garden, the car, and other consumer items as they came along, were all the stuff of which their dreams were made.

The long boom and educational reform
It was the evident reform of capitalism that the postwar parents came to enjoy and that provided the context of socialisation for their children, who, at the end of the century, are the parents of young adults; this new generation is once again struggling for jobs and tertiary education, and facing an uncertain future in relation to housing, health, and welfare. The postwar parents assessed their freedoms and the economic opportunities in the 1950s and 1960s against the terrible period of capitalist recession that maimed and claimed the lives of millions in poverty, starvation, and war. From 1950, social democracy and its educational system was the answer given to the question of where to find opportunity and happiness. It is quite correct to observe that in what are called the golden years of capitalism education opened up promises for a better future to the mass of young people (Armstrong et al., 1984). From 1945 to 1968, the percentage of New Zealanders who participated as students in any form of education rose from 19.3 per cent to 30.9 per cent (Department of Statistics, 1950 and 1970).

This is not to say that education during this period was anything like equally available, or that class and ideology were at an end, as some commentators claimed. With the benefit of hindsight, it is easy to see that the inequalities of race and gender, and of class, were hardly alleviated, and even deepened in new ways. Consider just one statistic, the percentage of school leavers with School Certificate or better. For the great majority of the population, School Certificate was regarded as the principal high school qualification. From the early 1960s until the late 1970s, the percentage of Maori and non-Maori school leavers with School Certificate or better increased. In 1961 the gap between the two groups was 26.4 per cent. In 1979 the gap had, in fact, increased to 38.9 per cent (Department of Education, 1962 and 1980). In addition, patterns of subject choice were highly differentiated as between boys and girls, as indeed they still are. Such differences reflected, and continue to reflect, occupational differences in work roles.

But these observations do not negate the general claim about the new freedoms that were emerging, both in thought and culture as well as in work. Expanded education and new layers of workers brought to the fore new forms of consciousness that eventually led to new ways of viewing and judging the world. It was the achievements of the welfare state and shifts in the labour market, for example, that provided a platform for the modern women's movement, out of which the feminist critique arose. For instance, in 1951, women constituted about 25 per cent of the labour force (Prime Ministerial Taskforce on Employment, 1994, p. 28). By 1991 this proportion had risen to 41 per cent, even if much of this work was part-time and paid at a lower rate, on average, than in the male workforce (see Chapter 8).

In general, education was a powerful force—along with universal health care, expanding consumerism, and access to housing—in conveying and shaping a sense that social democracy was the path to equality. Labour and National politicians announced that New Zealand was a 'land free of what used to be called the class struggle' and upward mobility was a widespread and believable phenomenon. New schools were being built in the new suburbs and new jobs were opening up in the expanding economy. From the early 1950s through to about the mid-1970s there was a steady growth in employment from nearly 500 000 jobs to nearly 900 000 jobs (Prime Ministerial Task Force on Employment, 1994, p. 29). Unemployment was minimal. Following the historic defeat of the militant wing of the trade union movement in the 1951 waterfront dispute, the sense of open class struggle, so emphatically a matter of experience and socialisation in earlier periods of capitalist growth, was mostly unconscious during the postwar years. It seemed that the dreaded class struggle had been confined to the vagaries of status symbols, feelings, and modes of consumption, rather than openly voiced in large movements of social discontent. The old socialist term had only residual meaning, if it had meaning at all. And the old socialists might write jeremiads against capitalism and its consumerist culture, but who, outside the isolated left, believed them? The social psychology of class seemed to confirm this, with its findings that feelings of class consciousness were disappearing, to be overtaken by a sense that everyone was now middle class. The problems of adolescents were seen as individual problems, at least until the end of the 1950s, when unexpected forms of social disaffection began to surface among the new generation of teenagers. Workers were thought by academics to be left with only psychological alienation, and even this was assumed to be disappearing.

Booming capitalism was dispensing redemption on a scale never before dreamt of. In the urban centres and the farming hinterlands, confidence, optimism, materialistic hope, and social amnesia variously limited what was taught and what was learned in schools. No one bothered to consider the meaning of capitalist development for those living in the forgotten areas of country life, especially in the Maori pa which was now, in any event, economically irrelevant. After all, where it mattered, in the centres of production—particularly in Mount Wellington and Lower Hutt, but also in Addington and South Dunedin—more and more Maori workers were standing at the same machines, disciplined by the same factory regimes of exploitation as their Pakeha brothers and sisters. In 1961 the Hunn Report declared that, within two generations, the Maori would be 'well nigh fully integrated' (Hunn, 1961, p. 14). The tribe and whakapapa belonged to a lost world. All that had been solid, for nearly 1000 years, just surviving the ravages of colonial administration and the New Zealand Wars, was now finally melting into air before the advances of profitable capitalism.

As has already been indicated, talk of equal opportunity and the virtues of free public education during these postwar years was inflated. Nevertheless, such notions did become common opinion among wide sectors of the population and conveyed a picture of class harmony, community, and one nation. It is possible to get some sense of just how much this meant to working people if the educational achievement of social democracy is compared with what, from the beginning of the socialist movement, was a central demand: 'free education for all children in public schools'. Mass secondary schooling in New Zealand has only been a fact since 1950. The election of the first Labour Government in 1935 led to a social program of educational opportunity that effectively began delivering after the Second World War. Thus, the commitment to universal education got its first great political push as the result of social democratic struggle emerging out of the labour movement. It is hardly surprising that postwar parents in particular, though also their children, saw schooling as more than simply a ticket into the economy. Certainly it was this, but it was also a road to the full enjoyment of a political economy defined by the wider and more humane aspirations of the welfare state. Take, for example, the following two statements (quoted by Vellekoop, 1971, p.15 and p. 75) by parents in the mid-1960s: 'I can only hope and pray that my son will seize the wonderful opportunities afforded the children of our country'; 'Any ambitions I have for my son will be guided entirely by his own attainments academically and by the gifts and talents he possesses'. Girls were thought to have wonderful opportunities, too, though in somewhat different directions from the boys.

During the postwar period, education and work provided a pattern of life and a direct entrance to the adult world of consumption and political participation. The typical model for understanding all this was some version of liberalism, according to which work in the capitalist economy, development by means of free education, and participation by means of voting in a representative democracy, were the guarantees of the good life. The theory of equality of opportunity was assimilated in a relatively unconscious way by teachers, administrators, parents, and children. The underlying assumption was that a profitable economy could fund expanded schooling. In order for the economy to run at maximum capacity, workers had to be distributed into positions of work relative to their interests, abilities, and patterns of motivation. It was in relation to this goal that the provision of universal education played such a central role. In 1951, for example, about 70 per cent of those aged between fifteen and nineteen were active in the labour market. By comparison, in the 1990s this proportion had fallen to 53 per cent, and much of it was part-time on minimum wages (Prime Ministerial Taskforce on Employment, 1994, p. 28). In the 1950s and 1960s, two or three years at high school was sufficient to guarantee employment for most school leavers.

According to the liberal theory of education, children enter this world with the impediments of class background, ethnic origin, and gender. An open system of education, available to all regardless of background, was presumed to be sufficient to overcome these impediments. In New Zealand education, this viewpoint was most famously expressed in the much quoted statement of the then Education Minister, Peter Fraser.

The Government's objective, broadly expressed, is that every person, whatever his level of academic activity, whether he be rich or poor, whether he live in town or country, has a right, as a citizen, to a free education of the kind for which he is best fitted and to the fullest extent of his powers . . . the present Government was the first to recognize explicitly that continued education is no longer a special privilege of the well-to-do or the academically able, but a right to be claimed by all who want it to the fullest extent that the State can provide (*Appendices to the Journals of the House of Representatives*, E-1, 1939, pp. 2–3).

If we come forward to the late 1970s, this ideology was still receiving wide support, as is shown by the following statement from the New Zealand Planning Council.

There is wide acceptance of the concept that a good education for all regardless of the financial means of parents is a prerequisite for equality of opportunity. Education is seen as an investment in tomorrow's producers as well as a way of assisting individuals to develop their talents and to find fulfilment in life (New Zealand Planning Council, 1979b, p. 49).

Hence it was the role of the state to ensure that the conditions of equal opportunity were embodied in the material infrastructures and curricula of the schools.

A potent social democratic belief during the long economic boom was that the state could be the agent of social transformation. This was commonly held without appreciating that, in a profitable economy, the state could operate partially on social democratic assumptions, well within the limits of capitalism itself. Indeed, the implicit social contract allowed everyone to be, or be seen to be, a political winner. Average expenditure (current and capital) on education in the period from 1950 to 1975, as a percentage of total central government expenditure, increased steadily from 13.6 per cent to 25 per cent (New Zealand Planning Council, 1979a, pp. 26–43). If education is seen rather more widely—as the range of ways in which societies shape and make their people—then health, education, law and order, and welfare together amounted, on average, to a much higher percentage of all government expenditure annually during the long boom.

If education achieved a distribution of talent into the economy then it was assumed, all things being equal, that the economy would expand and, with it, the capacity of the state to fund further developments in education. Beyond this, the state was assumed to provide further conditions relating to what has been earlier referred to as freedom. The first of these conditions is social integration, what is labelled in Figure 11.1 as social equality and political participation. This might be thought of as a form of positive freedom

Figure 11.1 The liberal theory of education

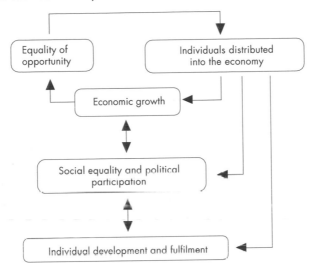

that comes from the ability to be part of a community. Crucial to this integration was home ownership and, from an educational perspective, this meant extending the nurturing and socialising environment across the whole suburb. Home and school could be linked together but also linked in with the fabric of other associations such as social clubs, sports teams, and churches. It was this richly woven fabric of social activity, intellectually and snobbishly dismissed by the cultural élite as suffocating, that made possible the theoretical idea that social life could be actually and intimately democratic. For millions, the welfare state and education made freedoms available for the first time, and on an unprecedented scale. Employing a Deweyan turn of phrase, we might say that the great community was being realised within the great society. The New Zealand vernacular for this was 'Godzone'.

Looking back from a distance of four decades, it is easy to criticise these achievements and their associated beliefs as naive. But the liberal theory was, and to some extent remains, a powerful ideal of the educational meaning of capitalist democracy, especially if the emphasis is placed on democracy. If the implicit compact between state, capitalists, and workers achieved industrial peace and wage stability in the private sector, then the benefits of educational opportunity and economic stability sustained the fabric of democratic opportunity in everyday life. Translated across communities as a whole, the consequences of educational opportunity were expected to underwrite an electoral democracy in which all citizens would have an investment, and which would translate into further involvement in the economy. Finally, this educational vision of society was to find its ultimate expression in the self-realisation of the individual whose abilities were being applied in the economy and expressed in the more immediate life of the community. In other words, the social democratic individual would have both the material and spiritual resources for full human development.

Collapse of the long boom and the crisis of social democratic educational policy

The end of the long economic boom in 1974 put all these propositions into question and for the two decades since then liberal educational theory has been deeply problematic. At the centre of this situation, however, is an essential continuity in the meaning of the state. In the golden years of capitalism, educational theory easily assumed what can be called the 'theory of the neutral state'. According to this, the state essentially lies beyond the reaches of particular interests and remains, over the long term, relatively untainted by biases of power and political machination. Put like this, it is hard to imagine that anyone would actually subscribe to this theory, but in one respect it does reflect an obvious reality about the postwar period. The development of public education was advancing and in the economy the class relation was largely hidden by national and collective forms of bargaining. Whatever the rhetoric between the two main political parties, across the political mainstream there was widespread commitment to liberal educational policies.

For the generation that grew up in postwar New Zealand, the economic boom came to be seen as an almost established fact of life. During the 1950s and 1960s incomes rose, consumer goods became increasingly available, fuels and raw materials were cheap, the rate of inflation was low, as was unemployment, and after 1951 industrial relations were quiet. Opportunities in education, work, and leisure expanded and poverty and hardship appeared to be disappearing into the past. In a single generation, it seemed, New Zealand had moved into an era of progress, plenty, and social mobility. Everyone seemed to be flourishing, to be receiving the same amount of the world's goods, and to be moving in the same direction. The vision of what was later called the 'half-gallon quarter-acre pavlova paradise' was much more than just a joke.

This is not the place for a detailed review of relevant statistics, but to take just a single index of the period, consider the annual real GNP growth. Assuming growth rates of around 4.5 per cent for the period 1950–75, each successive generation could expect to be roughly twice as well off as its parents and four times as well off as its grandparents. This bald economic reality carried with it an enormously powerful educational message, and it is suggestive of the material basis underlying the sentiments expressed by the two parents quoted earlier. In 1968 the Minister of Finance, Robert Muldoon, characterised the political economic conditions surrounding the educational ideology of the state—that equality of opportunity is the touchstone of government policy—when he said that '. . . the basic objective of economic policy will continue to be full employment, a steady rate of growth, reasonable stability of costs and prices, and a balance of payments in approximate equilibrium' (1968, pp. 43–4). Schools played their part in this scenario of golden capitalism by developing a whole new generation of well-trained, literate and numerate students, ready to enter society as workers, consumers, and voters.

By the late 1960s the avenues of profitability had begun to close. Boom gave way to slump, inflation accelerated, unemployment rose alarmingly from the mid-1970s, wages were lowered, and workers, the great majority of consumers, found that they could no longer afford to buy all the commodities necessary to sustain the New Zealand version of the good life. The average rate of profit across the economy as a whole declined, production slowed, stagnated, and failed (see Chapter 1). As more and more workers and their families were affected by the economic recession, they began to wonder whether education could help and what forms of training were best in the competitive search for jobs. Then they discovered that they had to worry about how to finance an education.

In 1986 the fourth Labour Government set up a royal commission to inquire into 'the extent to which New Zealand meets the standards of a fair society' (Royal Commission on Social Policy, 1988, p. v). At the same time, social democracy was moving to the right. In a telling comment for a social democrat, although it was hardly news to the political left or right, the Prime Minister, David Lange, said that social democrats 'must accept the existence of economic inequality because it is the engine which drives the economy' and that 'their goal is to reduce as much as possible the socially-damaging and disruptive effects of an economy which depends on self-interest without intervening to the point where the economy loses its motive force' (1986, p. 7). It had long been an article of social democratic faith that the state could manage a humane welfare society. In practice, equality of opportunity was far from being a touchstone of everyday life for most people, although what a person lacked today could still plausibly be hoped for in the future.

As has been argued, capitalist profits sustained a set of relationships between the state, employers, and workers that was reflected in the liberal theory of education. It was this practice of education that socialised the sense of hope already referred to. Because the economic machine was expanding with no expectancy of future crises, it seemed possible, during the long boom, to project a relatively smooth course for future development. But nothing in capitalist society is solid forever and the partial achievements of social democracy during the long boom were, by the mid-1980s, beginning to look insecure. Inevitably, economic crisis leads to educational crisis, to a demand for cutbacks, for a return to basics and vocational relevance. What had been declared to be the right of all was now argued to be the right of those who could pay for it. Social crisis undermines confidence in existing relationships and social institutions, including education.

In attempts to reconfigure the economy, educational thinking and attitude have been affected in two ways. First, it has increasingly been argued that the state can no longer support anything more than a minimum welfare programme. Second, it is demanded that education be restructured in line with new demands for school leavers to think, act, and react more flexibly and competitively. The Minister of Education during much of the fourth National Government (1990–96) argued that

> We have reduced substantially the protection of our domestic economy, we have deregulated our labour market, reducing union power, and allowed individuals and enterprises to negotiate employment arrangements that suit them best. We aim to build a highly skilled, highly innovative and highly adaptive workforce through a reformed education system (Smith, 1992).

Two examples illustrate the debate over skill. The Porter Report, entitled *Upgrading New Zealand's Competitive Advantage,* argued that New Zealand had not invested in 'creating the pools of human-resource skills needed to be internationally competitive' (Crocombe et al., 1991, p. 99). Using the relationship between the level of educational qualification and potential participation in the workforce, the report estimated that only 20 per cent of New Zealanders were likely to contribute towards developing New Zealand's economic base. But the situation was thought to be even worse than this simple statistic suggested. New Zealand's education system, it turned out, had not focused on subjects with direct economic value such as the sciences, engineering, mathematics, and agriculture. The report concluded that the New Zealand 'educational system is not equipping people with the skills necessary to compete successfully in the global economy' (p. 105).

The second illustration is drawn from a Ministry of Education document that is worth quoting at length:

> The school curriculum will give all students the opportunity of a broad and balanced education . . . to continue learning throughout life, and to play their

full part in our democratic society and in a competitive world economy . . .
Change will continue to accelerate. Schools can no longer provide people with
the specific skills they will need in adulthood, because we can no longer predict
what those skills will be. People are going to have to re-train several times through
their working lives. If change is constant, education and training must be too.
We must learn to make change our friend . . . The tertiary sector must be the
driving force of research, discovery and innovation. Our academics and researchers
must work at the leading edge of international thinking. The workplace must
also be integrated into the educational system to ensure that we have a population
skilled enough, adaptable enough, and innovative enough to be successful in
international competition. In this business, enterprise must take the lead and
responsibility for the development of skills relevant to industry . . . We must
ensure that our workforce is suitably skilled in science, technology, and engineering,
. . . These ideas are recognised in most countries around the world. That in itself
poses challenges to New Zealand. We live in a global community and a global
marketplace. If we seek to improve our economic standing relative to that of our
competitors, our commitment to education and training must be greater than
that of other countries. We must adapt more quickly to change than our
competitors, and the skills of our workforce must improve faster than the skills
of other workforces. We must invest in people, our greatest economic resource
(Ministry of Education, 1993, pp. 7–8).

The economic boom had made all things relatively possible for educationists
and it appeared to give the state's educational enterprise an efficacy on its
own terms. The prolonged crisis of capitalism has had just the opposite
effect, as the statement above so clearly expresses. In fact, the liberal hope
for education almost totally disappeared during the economic crisis that
began in the 1970s. Not only do dramatic inequalities of opportunity and
achievement now go unchallenged, but, in the name of flexibility and global
competitiveness, these inequalities are now accepted as necessary, and even
celebrated.

There are no grounds for imposing a mechanical scheme on economic
and educational history and supposing, therefore, that the long downswing
in capitalist development will automatically be followed by an upswing. In
the advanced capitalist societies, New Zealand included, it seemed almost
mandatory in the mid-1990s to announce that the recovery had begun,
although this was typically done using a highly selective range of statistics.
Little mention was made of long-term growth rates, unemployment and
underemployment, poverty, housing, racism, educational costs, and faltering
health systems. It may be that the crisis of capitalist economies has reached
a point where minimal profitability is impossible without lowering wages,

restricting working conditions, keeping unions weak if not totally ineffective, and reducing the provisions of social democracy through programs of restructuring, restraint, privatisation, and devolution. Even though these moves are made in support of capitalist restructuring, they are passed off as being democratic—in the name of community control, parental choice, participation and individual responsibility. Without these shifts it will be, as the Ministry of Education indicated, impossible to compete in the international economy. None of this is new in conservative economic thinking. But it is an indication of how far things have shifted to the right that mainstream social democrats, unionists, teacher advocates, and academics, are found giving voice to similar sentiments. For instance, the common argument, that New Zealand needs to develop a high skill, high wage competitive economy that will attract capital investment, is largely indistinguishable from anything for which the most enthusiastic representatives of capital have argued. After all, who cares where the investment capital comes from or how it gets here? The idea that education is the solution to New Zealand's economic and social woes is, perhaps, attractive to educationists, but it is an idle dream. As Wood (1995) concluded, 'In a context of mass unemployment, the logic of a theory that places the supply of skilled workers before the demand is at best illusive. Is it reasonable to suppose that jobs that do not exist for structural reasons will suddenly be created to absorb a newly skilled workforce?' (p. 286).

Social democrats might constantly bemoan the neoliberal revolution but it seems that the New Right has actually done something that the best of left-wing thinking has always placed great store by. The New Right has shown the limits of capitalism, albeit in a celebratory key. Capitalist profitability comes at a cost and that cost is lowered social provision and, along with other policies, the translation of this into the various means by which education is restructured. As Frederic Jamieson once put it, 'history is what hurts' (cited in Eagleton, 1995, p. 63).

Conclusion

This chapter has suggested that, under conditions of expansion and recession social democratic education and educational restructuring can be seen as two solutions to the continuing problem of achieving a relative correspondence with capitalist economic structures. And it is this continuing historical problem that has established the limits within which educational theories and practices have developed over half a century.

The critical issue is not what particular policies and details are being pursued, though most educational discussion, academic and professional, is at this level. Instead, those who see education as an unambiguous democratic and public good must use tactics that take the limits of capitalism every bit as seriously as do the advocates of capital themselves. So far this has not been done. So long will education, with the freedoms and engagements that its social democratic version has anticipated, lie in the shadow of an encroaching capitalist state.

Guide to Readings

For the original statement of the correspondence theory, see Bowles and Gintis (1976). For a range of theoretical and political responses to the theory together with a reply from Bowles and Gintis, consult Cole (1988). Fisk (1989) sets out a sophisticated defence of historical materialism that circumvents old debates between various positions on the role of material factors in explanation.

There is a large technical and critical literature on the theory of long waves of economic development. A recent survey can be found in Kleinknecht, Mandel, and Wallerstein (1992). For a sympathetic application within a Marxian framework see Mandel (1978, 1995). On post-1945 capitalism, see Armstrong, Glyn, and Harrison (1984), Marglin and Schor (1992), Mandel (1978) and, at the level of world history, Part Two of Hobsbawm (1994). For examples of recent educational policy analysis, see Dale (1994), Grace (1990), the essays in Codd, Harker, and Nash (1990), and the essays in Gordon and Codd (1991). Openshaw (1995) discusses state postprimary education for the period traversed by this chapter.

CHAPTER TWELVE

WOMEN, FEMINISM, AND THE STATE

ROSEMARY DU PLESSIS

Feminists have had an uneasy and sometimes contradictory relationship with 'the state' (Sassoon, 1987; Watson, 1990; Yeatman, 1990; Armstrong, 1992; Curthoys, 1993). Some feminists have argued that social democratic states have privileged men's interests (Bryson, 1992) and that they consolidate the power of capitalist employers at the expense of women (Wilson, 1977). This has not prevented feminists from arguing for state intervention to end discrimination in the workplace, income support for women involved in unpaid caring work, and government funding for childcare facilities (Baldock and Cass, 1983; Piven, 1984; Franzway et al., 1989; Yeatman, 1994).

As a consequence of feminist claims over the last twenty-five years, states in most social democracies have embarked on programs of legal reform directed at outlawing gender discrimination. Women's refuges, women's health centres, and rape crisis workers have received government funding and public money has been used to send women's delegations to international conferences that charge states with responsibility for women's health and economic development. Franzway, Court, and Connell argue that, 'While law, police, state employment practices, school curricula, housing policy have all been direct agents of the oppression of women, they have also been vehicles for reform' (1989, p. 12). Hence the ambivalence among feminists to state policy and state structures (Brown, 1992).

This chapter explores the relationship between 'women', 'feminism', and 'the state', and disrupts the unity often associated with each of these terms. Differences between women, divergent feminisms, and understandings of states that focus on complexity and diversity are discussed. This focus on states as practices, organisational forms, social relations, and arenas of power resonates with aspects of the state sector restructuring experienced in Aotearoa over the last decade. Feminist political analysts in Australasia are increasingly attracted to theories about state policy and state structures that address contradiction and specificity. This is not just because generalisations about patriarchy have proved problematic and attention to specificity is fashionable in contemporary social theory (Yeatman, 1994; Pringle, 1995), but also because citizens in the 1990s are constantly challenged to negotiate complexity, difference, and the specific features of regionally based, state-funded organisations.

Women, the State, and the Construction of 'Interested Universalism'

Feminist criticisms of state policy have frequently drawn on a universalistic rhetoric to articulate women's interests *as women* (Yeatman, 1993, pp. 234–5). Claims about women's common interests have been used as a strategy to ensure that international organisations such as the United Nations attend to the political status of women. It has also been vital in developing women-focused structures in particular nation states (such as New Zealand's Ministry of Women's Affairs) and at the level of local community organisations, trade unions, churches, workplaces, professional associations, and educational institutions (Olsson, 1992, pp. 103–46).

Feminist claims about 'women's interests' were subjected to considerable criticism in the 1980s by women who identified as African-American or Black women, Third World women, 'women of colour', Maori, and Aboriginal women (hooks, 1981; Joseph and Lewis, 1981; Moraga and Anzaldua 1981; Hull et al., 1982; Awatere, 1984; Lorde, 1984). The focus of this debate with Western feminism was the obliteration of significant differences between women. The rights of Western feminists to speak on behalf of 'all' women were criticised by women whose ancestors had experienced slavery and colonisation, whose villages were currently being destroyed by weapons produced in capitalist social democracies, and whose lives were disrupted by forms of multinational offshore investment in developing countries. As a consequence, feminist scholars have increasingly focused on the need to acknowledge differences associated with ethnicity, class, religion, colonial conquest, sexualities, and disabilities (Fine and Asch, 1988; Williams, 1989; Spelman, 1990; Bottomley et al., 1991; Bock and James, 1992; Flax, 1992; Pettman, 1992, pp. 78–105; Gunew and Yeatman, 1993; Afshar and Maynard, 1994; Johnston and Pihama, 1994).

Ang argues that '. . . differences between women undermine the homogeneity and continuity of "women" as a social category' (1995, p. 58), but she states that differences between women cannot easily be 'resolved'. Suspicious of a politics of inclusion that potentially obliterates differences between women, Ang says that feminists need to recognise the partiality of feminism as political practice and its limitations as a vehicle for addressing *all* the political issues that women confront.

Johnston and Pihama (1995) explore similar issues in a paper on the politics of difference. Challenging assertions about any simplistic commonality between Maori and Pakeha women as women, Johnston and Pihama state that, 'Pakeha women may well be in the same boat but Pakeha and Maori women definitely do not come from the same waka, and for Maori women that is a difference that counts' (p. 83).

Women Inside and Outside State Structures

It is against this kind of background that contemporary feminists engage in critical analyses of state policy (Yeatman, 1994). They also participate in forms of contestatory politics at a time when some feminists' claims have become state policy, part of the established process of governance. The requirement, under the State Sector Act 1988, that government-funded institutions be 'good employers', promote equal employment opportunities, and recognise the employment requirements of women, Maori, and those with disabilities, provides a climate in which feminists are likely to be both the custodians of established policy and those who contest policies in the interests of emancipatory agendas. Some analysts have looked critically at the outcome of this institutionalisation of feminist claims. They have argued that, although equal employment opportunities initiatives have benefited some women, those most advantaged have tended to be the women who most resemble those who fill the equal employment opportunities (EEO) positions in organisations (Yeatman, 1990; Poiner and Wills, 1991). In the New Zealand context, the way 'difference' is produced in employment policies in government organisations has been explored by Jones (1995), who has analysed the uneasy relationship between EEO programs and biculturalism. Jones argues that EEO is both 'the major and critical attempt to address issues of inequality in employment' (p. 97) and a way in which dominant groups name 'difference' and interpret the 'needs' of 'target groups' (women, people with disabilities, and Maori). She argues that the construction of Maori as an 'EEO target group' is inconsistent with the concept of rangatiratanga, which is guaranteed in the Treaty of Waitangi and often interpreted by Maori as the right to sovereignty, to parallel Maori institutions, and to the opportunity to 'determine one's own destiny' (Jones, 1995, pp. 107–8.)

Feminist political pressure on politicians and bureaucrats, and their activism in community organisations, occupational groups, unions, political parties, and research organisations, has resulted in some institutional recognition within state structures of 'women' as a political category, with actual or potential interests that need to be addressed by those charged with policy development. This institutionalisation of feminist claims on the state is most obviously represented by the Ministry of Women's Affairs, a policy-focused agency with particular responsibility to provide gender-specific advice to the government on public policy issues and develop strategies for analysing the possible effects of policy initiatives on women (O'Regan, 1992; Ministry of Women's Affairs/Minitatanga mo nga Wahine, 1996). The ministry can be seen as a vehicle for the articulation of feminist analysis within the body of the state or, alternatively, as a way in which feminist contestation is contained by state bureaucrats, who appropriate the voice of protest and resistance and speak for 'women' (Saville-Smith, 1987; Franzway et al., pp. 133–55; Yeatman, 1990, pp. 80–97; Yeatman, 1993, p. 235).

As outlined above, analysis of issues associated with 'women' and 'the state' demands attention to differences between women and between feminists. It requires attention to women as custodians of new gender-sensitive state policies and those who criticise those policies. Any engagement with the relationship between feminists and state policies must attend not only to differences between women, but also to theoretical debates among feminists. These debates involve both the construction of generalisations about 'the state' and their critical 'deconstruction' by other feminists.

Liberal Feminist Theory

Liberal feminist approaches to the state have focused on women's rights as citizens and the need to institutionalise what some theorists have referred to as 'gender justice' (Franzway et al., 1989, pp. 14–17; Hawkesworth, 1990, pp. 157–60 and 171–97). According to liberal theory, the state is ideally gender-neutral. In the past, however, states often legitimated discrimination by employers, unions, schools, and financial institutions. In New Zealand, differential pay rates for women and men doing the same job were legal in the private sector until the Equal Pay Act was passed in 1972 (Hyman, 1994, pp. 79–100).

State policy that treated women and men differently with respect to their access to the vote, political office, employment, earnings, benefits, pensions, or superannuation has been consistently challenged by liberal feminists for more than a century (Armstrong, 1992, pp. 226–8, Macdonald, 1993). Feminists have used liberal theory to argue for the right of women to half the matrimonial property on the break-up of a marriage, equal pay for equal work, equal employment opportunities programs and pay equity (Clark, 1993; Else, 1993, pp. 80–4, 98–9; Hyman, 1994, pp. 79–100).

Liberal feminists also lobbied for legislation to outlaw gender discrimination in the provision of financial services, housing, education, and employment. The Human Rights Commission Act 1977 was at least in part a response to liberal feminist claims on the state in the early 1970s. It prohibited discrimination in housing, education, employment, and access to goods and services on the basis of ethnicity, religion, gender and marital status, and provided a framework for complaints of discrimination. Although this legislation did not end discriminatory treatment, the Human Rights Commission Act and the Human Rights Act 1993, which made discrimination on the basis of sexual orientation, age, and disability illegal, challenged many people's assumptions about the legitimacy of differential treatment for women, gay men, lesbians, Maori, Pacific Islanders, Indians, and Chinese.

Liberal feminist arguments for equality arose out of women's experience of legal discrimination. Feminists argued for an end to legal discrimination with respect to access to trade apprenticeships, housing loans, and unemployment benefits, and asserted their rights to rates of pay equivalent to male workers. These claims, however, drew upon understandings of equality that assumed a gender-undifferentiated 'citizen' with generic 'rights'. Increasingly, feminist theorists have considered how citizenship implies a male subject and inhibits attention to forms of difference between women and men that might legitimate the two sexes making different claims on the state.

'Patriarchal States'—Radical Feminists Theorise the State

Radical feminists are likely to be much more sceptical than liberal feminists about the extent to which women can recruit state actors as allies in struggles around gender equality (Franzway et al., 1989, pp. 27–32). They argue that it is not just an unfortunate mistake that women have had to battle for recognition of their rights as citizens, an oversight easily corrected by granting women the right to vote, to hold political office, to earn the same amount as men doing the same job, or to have access to half the matrimonial property on the dissolution of a marriage. According to MacKinnon (1989), modern capitalist social democracies have at their core a legal system that systematically authorises men's experience of the world, while appearing to be impersonal and objective.

Pateman (1988) has argued that conceptions of citizenship developed in the seventeenth century assumed sexual difference and excluded women from participation as individuals in the public sphere of the economy and politics. According to Pateman, the 'social contract', the basis of citizenship, challenged the power of fathers and the claims of kinship and established modern 'fraternal patriarchy' (Pateman, 1988, p. 3; Pringle and Watson,

1990, pp. 230–3). A core component of this fraternal patriarchy was the marriage contract, a 'sexual contract' organised around men's rights over women and their subordination.

This sexual contract has been consistently challenged, particularly by feminists who worked in the nineteenth century for married women's access to divorce on the same terms as men, for their right to enter into legal contracts, to vote, to control inherited property, and to have guardianship rights over their children. These struggles for women's rights were fought by New Zealand feminists such as Mary Colclough, Kate Sheppard, Jessie Mackay, Meri Mangakahia, and Margaret Sievwright, who worked for the recognition of women's right as citizens to vote, their right to paid work, their right to control their own earnings, and their right to legal autonomy (Lovell-Smith, 1992; Macdonald, 1993, pp. 13–67; Rei, 1993a).

Pateman has argued that the achievement of these rights has often involved treating women like men and accepting male definitions of what constitutes 'citizenship' and 'work'. This echoes what Schirmacher, a German feminist, stated in 1905: 'We live in a "man's world", created by man in the first place for himself . . . For him value lay only in sameness; only assimilation could count for him as equality' (cited in Bock and Thane, 1991, p. 14).

Although women have achieved legal equality with men, men are still more frequently found in positions of formal power, women's work is still lower paid, and women, as a consequence, are likely to be worse off at the end of marriage, even though they have the legal right to half the matrimonial property. The freedom to enter into contracts may be a limited freedom in a context of inequalities in power, property, and rates of pay (Statistics New Zealand, 1993, pp. 79–117).

Pateman (1992) argues that a crucial feature of the social contract is the construction of 'motherhood' as a political status, a status through which women can be connected to the structure of modern states. States have attached considerable importance to the regulation of reproduction. In the New Zealand context, pro-natalist policies in the 1930s discouraged women's access to contraception and outlawed abortion. A Committee of Inquiry into Abortion concluded that women should consider 'the grave physical and moral dangers, not to speak of the dangers of race suicide' posed by abortion and birth control (cited in Brookes, 1986, p. 132). Voluntary organisations such as the Family Planning Association struggled to provide information and contraceptive advice to women who wanted to control their fertility (Fenwick, 1980; Else, 1993, pp. 261–9). The state has also played a key role in regulating adoption with significant consequences for the lives of many birth mothers (Else, 1991).

By the 1990s, the state had provided some women with access to free contraceptives and state-funded terminations. While regulating abortion (Dann, 1985, pp. 51–64), governments have responded to claims that they have a responsibility to provide a state-funded abortion service and to facilitate women's access to contraception. The state is also subject to claims by individuals experiencing infertility to provide state resources for infertility programmes. Arguments for these programs often draw on a new rights discourse—the right to experience parenthood or full participation in intergenerational reproduction (Robertson, 1994). The state has also started to respond to the moral and political challenges associated with regulating the use of new reproductive technologies (Ministerial Committee on Assisted Reproductive Technologies, 1994).

Women's engagement with the state since the late eighteenth century has involved women both claiming equality with men as citizens and arguing that the state should recognise differences between them and men (Cass, 1995). Bock and Thane argue that 'Despite all the differences between the women's movements of the first and second waves, there is a line of continuity in the search for the difficult conceptual, cultural, political and social balance between the "right to be equal" and the "right to be different"'(1991, pp. 14–15). Sometimes the search for the 'right to be different' has generated heated debate among women, for example, debates about protective labour legislation that restricted women's hours of work in the interests of their health and their families' claims on their time, but also reduced their earnings and access to jobs (Pateman, 1992; Wikander et al., 1995).

Although radical feminists have often focused on differences between women and men, they have also argued for the recognition of both 'equality' and 'difference'. According to Pateman, 'for citizenship to be of equal worth, the substance of equality must differ according to the diverse circumstances and capacities of citizens, men and women' (Pateman, 1992, p. 29). Equality, according to this view, is not being treated 'the same', but in ways that recognise different needs and ensure material security for citizens with differing levels of responsibilities and opportunities to enter paid work.

It was this understanding of citizenship that lay behind the provision of the means-tested Widows' Benefit in 1911, initially available only to women 'of good repute' with dependent children (Koopman-Boyden and Scott, 1984, p. 112). This benefit recognised many women's dependence on their partners' earnings and was not available to married men who lost their wives, although an exception was made in 1918 after the influenza epidemic, when eighty-nine widowers with children were granted pensions.

State regulation relating to parental leave first took the form of a gender-specific piece of legislation that involved recognising differences between women and men. The Maternity Leave and Employment Protection Act 1981, passed by a National Government, protected women from dismissal for reasons of pregnancy, granted them the right to leave without pay in the later stages of pregnancy, and protected their jobs for up to one year while they took unpaid parental leave. The fourth Labour Government modified this legislation, extending to either parent the legal right to unpaid leave and the opportunity to share this twelve-month leave. The Parental Leave and Employment Protection Act 1987 still differentiates between women and men with respect to the length of leave available at the time of childbirth and the protection of pregnant women from dismissal on the grounds of their pregnancy. In this respect it attends to both 'equality' and 'difference'.

The relation between state policy and the physiology of reproduction are the subject of Galtry's reflections on breastfeeding and paid maternity leave (Galtry, 1995). She focuses on the conflict between the promotion of breastfeeding and the social and economic pressures on women to return to paid work within the first year of a child's life. Access to the 'choice' to continue breastfeeding may rest on access to state support as an alternative to paid work. In this case, a liberal discourse of individual 'choice', radical feminist critiques of 'equal' treatment for women and men, and a collective discourse of community responsibility for infant welfare are used to construct a case for paid maternity leave.

Shaver (1995) has argued that there has been an increasing shift in Australian social policy from differential treatment of women and men to policies that treat them equally with respect to income support. A decreasing state focus on women as economic 'dependants' intensifies women's dependence on paid work as a means of access to income and material security. She suggests that this equal treatment does not take account of women and men's 'greatly unequal circumstances in the society beyond the safety net' (Shaver, 1995, p. 156).

The Patriarchal Capitalist State—Marxist and Socialist Feminist Theory

Feminists have also used forms of Marxist theory to criticise liberal feminists' attempts to 'reform' the state and radical feminist constructions of the patriarchal state. Marxist and socialist feminists have tended to focus on the ways in which states represent the interests of those with capital, not just men. They have also highlighted the way in which welfare states in social democracies like New Zealand diffuse attention to class differences and the different interests of employers and employees. According to this analysis, women's position in paid work and in the family will not improve just by including women as citizens, nor through state responses to 'women's' needs. The dynamics of private enterprise and state protection of capitalists are seen as contributing significantly to women's vulnerable position within households and the labour market (Wilson, 1977; Barrett, 1980; Franzway et al., 1989, pp. 19–26).

According to Marxist feminists, women's unpaid labour contributes to capitalist accumulation. Women engage in the reproduction of the workforce, sustaining the capacity to work of the adults in their households, and rearing a new generation of workers. Women's domestic labour is not just of benefit to individual men, but functional for the capitalist system. The state reinforces this form of patriarchal capitalism through the education system, through benefit structures that privilege nuclear families, and through the regulation of marriage and divorce. Wilson articulated an early version of this form of socialist feminist analysis in the late 1970s when she argued that the state

> . . . operates in a subtle and in some ways a more coercive fashion to keep women to their primary task as adults. This is the task of reproducing the work force. That the workforce should be reproduced is obviously essential to the continuation of the economy and of society itself, but in doing this job in a very particular way for the capitalist economy, women are guided by the State (Wilson, 1977, p. 8).

This view of the welfare state focuses on the way the state makes women responsible for sustaining family life and for ensuring children's access to such services as immunisation and schooling. State services directed at women and children are, according to this view, means of regulation and control that ensure the production of a healthy, well-disciplined, and educated workforce. In this way the state, while appearing to offer services and benefits, organises private domestic life in ways that benefit employers. Welfare provision is seen as 'an essential part of modern capitalism . . . part of the tightrope act . . . performed by bourgeois democratic governments in their attempts to balance working-class demands and the reproduction of capital' (Wilson, p. 39).

The application of this analysis to New Zealand would look at public education, health care, and income support as aspects of the welfare state for which working class people have struggled *and* as strategies for regulating women and households. Women may have access to free maternity care, but the state has regulated the conditions under which they will give birth and, until recently, differentiated sharply between the autonomy of doctors and midwives, and the rates of pay available to them. Women who refuse to immunise their children encounter the disapproval of Plunket and public health nurses. Income support for women has been used as a form of moral regulation available only to 'good' women. For many years, income support for women alone with children was confined to widows and deserted wives, and not available to single mothers (Du Plessis, 1993, p. 214). In the 1990s, mothers claiming the domestic purposes benefit (DPB) have been penalised if they do not supply information about the fathers of their children so that these men can be made liable for a proportion of the benefit. These are just a few of the ways in which state organisations subject women to forms of regulation and surveillance, while at the same time providing them with necessary social services and income support.

Some socialist feminists have explored the complex relationship between the state, capitalist economic relations, and families. McIntosh suggested in the late 1970s that the state does not always act in the interests of capitalist employers nor investors, but has to balance the demands of families and the economy, demands that frequently conflict (McIntosh, 1978). This model of the relationship between states, families, and economic activity challenges the view that states consistently ensure that families function to meet employers' needs for cheap labour. McIntosh's analysis directs attention to the complexity of state policy, an aspect of socialist feminist analysis that received considerably more attention in the 1980s (Walby, 1986). By the late 1980s, Franzway, Court and Connell (1989) asserted that 'the capitalist state is not smoothly running; it is racked by crisis and difficulty . . . patriarchy and capitalism often cut across and undermine each other' (Franzway et al., 1989, p. 24).

In the 1990s, feminists interested in studying what Armstrong (1992) has referred to as the many-headed 'hydra' of the state, are less interested in determining the effects of capitalism and are more focused on the state as a set of contradictory relationships and organisational forms—a site of struggle between different interests, organisational agendas, needs claims, and rights discourses. This approach involves analysing the sometimes inconsistent responses of state actors to demands from capitalist entrepreneurs, feminists, and other groups seeking to influence state policy (Franzway et al., 1989, pp. 41–2; Curthoys, 1993, p. 34; Yeatman, 1994, p.180–4).

Feminism and Neoliberal Resistance to the 'Maternal' Welfare State

Liberal, radical, and socialist feminists have subjected the welfare state to considerable criticism. Since the late 1980s, however, feminists with very different orientations to 'the state' have often found themselves defending the welfare state against neoliberal or new right theorists who argue that welfare states undermine independence and self-reliance (Richardson, 1995; Green, 1996). Neoliberal theories acknowledge the need for states to protect existing property rights and regulate contractual relationships between citizens, but resist expectations that states should assume responsibilities for the economic support of citizens or provide housing, schooling, or health care (Nozick, 1974).

The neoliberal citizen is an autonomous and self-reliant individual involved in paid work, entering into contracts as employer or employee in a capitalist labour market. Those whose lives are organised around juggling paid and unpaid work, whose economic support depends on non-market exchanges that sometimes succeed and sometimes fail, have little place within this construction of state/citizen relations (Else, 1992; Cass, 1995).

Women are overrepresented among those whose lives are not organised primarily around formal contracts of employment and who forgo paid work to respond to the needs of dependants (Briar, 1992). They are also more likely than men to be dependent on income support from the state (Statistics New Zealand, 1993, p. 115). They were, therefore, among those most affected by the benefits cuts initiated in the 1991 Budget, ironically referred to by Finance Minister, Ruth Richardson, as 'the Mother of all Budgets' and defended by Jenny Shipley, the Minister of Social Welfare, as a strategy directed at encouraging 'autonomy' and 'independence' (Shipley, 1991).

Maori women are particularly likely to rely on the state for economic support. In the year to March 1992, 40 per cent of the regular and recurring income of Maori women came from government income support programs. This was a significant increase on levels of state dependency in the year to March 1984, when only 26 per cent of Maori women's income came from this source (Statistics New Zealand, 1993, pp. 115–18). Women and their children are also major users of state services such as public health care, partly as a consequence of their use of maternity services (Else, 1992, pp. 239–40; Statistics New Zealand, 1993, p. 159). Many women, therefore, have a vested interest in states organised around assumptions of inter-dependence rather than individual autonomy and orientations to state policy that assume a commitment to the redistribution of income and provision of public services.

An explicit philosophy of self-reliance and autonomy is articulated in Aotearoa by politicians and supporters of the neoliberal party, ACT (Prebble, 1996; Awatere Huata, 1996). But both Labour and National Governments since 1984 have embraced aspects of neoliberalism, withdrawing from active control over interest and exchange rates, lifting subsidies on agricultural production and exports, reducing direct taxation, increasing user charges for education and health, reducing state intervention in industrial relations, and privileging those involved in paid work over those on benefits. A multiparty agreement on retirement income has at its base the assumption that state support is there to complement individual responsibility for retirement savings.

Maori and non-Maori women have played a significant part in the creation of the New Zealand welfare state. Since the nineteenth century, women's organisations have urged the state to support a range of public health measures such as ante-natal classes, nursing assistance for women with babies, immunisation and food handling regulations, the distribution of nutritional information, contraceptive advice, and cervical screening (Else, 1993, pp. 239–86). They have also highlighted the relationship between health status and other social indicators such as housing, unemployment, and poverty. The Maori Women's Welfare League, founded in 1951 to promote the health, education, and well-being of Maori women and children, and supported by government funding, has had a particularly important role to play in highlighting the relationship between health status and socio-economic status (Rei, 1993b; Szaszy, 1993).

Women have a long history of involvement in the provision of social services in both a voluntary and paid capacity (Tennant, 1993, pp. 109–19). Women are not just the recipients of state services, but are significantly represented among employees in state funded organisations and professionally involved in these services (Hernes, 1987, p. 86). It is hardly surprising, therefore, that nurses, kindergarten, primary and secondary teachers have been in the forefront of struggles with the state since the late 1980s, as successive governments in New Zealand have sought to contain state spending, exert control over state workers, reduce state provision of services, and organise state institutions as businesses. Such struggles have often involved female-dominated professional groups in confrontations with female politicians. This highlights the complexity of the gendered features of contemporary state politics and the diversity of positions that women might occupy *vis-à-vis* 'the state', as clients, as state employees, as politicians, and as community-based political activists (Du Plessis, 1993, pp. 223–5).

From Theorising 'the State' to Deconstructing '*the State*'

Some analysts have looked critically at attempts to develop gender-focused theories of the state and asked whether feminists need 'a theory of the state'

(Allen, 1990). Allen has argued that 'the state' is 'a category of abstraction that is too aggressive, too unitary and too unspecific to be of much use in addressing the disaggregated, diverse and specific (or local) sites that must be of most pressing concern to feminists' (Allen, 1990, p. 22). Feminists need to pay attention to specificity, to particular state institutions and strategies with respect to birthing, childcare, health, and housing.

Curthoys has looked at the challenges for feminists in Canada, the USA, Australia, and New Zealand of claims by indigenous people 'demanding sovereignty, compensation, and self-determination' (1993, p. 35). She argues that feminist theorising about 'the state' and feminist claims on the state are often based on understandings of 'state', 'property', and 'citizenship' which have been imposed on colonised peoples. These discourses were used to construct the identities of settler women as citizens and assert their rights *vis-à-vis* men. In the New Zealand context, citizenship for non-Maori, whether recent settlers or the descendants of settlers, has become entwined around interpretations of the Treaty of Waitangi. Yeatman (1995) has discussed some of the complex connections between feminist critiques of conceptions of sovereign selfhood and Maori challenges to the sovereignty of a predominantly Pakeha state. Others have also addressed the challenge for feminists of the constitutional, analytical, and political issues surrounding the Treaty of Waitangi (Elvidge, 1987; Irwin, 1992; Jones, 1992 and 1995; Evans, 1994; Johnston and Pihama, 1994 and 1995).

Some of these challenges were acted on by those establishing the Ministry of Women's Affairs in 1984. Maori women presented a detailed case for a separate Maori women's secretariat, Te Ohu Whakatupu, an autonomous structure within the ministry directed at providing government with policy advice relating to Maori women (McDowell, 1995). This secretariat was established in 1986 (Rosier, 1986; Washington, 1988; O'Regan, 1992). Te Ohu Whakatupu was informed by understandings of what was involved in practising 'biculturalism', 'rangatiratanga', 'partnership', or 'Maori sovereignty' in the context of a state bureaucracy (Ministry of Women's Affairs, 1988). Its formation was, however, also shaped by Pakeha feminists' engagement with 'the state' and the arguments developed during the 1970s by radical feminists for autonomous women-focused structures.

Needs Discourse and Feminist Claims on the State

Feminist demands on the state have often been based on claims about women's 'needs'—their need for inexpensive, high-quality childcare in order to combine paid work and responsibilities as parents, their need for preventative health services such as cervical screening, non-interventionist birthing services, and freedom from sexual harassment at work. Much state action in social democracies such as New Zealand is driven by what Fraser has referred to as 'needs discourses'—sets of statements that 'construct' the needs of various sections of the population. Fraser has argued that the combination of 'needs talk' and claims about 'rights' and 'interests' is crucial to political life in contemporary social democracies (Fraser, 1989, p. 162). Feminists are now analysing the processes involved in defining needs and the mechanisms by which some people are constituted as authorities on the definition of the needs of 'families', 'women', 'Maori', and so on (Fraser, 1989; Watson, 1995; Jones, 1995).

Needs discourse can be used to construct women as 'victims' or as 'lacking' qualities that are better represented among men. Talk about women's needs may focus on problems concerning vocational qualifications, women's concentration in work that does not demand high levels of technical expertise, or their needs for part-time and flexible work in order to meet demands on them in their homes. While state intervention is demanded as a way of remedying these 'lacks', these arguments may also reinforce the forms of differentiation that generate the demands in the first place (Jones, 1995, p. 108). Watson has argued that, '[n]eeds discourse has operated to provide women with all sorts of benefits and to shift back the boundaries of the domestic. But it has also confirmed women as lacking, marginal and powerless, as subjects to be regulated' (1995, p. 169). Constructions of women as the victims of men, employers, or the state are challenged by poststructuralist analyses of power that have been used extensively by feminist analysts since the mid-1980s.

Power, Women, and State Processes

Poststructuralist analyses draw on Foucault's idea that 'power' does not lie solely with those in positions of structural control, but works 'in a capillary fashion from below' (Pringle, 1995, p. 207). Women, according to this view, are both constrained by gender conventions and are active agents in producing gender differences. While 'men' and 'patriarchy' can no longer be objectified and blamed, this analysis suggests the possibility of different forms of action— the potential of different ways of 'doing' power. It defuses the force of some women's resentment against 'men' and 'the state', but it also opens up the possibility of seeing the power of politicians, bureaucracies, and individual men as contingent, fragile, less inevitable.

These moves in feminist theory are sometimes seen as the indulgent pursuit of academics far removed from the everyday realities of women battling to house themselves and their children, extract necessary services from health providers and meet the electricity bill (Smyth, 1996). They are, however, relevant when viewed with regard to the diverse range of state-funded institutions with which individuals interact in a restructured New Zealand, and the different positions they occupy with respect to these organisational forms. Negotiating a relationship with state-funded organisations may mean that individuals must place themselves in a variety of identity categories (sole parent, woman, sportswoman, asthmatic, factory worker, accident victim, beneficiary, social worker, kindergarten teacher, community activist) in order to negotiate access to resources from Housing New Zealand, the Hillary Commission, Crown health enterprises, the Ministry of Education, the New Zealand Employment Service, the Accident Compensation Corporation, and the Department of Social Welfare. Women's access to resources made available by government departments, quasi-state organisations, local government, and voluntary agencies may depend on their skills in constructing themselves as a variety of different 'subjects', telling a variety of narratives about themselves and their personal circumstances, drawing on different discourses or sets of understandings about gender, family, health, and employment status. In constructing these stories, women may draw on traditional understandings of women as unpaid family caregivers, but they may also use discourses that challenge the inevitability of such responsibilities and assert their right to resources that would facilitate their access to vocational training, tertiary education, sporting facilities, and paid work.

Research with women in Queensland mining communities has convinced Gibson-Graham that feminism involves the undermining of an accepted 'gender discourse' about differences between women and men (Gibson-Graham, 1995, pp. 219–20). They focus on the subversive features of the different identities, interests, and needs that develop when people resist the actions of employers or state actors. The destabilisation of gender advocated by Gibson-Graham undermines the rhetorical force of arguments about 'women', 'men', 'capitalism', and 'patriarchy', but it also suggests that inequalities between women and men, and constraints on women, are processes, understandings, and forms of organisation that can be changed.

These ideas about mechanisms, processes, and specificity have particular relevance in contemporary New Zealand. 'The state' may always have been more complex and less coherent than some social theorists recognised, but over a decade of deregulation and devolution has produced increasingly diverse forms of state-funded institutions. Large government departments have been divided up into policy-focused ministries and a variety of state-funded businesses or autonomous institutions engaged in quality control of state-funded organisations. There is no longer a Department of Education, but a Ministry of Education, a New Zealand Qualifications Authority, a standards review body that audits educational institutions, and boards of trustees that run thousands of school businesses.

While feminists focusing on women's health may have previously made claims on the minister and officials in the Department of Health, they may now have to take up particular issues with their regional health authority or the Crown health enterprise in their city or district. Although all regional health authorities and Crown health enterprises are subject to monitoring by the Ministry of Health, the new structures of health care delivery are supposed to attend to regional and local differences. This requires attention to specificity by both administrators and political actors.

Feminists who want to study how taxes are spent to sustain or develop public services require theories that address the complexity of the state and quasi-state organisations with which they interact. Women have often been consummate local networkers. Their work in voluntary organisations and small activist groups is sustained through grassroots networks. They may, therefore, respond well to the challenges of attending to the specifics of local context, the strategies of different Crown health enterprises, and the organisational culture of different boards of trustees.

Watson (1995) has argued that diversity within the complex and contradictory set of organisational forms that is 'the state' is likely to produce similar diversity in the discourses and practices of feminists who are state officials, politicians, appointees to quasi-state institutions, teachers, health activists, welfare beneficiaries, church members, voluntary workers, employers, academics, local body politicians, managers, and social workers. This opens up the possibility of a feminist politics that embraces a variety of interventions directed at particular forms of social change.

Pringle has argued that a feminist politics directed at 'overthrowing' 'the state', 'capitalism', or 'patriarchy' is misplaced. Feminists can, however, direct themselves to 'contesting specific instances of power' (Pringle, 1995, p. 211). Although this may appear to be an easier task than confronting 'capitalism' and 'patriarchy' or 'the state', it still requires a sharp understanding of the way different people are positioned, the styles of talk that are used, the rules of the game, and a capacity to conceive of alternatives. Against the background of these challenges, women who differ with respect to ethnicity, bureaucratic power, sexual orientation, age, and socio-economic status daily combine visions for the future with fragments of the ideas discussed in this chapter as they interact with the complex set of practices and organisational forms that are referred to as 'the state'. In the process they contest, reproduce, and remake the dynamics of power between women and men, shifting the ground for a new set of political actors.

Guide to Readings

In the last twenty years there has been a rapid expansion in feminist literature on women and 'the state'. Debates in the 1970s and early 1980s were dominated by the work of socialist feminists based in Britain (see Wilson, 1977; McIntosh, 1978; Barrett, 1980). An early edited collection was Holter (1984). International comparisons of welfare policies relating to women was the focus of Sassoon's (1987) text. Baldock and Cass (eds) (1983) was the first significant Australian collection of feminist writing on the welfare state.

Theoretical engagement with state policies and political theory in these collections was extended by Fraser (1989). Pateman (1988) and MacKinnon (1989) also produced extended philosophical essays on the limitations of liberal and Marxist theory for feminists interested in analysing 'the state'.

Franzway et al. (1989) reviewed feminist theories on the state. Their attempt to identify the criteria for 'a theory of the state' and their analysis of the state as 'complex' and 'contradictory' met with a critical response in a number of the contributions to Watson's collection (1990). Other texts appearing at this time analysed femocracy as the professionalisation of feminist ideology (Yeatman, 1990), looked sceptically at the institutionalisation of EEO initiatives (Poiner and Wills, 1991), or challenged feminists to look more carefully at differences between women (Pettman, 1992). Eisenstein (1991) wrote about her experience as a feminist bureaucrat in Australia.

An analysis of family policy in New Zealand is found in Koopman-Boyden and Scott (1984). More explicitly feminist analyses of state policies in the context of Aotearoa are found in Du Plessis et al. (1992), Briar et al. (1992), and Olsson (1992). The only text produced in New Zealand by a feminist economist provides excellent insights into, among other things, struggles with respect to equal pay and pay equity (Hyman, 1994). Two recent collections edited by Edwards and Magarey (1995) and Caine and Pringle (1995) are useful as introductions to contemporary international literature analysing feminism, state policy, and state institutions.

CHAPTER THIRTEEN

THE WELFARE STATE

CHRIS RUDD

It may be thought that policies directed towards health, education and welfare are not directly part of the political-economy nexus; they are 'social policies' and, as such, are only indirectly related to the economic sphere. This would be to take an extremely narrow view of the term political economy. For example, as the chapter on education (Chapter 11) clearly demonstrates, policy-making in this 'social' area has directly reflected the changing needs and imperatives of the New Zealand economy over the postwar period. This chapter will similarly endeavour to show how political involvement in economic management has shaped social welfare policy in postwar New Zealand. The chapter begins by looking at the definitions and different types of welfare state. It then goes on to examine the various historical stages of the development of the New Zealand welfare state from its origins in the 1930s to the changes made to the provision of welfare by the fourth National Government in the 1990s.

Definitions and Types

In approaching a definition of the welfare state, it becomes clear why the 'social', the 'economic', and the 'political' cannot be treated separately. The welfare state is more than just the sum of government expenditure on social security systems designed to maintain a minimum income for those suffering from sickness or injury, for those unable to work owing to old age or unemployment, and for those requiring public assistance for other personal services such as childcare. If this was all that a welfare state stood for, it would indeed be 'marginalist' or 'residual'. The welfare state in this chapter, however, is viewed from a social democratic perspective as encompassing a range of government policies other than those that ensure a minimum income for all. Such policies are designed to protect a citizen's income and employment status through a variety of measures ranging from import protection and export promotion, to health and safety regulations at work, public works programs, and compulsory wage arbitration. A welfare state in this sense, first tries to protect citizens from the unwelcome effects of the operation of market forces, and, second, to compensate those who have been adversely affected by market forces (the unemployed) as well as those unable or unwilling to participate in paid work (sole parents, the sick, the elderly). In this expanded definition of a welfare state, the citizen is viewed as having a right to a 'decent' standard of living, irrespective of their status in the labour market. In other words, social needs (for example, to enjoy a healthy and happy life) are not subordinated to or dependent upon a person's economic power or status in the labour market.

It will be apparent from the above discussion of definitions that there are different types of welfare state. Following the pioneering work of Esping-Andersen, four factors can be identified with which to create a typology of welfare states (Esping-Andersen, 1985, 1989 and 1990). The first factor measures the extent of decommodification of labour. Decommodification relates to the universalism of welfare benefits. Are the benefits available to all citizens, irrespective of demonstrable need, or are the benefits means-tested (or needs-based)? The introduction of free health care would be an example of a move towards decommodifying welfare provision; so, too, would measures entitling citizens to income support should they choose to opt out of work to raise children or care for elderly parents. Furthermore, in a decommodified welfare system benefit levels are not determined by length of participation in the workforce, as this would create inequalities between those in paid and unpaid employment.

The second factor is the degree of solidarity or social stratification embedded in the system of welfare provision. Stratification refers to the development of a dual welfare system in which low-income groups rely on the state for welfare whereas more prosperous groups of workers buy supplementary welfare in the market, for example private pensions and private health care. The state may also single out particular groups of workers for privileged provision, most typically state employees themselves. In such a welfare set-up, welfare policies serve to reinforce social inequalities that already arise from the unequal distribution of market power among citizens.

Income redistribution is linked to the third feature that helps to determine the type of welfare state—the nature of the taxation system, whether it is progressive or regressive. 'Taxing the incomes of the rich to subsidise the incomes of the poor' may be stating it simplistically but this nevertheless encapsulates the way a government can use fiscal policy to achieve welfare policy goals. Flattening the personal income tax scale and increasing indirect taxes, particularly broad-based taxes on goods and services, are two ways in which a government might signal its lack of commitment to income redistribution.

The fourth and final criterion by which to typify welfare states concerns the state's commitment to a policy goal of full employment. A government may seek to achieve full employment through a variety of measures, some of which were mentioned earlier, for example, public works and import protection. Job security provides citizens with the psychological and financial wherewithal to pursue a 'healthy and happy life'. This is not to suggest that some governments may have unemployment as a policy goal but some governments have made price stability and market deregulation the priority and have accepted the adverse consequences this has had on employment as 'unfortunate, but necessary'.

Using the above four criteria, two ideal types of welfare state can be identified.[1] At one end of the welfare state spectrum is the liberal, residualist, or minimal welfare state, characterised by:

(i)   welfare benefits that are means-tested (non-universal) with strict eligibility criteria;
(ii) promotion of a work ethic resulting in stigma associated with being a welfare beneficiary which, combined with
(iii) modest amounts paid to beneficiaries, 'encourages' people both to work and
(iv) to supplement or top up state welfare with private welfare purchased in the marketplace (reinforcing stratification);
(v)   a taxation system with a flattened personal tax scale and significant emphasis on indirect taxes;
(vi) full employment is not a specified policy goal of government (price stability, on the other hand, may be).

At the other end of the spectrum is the social democratic welfare regime characterised by the opposite features to those of the liberal welfare state:

(i)   welfare benefits are universal with every citizen treated equally;
(ii) everyone has a right to receive state welfare with no moral stigma associated with being a welfare recipient;
(iii) benefits are sufficiently adequate so that there is little need to supplement them by purchasing additional benefits in the private sector;
(iv) a system of progressive taxation consisting of steeply graduated personal tax rates and little reliance on indirect taxes as a means of raising revenue;
(v)   a variety of legislative and regulatory measures used by governments to pursue an economic policy goal of full employment.

Although it may not be possible to identify countries that completely satisfy the criteria of either extreme types of welfare regime, it is feasible to locate countries approximately closer to one particular end of the welfare state spectrum. Britain and its former colonies—Canada, Australia, Ireland, and the USA—approximate the residual or liberal welfare state. The Scandinavian countries—Norway, Sweden, Denmark, and Finland—come closest to examples of the social democratic welfare state. Other OECD countries, such as Austria, Germany, France, Belgium, and the Netherlands, tend to fall somewhere in between, combining a mix of the two extreme types. Where does New Zealand fit in this welfare state scheme? The remainder of this chapter seeks to answer this question by examining the development of the New Zealand welfare state since the 1930s. An equally important question is, of course, whether New Zealand has shifted along the welfare regime dimension over the last sixty years and, if so, in what direction and how far?

Laying the Foundations of a Welfare State: The First Labour Government

New Zealand's first Labour Government entered office in 1935 in the wake of a severe economic recession. Labour's major achievement in its fourteen years of office was to use the powers of the state to pursue an economic policy designed to help create, finance, and maintain a range of welfare services that had hitherto been either virtually non-existent in New Zealand or accessible only to a limited few.

The view that New Zealand's economic woes could be attributed to its vulnerability in the international economic environment led the Labour Government to introduce a wide range of measures intended to increase state control of the domestic economy, for example, import licensing, exchange controls, and controls over domestic credit, interest rates, prices, and incomes. The exigencies of war considerably paved the way for the government to increase its economic activities without facing undue popular or political opposition. Some of the government controls such as rationing were removed soon after the war but many others remained in force until the 1980s (for example, import licensing and financial controls).

This increase in government intervention in the economy was a direct response to the Depression of the 1930s and the perceived failure of previous governments to combat such a recession with neoclassical economic remedies. The overriding priority was to achieve full employment and to avoid a return to the mass unemployment and widespread poverty of the early 1930s. This commitment to what would later be called a Keynesian, as opposed to a monetarist, approach to economics, was embodied in the nationalisation of the Reserve Bank by the Labour Government in 1936. Both comment in Parliament and the actual wording of the revised Reserve Bank Act made it clear that the government intended to directly use the bank to promote and maintain 'the economic and social welfare of New Zealand' (Dalziel, 1993, p. 80).

One element in the Labour Government's greater control of economic activity that has not been mentioned so far was the incorporation of organised labour into a compulsory arbitration system. The Labour Government restored compulsory arbitration and compulsory union membership for occupations covered by awards. This strengthened a union movement that had been severely weakened by the Depression but at the price of reduced autonomy. A reinvigorated union movement supporting a government committed to full employment fostered a level of social solidarity that had been absent during the previous decade.

As regards taxation, the first Labour Government was forced to raise taxation rates in general and to levy a new social security tax to help pay for its new comprehensive system of welfare benefits. This, however, also coincided with a decisive shift from a heavy reliance on indirect taxes levied on a wide range of everyday goods and services, to taxes on income. It was during the Second World War that revenue from direct taxation overtook that from indirect taxation (Hawke, 1983, p. 170). So, although there was a considerable increase in the amount of tax raised under the first Labour Government, it was taxation based on the progressivity principle.

The first Labour Government paid particular attention to the problem of substandard, overcrowded housing conditions that were a legacy of the Depression years. The government did not opt to build state houses itself but to administer and regulate the private production of housing (Davidson, 1994, p. 68) and to make these homes available at affordable (that is, below the market rate) rents to low-income workers. At the same time, the State Advances Corporation set up in 1936 provided low-interest loans to first-time buyers. During the first Labour Government's fourteen years in office, over 30 000 state houses were built in what was a determined effort to decommodify housing in New Zealand. There was the presumption that every citizen had a right to a decent standard of housing, regardless of their earning power in the marketplace. State housing was to be of a good quality, not just reserved for the very poor—it was not intended to lead to a ghettoisation of the poor. The reflection of social stratification in housing tenure was to be minimised.

The 1938 Social Security Act was the central piece of legislation underpinning Labour's social policy. The act 'included benefits for the elderly, widows, orphans, children, invalids, miners, the sick, the unemployed, those who had fought in the Land Wars, and an emergency benefit' (O'Brien and Wilkes, 1993, pp. 53–4). Some of the benefits were new (for example, sickness benefits, unemployment benefits to women) and the benefit rates were generous. In addition to the welfare benefits, there were reforms to the health system and, by the end of the war, New Zealand had probably the world's first national health system consisting of free medical treatment in hospitals for both in- and out-patients, a partly subsidised general practitioner's service, free prescriptions, and a range of medical benefits for maternity, physiotherapy, district nursing, X-ray diagnostics, district nursing, and domestic assistance.

Sutch lauded the new social security and health benefits as meaning 'more dignity and serenity in old age, less anxiety and suffering during working life, less pinching and scraping and undernourishment, more freedom and humanity in family relationships, and, to the individual person, greater opportunity for self-expression' (Sutch, 1966, p. 237). Sutch's praise was no doubt justified and New Zealand did, after the Second World War, have a welfare system that was 'more extensive and more generous than the country had known before' (Oliver, 1988, p. 29). But at the same time, it was closer to a residual than to a social democratic welfare state. This was particularly the case with the welfare benefits, all of which were means-tested except for pensions for those aged over sixty-five and the family benefit, which became universal after 1946. Furthermore, the distinction between the deserving and undeserving poor, which had been such a salient feature of the poor laws of nineteenth-century Britain and the public assistance programs of New Zealand at the turn of the century, was still be found in the 1938 Social Security Act. As O'Brien and Wilkes note, the family benefit could be stopped if the authorities believed it was not being used for the children; the unemployment benefit could be postponed if it was thought that the applicants had become unemployed because of misconduct or had made themselves unavailable for work; an invalid's benefit was to be forfeited if it was thought a person's incapacity was self-induced (O'Brien and Wilkes, 1993, p. 54).

The irony was, therefore, that while the first Labour Government's economic policy of full employment, its progressive taxation system, and state-regulated labour relations were all conducive to a social democratic welfare regime, with the possible exception of housing this was not matched by a social policy designed to decommodify labour. A further irony was that, during the first two postwar decades, this asymmetry between the two policy fields did not greatly matter as full employment meant that few people were forced to rely on the minimal welfare safety net provided by the state.

1950s–1960s: Enjoying the Golden Weather

Until the oil crisis of 1973, official registered unemployment in New Zealand never exceeded 1 per cent of the workforce. Economic growth averaged 4.5 per cent per annum (see Chapter 1). Following the waterfront strike of 1951, industrial unrest was minimal throughout the 1950s and most of the 1960s (see Chapter 7). The cause of this was not the arbitration system per se but the fact that, during this period, workers enjoyed rising real wages and employers historically high levels of profitability.

Both National and Labour Governments pursued a full employment policy during this period and full employment was the cornerstone of the welfare state. Castles coined the term 'wage earners' welfare state' to characterise New Zealand's welfare system at this time (1985, p. 103). Even more precisely, it was a welfare state for workers in unions, covered by awards and predominantly for males. An able-bodied, full-time employed male received a 'social wage' as determined by the arbitration courts, a wage sufficient to care for his dependants, that is, a wife and three children. For people who did not fit into this category, the state provided an array of welfare benefits that remained largely unimproved during the 1950s and 1960s. Women, in particular, were disadvantaged under such a welfare regime as they either had to conform to the cult of domesticity, irrespective of how unsatisfactory or unequal their relationship was with their male 'breadwinner' and 'head of household', or they could face moral opprobrium and financial insecurity by voluntarily leaving such a relationship and placing themselves at the discretionary mercy of the Social Security Department.

As regards the range of welfare benefits introduced under the first Labour administration, little was done throughout the 1950s and 1960s to make them less selective and more decommodifying. This reinforces a point made by Thomson that what follows after being the 'first' with comprehensive social security also matters (1991, p. 100). From 1950 until the early 1970s, there was a steady erosion of welfare benefit levels. The National Party was in government for all but three years from 1949 to 1972 and while it maintained its commitment to full employment, it failed to ensure that the value of welfare and medical benefits kept pace with changes in real wages and living standards (see Sutch, 1966, pp. 461–2; Hanson, 1980, Ch. 9; Easton, 1981, Ch. 4; Martin, 1981; Castles, 1985, p. 35). In comparative terms, benefit expenditure as a percentage of gross national product (GNP) increased by just less than 2 percentage points in New Zealand between 1949/50 and 1965/66, a record matched only by Japan of other OECD member countries (ILO, 1964–66). Between 1962 and 1972 New Zealand was only one of two OECD countries whose public income maintenance expenditure as a ratio to GDP actually declined (OECD, 1976, p. 35).

The National Government during this period also did little to extend or continue the housing policy of the first Labour Government. In fact, there was a switch in emphasis in the affluent 1950s and 1960s from state provision of housing to state promotion of owner-occupied housing. This recommodification of housing was reflected in the decline of state houses built after 1950 and the sale of state houses to private owners (27 000 between 1950 and 1970). Even the second Labour Government (1957–60) fostered private over state housing when it allowed the capitalisation of family benefits to provide a deposit for house purchase (Davidson, 1994, p. 103). All this was to benefit middle-income earners and increasingly to restrict state housing to the poorest sections of New Zealand society. State housing was becoming the last resort for the 'needy'.

The conclusion to be drawn from all this is that the golden weather shone rather more brightly on the 'typical' family headed by an able-bodied, unionised, award-covered, waged working male, than it did on those who did not fall into such a category. It was not a welfare regime that decommodified labour and it fostered stratification by creating inequalities between workers in different occupations, between unionised and non-unionised workers, between owner-occupiers and state house tenants, and between males and females. Towards the end of the 1960s, pressures were emerging to improve the value of benefits and to remove the gender discrimination embedded in the administration of welfare. Although such pressures for change were largely successful in the short run, in the long run, changes to economic policy first undermined, and then reversed, many of the gains made during the 1970s.

The 1970s: A Decade of Change

Changes in social policy during the 1970s indicated a shift towards a more social democratic model of welfare provision. In 1969, a Royal Commission of Inquiry on Social Security had been established and this reported its findings in 1972. The commission supported a continuation of the existing welfare set-up but with specific recommendations that (a) benefit rates be increased; (b) the 'morals clause' (whereby the 'moral character and sober habits' of a claimant be assessed to determine eligibility) be removed; and (c) a statutory domestic purposes benefit (DPB) be introduced for sole parents, women caring for infirm and sick persons, and women alone.

Although all but two statutory benefits remained income- or means-tested, the increase in the value of benefits was a move towards decommodifying labour. The DPB treated women as independent citizens and not just as dependants of men. Women were now free, at least in theory, to leave an unsatisfactory relationship and, by right to receive support from the state without being subject to an investigation of personal circumstances in order to determine whether they were 'deserving'.

That women were to be treated as full citizens,[2] reinforcing the principle of social solidarity, was also to be found in the newly created Accident Compensation Scheme which came into effect on 1 April 1974. The scheme was the result of another royal commission, this time on Compensation for Personal Injury. The commission had reported in 1967, but years of political and technical debate had followed. What resulted was an innovative scheme (both for New Zealand and internationally) of state assistance for the disabled. First, the private right to sue for accident compensation was abolished and replaced with a 'no fault' principle. Second, all citizens were covered for the costs of accidents, twenty-four hours a day. Third, for accidents at the workplace there was provision for earnings-related compensation. Finally, the scheme was to be funded by a combination of levies on employers and motor vehicles, and direct taxation.

From the perspective of the welfare state, the key factor in the new scheme was the replacement of individual liability with community responsibility for the accident victim. In the words of the commission, 'the community must protect all citizens (including the self-employed) and the housewives who sustain them from the burdens of individual losses when the ability to contribute to the general welfare by their work has been interrupted by physical incapacity' (Royal Commission of Inquiry Upon Workers' Compensation, 1967, para. 55). From a feminist perspective, this was an acknowledgment, albeit in sexist language, of the contribution to society of unpaid 'housewives'.

The final major change in social policy in the 1970s concerned pensions. Pensions, like other welfare benefits, had fallen in real value during the 1950s and 1960s. With an eye to gaining the support of such a significant minority of voters, the National and Labour parties had tried to outbid one another as to what they could offer the elderly. The outcome was the National Party's proposal, during the 1975 election campaign, of a national superannuation scheme, which was duly introduced in 1977 following National's election victory.

Like Accident Compensation, national superannuation treated women equally. National superannuation was also a very generous scheme financially. Before national superannuation there was a universal (but taxed) superannuation available to those aged over sixty-five and an income-tested (but not taxed) old age pension for those sixty and over. National super-annuation replaced both these with a single, universal, taxable pension available to all over the age of sixty and paid at the relatively generous rate of 40 per cent of the average wage for a married person and 48 per cent for a single person (the old age pension was 32 per cent of the average wage) (St John, 1992, p. 128). The impact on public expenditure was considerable. In 1975, 289 340 people received either universal superannuation or the old age benefit for a total cost of $365.8 million. Five years later, the number of national superannuants was 405 834 and the cost $1334 million (Department of Social Welfare, 1996, pp. 8–9). This was an increase of over 80 per cent in real terms.

The commitment to full employment was once more affirmed during the 1970s with a change to the Reserve Bank Act in 1973. Previously the bank was required to promote 'employment'; now it was to promote 'full employment'. This, together with a taxation regime that remained progressive and the changes to the welfare benefits already discussed, suggest a welfare state looking more like the social democratic than the liberal ideal. But although the 1970s offered the promise of a more rights-based welfare state, this promise remained unfulfilled. The reasons for this lay in New Zealand's changing political economy. During the 1950s and 1960s New Zealand economy had been protected by an array of regulations—import licensing, exchange controls and the like—that had enabled it to operate at near full employment levels. Protections safeguarded the balance of payments against 'crises' and, in the long term, fostered domestic industries by encouraging industrialisation (see Chapter 2). And governments during this period used the public sector to absorb labour unwanted in the private sector.[3] With a guaranteed export market in Britian and a healthy balance of payments, New Zealand governments had sufficient overseas earnings to be able to afford high levels of public sector employment.

The government's handling of the economy came into question as New Zealand's increasing integration into a global economy, its loss of privileged access to the British export market, and resulting balance of payments problems all contributed to growing unemployment. Despite what the Reserve Bank Act said, full employment could not be created by legislation. Whereas fewer than 10 000 New Zealanders were unemployed and seeking work during the 1950s and 1960s, by 1971 the figure had risen to over 16 000; a decade later the number had reached 60 000, and by 1986 over 100 000 New Zealanders were unemployed and seeking work (Department of Statistics, 1987–88, p. 338). Over this same period there was a downturn in economic growth, high inflation, declining profitability, and a cessation of real wage growth. There was also a 'fiscal crisis', with a small Budget surplus in 1976/77 becoming a Budget deficit amounting to 6.9 per cent of GDP in 1983/84 (Dalziel, 1992, p. 20). Not surprisingly, the major component of government expenditure showing significant growth during this period was social welfare spending. Expenditure in this area (excluding health and education) already accounted for 21 per cent of total government expenditure in 1971/72. By 1980/81 it had increased to 28.3 per cent and 30 per cent by 1986/87 (see Table 13.1). As a percentage of GDP, welfare spending had risen from 6 per cent to over 11 per cent during the same period.

Table 13.1 Social welfare expenditure as a percentage of total government expenditure and GDP (selected years)

	1971/72	1974/75	1977/78	1980/81	1983/84	1986/87	1989/90	1992/93	1995/96
As a percentage of total government expenditure	21.0	23.2	27.7	28.4	28.4	31.0	40.5	38.7	37.6
As a percentage of GDP	5.7	7.8	10.5	11.2	11.6	11.8	14.4	13.9	13.0

Source: Data provided by Treasury, projection for 1995/96.

The critics of the Keynesian direction of the government's economic policies advocated reforms that would, if implemented, have a significant impact on the welfare state. In fact, as will be shown in the next section, all the main pillars of the welfare state were subjected to major change: the abandonment of full employment as a priority policy goal and the consequent deregulation of the labour market, the shift away from progressive taxation, and changes to welfare benefits leading to a greater commodification of labour and growing social inequality.

The Fourth Labour Government: 1984–90

Looking at the overall record of the fourth Labour Government might leave the impression that, while there were radical changes in the sphere of economic policy, social policy was left relatively untouched. It was, after all, the defence of social policy from encroachment by 'Rogernomics' that led the Prime Minister, David Lange, to force the resignation of his Finance Minister, Roger Douglas, in December 1988. It was also Lange who, in 1986, set up the Royal Commission on Social Policy that both Douglas and Treasury opposed (Easton, 1989b, p. 174). The commission's report (1988), although critical of some aspects of the way in which welfare was administered in New Zealand, nevertheless expressed clear support for a substantial state role in the provision of social welfare and an antipathy towards attempts fundamentally to restructure the existing welfare system.

Yet any impression that the fourth Labour Government successfully protected social policy against Rogernomics would be highly misleading. This government's abandonment of full employment and the shift towards a more regressive taxation system directly affected the welfare state in New Zealand. In addition, changes to welfare benefits were made, although it was not until the fourth National Government that systematic changes to welfare benefits were proposed as part of a 'grand redesign' of the welfare state.

The range of measures adopted by the fourth Labour Government to deregulate the New Zealand economy have been extensively discussed elsewhere in the literature (for example, Bollard and Buckle, 1987; Holland and Boston, 1990). The removal or reduction in tariffs, import licensing, exchange controls, and export incentives were all designed to improve the international competitiveness of New Zealand firms and their products. Whether this was successful and whether alternative strategies would have achieved the same goals is not the point at issue here. The point is that this program of deregulation was to have a profound effect on the financial and psychological security of many New Zealanders. Labour's two terms in office witnessed increases in poverty, income inequality, and unemployment (see Chapter 5). Labour abandoned Keynesianism for monetarism and, with it, the commitment to full employment. It was not just that control of inflation now had a higher priority than promoting employment; the new Reserve Bank Act 1989 laid down only one statutory objective of monetary policy: achieving and maintaining stability in the general level of prices (Dalziel, 1993, p. 84).

The fourth Labour Government also made changes to the taxation system that shifted the New Zealand welfare regime further towards a residual model. For monetarist economists whose thinking imbued the Treasury briefing papers (see Chapter 4), the impact of fiscal policy on the economic activity of firms and individuals is of crucial importance. High direct taxes, such as taxes on incomes and profits, discourage production and investment and reduce the incentive to work, while encouraging tax avoidance. For this reason, the fourth Labour Government introduced measures to reduce direct taxes and increase indirect taxes. In 1987 the Finance Minister announced that the government was going to introduce a single income tax rate. This was an extremely radical proposal as it removed completely the progressivity of the tax system, the principle that the more people earn, the more they should pay in tax—redistributing from the rich to the poor. Although the proposal was defeated and brought to a climax the conflict between the Finance Minister and the Prime Minister, personal tax rates were flattened with the top marginal rate reduced from 48 to 33 per cent.[4] This led to a significant fall in income tax as a source of revenue, from 74 per cent of total tax revenue in 1980, to 64 per cent in 1990 (Birks, 1992, p. 273). The second major tax change had occurred earlier in 1986, with the introduction of the goods and services tax (GST).[5] GST is an indirect tax levied at a flat rate on all goods and services purchased. Originally the GST rate was 10 per cent, raised to 12.5 per cent in 1989. It is a potentially regressive tax, with people on lower incomes paying a larger proportion of their income in GST than those on higher incomes.[6]

Welfare payments are intended to redistribute income and if the taxation system does little to ameliorate income inequalities, welfare benefits take on an added importance. But even before the fourth Labour Government came to power, the previous National Government had taken measures to make some welfare benefits less generous, for example, the reductions in DPB in 1977 and the relative level of superannuation in 1979. Reducing the value of benefits and tightening eligibility criteria were measures pursued further by the fourth Labour Government. An income test was introduced for national superannuation in 1985 and it was announced that the age of eligibility was to be increased, in stages, from sixty to sixty-five. All income-tested benefits were to be taxed as from October 1986. By the end of the fourth Labour Government's term of office in 1990, the Minister of Social Welfare was able to claim annual 'savings' in his portfolio of at least $800 million (*Dominion Sunday Times*, 4 March 1990).

There was also pressure from employers to reform the Accident Compensation Scheme. The amount paid out in compensation and medical expenditure had increased considerably since the scheme's introduction—between 1985 and 1990 at an average rate of 25 per cent per annum. Although there were no major changes to the scheme under the fourth Labour Government, neither did the government attempt to place the scheme on a securer financial basis, relying instead on increases in employer contributions, which simply increased employer hostility to the scheme's perceived 'generosity'. As with labour deregulation, it was left to the fourth National Government to pursue more fundamental changes in this area.

The 1970s saw a dramatic rise in the price of land and houses. Many people were trapped into rental accommodation as state assistance to buy was now very limited and private finance for a mortgage was out of their reach (or led to a large portion of income going to service the mortgage). The fourth Labour Government's economic policy of deregulation of the financial markets, and the subsequent rise in interest rates, worsened the situation of those seeking to buy their own home. The Labour Government also cut direct government expenditure on housing, which fell below 1 per cent of GNP after 1987. Funds allocated to the Housing Corporation were less in nominal terms in 1987/88 than in 1984/85. Housing in New Zealand was being recommodified and, with it, the deterioration of the housing opportunities of the working class both in the rental and ownership section of the market' (Davidson, 1994, p. 146).

At the end of the second term of the fourth Labour Government, one thing was clear: any expectation of a movement towards a social democratic welfare state, which the innovations of the 1970s might have engendered, was completely quashed. Quite the opposite occurred. Abandonment of full employment, a more regressive tax system, a leaner and meaner welfare benefit system, recommodified housing, and faltering steps towards reassessing the traditional role of the state in industrial relations[7] were all moves in the direction of a liberal welfare state. The fourth National Government was to continue this movement.

The Fourth National Government: 1990–96

The fourth National Government continued to support the Reserve Bank's pursuit of price stability as the aim of government monetary policy. Both New Zealand's main parties now embraced monetarism and rejected Keynesian economic policy prescriptions. The tax regime remained skewed in the regressive direction, with the announcement of income tax cuts in February 1996.[8] Furthermore, in announcing the package of tax changes, the Finance Minister made it clear that increasing the incomes of beneficiaries was not the purpose of the changes, as this might encourage people to leave work and go on benefits (*Otago Daily Times*, 20 February 1996).[9] The aim was to reward working families. This is a clear illustration of the commodification of labour. Citizens have no option but to participate in the workforce or become dependent on those who do participate.

From the neoclassical perspective, benefits should not be so generous as to encourage 'idleness' but instead should be sufficiently marginal to create an incentive to work. In this respect, National continued the fourth Labour Government's efforts to cut welfare benefits, but in a much more comprehensive fashion. It was made explicit that the aim of welfare changes was to shift people 'out of welfare into work'. What was made less explicit was that this was to be achieved primarily by making life on welfare as financially uncomfortable as possible. The December 1990 Economic and Social Initiative and the 1991 Budget introduced or proposed measures that were intended, in the words of the Prime Minister, to 'redesign the welfare state' (quoted in *Otago Daily Times*, 24 July 1991). The Minister of Social Welfare was equally explicit in her statement that the 'state will continue to provide a *safety net*—a modest standard below which people will not be allowed to fall provided they demonstrate they are prepared to *help themselves*' (Shipley, 1991, p. 13, emphasis added). This is a residual welfare state, with its distinction between the deserving and undeserving poor. Furthermore, the Minister of Welfare tried, with little success, to recreate the typical family or 'core family unit' as a basis for assessing welfare needs.

The changes made to the health and welfare benefits under the fourth National Government are too numerous to list (for details, see Boston and Dalziel, 1992; Kelsey, 1995). The main thrust of the changes, however, can be summarised as an intention to introduce stricter eligibility criteria (for example, increasing the stand-down period for the 'voluntary' unemployed from six weeks to six months), an increase in targeted as opposed to universal provision (abolition of the family benefit), and direct cuts in the rate (and indirect cuts through the refusal to adjust for inflation) for nearly all benefits, including pensions. Stricter targeting and the introduction and increase in user charges also occurred in the health and education areas.

The Accident Compensation Scheme had come under attack by employers during the 1980s as the cost of the scheme, and employer levies, increased. There was growing pressure to change those very features that had made the scheme so innovative when it was introduced—community (that is, public) responsibility for compensation for injuries both in the workplace and elsewhere, along with a no fault principle. Such a decommodified-style benefit sat uneasily in the residual welfare state that National was designing in the 1990s. In its 1991 Budget, National stated that it would introduce competition for the supply of accident insurance, a proposal supported by both the New Zealand Business Roundtable and the New Zealand Employers' Federation. Although the proposal was not acted upon within the term of the fourth National Government, National did introduce changes that had the effect of making the scheme less generous, less comprehensive and more vulnerable to future cost-cutting (and possible privatisation) than it had been twenty years earlier (see Kelsey, 1995, pp. 203–6 for details).

Under the fourth National Government the process of limiting the state's involvement in housing continued. The Housing Corporation was directed to charge market rents for the remaining stock of state housing; the corporation was commercialised in 1992 and sold its mortgages. What remained, therefore, in the 1990s, of the first Labour Government's 'State Housing Project', designed to obliterate the slum dwellings of the 1930s, was 69 000 state-owned dwellings, the overwhelming majority of which formed ghettos in the poorest areas of New Zealand's major cities.

The changes to welfare benefit entitlements noted above force many workers to accept what they may feel to be unsatisfactory conditions of employment. In a deregulated labour market, they lack the resources to improve their conditions of employment; in a residual welfare state they lack any realistic alternative but to accept their disadvantaged dependency on the labour market.

The 1990s also witnessed the erosion of some of the gains women had made in the 1970s in their quest for social and economic equality. Labour market deregulation did not benefit women (see Chapter 8) and the benefits cuts also impacted heavily on women, a larger proportion of whom receive some type of state income support compared with men. As the state cut back on the funding and provision of such social services as care for children, the sick, and the elderly, women were the most likely to be placed in the position of providing such services themselves, unpaid and unrecognised.

The shift of part responsibility for welfare provision to women (or the 'core family unit', as the Minister of Social Welfare called it) was only one strand of an attempt to 'privatise' welfare in New Zealand during the 1990s. The church and voluntary organisations in the private sector were mobilised to meet the needs of those no longer catered for by the state or families. Charitable organisations have a long history in New Zealand as providers of health and welfare services (Tennant, 1989). The increased activity of such bodies was symbolised by the mushrooming of food banks and the number of food parcels distributed (see Whale, 1993; Kelsey, 1995). This could be interpreted as community groups having to step in as bodies of 'last resort', to fill the gap left by state withdrawal. But it was more than just this, as voluntary bodies came to provide frontline services, the first rather than the last resort for many people. This, again, formed a part of the government's strategy of trying to make individuals, their families, and their local community responsible for their own well-being, rather than the state. Such state inaction in welfare leads to 'privatisation by default' (Laws, 1988) and to what Wolch (1990) called the 'shadow state'. Many voluntary agencies depend upon government contracts for funds and, through this financial dependency, come to occupy a grey area in the state apparatus. The state can devolve to these agencies the responsibility for delivering services to the community more cheaply than if it performed them itself. At the same time, the state can stifle criticism of government policy by these financially dependent agencies.

Another way in which the fourth National Government sought to privatise welfare was by encouraging individuals to purchase welfare services from the private sector, for example, private medical insurance and pension schemes. Efforts to persuade people to take up private medical insurance began in the 1960s, when cuts in funds to public hospitals (and subsequent increases in hospital waiting lists) were combined with making medical insurance premiums a tax-deductible item. At the end of 1982, an estimated 36 per cent of New Zealand's population belonged to private medical schemes (Hay, 1987, p. 159). By 1995, the figure was estimated to be 55 per cent (Kelsey, 1995, p. 216). Under the fourth National Government the increased use of user part-charges, the uncertainty surrounding the public health sector following years of reforms and restructuring, and the media coverage of growing hospital waiting lists led many people to heed the signals coming from the government to purchase private medical insurance.

Both the fourth Labour and National Governments sent a similar message with regard to pensions—citizens should look to provide for their own retirement rather than expect automatic provision by the state. Frequent changes to the eligibility criteria for superannuation were combined with gloomy predictions about a future New Zealand society burdened with an ageing population. This did not, however, bring about a similar increase in private pension coverage as occurred for private medical insurance. There were a number of reasons for this, one of the most important being the political clout of the elderly electorate ('Grey Power'), which successfully resisted radical change to the government superannuation scheme.[10] Also, visits to the doctor and hospital are likely occurrences for young people and therefore provide a tangible motivation to try to insure against such events. It is much harder to interest the young in something they have yet to experience and probably have little desire to think about.

Conclusion

The welfare state set up by the first Labour Government was a residual one. It was a great improvement on what existed before; it provided a comprehensive package of welfare benefits and health services, and clearly identified the state as having a legitimate role to play in providing such benefits and services. It was, however, a limited role and responsibility. Benefits were not given as part of a citizen's right but on an assessment of whether they were 'needy' or 'deserving'. Citizens were still dependent on their position in the marketplace—or dependent on someone else's market power as the male wage earners' welfare state exemplified.

During the 1950s and 1960s little was done to expand the welfare state in New Zealand but full employment and state regulation of industrial relations ensured there was little demand for the safety net that the state did provide. In other words, the limitations of the New Zealand welfare system were not exposed during this period.

As a result of a number of factors, such as the growth of the feminist movement and party competition, the 1970s witnessed an improvement in existing welfare services as well as innovative additions (the Accident Compensation Scheme and the DPB). This was a move towards the decommodification of labour and the removal of social and gender inequalities. But unemployment and the fiscal crisis curtailed developments in the direction of a social democratic welfare state. In fact, reforms during the 1980s and 1990s returned the New Zealand welfare state firmly to the liberal category, precisely where the fourth National Government wanted it to be.

---

1 Esping-Andersen (1990) identifies three to which Castles and Mitchell (1992) add a fourth. For a critique of both, see Bolderson and Mabbett (1995).

2 The relationship between women and the welfare state is critically discussed in Chapter 13.

3 Until the mid-1980s, employment in the public sector accounted for one-quarter of the total labour force (Department of Statistics, 1970, 1975, 1981, 1985). The fourth Labour Government introduced various measures to reduce staff numbers in the core public service departments and these led to the virtual halving of permanent staff from 66 102 in 1983 to 34 505 in 1994 (Boston et al., 1996, p. 55). Corporatisations and privatisations since 1987 have also dramatically reduced the number of public sector employees. For example, the Railways Department in 1981 had a staff of over 21 000; as New Zealand Rail Ltd in 1991 this figure was just 5900 (Duncan and Bollard, 1992, p. 131). In 1993 New Zealand Rail was privatised. The Post Office in 1986 employed 40 000 people. In 1986 it was separated into three parts, two of which (Postbank and Telecom) were later privatised, leaving NZ Post in 1991 with just 8200 employees.

4 The top company tax rate was also reduced from 48 per cent to 28 per cent (later increased to 33 per cent).

5 The introduction of user charges for previously free public services, such as medical prescriptions, was another form of taxation imposed by the fourth Labour Government.

6 GST also replaced existing discriminatory indirect taxes that were progressive in that they were levied on luxury goods.

7 The regulation and deregulation of labour over the postwar period is discussed in detail in Chapter 10.

8 For a scathing critique of the fourth National Government's *Tax Reduction and Social Policy Programme* see Dalziel (1996).

9 Various empirical studies have found the link between the disincentive to work and the benefit system to be rather small, insignificant or insubstantial (Brosnan, Wilson, and Wong, 1989; Atkinson and Micklewright, 1991; Dilnot and Duncan, 1992).

10 The main political parties—National, Labour and Alliance—also sought to take the pension issue off the political and electoral agenda by entering into *An Accord on Retirement Income Policies* in August 1993.

Guide to Readings

Esping-Andersen (1985, 1989, and 1990) provides the most sophisticated typology of welfare regimes. Castles and Mitchell (1992) offer an interesting refinement to Esping-Andersen's typology.

For empirical data on welfare spending the International Labour Office's (ILO) series of publications *Costs of Social Security* contain information for a wide range of countries going back to the late 1940s. For data specific to New Zealand, see Martin (1982) and Table 1 in the annual Budget paper B6.

Historical overviews up to and including the fourth Labour Government are found in O'Brien and Wilkes (1993) and Oliver (1988). For historical overviews with a comparative perspective, see Castles (1985) and Davidson (1989). For the first Labour Government, see Sutch (1966) and Hanson (1980). Easton (1981) is indispensable for the 1970s. For the fourth National Government, Boston (1992a) provides an early assessment, Kelsey (1995) a later one. Kelsey is also very good on the fourth Labour Government.

CHAPTER FOURTEEN

STATE AND DEMOCRACY IN NEW ZEALAND

RICHARD MULGAN

This chapter examines the issue of democracy in relation to the New Zealand state, beginning with the question of whether, or to what extent, New Zealand may be characterised as a democracy and then looking at whether the change to a mixed member proportional (MMP) electoral system is likely to make New Zealand more or less democratic.

In any discussion of democracy, questions of definition are fundamental. An initial understanding of the term may be derived from common usage, whereby some countries, but not others, are classified as democracies. In this sense, democracy is usually identified with a system of government in which supreme political authority is formally in the hands of popularly elected leaders. More specific tests of such democracy include whether elections are held regularly and operated fairly, whether opponents to the existing regime are free to organise and present themselves to the voters, and whether the right of election winners to govern is unequivocally accepted by their political opponents as well as by other state institutions, such as the armed services, the bureaucracy, and the courts.

Democracy in this sense is sometimes described as representative or indirect democracy, to indicate that the voters delegate the functions of government to elected representatives and do not normally play a direct role in decision-making themselves. It is also referred to as liberal democracy, indicating its close association with liberal capitalist societies in which individual rights and private property are particularly valued. Although the right to such democratic government is internationally proclaimed in documents such as the United Nations Declaration of Human Rights, most countries have either never experienced such a system or have done so only precariously and intermittently. Of the world's nations, only twenty-one (including New Zealand) have had unbroken democratic government for the last half century or more (Lijphart, 1984, Ch. 3).

Although democracy understood in this way may be of undoubted value and importance, particularly to those who have not yet achieved it, for those who can take it for granted, such as New Zealanders, it may look less impressive. The concept of democracy appears to involve more than simply locating power in the hands of an elected government; it also implies political equality for all citizens, and yet some citizens clearly have much more power than others. Government may be formally in the hands of popularly accountable politicians but the political agenda remains dominated by unelected bureaucratic and business élites. How can this be a genuine democracy? We need to distinguish two uses of the term 'democracy' (Mulgan, 1989a, pp. 16–23). The first is a minimum conception that identifies democracy with certain basic, though far from negligible, requirements, particularly free and fair elections, freedom of political speech and organisation, and acceptance of the legitimacy of elected governments. In this sense, New Zealand, like France and India, is clearly a democracy, whereas China and Iraq are clearly not democracies. Other countries may be borderline instances, either because the electoral system is less than fully fair, as in Fiji, or because freedom of speech and organisation are circumscribed, as in Singapore, or because the legitimacy of elected governments is not yet fully established, as in Russia. The second sense is an ideal conception of democracy in which all citizens are equal politically and no one person or group has any more power than any other. In this sense, no country is a true democracy but all fall short of the democratic ideal to a greater or less extent, and in different respects. It is this latter, ideal, sense of democracy that can provide a standard against which to assess the extent of democracy in a country such as New Zealand.

More than one such ideal of democracy can be chosen as a standard of assessment. Western democratic theory has produced a variety of ideal conceptions or models of democracy (Held, 1987). All share a commitment to the basic principle of political equality but they differ according to their theory of society and their view of the main threats posed to the achievement of equality. Thus the Marxist model of democracy is grounded in the Marxist assumption that the main cause of inequality in capitalist societies has been the division between those who own and control the means of economic production, the capitalist class, and those whose labour is exploited by them, the proletariat or working class. In a capitalist economy, any government, whether elected or not, will be bound to pursue the interests of capital. True political equality requires the radical transformation of capitalist society and the establishment of a radically democratic workers' state as the first step towards building a classless, stateless communist society. From this perspective, 'socialist democracy would both incorporate key elements of liberal democracy—citizenship rights, freedom of political expression and assembly, regular multi-party elections—and ultimately transcend it by democratizing the whole of society, not just the political sphere' (Roper, 1996, p. 64). Only when the classless society of communism has brought an end to the economic exploitation of workers will genuine democracy be possible. In the classless society, there will be no major political conflicts and power will be dispersed throughout society. In the meantime, however, progress may be made towards greater political equality by reducing the extent of economic and social exploitation in liberal capitalist societies. Reform-minded Marxists and social democrats generally have concentrated on using the institutions of political democracy, such as competitive elections and parliaments, to reform and make society less unequal.

A related participatory model is associated with anarchism and with the New Left of the 1960s and 1970s; these theories place particular weight on the coercive effects of governments and other large organisations and wish to devolve power to the grassroots of the community. Large authoritative institutions are seen to be undemocratic in that they place power in the hands of organisational élites and reduce the bulk of the population to a passive and powerless mass. The solution is to empower ordinary citizens by reducing the scale of political and economic institutions and to encourage the direct participation of citizens in the control of their daily lives. The ideal political unit, therefore, is the small community that avoids specialised bureaucracy and allows everyone to participate in decision-making. Although anarchists and participatory democrats share many of the same ideals as Marxists and socialists, their analyses of the reasons for the inequalities in present-day societies tend to concentrate on state power and the coercive effects of ruling élites, whereas Marxists and socialists emphasise economic inequality and exploitation as the root cause of political inequality.

Various forms of radical feminism have adapted elements of these models while emphasising the inequality between men and women.[1] In particular, the anarchist emphasis on participation and hostility to hierarchical authority structures have struck a chord with feminists seeking to establish more egalitarian and inclusive patterns of decision-making. Radical feminists have advocated collective decision-making in which all members of the group share equally. They have been suspicious of all forms of delegated authority, even in the hands of elected representatives. Socialist feminists, like socialists generally, have shared many of the democratic ideals of the radicals. At the same time, they have adopted the Marxist assumption that the economic structures of capitalism are the main impediment to political equality. They identify the economic exploitation of women due to their reproductive capacity as a particularly important aspect of capitalism, an aspect that was neglected by earlier Marxists and socialists. Their agenda is thus similar to that of other socialists, but with the added dimension that the socialist transformation of the economy and society requires an equally fundamental transformation of the relations between the sexes.

All such theories of democracy presuppose a fundamental transformation of the existing social and economic structure before a truly democratic society can be achieved. There are other models of democracy, however, that do not seek to change the underlying structure of liberal capitalist society but instead hope to maximise democratic equality within it. This is the approach associated with less radical forms of socialism and feminism, such as social democracy and liberal feminism, as well as with the political theory of pluralism that provides the perspective adopted in this chapter. Pluralism is a loosely defined body of theory located in American political science of the mid-twentieth century. There is no single authoritative text and the views of the movement's leading figures, notably David Truman (Truman, 1951) and Robert Dahl (Dahl, 1956) evolved over time. In general terms, however, most pluralists agree that society is divided into different groups with different interests and that power is dispersed through society rather than located within one particular group or institution. Membership of groups overlaps, with individual members of society belonging to a number of different groups, for instance, a particular occupational class, a regional locality, a gender, a religion, and so on. Institutions of government operate at a number of different levels—local, regional, national, and international—and respond to pressure from different groups pursuing their own special interests. The democratic ideal implicit in the pluralist model is that each group in society will be able to wield equal power over the political system, or, more strictly, will be able to wield power in equal proportion to the size of the group and the degree to which it is affected.

According to some earlier versions of pluralism, the government is essentially passive in the policy-making process, receiving inputs from conflicting interest groups in society and, like a weather vane, pointing in the direction of the strongest pressure. Other versions, however, more realistically attribute a positive political role to governments, particularly if the government is understood to encompass the state sector as a whole. In this sense, the government itself may be said to include powerful state institutions such as the bureaucracy, the armed forces, and institutions of public education and health, all of whose members have their own independent interests that impinge directly on public policy. Again, some versions of pluralism have held that politics is simply about the accommodation of sectional interests and ignore any possible role for an overarching public interest. It is more plausible, however, to admit the existence of a communitywide public interest that governments may be called on to implement, sometimes in opposition to sectional interests.

By working within a liberal capitalist framework, pluralists can avoid the criticism of utopianism and irrelevance that can be made against those, such as Marxists or radical feminists, whose ideals call for a complete trans-formation of society. There is little realistic likelihood that a society such as New Zealand's will cease to be a liberal capitalist society, more or less closely integrated into an international capitalist economy and a global culture. On the other hand, pluralists can also be accused of naïveté and overconfidence if they assume that all social groups and classes within a capitalist society can achieve the political equality implicit in their model of democracy. Capitalism's commitment to the dominance of private property, and the limits it places on the role of the state in the redistribution of wealth, inevitably lead to disparities in economic power, which generate inequalities in political power. Pluralists, especially those known as neopluralists, have retreated from the complacency of the immediate postwar period and now generally admit the privileged position occupied by business interests in capitalist democracies (Lindblom, 1977; Dahl, 1985). By implication, they accept that the pluralist ideal of political equality is unattainable.

Indeed, recent writing on democracy from almost all theoretical perspectives has exhibited a growing scepticism about the possibility of achieving an ideally democratic society and an increasing concern with the more modest goal of partially reducing the degrees of inequality within existing structures (Hindess, 1993). Pluralists are not the only democratic theorists to think that half a loaf of democracy, or even just a slice, may be better than no loaf at all. NeoMarxists and market socialists have been readier to join with social democrats in acknowledging the value of representative government to working people. Many socialists and Marxists were always critical of the undemocratic nature of self-proclaimed communist regimes (Callinicos, 1991). As the experience of those living under such regimes has underlined, the rights of citizens are less likely to be abused or their interests neglected if state institutions operate within the limits set by a system of democratic government subject to the rule of law. Individual political freedoms upheld by a robust civil society independent of the state are a potent protection for the worker (Hirst, 1990; Pierson, 1993). Similarly, the more radical strands of feminism, while not necessarily abandoning the search for more direct participation, have been more willing to join with pluralists in recognising the concrete achievements produced by liberal democratic institutions (Phillips, 1991). Thus, although democratic theorists may differ in their conceptions of the ideally democratic society, they are much more likely to agree both on the basic value of liberal democratic institutions and on the immediate practicable steps that might be taken to ameliorate their more glaring inadequacies.

In the New Zealand context, however, there is an important exception to this general democratic consensus in that some sections of the Maori people are not necessarily fully committed to democratic principles. The fundamental importance of individuals and individual rights, on which democracy is based, is less prominent in the more group-centred Maori culture. Maori political traditions lay great considerable weight on concepts of inherited chiefly authority, which are contrary to democratic notions of equality and equal opportunity. Some Maori tribes prohibit women from the basic political right of speaking formally on the marae. On the other hand, as in democracies, fundamental legitimacy lies with the community as a whole. The authority of chiefs and elders is ultimately dependent on the consent of their followers and new leaders can acquire authority through effective service to the group (Metge, 1976, Ch. 14).

More problematic than the issue of democracy within Maori society is the application of democratic principles to Maori within New Zealand as a whole. Maori nationalists, for instance, reject the legitimacy of New Zealand's system of government and the equal democratic rights of all New Zealanders implicit in this system (see Chapter 9; Awatere, 1984). According to this view, the existing structure of government was imposed by force on the original inhabitants, the tangata whenua, in breach of the assurances guaranteed in the Treaty of Waitangi. The concept of equal democratic rights is merely a pretext for asserting the superior rights of the invading majority and for marginalising the Maori minority. The restoration of Maori sovereignty (tino rangatiratanga) within the existing New Zealand state may, in turn, require breaches of the principle of equal democratic citizenship, for instance through the creation of a joint senate with equal representation for Maori and non-Maori, as proposed by the New Zealand Maori Council (Mulgan, 1989b, pp. 133–4).

In response to the Maori nationalist critique, it may be pointed out that the unqualified equation of democracy with majority rule is a mistake. Democratic principles, properly understood, imply the protection of everyone's rights equally, including the rights of minorities, and do not license the oppression of a minority by a majority (Mulgan, 1989b, Ch. 3). Moreover, most Maori leaders take a more conciliatory line, accepting democratic principles for all New Zealanders and concentrating their efforts on seeking to achieve fair treatment for Maori in accordance with these principles. For them, democratic principles are part of the solution rather than the problem. Nonetheless, there are at least some Maori who reject democracy as an alien import.

From a pluralist perspective, then, how equally is power distributed in New Zealand? Given the complexity of both New Zealand society and the dimensions of political power, it is possible only to offer a few broad generalisations. Although all adults have equal voting rights and are equally entitled to organise with like-minded fellow citizens to influence government policy in their favour, certain sections of society are systematically more influential than others. Most significant is the dominant role played by economically powerful interests. New Zealand governments, like other governments in capitalist democracies, depend for their electoral survival on maintaining a reasonable degree of economic prosperity. Voters look to governments to provide the economic conditions necessary to sustain their living standards; they also expect governments to provide extensive public services, an expectation that is much easier for governments to meet if the economy is growing. The overriding political imperative of encouraging economic growth makes governments particularly sensitive to the interests of those who have the power to make or break their economic strategies. Investors must be induced to invest their capital in New Zealand rather than elsewhere; this means that governments must provide economic policies, such as low inflation, low taxation, and minimum regulation of the private sector, which will make investment attractive. Sectors of the economy that are vital for national prosperity, such as farming or forestry, must be helped to prosper and their representatives given particular attention when they lobby on government policy.

Apart from the political leverage that can be derived from holding an economically strategic position, those who possess superior wealth also have more direct advantages in the general competition between different groups for political influence over government. Much of this competition is carried on between organised interest groups that seek to lobby politicians, public servants, and the media. Successful organisation requires substantial resources, for instance to conduct soundly based research, to publish attractive and convincing submissions and media releases, and so on. This gives a clear advantage to the wealthier producer groups and professions over those representing disadvantaged sectors or the general public as a whole. Again, political parties depend heavily on substantial donations from individual businesspeople and from private companies to mount their election campaigns. Such donations are unlikely to be forthcoming if ministers do not grant privileged political access to business leaders.

There are other social divisions, besides economic wealth and power, that also translate into political inequalities. Women have been largely excluded from positions of power in politics and the bureaucracy, which has helped to reinforce the neglect of women's interests by the political system (Julian, 1992; Catt and McLeay, 1993). Maori have been alienated from the Pakeha-dominated political system (Walker, 1992), exhibiting consistently lower rates of turnout at elections than the rest of the population (Vowles and Aimer, 1993, pp. 51–2). The seclusion of Maori voters on a separate Maori roll, while it has guaranteed Maori representation in Parliament, has arguably marginalised Maori voters and their interests from the mainstream of democratic political competition because the National Party has had no realistic chance of winning a Maori seat and therefore no incentive to appeal to Maori voters.

These systematic inequalities—economic, gender, and ethnic—provide the bases of radical critiques of liberal democracy and the inspiration for radical models of democracy. A pluralist approach recognises the evidence of inequality where it occurs without subscribing to the predominance of any one social division and without overlooking the importance of countervailing factors. For instance, the extent of political advantage enjoyed by the economically powerful should not be exaggerated. Members of powerful business groups, such as the Business Roundtable, regularly complain about government unwillingness to adopt their preferred policies. Business interests are far from monolithic and different sectors will often be found to be favouring conflicting policy directions, each with the support of different sections of the bureaucracy. Groups that lack economic clout can use other means of exerting leverage over governments. For instance, they may consider withdrawing their electoral support, as senior citizens did in relation to superannuation policy during the 1980s and 1990s.

Similarly, while still undoubtedly disadvantaged by male power structures, women have been able to mobilise alternative networks of political support within the bureaucracy and political parties (Wilson, 1992). Women comprise half the electorate which means that their votes must be actively sought by all parties. In this respect, the relative lack of women MPs does not necessarily translate into lack of power for women, so long as the interests of women voters are articulated and competed for by political parties. In a system of competitive party politics, it is more important to be represented by a political party committed to pursuing one's interests rather than to be represented by an MP who happens to share one's social position but may have little capacity or inclination to act on one's behalf.

Nor are Maori powerless to influence governments. Their voting power may have been limited in effect, particularly with the National Party, but they have other means of exerting leverage, for instance through the desire of all New Zealand governments to preserve the country's reputation for harmonious race relations. Angry demonstrations by Maori and claims of unjust treatment, particularly when they are backed up by international condemnation through forums such as the United Nations Working Group on Indigenous Peoples, bring New Zealand into disrepute and provide a powerful motive for governments to make decisions in favour of Maori interests. Although Maori have suffered disproportionately in terms of rising unemployment and relative decline in wages for unskilled labour, they have developed a notable capacity for countervailing political pressure centred on the increasing political and legal prominence of the Treaty of Waitangi. Like leaders of all successful interest groups, Maori leaders are reluctant to admit to their success publicly, for fear of letting the government off the hook and ceding ground to their opponents. Nonetheless, both ministers and bureaucrats would testify to the capacity of Maori groups to make life difficult for governments (Palmer, 1992, Ch. 4).

The question of the distribution of political power, and thus the extent of democracy in New Zealand, is, therefore, a very complex one. No group or section is entirely powerless and yet some have a marked advantage, at least in some areas and in some respects. In general, the most persistent and fundamental form of inequality relates to the inequality of economic power. Most other types of disadvantage, such as those resulting from gender and ethnicity, also have a significant economic aspect that reinforces the original disadvantage (James and Saville-Smith, 1989). Moreover, while the political power of business interests is a feature of all capitalist democracies, it has become particularly marked in New Zealand (see Chapter 6; Roper, 1993a). As a result of the restructuring of the economy and the public sector since 1984, New Zealand has become noted among the developed countries as a country that provides an especially favourable environment for business investment through measures such as the Reserve Bank Act 1989 and the Employment Contracts Act 1991 and through relatively unregulated financial and investment markets (World Economic Forum, 1995).

At the same time, the New Zealand political system itself has become particularly susceptible to the political influence of those representing the interests of international investors. The scope for countervailing pressure from groups representing interests opposed to those of international investors has been significantly reduced by the restructuring process. The floating of the dollar, by making the economy much more vulnerable to immediate shifts in investor confidence, has correspondingly increased the reluctance of governments to implement policies that would threaten such confidence. Deregulation, by removing the need for government decisions on matters such as interest rates, wage rates, and import quotas, has deprived organised groups such as manufacturers, farmers, and trade unions of the opportunity to influence economic outcomes through political means. The extensive corporatisation and then privatisation of state enterprises, by removing them from day-to-day ministerial control, have prevented interest groups and members of the general public from seeking to influence the decisions of such enterprises by political pressure relayed through politicians.

Supporters of the deregulation and restructuring program were explicit about their political aim of reducing the scope for politicians and sectional interest groups to intervene in economic decisions (Boston, 1991a). According to the neoliberal theory that underpinned the reform program, democratically responsive government, in the sense of policy control by politicians subject to pressure from voters and interest groups, was harmful to long-term economic prosperity. Sound economic policy required a political system in which major decisions were either taken by politically independent statutory bodies, such as the Reserve Bank, or left entirely to the market.

The neoliberal agenda of reform was international but New Zealand was able to carry it further than almost any other country. The reasons for New Zealand's exceptional radicalism are complex. Some are personal, concerning the personalities of individual politicians concerned, such as Roger Douglas and David Lange, Finance Minister and Prime Minister respectively during the fourth Labour Government's first term of office (1984–87). Others are economic, related to the structural weakness of the New Zealand economy. Political factors were also important, particularly the fact that the initial restructuring was carried out by a Labour Party acting against its traditional principles. This led to Labour's eventual defeat in 1990 and provided the incoming National Government with a policy base from which to mount still further reforms. Most significant of all, perhaps, was New Zealand's constitutional structure, which enabled a determined government to enact radical reforms at great speed and in the teeth of considerable opposition.

The extent of constitutional power accorded to New Zealand governments can be gauged from international comparisons. In his analysis of democracies, the Dutch political scientist Arendt Lijphart (1984 and 1989) classifies them according to two contrasting tendencies, which he labels majoritarian and consensual. Majoritarian democracies are so named because power is supposedly concentrated in the hands of the majority; in consensual democracies political power tends to be shared, dispersed, and limited in various ways. The majoritarian model is explicitly designed to isolate the main characteristics of the British Westminster system of government in which a typically single-party Cabinet dominates a legally sovereign Parliament through its control of a disciplined party holding a majority of parliamentary seats, the *elective dictatorship*. (The term majoritarian is something of a misnomer in that single-party governments, although they have a majority in Parliament, typically have the support of less than a majority of voters; in this respect, *pluralitarian* might be more accurate (Nagel, 1994).) This system is sharply contrasted with a mainly continental European model of multiparty coalition governments subject to constitutional limits on their powers. Until the change to MMP in the mid-1990s, New Zealand provided the most extreme version of majoritarian democracy, a purer form of the Westminster model than the British prototype at Westminster (Lijphart, 1984, pp. 16–24). Although New Zealand's system of separate Maori seats is a non-majoritarian element, designed to guarantee parliamentary representation of a minority, in other respects, particularly the parliamentary dominance of the two major parties and the absence of a second parliamentary chamber, the New Zealand system has concentrated extraordinary power in the hands of a single-party Cabinet.

Such a concentration of political power may have democratic or undemocratic consequences, depending on the use to which it is put. Studies of New Zealand politics of the 1960s and 1970s (Mitchell, 1969; Jackson, 1973) suggested that New Zealand governments were constrained by populist conventions embedded in the political culture. Turnout in elections was very high by world standards and signified an electorate that kept a comparatively close watch on its governments. Parties offered detailed manifestos to the voters and, if elected, could be relied on to use their constitutional dominance to implement their election promises. Ministers were expected to keep close to the grassroots of public opinion, through close consultation with their backbench colleagues in caucus and with the party rank and file in the constituencies. The public were also represented by a plethora of organised interest groups. Each area of government policy-making had its own constellation of groups, which expected to be consulted by relevant ministers. Admittedly, not all sectors of society were equally organised and the political system was still heavily influenced in favour of dominant economic interests, but a case could be made that the weaker interests in society received more favourable political attention from New Zealand's elective dictatorship than in other countries with more fragmented systems of government.

Because, however, the popular responsiveness of New Zealand governments was due more to convention than to any constitutional requirement, it was vulnerable to a change of political values, particularly from within the government itself. Fortified by the anti-democratic ideology of neoliberalism, which treats organised public opinion as the expression of illegitimate vested interests, leading members of the fourth Labour Government gradually weakened the informal political structures of populism, by disregarding electoral commitments, overriding opposition from the party rank and file, and excluding interested parties from involvement in reforms that directly affected them. The Finance Minister, Roger Douglas, and his associates were usually able to carry the main Cabinet committee, the Cabinet Policy Committee, which, in turn, dominated Cabinet, which, in turn, controlled a majority in the Labour caucus. Armed with a parliamentary majority, the reformers faced no legal impediment to implementing their neoliberal program. Ultimately, after winning a second term in the 1987 election, many of them even abandoned the desire for re-election, which is the mainspring of democratic responsiveness. The fourth National Government, after its election in 1990, continued along a similar path, radically restructuring the welfare and health systems, as well as the system of industrial relations, to an extent largely unheralded before the election. New Zealand's extreme version of the Westminster system had proved an ideal instrument for imposing unwelcome reforms on an unwilling public (Mulgan, 1992).

The assault on democratic conventions by both Labour and National Governments produced a vigorous public reaction in the form of support for radical electoral reform in the referendums of 1992 and 1993. Though the ultimate margin of support for MMP was relatively slight (54 per cent over 46 per cent), this change marked a deep public alienation from the existing political system. In general, democratic electorates tend to be constitutionally conservative and reluctant to accept fundamental change unless it is precipitated by a major political crisis, such as defeat in war or a revolution. Some elements of New Zealand's democratic constitution may have come under periodic criticism, for instance the absence (since 1951) of a second chamber, the lack of a written constitution or a bill of rights, the comparative shortness of the parliamentary term (three years), and the disproportionate nature of a single-member electoral system. But, hitherto, there was no major pressure for reform. That New Zealand voters, living in a stable democracy with consistently high levels of voter turnout, rejected the existing system in such numbers indicates an exceptional degree of public disillusion and anger. The fact that reform was opposed by the leaders of both major parties and by influential members of the Business Roundtable (who were able to outspend the reformers by an estimated ratio of five to one (Vowles and Aimer, 1994b, pp. 96–7)) serves to underline both the strength of public feeling and its anti-élitist tenor.

Will the change to MMP help to enhance the level of democracy in the New Zealand political system? The fact that the number of seats held by the parties more closely reflects their levels of support in the electorate as a whole makes the electoral system fairer and more in accordance with the democratic principle of 'one vote, one value'. Maori voters and Maori interests may be expected generally to gain from the new system of allocating constituency seats, which has increased the number of their seats from four to five. More important, the new nationwide competition for the crucial party vote may encourage all parties to compete for Maori support in a way that was less likely when Maori voters were 'ghettoised' in Maori seats safely held by the Labour Party. It is not clear, however, that this did in fact happen at the 1996 election. Nor is it clear that this feature of MMP, that all votes are counted in the competition between the parties, increased levels of political interest throughout the electorate, although it did possibly contribute to arresting the declining trend in voter turnout (Vowles and Aimer, 1994a, Ch. 8). Nevertheless, the system of nationwide party lists, from which half the MPs were selected, did encourage parties in 1996 to put forward lists of candidates that were balanced in terms of major social distinctions such as gender and ethnicity. The 1996 election did see a significant increase in the representation of women in Parliament, the overwhelming majority of whom were elected from party lists. There was also an increase in the number of Maori elected and one National Party candidate of Asian descent became what is believed to be New Zealand's first Asian MP.

Many hopes for increased levels of democracy turn on the end to single-party government. As predicted, no one party had a parliamentary majority, so a government had to be formed that had the support of more than one party in Parliament, either a majority coalition government containing more than one party or a minority government depending on parliamentary support from a party or parties not represented in Cabinet. Ultimately, the first type of government was formed. The political dynamics of coalition or minority governments can vary widely, depending on factors such as the number of parties involved, their relative sizes, their placement on the ideological spectrum, and so on (Harris and McLeay, 1993; Boston, 1994). Predictions of how government and parties will continue to behave under the new system must therefore be treated with caution.

One consequence of multiparty government is the inability of any one party to deliver all its preferred policies. (Paradoxically, it was the failure of the fourth Labour and National single-party governments to keep their election commitments that led voters to prefer a new system in which the keeping of election policies becomes much more difficult (Vowles et al., 1995, pp. 195–6).) Instead, governing parties are required to negotiate with each other and make compromises on policy. Such negotiation and compromise, it is held, increase the level of consensus in government decision-making and therefore implicitly make governments more responsive to the voter's wishes (McRobie, 1993, p. 120 and p. 187; Nagel, 1994, p. 527). It is to be hoped that political opponents will deal with each other in a less adversarial and more conciliatory style, a trend that began immediately after the 1993 election as a result of the closeness of the result (National had a majority of only one seat) (Vowles et al., 1995, pp. 1–2). This trend was intensified from 1995 when defections from National turned the government into a minority government.

More significant than a change in style will be a greater tendency for policy issues, particularly those on which the governing parties are divided, to be debated more publicly and at greater length. This should give greater opportunity for public opposition to be aroused, for interest groups to be heard, and for pressure to be put on parties to reconsider their support for the government. To this extent, former conventions of consultation will be reasserted and governments will be less prepared to ride roughshod over public opposition. Again, the the fourth National Government provided examples of such caution when fear of being outvoted in Parliament made it draw back from unpopular policies concerning the wholesale privatisation of Electricorp and the deregulation of postal services.

But although governments are likely to be more conciliatory in tone and more cautious in policy, the extent of such change should not be exaggerated. All parties will have a strong electoral incentive to remain united and disciplined, and parliamentary alignments should be much less uncertain and unpredictable than they were during the transitional period, 1994–96. Moreover, Parliament is still likely to incorporate a recognisable division between government and opposition. Despite the fact that New Zealand First held the balance of power following the 1996 election, the long-standing adversarial relationship between National and Labour is set to continue with each side providing the centre or nucleus of a government and of an opposing alternative government respectively. In addition, New Zealand's constitution will continue to be highly centralised. Provided only that their majority in the House of Representatives is secure, Cabinet ministers, collectively and individually, will be able to exert the same degree of control over Parliament and the bureaucracy as before. The basic constitutional structure of the Westminster system, the fusion of legislative and executive functions in the Cabinet, and the relative immunity of legislation and government decisions from judicial review, will be unaffected. In terms of Lijphart's distinction, New Zealand will be less pure a specimen of the majoritarian model but will still remain indisputably in the majoritarian camp.

The limitations on the extent of change are not necessarily to be regretted. For instance, consensus between parties will not always benefit the wider community. Indeed, interparty agreements may be designed to frustrate the influence of sections of the electorate. A few months before the 1993 election, the National, Labour, and Alliance parties entered into an accord on government-funded superannuation, agreeing to raise the age of eligibility to sixty-five by 2001 and to set the level of payments at between 65 per cent and 72.5 per cent of the average wage. While this can be seen as an example of interparty consensus and a new politics of accommodation, it was clearly motivated by the parties' desire to avoid electoral competition on the issue of superannuation. In this respect, by taking an important issue off the political agenda, the accord could be said to mark a reduction in voter leverage and in the democratic responsiveness of governments. Consensus politics, while it can open decisions up to greater public discussion and public influence, can also be a means whereby élites join ranks to resist inconvenient popular pressure. For this reason, there is democratic advantage in maintaining an adversarial division between government and opposition parties in Parliament. An effective opposition party or parties, dedicated to defeating the incumbent government at the ballot box, can provide a powerful mechanism for representing interests that governments might otherwise neglect. In this respect, governments can exercise consensus politics in relation to interest groups and the public while maintaining a non-consensual, adversarial stance towards political opponents.

The change to MMP and multiparty government thus has the potential to increase the extent of democratic responsiveness in the political system by forcing governments into more open discussion and by increasing the likelihood of political resistance to deeply unpopular policies. The capacity for governments to impose the type of radical restructuring carried out between 1984 and 1993 will be curtailed. To this extent, electoral reform marks a victory for the populist element in New Zealand's political culture, for the expectation that politicians should keep close to the grassroots of public opinion. Any expectation that governments will return to pre-1984 levels of government consultation and responsiveness must, however, be tempered by the fact that the scope for government action has been significantly altered.

In relation to economic policy, for instance, a decade of deregulation and privatisation has considerably reduced the effective role of government. Issues such as exchange rates, interest rates, and wage rates, which were once the province of government decision or at least substantial government influence, often in consultation with producer groups, are now left by governments for the Reserve Bank and markets to decide. So, too, are most of the investment and customer service decisions of former government departments, such as the post office, the railways, or state forests. Although there may be some weakening of this pro-market stance, for instance through increased government regulation along the lines of other less deregulated market economies, complete reversal is politically out of the question. Repurchase of privatised state assets would place an unpalatable burden on taxpayers. More generally, any substantial attempt to roll back the free play of markets would provoke an immediate and hostile response from international financial markets sufficiently damaging to the economy to bring any government quickly to heel.

At the same time, the government will be pressured against change by the new constellation of interested parties to which the newly deregulated environment has given rise. Groups that benefit from deregulation, such as the Business Roundtable, have established strong links with governments at the expense of groups whose scope for policy input has been removed, most notably trade unions, but also some producer groups such as manufacturers. In the public service, many of the departments that were involved in the former more interventionist policies, for instance the former Department of Trade and Industry and the Ministry of Works and Development, have been radically restructured themselves and are no longer a potent political voice. Conversely, Treasury, the department that has spearheaded the restructuring process, has become even more dominant in government policy making (Boston, 1991b). Thus, as Treasury's own favoured public choice theory would predict, a new entrenched institutional structure has emerged, committed to a new status quo.

MMP, by encouraging multiparty government, is likely to lead to more open discussion of public policy matters and will increase the political risks for governments contemplating radically unpopular measures. To this extent, there will be greater responsiveness to voters and to community groups and thus an increase in democracy and trust. With the possible exception of increased leverage for Maori interests, however, the change is unlikely to affect the major political inequalities in New Zealand society, which result from the unequal division of economic power and the limited capacity of elected government to redress such inequality. Sceptical pluralists, not to mention Marxists and other radical critics of liberal democracy, will not be expecting any substantial redistribution of power.

1 See Bryson (1992) for an overview of various feminist political theories.

Guide to Readings

Modern theories of democracy are discussed in Held (1987 and 1993). Pluralist democracy is particularly associated with Robert Dahl, whose more recent thoughts on democracy (for example, 1989) are more relevant than his earlier work (for example, 1956). A theory of pluralist democracy is applied to New Zealand in Mulgan (1989a). The distinction between 'majoritarian' and 'consensual' democracies is elaborated by Lijphart (1984, 1989) and its relevance to electoral reform in New Zealand is discussed by Nagel (1994) and Vowles et al. (1995).

REFERENCES

Aberbach, J. and Rockman, B. (1988), 'Image IV Revisited: Executive and Political Roles', *Governance: An International Journal of Policy and Administration*, 1:1, pp. 1–25.

Adams, P. (1977), *Fatal Necessity: British Intervention in New Zealand 1830-47*, Auckland University Press, Auckland.

Adams, R. (1992), 'The role of the state in industrial relations', unpublished paper, McMaster University, Hamilton, Canada.

Afshar, H. and Maynard, M. (1994), *The Dynamics of 'Race' and Gender: Some Feminist Interventions*, Taylor & Francis, London.

Allen, J. (1990), 'Does feminism need a theory of "the state"?', in *Playing the State: Australian Feminist Interventions*, ed. S. Watson, Allen & Unwin, Sydney.

Anderson, G. (1991), 'The Employment Contracts Act 1991: An Employers Charter?', *New Zealand Journal of Industrial Relations*, 16:2, pp. 127–42.

Anderson, G. (in press), 'Trade unions, collective bargaining and the law', in *Trade Unionism in Australia and New Zealand: Roads to Recovery*, eds T. Bramble and B. Harley, ACIRRT Monograph, University of Sydney.

Anderson, P. (1967), 'The limits and possibilities of trade union action', in *The Incompatibles: Trade Union Militancy and the Consensus*, eds R. Blackburn and C. Cockburn, Harmondsworth, Penguin.

Ang, I. (1995), 'I'm a feminist but . . . "Other" women and positional feminism', in *Transitions: New Australian Feminisms*, eds B. Caine and R. Pringle, Allen & Unwin, St Leonards.

Armstrong, N. (1992), 'Handling the hydra: feminist analyses of the state', in *Feminist Voices: Women's Studies Texts for Aotearoa/New Zealand*, eds R. Du Plessis, P. Bunkle, A. Irwin, K. Laurie, and S. Middleton, Oxford University Press, Auckland.

Armstrong, P., Glyn, A. and Harrison, J. (1984), *Capitalism Since World War II*, Fontana, London.

Armstrong, P., Glyn, A. and Harrison, J. (1991), *Capitalism Since World War II*, 2nd ed., Basil Blackwell, Oxford.

Armstrong, W. (1980), 'Land, class, colonialism: the origins of dominion capitalism', in *New Zealand and the World*, ed. W. Willmott, University of Canterbury, Christchurch

Atkinson, A. and Micklewright, J. (1989), 'Turning the screw: benefits for the unemployed, 1979–1988', in *The Economics of Social Security*, eds A. Dilnot and I. Walker, Oxford University Press, Oxford.

Awatere, D. (1984), *Maori Sovereignty*, Broadsheet, Auckland.

Awatere, D. Huata (1996), *My Journey*, Seaview Publishers, Auckland.

Bachrach, P. and Baratz, M. (1970), *Power and Poverty: Theory and Practice*, Oxford University Press, New York.

Baker, J. (1965), *The New Zealand People at War: War Economy*, Department of Internal Affairs, Wellington.

Baldock, C. and Cass, B. (eds) (1983), *Women, Social Welfare, and the State*, Allen & Unwin, Sydney.

Ballara, A. (1986), *Proud to be White? A Survey of Pakeha Prejudice in New Zealand*, Heinemann, Auckland.

Barber, K. (1989), 'New Zealand "Race Relations Policy" 1970-1988', *Sites*, 18 (Winter), pp. 5–16.

Barnes, J. (1987), Never a White Flag, unpublished mimeo available from author.

Barrett, M. (1980), *Women's Oppression Today: Problems in Marxist Feminist Analysis*, Verso, London.

Barth, F. (ed.) (1969), *Ethnic Groups and Boundaries*, Little, Brown, Boston.

Bassett, M. (1972), *Confrontation '51: The 1951 Waterfront Dispute*, A.H. & A.W. Reed, Wellington.

Baumol, W., Nelson, R. and Wolff, E. (eds) (1994), *Convergence of Productivity: Cross-National Studies and Historical Evidence*, Oxford University Press, New York.

Bayliss, L. (1994), *Prosperity Mislaid: Economic Failure in New Zealand and What Should be Done About It*, GP Publications, Wellington.

Bedggood, D. (1978), 'New Zealand's semi-colonial development: a Marxist view', *Australian and New Zealand Journal of Sociology*, 14:3 (2), pp. 285–9.

Bedggood, D. (1980), *Rich and Poor in New Zealand*, Allen & Unwin, Auckland.

Belich, J. (1986), *The New Zealand Wars, and the Victorian Interpretation of Racial Conflict*, Auckland University Press, Auckland.

Bell, S. (1995), 'The collective capitalism of Northeast Asia and the limits of orthodox economics', *Australian Journal of Political Science*, 30:2 pp. 264–87.

Bergmann, B. (1989), 'Why do economists know so little about the economy?' in *Unconventional Wisdom: Essays on Economics in Honour of John Kenneth Galbraith*, eds S. Bowles, R. Edwards, and W. Shephard, Houghton Mifflin, Boston.

Bertram, G. (1993), 'Keynesianism, Neoclassicism and the state', in *State and Economy in New Zealand*, eds B. Roper and C. Rudd, Oxford University Press, Auckland.

Bhaskar, R. (1989), *Reclaiming Reality: A Critical Introduction to Contemporary Philosophy*, Verso, London.

Bina, C. and Yaghmarian, B. (1990), 'Postwar global accumulation and the transnationalization of capital', *Review of Radical Political Economy*, 22:1, pp. 78–97.

Birch, B. (1994), *Budget B6*, Wellington.

Birch, B. (1996), *Tax Reduction and Social Policy Programme: details*, GP Print, Wellington.

Birks, S. (1992) 'The public sector: an overview', in *The New Zealand Economy*, eds S. Birks and S. Chatterjee (2nd ed.) Dunmore Press, Palmerston North.

Blaug, M. (1985), *Economic Theory in Retrospect* (4th ed.), Cambridge University Press, Cambridge.

Bock, G. and James, S. (1992), 'Introduction: contextualizing equality and difference', in *Beyond Equality and Difference: Citizenship, Feminist Politics and Female Subjectivity*, eds G. Bock, and S. James, Routledge, London.

Bock, G. and Thane, P. (1991), 'Editors' Introduction' in *Maternity and Gender Politics: Women and the Rise of the European Welfare States 1880s-1950s*, eds G. Bock and P. Thane, Routledge, London.

Bolderson, H. and Mabbett, D. (1995), 'Mongrels or thoroughbreds: A cross-national look at social security systems', *European Journal of Political Research*, 28:1, pp. 119-39.

Bollard, A. (ed.) (1988), *The Influence of United States Economics on New Zealand: The Fulbright Anniversary Seminars*, New Zealand Institute of Economic Research, Research Monograph 42, Wellington.

Bollard, A. and Buckle, B. (eds) (1987), *Economic Liberalisation in New Zealand*, Allen & Unwin, Wellington.

Boon, B. (1992a), Remedies for Unjustifiable Dismissal under the Labour Relations Act, *New Zealand Journal of Industrial Relations*, 17:1, pp. 101-7.

Boon, B. (1992b), Procedural Fairness and the Unjustified Dismissal Decision, *New Zealand Journal of Industrial Relations*, 17:3, pp. 301-17.

Boston, J. (1984), *Incomes Policy in New Zealand: 1968-1984*, Institute of Policy Studies, Wellington.

Boston, J. (1989) 'The Treasury and the organization of economic advice: some international comparisons', in *The Making of Rogernomics*, ed. B. Easton, Auckland University Press, Auckland.

Boston, J. (1990), 'The Cabinet and policy making under the fourth Labour Government', in *The Fourth Labour Government* (2nd ed.), eds M. Holland and J. Boston, Oxford University Press, Auckland.

Boston, J. (1991a) 'The theoretical underpinnings of public sector restructuring in New Zealand', in *Reshaping the State: New Zealand's Bureaucratic Revolution*, eds J. Boston, J. Martin, J. Pallot, and P. Walsh, Oxford University Press, Auckland.

Boston, J. (1991b), 'Reorganizing the machinery of government in New Zealand: objectives and outcomes', in *Reshaping the State: New Zealand's Bureaucratic Revolution*, eds J. Boston, J. Martin, J. Pallot, and P. Walsh, Oxford University Press, Auckland.

Boston, J. (1992a), 'Redesigning New Zealand's welfare state', in *The Decent Society?*, eds J. Boston and D. Dalziel, Oxford University Press, Auckland.

Boston, J. (1992b), 'The Treasury: its role, philosophy and influence', in *New Zealand Politics in Perspective* (3rd ed), ed. H. Gold, Longman Paul, Auckland.

Boston, J. (1993), 'Decision-making and the budgetary process in New Zealand', in *Decision Making in New Zealand Government*, eds J. Nethercote, B. Galligan, and C. Walsh, Federalism Research Centre, Canberra.

Boston, J. (1994), 'Electoral reform in New Zealand', *Australian Quarterly*, 66:3, pp. 67-90.

Boston, J. and Cooper, F. (1989), 'The Treasury: advice, coordination and control', in *New Zealand Politics in Perspective* (2nd ed.), ed. H. Gold, Longman Paul, Auckland.

Boston, J. and Dalziel, P. (eds) (1992), *The Decent Society?* Oxford University Press, Auckland.

Boston, J., Martin, J., Pallot, J. and Walsh, P. (1996), *Public Management: The New Zealand Model*, Oxford University Press, Auckland.

Boston, J., Martin, J., Pallot, J. and Walsh, P. (eds) (1991), *Reshaping the State. New Zealand's Bureaucratic Revolution*, Oxford University Press, Auckland.

Bottomley, G. et al. (eds) (1991), *Intersextions: Gender/Class/Culture/Ethnicity*, Allen & Unwin, Sydney.

Bowles, S. and Gintis, H. (1976), *Schooling in Capitalist America*, Routledge & Kegan Paul, London.

Boxall, P. (1991), 'New Zealand's Employment Contracts Act 1991: an analysis of background, provisions and implications', *Australian Bulletin of Labour*, 17:4:, pp. 284–309.

Bramble, T. (1993) The contingent conservatism of full-time trade union officials: a case study of the Vehicle Builders Employees' Federation of Australia, 1963 to 1991, unpublished PhD thesis, La Trobe University, Melbourne.

Bray, M. and Howarth, N. (1993), *Economic Restructuring and Industrial Relations in Australia and New Zealand*, Australian Centre for Industrial Relations Research and Teaching, Sydney.

Bray, M. and Walsh, P. (1992), Accord and discord: the differing fates of corporatism under Labour governments in Australia and New Zealand, unpublished paper presented to the Ninth World Congress of the International Industrial Relations Association, Sydney.

Bray, M. and Walsh, P. (1995), 'Accord and discord: the differing fates of corporatism under Labour governments in Australia and New Zealand', *Labour and Industry*, 6:3, pp. 1–26.

Briar, C. (1992), 'Women, economic dependence and social policy', in *Superwoman Where are You? Social Policy and Women's Experience*, eds C. Briar, R. Munford, and M. Nash, Dunmore Press, Palmerston North.

Briar, C., Munford, R. and Nash, M. (eds) (1992), *Superwoman Where are You? Social Policy and Women's Experience*, Dunmore Press, Palmerston North.

Brittan, S. (1975), 'The economic contradictions of democracy', *British Journal of Political Science*, 5:2, pp. 129–59.

Britton, S., Heron, R. and Pawson, E. (eds) (1992), *Changing Places in New Zealand: A Geography of Restructuring*, New Zealand Geographical Society, Christchurch.

Brook, P. (1989), 'Reform of the labour market. in *Rogernomics: Reshaping New Zealand's Economy*, ed. S. Walker, Government Print Books, Wellington.

Brook, P. (1990), *Freedom at Work*, Oxford University Press, Auckland.

Brookes, B. (1986), 'Reproductive rights: The debate over abortion and birth control in the 1930s', in *Women in History: Essays on European Women in New Zealand*, eds B. Brookes, C. Macdonald, and M. Tennant, Allen & Unwin, Wellington.

Brooking, T. (1992), 'Economic transformation', in *The Oxford History of New Zealand*, ed. G. Rice, Oxford University Press, Auckland.

Brosnan, P. and Rea, D. (1991), 'An adequate minimum code: a base for freedom, justice and efficiency in the labour market', *New Zealand Journal of Industrial Relations*, 16:2, pp. 147–66.

Brosnan, P. and Wilson, M. (1989), *The Historical Structuring of the New Zealand Labour Market*, Working Paper 4/89, Industrial Relations Centre, Victoria University, Wellington.

Brosnan, P., Smith, D. and Walsh, P. (1990), *The Dynamics of New Zealand Industrial Relations*, John Wiley, Auckland.

Brosnan, P., Wilson, M. and Wong, D. (1989), 'Welfare benefits and labour supply: a review of the empirical evidence', *New Zealand Journal of Industrial Relations*, 14:1, pp. 17–35.

Brown, W. (1992), 'Finding the man in the state', *Feminist Studies*, 18:1, pp. 7–34.

Bryson, L. (1992), *Welfare and the State: Who Benefits?*, Macmillan, London.

Bryson, V. (1992), *Feminist Political Theory*, Macmillan, Basingstoke.

Buchanan, J. (1975), *The Limits of Liberty: Between Anarchy and Leviathan*, University of Chicago Press, Chicago.

Buchanan, J. (1988), 'The economic theory of politics reborn', *Challenge*, March/April, pp. 4–10.

Buchanan, J. and Tullock, G. (1962), *The Calculus of Consent: Logical Foundations of Constitutional Democracy*, University of Michigan Press, Ann Arbor.

Buchanan, J. and Tullock, G. (1984), 'An American perspective: from 'markets work' to 'public choice', in *The Emerging Consensus (2nd ed.)*, ed. A. Seldon, Macmillan, London.

Buchanan, J. Tollison, R. and Tullock, G. (eds)(1980), *Towards a Theory of the Rent-Seeking Society*, A. & M. University Press, Austin, Texas.

Buchele, R. and Aldrich, M. (1985), 'How much difference would comparable worth make?', *Industrial Relations*, 24:2, pp. 222–33.

Buckle, R. (1988), *Expectations and Credibility in the Disinflation Process*, Discussion Paper No. 33, New Zealand Institute of Economic Research, Wellington.

Buckle, R. (1995), 'Old views and new facts about prices and business cycles', *Victoria Economic Commentaries*, 12:3, pp. 3–10.

Buckle, R., Assendelft, E. and Jackson, L. (1990), 'Manufacturer's expectations of prices and quantities: New Zealand experience, 1964-1987', *Applied Economics*, 22:5, pp. 579–98.

Burns, J. and Coleman, M. (1991), *Equity at Work—an Approach to Gender Neutral Job Evaluation*, State Services Commission and Department of Labour, Wellington.

Butterworth, G. (1967), *The Maori in the New Zealand Economy*, Department of Industries and Commerce, Wellington.

Caine, B. and Pringle, R. (1995), *Transitions: New Australian Feminisms*, St Martin's Press, New York.

Callinicos, A. (1987), *Making History*, Polity Press, Cambridge.

Callinicos, A. (1991), *The Revenge of History*, Polity Press, Cambridge.

Callinicos, A. (1992), 'Race and class', *International Socialism*, 55, pp. 3–39.

Callinicos, A. and Harman, C. (1987), *The Changing Working Class*, Chicago Press, London.

Cammack, P. (1989), 'Review article: bringing the state back', in *British Journal of Political Science*, 2:19, pp. 261–90.

Campbell, R. and Kirk, A. (1983), *After the Freeze*, Port Nicholson Press, Wellington.

Cantwell, J. (1989), *Technological Innovation and Multinational Corporations*, Blackwell, Oxford.

Carnoy, M. (1984), *The State and Political Theory*, Princeton University Press, Princeton.

Carpinter, P. (1979), Trade protection and growth—the New Zealand experience, paper presented to the ANZAAS Congress, Auckland.

Cass, B. (1995), 'Gender in Australia's restructuring labour market and welfare state', in *Women in a Restructuring Australia: Work and Welfare*, eds A. Edwards and S. Magarey, Allen & Unwin in association with the Academy of Social Sciences in Australia, St Leonards.

Castles, F. (1985), *The Working Class and Welfare*, Allen & Unwin, Wellington.

Castles, F. and Dowrick, S. (1990), 'The impact of government spending levels on medium-term economic growth in the OECD, 1960-85', *Journal of Theoretical Politics*, 2:2, pp. 173–204.

Castles, F. and Mitchell, D. (1992), 'Identifying welfare state regimes: the link between politics, instruments and outcomes', *Governance*, 5:1, pp. 1–26.

Castles, F., Gerritsen, R. and Vowles, J. (eds) (1996), *The Great Experiment: Labour Parties and Public Policy Transformation in Australia and New Zealand*, Allen & Unwin, St Leonards.

Catt, H. and McLeay, E. (1993), 'Women and politics in New Zealand', *Political Science*, 45:1.

Chapman, R. (1962), 'New Zealand since the war: politics and society', *Landfall*, 16:3, pp. 252–77.

Chapman, R. (1981), 'From Labour to National', in *The Oxford History of New Zealand*, eds W. Oliver and B. Williams, Oxford University Press, Wellington.

Chapple, S. (1993), Kalecki's macroeconomics, unpublished PhD thesis, Victoria University, Wellington.

Chernomas, R. (1987), 'Is supply-side economics rational for capital?', *Review of Radical Political Economics*, 19:3, pp. 1–17.

Clark, H. (1993), 'Employment Equity Bill: introduction', in *The Vote, the Pill and the Demon Drink: A History of Feminist Writing in New Zealand, 1869-1993*, ed. C. Macdonald, Bridget Williams Books, Wellington.

Clarke, S. (1988), *Keynesianism, Monetarism and the Crisis of the State*, Edward Elgar, Aldershot.

Cleveland, L. (1972), *The Anatomy of Influence: Pressure Groups and Politics in New Zealand*, Hicks Smith, Wellington.

Cockburn, C. (1983), *Brothers—Male Dominance and Technological Change*, Pluto Press, London.

Cocker, A. (1995), Oh what the Hayek! Public exasperation, exclusion and elite capture; the formulation of New Zealand's broadcasting policy, paper presented to the New Zealand Political Studies Association Annual Conference, Wellington.

Codd, J., Harker, R. and Nash, R. (eds) (1990), *Political Issues In New Zealand Education* (2nd ed.), Dunmore Press, Palmerston North.

Coddington, D. (1993), *Turning Pain into Gain: The Plain Person's Guide to the Transformation of New Zealand, 1984–1993*, Alister Taylor, Auckland.

Cohen, A. (1974), *Urban Ethnicity*, Tavistock, London.

Cohen, G. (1978), *The Revenge of History*, Oxford University Press, Oxford.

Cole, K., Cameron, J. and Edwards, C. (1991), *Why Economists Disagree* (2nd ed.), Longman Paul, London,

Cole, M. (ed.) (1988), *Bowles and Gintis Revisited: Correspondence and Contradiction in Educational Theory*, Falmer Press, Brighton.

Commission for Employment Equity (1990), *Into the '90s—a Report on Equal Employment Opportunities*, Wellington.

Considine, M. (1994), *Public Policy: A Critical Approach*, Macmillan, Melbourne.

Cooke, P. and Morgan, K. (1993), 'The network paradigm: new directions in corporate and regional development', *Environment and Planning D: Society and Space*, 11, pp. 543–64.

Council of Trade Unions (1988a), *Towards a Compact*, Wellington.

Council of Trade Unions (1988b), *The Need for Change*, Wellington.

Council of Trade Unions (1989), *Strategies for Change: Challenges for the Trade Union Movement of Today*, Wellington.

Council of Trade Unions (1991), *Minutes of the Second Biennial Conference*, Wellington.

Council of Trade Unions (1993), *Biennial Report*, Wellington.

Crawford, A., Harbridge, R. and Hince, K. (1996), *Unions and Union Membership in New Zealand: Annual Review for 1995*, Industrial Relations Centre Working Paper 2/96, Victoria University, Wellington.

Crocombe, G., Enright, M. and Porter, M. (1991), *Upgrading New Zealand's Competitive Advantage*, Oxford University Press, Auckland.

Curthoys, A. (1993), 'Feminism, citizenship and national identity', *Feminist Review*, 44, pp. 19–38.

Dahl, R. (1956), *A Preface to Democratic Theory*, University of Chicago Press, Chicago.

Dahl, R. (1985), *A Preface to Economic Democracy*, Polity Press, Cambridge.

Dahl, R. (1989), *Democracy and its Critics*, Yale University Press, New Haven and London.

Dale, R. (1994), 'The state and education', in *Leap Into the Dark: The Changing Role of the State in New Zealand Since 1984*, ed. A. Sharp, Auckland University Press, Auckland.

Dalziel, P. (1991), 'The Rhetoric of Treasury: A Review of the 1990 Briefing Papers', *New Zealand Economic Papers*, 25:2, pp. 259–74.

Dalziel, P. (1992), 'National's macroeconomic policy', in *The Decent Society?*, eds J. Boston and P. Dalziel, Oxford University Press, Auckland.

Dalziel, P. (1993), 'The Reserve Bank Act: reflecting changing relationships between state and economy in the twentieth century', in *State and Economy in New Zealand*, eds B. Roper and C. Rudd, Oxford University Press, Auckland.

Dalziel, P. (1996), *Poor Policy. A Report for the New Zealand Council of Christian Social Services on the 1991 Benefit Cuts and the 1996 Tax Cuts*, NZCCSS, Wellington.

Dalziel, P. and Clydesdale, G. (1991), New Zealand's Low Growth and High Unemployment: Supply or Demand Side Constraints?, paper presented at the 1991 Residential Conference of the New Zealand Association of Economists, Lincoln University, 26-28 August.

Dalziel, P. and Lattimore, R. (1996), *The New Zealand Macroeconomy*, Oxford University Press, Auckland.

Dann, C. (1985), *Up From Under: Women and Liberation in New Zealand 1970-1985*, Allen & Unwin, Wellington.

Dannin, E. (1992), 'Labor law Reform in New Zealand', *New York Journal of Comparative and International Law*, 13:1, pp. 1–45.

Dannin, E. (1995), 'We can't overcome? A case study of freedom of contract and labor law reform', *Berkeley Journal of Employment and Labor Law*, 16:1, pp. 1–168.

Dannin, E. (1996), 'Solidarity forever? Unions and bargaining representation under New Zealand's Employment Contracts Act, *Loyola of Los Angeles International and Comparative Law Journal*, 18:1, pp. 2–79.

Darlington, R. (1994), *The Dynamics of Workplace Unionism*, Mansell Publishing, London.

Davidson, A. (1989), *Two Models of Welfare*, Almqvist & Wiksell International, Uppsala.

Davidson, A. (1994), *A Home of One's Own: Housing Policy in Sweden and New Zealand from the 1840s to the 1990s*, Almqvist & Wiksell International, Stockholm.

Davidson, C. and Bray, M. (1994), *Women and Part Time Work in New Zealand— A Contemporary Insight*, New Zealand Institute for Social Research and Development, Wellington.

Davies, L. with Jackson, N. (1993), *Women's Labour Force Participation in New Zealand: The Past 100 Years*, Social Policy Agency, Wellington.

Deane, R. (1970), *Foreign Investment in New Zealand Manufacturing*, Sweet & Maxwell, Wellington.

Deeks, J. (1990), 'Old tracks, new maps: continuity and change in New Zealand labour relations, 1984-1990', *New Zealand Journal of Industrial Relations*, 15:2, pp. 99–116.

Deeks, J. (1992), 'Business, government and interest-group politics', in *Controlling Interests*, J. Deeks and N. Perry, Auckland University Press, Auckland.

Deeks, J., Boxall, P. and Ryan, R. (1984), *Labour Relations in New Zealand*, Longman Paul, Auckland.

Deeks, J., Parker, J. and Ryan, R. (1994), *Labour and Employment Relations in New Zealand* (2nd ed.), Longman Paul, Auckland.

Department of Education (1962, 1980), *Education Statistics of New Zealand*, Wellington.

Department of Labour (1996) *Contracts*, vol. 16, February, Wellington.

Department of the Prime Minister and Cabinet (1993), *An Accord on Retirement Income Policies*, Wellington.

Department of Social Welfare (1993), *A Profile of Sole Parents from the 1991 Census*, Wellington.

Department of Social Welfare (1996), *Fiscal 1995 Statistical Information Report*, Wellington.

Department of Statistics (1950, 1970, 1975, 1981, 1987–88, 1985), *New Zealand Official Yearbook*, Government Printer, Wellington.

Dicken P. (1992), *Global Shift: The Internationalization of Economic Activity*, Guilford Press, New York.

Dilnot, A. and Duncan, A. (1992), 'Thinking about labour supply', *Journal of Economics Psychology*, 13, pp. 687–713.

Dornbusch, R. (1990), 'Policies to move from stabilization to growth', *Proceedings of the World Bank Annual Conference on Development Economics*, Washington DC.

Douglas, K. (1991), President's Address to the 1991 CTU Biennial Conference, Conference Minutes.

Douglas, K. (1993a), 'Organising workers: the effects of the act on the Council of Trade Unions and its membership', in *Employment Contracts: New Zealand Experiences*, ed. R. Harbridge, Victoria University Press, Wellington.

Douglas, K. (1993b), Presidential Address. Minutes of the Proceedings of a Special Conference, Wellington.

Douglas, R. (1993), *Unfinished Business*, Random House, Auckland.

Douglas, R. and Callan, L. (1987), *Towards Prosperity*, David Bateman, Auckland.

Du Plessis, R. (1993), 'Women, politics and the state', in *State and Economy in New Zealand*, eds B. Roper and C. Rudd, Oxford University Press, Auckland.

Du Plessis, R., Bunkle, P., Irwin, K., Laurie, A. and Middleton, S. (eds) (1992), *Feminist Voices: Women's Studies Texts for Aotearoa/New Zealand*, Oxford University Press, Auckland.

Du Plessis Novitz, R. and Jaber, N. (1990), 'Pay equity, the "free" market and state intervention', *New Zealand Journal of Industrial Relations*, 15:3, pp. 251–62.

Dugger, W. (1989), 'Instituted process and enabling myth: the two faces of the market', *Journal of Economic Issues*, 23:2, pp. 607–15.

Duncan, I. and Bollard, A. (1992), *Corporatization and Privatization*, Oxford University Press, Auckland.

Dunning, J. (1981), *International Production and the Multinational Enterprise*, Allen & Unwin, London.

Eagleton, T. (1995), 'Where do postmodernists come from?', *Monthly Review*, 47:3, pp. 59–70.

Easton, B. (1980), 'Three New Zealand depressions', in *New Zealand and the World*, ed. W. Willmott, University of Canterbury Press, Christchurch.

Easton, B. (1981), *Pragmatism and Progress: Social Security in the Seventies*, University of Canterbury, Christchurch.

Easton, B. (1983), *Income Distribution in New Zealand*, New Zealand Institute of Economic Research, Wellington.

Easton, B. (1985), *A Critique of the New Victoria School*, Working Paper 85/31, New Zealand Institute of Economic Research, Wellington.

Easton, B. (1988), 'From Reaganomics to Rogernomics', in *The Influence of American Economics on New Zealand Thinking and Policy*, ed. A. Bollard, New Zealand Institute of Economic Research, Wellington.

Easton, B. (1989a), 'The commercialisation of the New Zealand economy: from think big to privatization', in *The Making of Rogernomics*, ed. B. Easton, Auckland University Press, Auckland.

Easton, B. (1989b), 'The Unmaking of Roger Douglas', in *The Making of Rogernomics*, ed. B. Easton, Auckland University Press, Auckland.

Easton, B. (1990a), *A GDP Deflator Series for New Zealand 1912/13-1976/77*, Economic Paper No. B9004, Massey University.

Easton, B. (1990b), '"Government management"; a review of its political content', *Political Science*, 42:2, pp. 35–42.

Easton, B. (1990c), Policy as revolution: two case studies, paper presented at New Zealand Political Studies Association Annual Conference, Dunedin.

Easton, B. (1994), 'Economic and other ideas behind the New Zealand reforms', *Oxford Review of Economic Policy*, 10:3, pp. 78–94.

Easton, B. (1997), *In Stormy Seas: The Post-War New Zealand Economy*, Otago University Press, Dunedin.

Easton, B. and Gerritsen, R. (1996), 'Economic reform: parallels and divergences', in *The Great Experiment: Labour Parties and Public Policy Transformation in Australia and New Zealand*, eds F. Castles, R. Gerritsen, and J. Vowles, Allen & Unwin and Auckland University Press, Auckland.

Econtech (1995), *New Zealand Model (NZM) Commissioned by the New Zealand Treasury: Report of 30 June 1995*, Kingston, Australia.

Edwards, A. and Magarey, S. (1995), *Women in a Restructuring Australia: Work and Welfare*, Allen & Unwin in association with the Academy of Social Sciences, St Leonards.

Edwards, S. and Holmes, F. (1994), *CER: Economic Trends and Linkages*, National Bank of New Zealand and Institute of Policy Studies, Wellington.

Edwards, S. and Van Wijnbergen, S. (1989), 'Disequilibrium and structural adjustment', *Handbook of Development Economics Volume 2*, eds H. Chenery and T. Srinivasan, Amsterdam, North-Holland.

Egeberg, M. (1995), 'Bureaucrats as public policy-makers and their self-interests', *Journal of Theoretical Politics*, 7:2, pp. 157–67.

Eisenstein, H. (1991), *Gender Shock: Practising Feminism on Two Continents*, Allen & Unwin, Sydney.

Eldred-Grigg, S. (1982), *A New History of Canterbury*, John McIndoe, Dunedin.

Elkan, P. (1972), *Industrial Protection in New Zealand 1952-67*, New Zealand Institute of Economic Research, Wellington.

Else, A. (1991), *A Question of Adoption: Closed Stranger Adoption in New Zealand 1944-1974*, Bridget Williams Books, Wellington.

Else, A. (1992), 'To market and home again: gender and the New Right, in *Feminist Voices: Women's Studies Texts for Aotearoa/New Zealand*, eds R. Du Plessis, P. Bunkle, K. Irwin, A. Laurie, and S. Middleton, Oxford University Press, Auckland.

Else, A. (1993), *Women Together: A History of Women's Organizations in New Zealand: Nga Ropu Wahine o te Mutu*, New Zealand Historical Publications Branch, Department of Internal Affairs, Daphne Brasell Associates Press, Wellington.

Elvidge, J. (1987), 'From the fire into the frying pan: on feminists, anti-racists and Maori nationalism', *Sites*, 15, pp. 76–81.

Employment Working Group (1989), *Work Today: Employment Trends to 1989*, New Zealand Planning Council, Wellington.

Endres, A. (1984), 'The New Zealand full employment goal', *New Zealand Journal of Industrial Relations*, 9, pp. 33–44.

Endres, A. (1989), 'Perceptions of full employment in relation to other major policy goals', in *The Making of Rogernomics*, ed. B. Easton, Auckland University Press, Auckland.

Epstein, R. (1984), 'In defense of the contract at will', *University of Chicago Law Review*, 51:4, pp. 947–87.

Esping-Andersen, G. (1985), 'Power and distributional regimes', *Politics and Society*, 14:2, pp. 223–56.

Esping-Andersen, G. (1989), 'The three political economies of the welfare state', *Canadian Review of Sociology and Anthropology*, 26:1, pp. 10–36.

Esping-Andersen, G. (1990), *The Three Worlds of Welfare Capitalism*, Polity Press, Cambridge.

Evans, R. (1994), 'The negotiation of powerlessness Maori feminism, a perspective', in *Hecate: An Interdisciplinary Journal of Women's Liberation*, Special New Zealand Issue, Arts Queensland Australian Council for the Arts, 20:2, pp. 53–65.

Ewer, P. et al. (1991), *Politics and the Accord*, Pluto Press, Sydney.

Fancy, H. (1993), 'The role of Treasury in the Budget process', in *Decision Making in New Zealand Government*, eds J. Nethercote, B. Galligan, and C. Walsh, Federalism Research Centre, Canberra.

Farrar, J. (ed.) (1993), *Takeovers, Institutional Investors, and the Modernization of Corporate Laws*, Oxford University Press, Auckland.

Fenwick, P. (1980), 'Fertility, sexuality and social control in New Zealand', in *Women in New Zealand Society*, eds B. Hughes and P. Bunkle, Allen & Unwin, Wellington.

Fine, B. (1975), *Marx's Capital*, Macmillan, London.

Fine, B. (1982), *Theories of Capitalist Economy*, Edward Arnold, London.

Fine, B. (1989), *Marx's Capital* (3rd ed.), Macmillan, London.

Fine, M. and Asch, A. (eds) (1988), *Women with Disabilities: Essays in Psychology, Culture and Politics*, Temple University Press, Philadelphia.

Fisk, M. (1989), *The State and Justice*, Cambridge University Press, Cambridge.

Flax, J. (1992), 'Beyond equality: gender, justice and difference', in *Beyond Equality and Difference: Citizenship, feminist politics and female subjectivity*, eds G. Bock and S. James, Routledge, London.

Fox, A. (1973), 'Industrial relations: a social critique of pluralist ideology', in *The Business Enterprise in Modern Industrial Society*, ed. J. Child, Collier Macmillan, London.

Franklin, S. (1978), *Trade, Growth and Anxiety: New Zealand Beyond the Welfare State*, Methuen, Wellington.

Franks, J. and Meyer, C. (1990), 'Corporate ownership and corporate control: a study of France, Germany, and the UK', *Economic Policy*, 10, pp. 189–231.

Franzway, S., Court, D. and Connell, R. (1989), *Staking a Claim: Feminism, Bureaucracy and the State*, Allen & Unwin, Sydney.

Fraser, N. (1989), *Unruly Practices: Power, Discourse and Gender in Contemporary Social Theory*, Polity Press, Cambridge.

Friedman, M. and Friedman, R. (1980), *Free To Choose*, Secker & Warburg, London.

Galtry, J. (1995), 'Breastfeeding, labour market changes and public policy in New Zealand: is promotion of breastfeeding enough?', *Social Policy Journal of New Zealand/ Te Puna Whakaaro*, 5, pp. 2–16.

Galvin, B. (1985), 'Some reflections on the operation of the executive', in *New Zealand Politics in Perspective* (1st ed.) ed. H. Gold, Longman Paul, Auckland.

Galvin, B. (1991), *Policy Co-ordination, Public Sector and Government*, Institute of Policy Studies, Wellington.

Gamble, A. (1988), *The Free Economy and the Strong State*, Macmillan, London.

Gandy, O. (1992), 'Public relations and public policy: the structuration of dominance in the information age', in *Rhetorical and Critical Approaches to Public Relations*, E. Toth and R. Heath, Lawrence Erlbaum Associates, Hillsdale, New Jersey.

Garrison, C. (1990), 'The defect in supply-side interpretations of the 1960s and 1970s', *Journal of Economic Issues*, 24:1, pp. 135-148.

Gibson-Graham, J. K. (1995), 'Beyond patriarchy and capitalism: reflections on political subjectivity', in *Transitions: New Australian Feminisms*, eds B. Caine and R. Pringle, Allen & Unwin, St Leonards.

Giddens, A. (1973), *The Class Structure of Advanced Societies*, Hutchinson, London.

Giddens, A. (1981), *The Class Structure of Advanced Societies* (2nd ed.), Hutchinson, London.

Giles, A. (1989), 'Industrial relations theory, the state and politics', in *Theories and Concepts in Comparative Industrial Relations*, eds J. Barbash and K. Barbash, University of South Carolina Press, Columbia.

Gobbi, M. (1994), The Cyclical Behaviour of Prices in New Zealand, unpublished MA thesis, Victoria University, Wellington.

Goldfinch, S., and Roper, B. (1993), 'Treasury's role in state policy formulation during the post-war era', in *State and Economy in New Zealand*, eds B. Roper and C. Rudd, Oxford University Press, Auckland.

Gordon, L., and Codd, J. (eds) (1991), 'Education policy and the changing role of the state', *Delta Studies in Education*, Number 1, Massey University Press, Palmerston North.

Gordon, P. and Klug, E. (1986), *New Right, New Racism*, Searchlight Publications, London.

Gottschalk, P. (1993), 'Changes in inequality of family income in seven industrialised countries', *American Economic Review*, 83:2, pp. 136–42.

Gould, J. (1982), *The Rake's Progress*, Hodder & Stoughton, Auckland.

Gould, J. (1985), *The Muldoon Years*, Hodder & Stoughton, Auckland.

Grace, G. (1990), 'Labour and education: the crisis and settlements of education policy', in *The Fourth Labour Government* (2nd ed.), eds M. Holland and J. Boston, Auckland University Press, Auckland.

Gramsci, A. (1920),'Unions and Councils' from L'Ordine Nuovo (12. 6. 20), in *Selections from Political Writings, 1910-20*, A. Gramsci (1977), International Publishers, New York.

Gramsci, A. (1971), *Selections from the Prison Notebooks*, Lawrence & Wishart, London.

Grant, W. and Nath, S. (1984), *The Politics of Economic Policymaking*, Basil Blackwell, Oxford.

Grassl, W. (1986), 'Markets and morality: Austrian perspectives on the economic approach to human behaviour', in *Austrian Economics: Historical and Philosophical Background*, eds W. Grassl and B. Smith, Croom Helm, London and Sydney.

Green, D. (1987), *The New Right: The Counter Revolution in Political, Economic and Social Thought*, Wheatsheaf Books, Sussex.

Green, D. (1996), *From Welfare Society to Civil Society: Towards Welfare that Works in New Zealand*, New Zealand Business Roundtable, Wellington.

Greenland, H. (1984), 'Ethnicity as ideology: the critique of Pakeha society', in *Tauiwi: Racism and Ethnicity in New Zealand*, eds P. Spoonley et al., Dunmore Press, Palmerston North.

Griffin, K. (1988/89), 'Monetarism', *Journal of Business Administration*, 18:1/2, pp. 67–109.

Gunew, S. and Yeatman, A. (eds) (1993), *Feminism and the Politics of Difference*, Bridget Williams Books, Wellington.

Gwartney-Gibbs, P. (1988), 'Sex segregation in the paid workforce: the New Zealand case', *Australia and New Zealand Journal of Sociology*, 24:2, pp. 264–78.

Hahn, F. (1984), *Equilibrium and Macroeconomics*, Basil Blackwell, Oxford.

Hale, M. and Kelly, R. (eds) (1989), *Gender, Democracy and Representative Bureaucracies*, Greenwood Press, New York.

Hall, P. (1986), *Governing the Economy: The Politics of State Intervention in Britain and France*, Polity Press, Cambridge.

Hall, S. (1988), 'The toad in the garden: Thatcherism among the theorists', in *Marxism and the Interpretation of Culture*, eds C. Nelson and L. Grossberg, Macmillan Education Ltd, London.

Hall, V. (1993), 'Some thoughts on the sustainability of economic growth', *Victoria Economic Commentaries*, 10:2, pp. 7–26.

Hall, V. (1995), *Economic Growth Performance in the Context of New Zealand's Economic Reforms*, Discussion Paper No. 329, Centre for Economic Policy Research, Australian National University, Canberra.

Hall, V. (1996), 'Growth', in *A Study of Economic Reform: The Case of New Zealand*, eds A. Bollard, R. Lattimore, and B. Silverstone, North-Holland, Amsterdam.

Hammond, S. and Harbridge, R. (1993), 'The impact of the Employment Contracts Act on women at work', *New Zealand Journal of Industrial Relations*, 18:1, pp. 15–30.

Hanson, E. (1980), *The Politics of Social Security*, Oxford University Press, Auckland.

Harbridge, R. (1990), 'Flexibility in collective wage bargaining in New Zealand: facts and folklore', *New Zealand Journal of Industrial Relations*, 15:3, pp. 241–50.

Harbridge, R. (1993b), 'Bargaining and the Employment Contracts Act: an overview', in *Employment Contracts: New Zealand Experiences*, ed. R. Harbridge, Victoria University Press, Wellington.

Harbridge, R. (1993c), *Service Workers Union Women Members Survey—Report*, Wellington.

Harbridge, R. (1994), *Labour Market Regulation and Employment: Trends in New Zealand*, Industrial Relations Centre, Victoria University, Wellington.

Harbridge, R. (ed.) (1993a), *Employment Contracts: New Zealand Experiences*, Victoria University Press, Wellington.

Harbridge, R. and Hince, K. (1992) *Decollectivisation of Industrial Relations in New Zealand: Issues of Union Membership and Structure*, Working Paper 1/92, Industrial Relations Centre, Victoria University, Wellington.

Harbridge, R. and Kiely, P. (1995), *Dynamism and Conservatism: The Role of the Judiciary in New Zealand's Employment Contracts Act*, Industrial Relations Centre, Victoria University, Wellington.

Harbridge, R. and McCaw, S. (1991), 'The Employment Contracts Act 1991: new bargaining arrangements in New Zealand', *Asia-Pacific HRM*, 29:3, pp. 5–26.

Harbridge, R., Hince, K. and Honeybone, A. (1995), *Unions and Union Membership in New Zealand*, Working Paper 2/95, Industrial Relations Centre, Victoria University, Wellington.

Harbridge, R., Honeybone, A. and Kiely, P. (1994), *Employment Contracts: Bargaining Trends and Employment Update: 1993/4*, Industrial Relations Centre, Victoria University, Wellington.

Harcourt, G. (1985), 'Post-Keynesianism: quite wrong and/or nothing new', in *Post-Keynesian Economic Theory*, eds P. Arestis and T. Skouras, Wheatsheaf Books, Sussex.

Harris, P. and McLeay, E. (1993), 'The legislature', in *Changing Politics? The Electoral Referendum 1993*, ed. G. Hawke, Institute of Policy Studies, Wellington.

Harvey, O. (1992), 'The unions and the government: the rise and fall of the Compact', in *Controlling Interests: Business, the State and Society in New Zealand*, eds J. Deeks and N. Perry, Auckland University Press, Auckland.

Hawke, A. (1991), *Male-Female Wage Differentials: How Important is Occupational Segregation?*, Discussion Paper 256, Australian National University Centre for Economic Policy Research, Canberra.

Hawke, G. (1985), *The Making of New Zealand: An Economic History*, Cambridge University Press, Cambridge

Hawkesworth, M. (1990), *Beyond Oppression: Feminist Theory and Political Strategy*, The Continuum Publishing Company, New York.

Haworth, N. (1992), 'National sovereignty, deregulation and the multinational: New Zealand in the 1980s', in *Controlling Interests: Business, the State and Society in New Zealand*, eds J. Deeks and N. Perry, Auckland University Press, Auckland.

Hay, I. (1989), *The Caring Commodity: The Provision of Health Care in New Zealand*, Oxford University Press, Auckland.

Hayek, F. (1976), *Law, Legislation and Liberty: Volume 2. The Mirage of Social Justice*, Routledge & Kegan Paul, London and Henley.

Hayek, F. (1979), *Law, Legislation and Liberty: Volume 3. The Political Order of a Free People*, Routledge & Kegan Paul, London and Henley.

Hayek, F. (1982), 'The use of knowledge in society', in *The Libertarian Reader*, ed. T. Machan, Rowman & Littlefield, New Jersey.

Heal, S. (1995), 'The struggle over the Employment Contracts Act 1987-1991', in *Labour, Employment and Work in New Zealand 1994*, ed. P. Morrison, Proceedings of the Sixth Conference, Department of Geography, Victoria University, Wellington.

Heap, S. (1989), *Rationality in Economics*, Basil Blackwell, Oxford.

Hechter, M. (1975), *Internal Colonialism: The Celtic Fringe in British National Development 1536-1966*, University of California Press, Berkeley and Los Angeles.

Hechter, M. (1987), *Principles of Group Solidarity*, University of California Press, Berkeley.

Hechter, M. and Levi, M. (1979), 'The Comparative Analysis of Ethnoregional Movements', *Ethnic and Racial Studies*, 2:3, pp.260–74.

Heery, E. and Kelly, J. (1994), *Working for the Union*, Cambridge University Press, Cambridge.

Held, D. (1987) *Models of Democracy*, Polity Press, Cambridge.

Held, D. (ed.) (1993), *Prospects for Democracy*, Polity Press, Cambridge.

Henning, J. (1995), 'The Employment Contracts Act and work stoppages', *New Zealand Journal of Industrial Relations*, 20:1, pp. 77–92.

Hernes, H. (1987), 'Women and the welfare state: the transition from private to public dependence', in *Women and the State: The Shifting Boundaries of Public and Private*, ed. A. Showstack Sassoon, Hutchinson, London.

Hettne, B. (ed.) (1995), *International Political Economy*, Zed Books, London.

Hicks, J. (1979), *Causality in Economics*, Basic Books, New York.

Higgot, R. (1991), 'International constraints on labor's economic policy', in *Business and Government under Labor*, eds B. Galligan and G. Singleton, Longman Cheshire, Melbourne.

Hill, R. and Novitz, R. (1985), Class, Gender and Technological Change, paper delivered to New Zealand Sociological Association Conference.

Hince, K. and Vranken, M. (1991), 'A controversial reform of New Zealand labour laws: The Employment Contracts Act 1991', *International Labour Review*, 130:4, pp. 475–93.

Hindess, B. (1993), 'Democratic theory', *Political Theory Newsletter*, 5:2, pp. 126–39.

Hirst, P. (1990), *Representative Democracy and its Limits*, Polity Press, Cambridge.

Hobsbawm, E. (1975), *The Age of Revolution 1789-1848*, Weidenfeld & Nicolson, London.

Hobsbawm, E. (1994), *Age of Extremes*, Michael Joseph, London.

Holland, M. and Boston, J. (eds) (1990), *The Fourth Labour Government* (2nd ed.) Oxford University Press, Auckland.

Holm, M. (1995), 'Share and share alike', *Listener*, 18 November.

Holt, J. (1986), *Compulsory Arbitration in New Zealand: The First Forty Years*, Auckland University Press, Auckland.

Holter, H. (1984), *Patriarchy in a Welfare Society*, Universitetsforlaget, Oslo.

hooks, B. (1981), *Ain't I a Woman: Black Women and Feminism*, South End Press, Boston, Massachusetts.

Hoover, K. (1988), *The New Classical Macroeconomics: A Sceptical Inquiry*, Basil Blackwell, Oxford.

Hosseini, H. (1990), 'The archaic, the obsolete and the mythical in neoclassical economics: problems with rationality and optimizing assumptions of the Jevons-Marshallian system', *American Journal of Economics and Sociology*, 49:1, pp. 81–92.

Hughes, J. (1991), 'The Employment Tribunal and the Employment Court', *New Zealand Journal of Industrial Relations*, 16:2, pp. 175–83.

Hull, G., Smith, B. and Bell-Scott, P. (eds) (1982), *All the Women are White, All the Blacks are Men, But Some of Us are Brave: Black Women's Studies*, Feminist Press, New York.

Hunn, J. (1961), *Report on Department of Maori Affairs*, Government Printer, Wellington.

Hyman, P. (1991), 'Enterprise bargaining and pay equity in New Zealand', in *Work, Work, Work: Women in the Nineties, Proceedings of the Fifth Annual Conference of the Women's Directorate*, New South Wales Department of Further Education, Training and Employment.

Hyman, P. (1993), 'Equal pay for women after the Employment Contracts Act: legislation and practice—the emperor with no clothes?', *New Zealand Journal of Industrial Relations*, 18:1, pp. 44–57.

Hyman, P. (1994), *Women and Economics: A New Zealand Feminist Perspective*, Bridget Williams Books, Wellington.

Hyman, R. (1971), *Marxism and the Sociology of Trade Unionism*, Pluto Press, London.

Hyman, R. (1979), 'The politics of workplace trade unionism: recent tendencies and some problems for theory', reprinted in *The Political Economy of Industrial Relations*, R. Hyman (1989), Macmillan, London.

Income Distribution Group (1990), *Who Gets What? The Distribution of Income and Wealth in New Zealand*, New Zealand Planning Council, Wellington.

Infometrics Business Services Limited (1991), Mitigating misery: a preliminary assessment of New Zealanders' capacity to absorb cuts in real income, unpublished paper, Wellington.

International Labour Office (ILO) (1964–66), *The Costs of Social Security*, ILO, Geneva.

Irwin, K. (1992), 'Towards theories of Maori feminism', in *Feminist Voices: Women's Studies Texts for Aotearoa/New Zealand*, eds R. Du Plessis, P. Bunkle, K. Irwin, A. Laurie, and S. Middleton, Oxford University Press, Auckland.

Iverson, S. (1987), 'Why women get paid less', *Broadsheet*, January–February: 146, pp. 24–40.

Jackson, K. (1973), *New Zealand Politics of Change*, A.H. & A.W. Reed, Wellington.

James, B. and Saville-Smith, K. (1989), *Gender, Culture and Power*, Oxford University Press, Auckland.

James, B. and Saville-Smith, K. (1992), 'Feminist perspectives on complex organisations', in *The Gender Factor—Women in New Zealand Organisations*, ed. S. Olsson, Dunmore Press, Palmerston North.

James, C. (1992), *New Territory*, Bridget Williams Books, Wellington.

Jesson, B. (1987), *Behind the Mirror Glass*, Penguin, Auckland.

Jesson, B. (1989), *Fragments of Labour: The Story Behind the Fourth Labour Government*, Penguin, Auckland

Jesson, B. (1992), 'Lobbying and protest: patterns of political change at the informal level', in *New Zealand Politics in Perspective* (3rd ed.), ed. H. Gold, Longman Paul, Auckland.

Johnston, P. and Pihama, L. (1994), 'The marginalisation of Maori women', *Hecate: Special Aotearoa/New Zealand Issue*, 20:2, pp. 83–97.

Johnston, P. and Pihama, L. (1995), 'What counts as difference and what differences count: gender, race and the politics of difference', in *Toi Wahine: The Worlds of Maori Women*, eds K. Irwin and I. Ramsden, Penguin Books, Auckland.

Jones, D. (1992), 'Looking in my own backyard: the search for white feminist theories of racism for Aotearoa', in *Feminist Voices: Women's Studies Texts for Aotearoa/ New Zealand*, eds R. Du Plessis, P. Bunkle, K. Irwin, A. Laurie, and S. Middleton, Oxford University Press, Auckland.

Jones, D. (1995), 'Setting up the targets: the construction of equal employment opportunity (EEO) "target groups" in the New Zealand Public Service', *Women's Studies Journal*, 11:1, 2, pp. 95–111.

Joseph, G. and Lewis, J. (1981), *Common Differences: Conflict In Black and White Feminist Perspectives*, Anchor Books, New York.

Julian, R. (1992), 'Women: how significant a force?', in *New Zealand Politics in Perspective* (3rd ed.), ed. H. Gold, Longman Paul, Auckland.

Katouzian, H. (1980), *Ideology and Method in Economics*, New York University Press, New York.

Keller, B. (1990), 'The state as corporate actor in industrial relations system', *Journal of Industrial Relations*, 32:2, pp. 254–68

Kelly, J. (1988), *Trade Unions and Socialist Politics*, Verso, London.

Kelsey, J. (1990), *A Question of Honour? Labour and the Treaty*, Allen & Unwin, Wellington.

Kelsey, J. (1993), *Rolling Back the State*, Bridget Williams Books, Wellington.

Kelsey, J. (1995), *The New Zealand Experiment*, Auckland University Press, Auckland Also published as *Economic Fundamentalism: The New Zealand Experiment— A world model for structural adjustment?*, Pluto Press, London.

Kendis, K. and Kendis, R. (1976), 'The street boy identity: an alternate strategy of Boston's Chinese-Americans', *Urban Anthropology*, 5, pp. 1–18.

Kerr, R. (1993a), 'A court for employment or unemployment?', *The Independent*, 7 May.

Kerr, R. (1993b), 'Employment contracts undermined by judicial activism', *The Independent*, 14 May.

Kim, K., Buckle, R. and Hall, V (1994), 'Key features of New Zealand business cycles', *The Economic Record*, 70:208, pp. 56–72.

Kim, K., Buckle, R. and Hall, V. (1995), 'Dating New Zealand Business Cycles', *New Zealand Economic Papers*, 29:2, pp. 143–72.

King, A., (1975), 'Overload: Problems of Governing in the 1970s', *Political Studies*, 23:2/3, pp. 284–96.

King, D. (1987), *The New Right: Politics, Markets, and Citizenship*, Macmillan, London.

King, M. (1992), 'Between two worlds', in *The Oxford History of New Zealand* (2nd ed.), ed. G. Rice, Oxford University Press, Auckland.

Kleinknecht, A., Mandel, E. and Wallerstein, I. (eds) (1992), *New Findings in Long-Wave Research*, St Martin's Press, London.

Koopman-Boyden P. and Scott , C. (1984), *The Family and Government Policy in New Zealand*, Allen & Unwin, Sydney.

Krasner, S. (1988), 'Sovereignty: an institutional perspective', *Comparative Political Studies*, 21:1, pp. 66–94.

Krueger, A. (1978), *Liberalization Attempts and Consequences*, National Bureau of Economic Research, Cambridge, Massachusetts.

Krueger, A. (1985), *Economic Liberalization Experiences: The Costs and Benefits*, New Zealand Treasury, Wellington.

Krueger, A. et al. (eds) (1981-83), *Trade and Employment in Developing Countries*, University of Chicago Press, Chicago.

Krugman, P. (1994), *Peddling Prosperity: Economic Sense and Nonsense in the Age of Diminished Expectations*, Norton, New York.

Kumon, S. and Rosovsky, H. (eds) (1994), *The Political Economy of Japan: Volume 3: Cultural and Social Dynamics*, Stanford University Press, Stanford.

Lal, D. (1983), *The Poverty of 'Development Economics'*, Institute of Economic Affairs, London.

Lamare, J. and Vowles, J. (1995), The Limits of Social Choice Theory: Electoral System Change in New Zealand, paper presented to the Australasian Political Science Association Annual Conference, Melbourne.

Lange, D. (1986), *The New Welfare State: The Mackintosh Memorial Lecture.*

Larner, W. (1996), 'Feminisation of the labour force', in *Changing Places: New Zealand in the Nineties*, eds R. Le Heron and E. Pawson, Longman Paul, Auckland.

Law, D. and Gill, S. (1988), *The Global Political Economy*, Harvester Wheatsheaf, Hemel Hemstead.

Laws, G. (1988), 'Privatisation and the Local Welfare State: the Case of Toronto's Social Services', *Transactions*, 13, pp. 433–48.

Le Heron, R. (1993), *Globalized Agriculture*, Pergamon Press, Oxford.

Le Heron, R. (1996), 'Globalisation and the economy', in *Changing Places: New Zealand in the Nineties*, eds R. Le Heron and E. Pawson, Longman Paul, Auckland.

Le Heron, R. and Pawson, E. (1996a), Introduction, in *Changing Places: New Zealand in the Nineties*, eds R. Le Heron and E. Pawson, Longman Paul, Auckland.

Le Heron, R. and Pawson, E. (eds) (1996b), *Changing Places: New Zealand in the Nineties*, Longman Paul, Auckland.

Lijphart, A. (1984), *Democracies*, Yale University Press, New Haven and London.

Lijphart, A. (1989), 'Democratic political systems: types, cases, causes and consequences', *Journal of Theoretical Politics*, 1:1, pp. 33–48

Lijphart, A. and Crepaz, M. (1991), 'Corporatism and consensus democracy in eighteen countries: conceptual and empirical linkages', *British Journal of Politics*, 21:2, 235–56.

Lindblom, C. (1977), *Politics and Markets*, Basic Books, New York.

Lindblom, C. (1988[1959]), 'The "Science" of muddling through', in *Democracy and Market System*, Norwegian University Press, London and New York.

Little, I. and Mirrlees, J. (1974), *Project Appraisal and Planning for Developing Countries*, London, Heinemann.

Little, I., Scott, M. and Scitovsky, T. (1970), *Industry and Trade in Some Developing Countries: A Comparative Study*, Oxford University Press, London.

Loomis, T. (1990), *Pacific Migrant Labour*, Averbury, Aldershot.

Lorde, A. (1984), *Sister Outsider*, The Crossing Press, New York.

Lovell-Smith, M. (1992), *The Woman Question: Writings by the Women who Won the Vote*, New Women's Press, Auckland.

Loveridge, A. and Scholffel, P. (1991), *Who Works at Home?: A New Zealand Profile*, DSIR Social Science, Christchurch.

Low, A. (1970), 'Indicative planning—the New Zealand experience', in *Proceedings of the Conference of Australian and New Zealand Economists*, Part 2, May.

Lukes, S. (1974), *Power: A Radical View*, Macmillan, London.

Lyman, S. and Douglas, W. (1973), 'Ethnicity: strategies of collective and individual impression management', *Social Research*, 40, pp. 344–65.

MacDonald, M. (1981), Implications of understanding women in the labour market: segmentation analysis—the unanswered questions, paper delivered to SSHRC Workshop on Women in the Canadian Labour Force, Vancouver.

Macdonald, C. (ed.) (1993), *The Vote, the Pill and the Demon Drink: A History of Feminist Writing in New Zealand, 1869-1993*, Bridget Williams Books, Wellington.

MacKinnon, C. (1989), *Toward a Feminist Theory of the State*, Harvard University Press, Cambridge, Massachusetts.

Maitra, P (1993), 'Internationalization of production and capitalism's dilemma', *International Journal of Social Economics*, 20:9, pp. 22–42.

Maitra, P. (1986), *Population, Technology and Development*, Gower, Aldershot.

Maitra, P. (1996a), *Globalisation of Capitalism in Third World Countries*, Praeger, London and Connecticut.

Maitra, P. (1996b), 'The end of the Cold War, the internationalisation of capitalism and the negation of nation states', in *Global Affairs: New World Order*, ed. R. Pettman, Occasional Publication No. 8, Department of Politics, Victoria University, Wellington.

Mandel, E. (1968), *Marxist Economic Theory*, Monthly Review Press, New York.

Mandel, E. (1969), *An Introduction to Marxist Economic Theory*, Pathfinder Press, New York.

Mandel, E. (1975), *Late Capitalism*, Verso, London.

Mandel, E. (1978), *Late Capitalism* (rev. ed.), Verso, London.

Mandel, E. (1979), Introduction, in *Capital*, K. Marx, Penguin, London.

Mandel, E. (1980), *Long Waves of Capitalist Development: The Marxist Interpretation*, Cambridge University Press, Cambridge.

Mandel, E. (1985), 'Marx, the present crisis and the future of labour', in *Socialist Register 1985-86*, eds R. Miliband et al., Merlin Press, London.

Mandel, E. (1995), *Long Waves of Capitalist Development* (2nd ed.), Verso, London.

Mannion, R. (1993), 'Breaking up is hard to do', *Sunday Times*, 25 July.

March, J. and Olsen, J. (1984), 'The new institutionalism: organisational factors in political life', *American Political Science Review*, 78:3, pp. 734–49.

Marglin, S. and Schor, J. (eds) (1992), *The Golden Age of Capitalism*, Clarendon Press, Oxford.

Martin, J. (1982), *State Papers*, Department of Sociology, Massey University, Palmerston North.

Marx, K. (1894), *Capital Volume 3*, International Publishers, New York.

Marx, K. (1973), *Grundrisse*, Pelican, London.

Marx, K. (1976), *Capital*, Penguin, London.

Mason, G. (1979a), 'Restructuring the New Zealand economy', *New Zealand Monthly Review*, April, pp. 6–7.

Mason, G. (1979b), Keynesianism and capitalist crisis: US arms production and the New Zealand construction sector, unpublished paper, University of Canterbury, Christchurch.

Mathias, P. (1969), *The First Industrial Nation*, Methuen, London.

McAndrew, I. and Hursthouse, P. (1991), 'Reforming labour relations: what southern employers say', *New Zealand Journal of Industrial Relations*, 16:1, pp. 538–55.

McCloskey, D. (1985), *The Rhetoric of Economics*, University of Wisconsin Press, Madison.

McDowell, T. (1985), Tokenism in the Ministry, *Broadsheet*, 128, pp. 28–30.

McIntosh, M. (1978), 'The state and the oppression of women', in *Feminism and Materialism: Women and Modes of Production*, eds A. Kuhn and A. Wolpe, Routledge & Kegan Paul, London.

McKenzie, P. (1993), 'Takeovers: the New Zealand experience', in *Takeovers, Institutional Investors, and the Modernization of Corporate Laws*, ed. J. Farrar, Oxford University Press, Auckland.

McRobie, A. (ed.) (1993), *Taking It to the People?*, Hazard Press, Christchurch.

Meiksins, P. (1986), 'Beyond the boundary question', *New Left Review*, 157, pp. 121–28.

Metge, J. (1976), *The Maoris of New Zealand* (rev. ed), Routledge & Kegan Paul, London.

Miles R. and Spoonley, P. (1985), 'The political economy of labour migration: an alternative to the sociology of "race" and "ethnic relations" in New Zealand', *Australian and New Zealand Journal of Sociology*, 21:1, pp. 3–26.

Miles, R. (1982), *Racism and Migrant Labour*, Routledge & Kegan Paul, London.

Miles, R. (1984), 'Summoned by capital: the political economy of labour migration', in *Tauiwi: Racism and Ethnicity in New Zealand*, eds P. Spoonley et al., Dunmore Press, Palmerston North.

Miles, R. (1989), *Racism,* Routledge, London.

Miles, R. (1993), *Racism After 'Race Relations'*, Routledge, London.

Miliband, R. (1989), *Divided Societies*, Clarendon Press, London.

Mills, C. (1948), *The New Men of Power America's Labor Leaders*, Harcourt Brace & Co., New York.

Ministerial Committee on Assisted Reproductive Technologies (1994), *Assisted Human Reproduction: Navigating Our Future*, Department of Health, Wellington.

Ministry of Education (1993), *Education for the 21st Century: A Discussion Document*, Ministry of Education, Wellington.

Ministry of Education (1995), *Education Statistics of New Zealand 1994*, Government Printer, Wellington.

Ministry of Women's Affairs (1996), *The Full Picture: Te Tirohanga Whanui: Guidelines for gender analysis*, Wellington.

Ministry of Women's Affairs/Minitatanga mo nga Wahine (1988), *Te Urupare Rangapu/Partnership Response*, Ministry of Women's Affairs, Wellington.

Ministry of Women's Affairs (1994), *New Zealand Report on Progress Towards the Implementation of the Nairobi Forward-Looking Strategies for the Advancement of Women—The Official Report to Beijing*, Wellington.

Mitchell, A. (1969), *Politics and People in New Zealand*, Whitcombe & Tombs, Christchurch.

Mitchell, B. and Deane, P. (1962), *Abstract of British Historical Statistics*, Cambridge University Press, Cambridge.

Moraga, C. and Anzaldua, G. (eds) (1981), *This Bridge Called My Back: Writings By Radical Women of Colour*, Persephone Press, Watertown, Massachusetts.

Moriarty, M. (1945), 'Administering the policy of economic stabilization', *New Zealand Journal of Public Administration*, 7:2, pp. 27–37.

Moriaty, M. (1956), 'Making economic policy in New Zealand', *Economic Record*, 32, pp. 224–38.

Morrison, A. (1987), 'Treasury forges a power base', *Dominion*, 9 November.

Moseley, F. (1985), 'The rate of surplus value in the postwar US economy: a critique of Weisskopf's estimates', *Cambridge Journal of Economics*, 9:1, pp. 57–79.

Moseley, F. (1991), *The Falling Rate of Profit in the Postwar United States Economy*, St Martin's Press, New York.

Muldoon, R. (1968), *Economic Review*, Government Printer, Wellington.

Mulgan, R. (1989a), *Democracy and Power in New Zealand* (2nd ed.), Oxford University Press, Auckland.

Mulgan, R. (1989b), *Maori, Pakeha and Democracy*, Oxford University Press, Auckland.

Mulgan, R. (1992), 'The elective dictatorship in New Zealand', in *New Zealand Politics in Perspective* (3rd ed.), ed. H. Gold, Longman Paul, Auckland.

Mulgan, R. (1993), 'A pluralist analysis of the New Zealand state', in *State and Economy in New Zealand*, eds B. Roper and C. Rudd, Oxford University Press, Auckland.

Mullard, M. (1992), *Understanding Economic Policy*, Routledge, London and New York.

Mumford, K. (1989), *Women Working—Economics and Reality*, Allen & Unwin, Sydney.

Murray, G. (1989), New Zealand corporate capitalism, unpublished PhD thesis, University of Auckland, Auckland.

Murray, G. (1996), 'Global "Who can I kill today?" capitalism: top business in the 90s', *Social Alternatives*, 15:1, pp. 26–30.

Nagel, J. (1994), 'What political scientists can learn from 1993 electoral reform in New Zealand', *PS: Political Science and Politics*, 27:3, pp. 525–9.

Nairn, M. and Nairn, R. (1981), 'The racism of economics and the economics of racism', in *The Challenge of the Third Depression*, ed. P. Davis, Ross, Auckland.

National Advisory Council on the Employment of Women (1990), *Beyond the Barriers: The State, the Economy and Women's Employment 1984–1990*, Department of Labour, Wellington.

Neilson, D. (1995), A Regulation School Perspective of State Autonomy, the Neo-Liberal Project, and the New Zealand Experience, paper presented to the New Zealand Political Studies Association Annual Conference, Wellington.

Nelson, J. (1993), 'Value-free or valueless? Notes on the pursuit of detachment in economics', *History of Political Economy*, 25:1, pp. 121–45.

New Zealand Business Roundtable (1987), *Freedom in Employment: Why New Zealand Needs a Flexible Decentralised Labour Market*, New Zealand Business Roundtable, Wellington.

New Zealand Business Roundtable (1988), *Employment Equity: Issues of Competition and Regulation*, Submission to Working Group on EEO and Equal Pay, New Zealand Business Roundtable, Wellington.

New Zealand Business Roundtable (1990), *The Pursuit of Fairness: A Critique of the Employment Equity Bill*, Submission to the Labour Select Committee, New Zealand Business Roundtable, Wellington.

New Zealand Employers' Federation (1987), *Submission on the Labour Relations Bill*, New Zealand Employers' Federation, Wellington.

New Zealand Employers' Federation (1990), *The Benefits of Bargaining Reform*, New Zealand Employers' Federation.

New Zealand Institute of Economic Research (1992), *Quarterly Survey of Business Opinion, Quarter Ending June 1992*, New Zealand Institute of Economic Research, Wellington.

New Zealand Institute of Economic Research (1995), *Special Survey on the Impacts of the Employment Contract Act*, December, New Zealand Institute of Economic Research, Wellington.

New Zealand Journal of Industrial Relations (1987), Papers from the Labour History Symposium, 12:3.

New Zealand Planning Council (1979a), *Public Expenditure and its Financing: 1950–1979*, New Zealand Planning Council, Wellington.

New Zealand Planning Council (1979b), *The Welfare State? Social Policy in the 1980s*, New Zealand Planning Council, Wellington.

New Zealand Planning Council (1986), *Labour Market Flexibility*, New Zealand Planning Council, Wellington.

Nozick, R. (1974), *Anarchy, State and Utopia*, Basic Books, New York.

O'Brien, M. and Wilkes, C. (1993), *The Tragedy of the Market*, Dunmore Press, Palmerston North.

O'Donovan, B. (1994), 'New Zealand price-output correlations over the business cycle', *New Zealand Economic Papers*, 28:2, pp. 165–80.

O'Regan, M. (1992), 'Daring or deluded: a case study in feminist management', in *Feminist Voices: Women's Studies Texts for Aotearoa/New Zealand*, eds R. Du Plessis, P. Bunkle, K. Irwin, A. Laurie, and S. Middleton, Oxford University Press, Auckland.

OECD (1976), *Public Expenditure on Income Maintenance Programmes*, OECD, Paris.

OECD (1990/91), *Economic Survey of New Zealand*, OECD, Paris.

OECD (1993) *OECD Economic Surveys: New Zealand*, OECD, Paris.

Offe, C. (1975), 'The theory of the capitalist state and the problem of policy formation', in *Stress and Contradiction in Modern Capitalism*, eds L. Lindberg, R. Alford, C. Crouch, and C. Offe, Lexington Books, Lexington.

Offe, C. (1984), *Contradictions of the Welfare State*, Hutchinson, London.

Offe, C. (1985) *Disorganized Capitalism*, Polity Press, Oxford.

Oliver, W. (1988), 'Social policy in New Zealand: an historical overview', in *The April Report*, Royal Commission on Social Policy, Government Printer, Wellington.

Oliver, W. (1989), 'The labour caucus and economic policy formation, 1981–1984', in *The Making of Rogernomics*, ed. B. Easton, Auckland University Press, Auckland.

Olson, M. (1965), *The Logic of Collective Action*, Harvard University Press, Cambridge.

Olson, M. (1982), *The Rise and Decline of Nations: Economic Growth, Stagflation and Social Rigidities*, Yale University Press, New Haven.

Olssen, E. (1977), 'Social class in nineteenth century New Zealand', in *Social Class in New Zealand*, D. Pitt, Longman Paul, Auckland.

Olssen, E. (1986a), 'The New Zealand labour movement, 1920–40', in *Common Cause: Essays in Australian and New Zealand Labour History*, ed. E. Fry, Allen & Unwin, Wellington.

Olssen, E. (1986b), 'Some reflections about the origins of the "Red" Federation of Labour, 1909–13', in *Common Cause: Essays in Australian and New Zealand Labour History*, ed. E. Fry, Allen & Unwin, Wellington.

Olssen, E. (1988), *The Red Feds: Revolutionary Industrial Unionism and the New Zealand Federation of Labour 1908–1913*, Oxford University Press, Auckland.

Olssen, E. and Richardson, L. (1986), 'The New Zealand labour movement, 1880–1920', in *Common Cause: Essays in Australian and New Zealand Labour History*, ed. E. Fry, Allen & Unwin, Wellington.

Olsson, S. (ed.) (1992), *The Gender Factor: Women in Organisations*, Dunmore Press, Palmerston North.

Openshaw, R. (1995), *Unresolved Struggle*, Dunmore Press, Palmerston North.

Orange, C. (1987), *The Treaty of Waitangi*, Allen & Unwin/Port Nicholson Press, Wellington.

Ormerod, P. (1994), *The Death of Economics*, Faber & Faber, London and Boston.

Osborne, C. and Wells, G. (1995), Debt and taxes in NZM, paper prepared for New Zealand Treasury's Modelling Workshop, Wellington.

Oxenbridge, S. (1996) New Zealand Unions and the Organization of the Low Wage Service Sector, paper presented to the AFL-CIO/Cornell University Research Conference on Organizing, Washington DC.

Palmer, G. (1979a), *Compensation For Incapacity: A Study of Law and Social Change in New Zealand and Australia*, Oxford University Press, Wellington.

Palmer, G. (1979b), *Unbridled Power*, Oxford University Press, Auckland.

Palmer, G. (1992), *New Zealand's Constitution in Crisis*, John McIndoe, Dunedin.

Panitch, L. (1977), 'The development of corporatism in liberal democracies', *Comparative Political Studies*, 10:1, pp. 61–90.

Pateman, C. (1988), *The Sexual Contract*, Polity Press, Cambridge.

Pateman, C. (1992), 'Equality, difference, subordination: the politics of motherhood and women's citizenship', in *Beyond Equality and Difference: Citizenship, Feminist Politics and Female Subjectivity*, eds G. Bock and S. James, Routledge, London.

Pawson, E. (1996), 'Labour', in *Changing Places.New Zealand in the Nineties*, eds R. Le Heron and E. Pawson, Longman Paul, Auckland.

Pearce, G. (1986), Where is New Zealand going, unpublished PhD thesis, University of Canterbury, Christchurch.

Pearson, D. and Thorns, D. (1986), 'A tale of two cities: marriage and mobility in New Zealand', *Australian and New Zealand Journal of Sociology*, 22:2, pp. 208–24.

Pearson, D. (1984), 'Two paths of colonialism', in *Tauiwi: Racism and Ethnicity in New Zealand*, eds P. Spoonley et al., Dunmore Press, Palmerston North.

Pearson, D. (1990), *A Dream Deferred: The Origins of Ethnic Conflict in New Zealand*, Allen & Unwin, Wellington.

Pearson, D. and Thorns, D. (1983), *Eclipse of Equality*, Allen & Unwin, Sydney.

Peetz, D., Quinn, D., Edwards, L. and Riedel, P. (1993), 'Workplace bargaining in New Zealand: radical change at work', in *Workplace Bargaining in the International Context*, eds D. Peetz, A. Preston, and J. Docherty, DIR, AGPS, Canberra.

Perry, M. and Goldfinch, S. (1996), 'Small business networking outside the industrial district', *Tijdschrift voor Economische en Sociale Geografie*, 87:3 pp. 222–36.

Pettman, J. (1992), *Living in the Margins*, Allen & Unwin, North Sydney.

Pettman, R. (1996), *Global Affairs: New World Order*, Occasional Publication No. 8, Department of Politics, Victoria University, Wellington.

Phillips, A. (1991), *Engendering Democracy*, Polity Press, Cambridge.

Pierson, C. (1993), 'Democracy, markets and capital: are there necessary economic limits to democracy?', in *Prospects for Democracy*, ed. D. Held, Polity Press, Cambridge.

Piven, F. (1984), 'Women and the state: Ideology, power and the welfare state', *Socialist Review*, 14:2, pp. 13–19.

Plowman, D. and Street, M. (1993), 'Industrial relations and economic restructuring in Australia and New Zealand: employers' agendas', in *Economic Restructuring and Industrial Relations in Australia and New Zealand*, eds M. Bray and N. Haworth, ACIRRT Monograph No. 8, University of Sydney, Sydney.

Poata-Smith, E. (1996a), 'Te ao marama? Cultural solutions to Maori educational inequality: a critique', *Access: Critical Perspectives on Cultural and Policy Studies in Education*, 15:1, pp. 34–56.

Poata-Smith, E. (1996b), 'He pokeke uenuku i tu ai: the evolution of contemporary Maori protest', in *Nga Patai: Racism and Ethnic Relations in Aotearoa/New Zealand*, eds P. Spoonley, D. Pearson, and C. MacPherson, Dunmore Press, Palmerston North.

Poiner, G. and Wills, S. (1991), *The Gifthorse: A Critical Look at Equal Employment Opportunities in Australia*, Allen & Unwin, Sydney.

Polaschek, R. (1958), *Government Administration in New Zealand*, Oxford University Press, London.

Polsby, N. (1963), *Community Power and Political Theory*, Yale University Press, New Haven.

Pontusson, J. (1991), 'Labor, corporatism and industrial policy: the Swedish case in comparative perspective', *Comparative Politics*, 23:2, pp. 163–79.

Porter, M. (1992), *Capital Choices: Changing the Way America Invests in Industry*, Council on Competitiveness, Washington DC.

Pound, J. and Zeckhouser, R. (1988), *The Market for Corporate Control, The Economics of Corporate Takeovers and the New Zealand Takeover Code: An Analysis and Proposals for Reform*, New Zealand Centre for Independent Studies, Auckland.

Powell, A. (1995), Some features of NZM, the New Zealand Treasury's model, paper presented to the conference to launch NZM, Wellington.

Prebble, R. (1996), *I've Been Thinking*, Seaview Publishers, Auckland.

Prichard, M. (1970), *An Economic History of New Zealand to 1939*, Collins, Auckland.

Prime Ministerial Task Force on Employment (1994), *Employment: The Issues*, Wellington.

Pringle, R. (1995), 'Destabilising patriarchy', in *Transitions: New Australian Feminisms*, eds B. Caine and R. Pringle, Allen & Unwin, St Leonards.

Pringle, R. and Watson, S. (1990), 'Fathers, brothers, mates: the fraternal state in Australia', in *Playing the State: Australian Feminist Interventions*, ed. S. Watson, Allen & Unwin, Sydney.

Rasmussen, E. et al. (1995), Industrial relations and labour market reforms in New Zealand, paper prepared for the PECC-HRD Task Force Meeting, Taipei.

Rayack, E. (1987), *Not so Free to Choose*, Praeger Publishers, New York.

Reder, M. (1982), 'Chicago economics: permanence and change', *Journal of Economic Literature*, 20:1, pp. 1–38

Rees, A. (1979), *The Economics of Work and Pay* (2nd ed.), Harper and Row, New York.

Rei, T. (1993a), *Maori Women and the Vote*, Huia Publishers, Wellington.

Rei, T. (1993b), 'Te Ropu Wahine Maori Toko i te Ora/Maori Women's Welfare League', in *Women Together: A History of Women's Organisations in New Zealand*, ed. A. Else, Daphne Brasell Associates Press, Wellington.

Renwick, W. (1986), *Moving Targets*, New Zealand Council for Educational Research, Wellington.

Reserve Bank (1960), 'Central banking practice in New Zealand', *Reserve Bank Bulletin*, 23:3, pp. 39–44.

Reserve Bank (1979), 'Foreign investment in New Zealand', *Supplement to Reserve Bank of New Zealand Bulletin*, November.

Richardson, L. (1981), 'Parties and political change', in *The Oxford History of New Zealand*, ed. W. Oliver, Oxford University Press, Wellington.

Richardson, R. (1995), *Making a Difference*, Shoal Bay Press, Christchurch.

Riddell, T. (1988), 'The political economy of military spending', in *The Imperiled Economy*, Book II, eds R. Cherry et al., Union for Radical Political Economics, New York.

Rinder, R. (1984), 'Supply-side economics: incentives and disaster', in *Free Market Conservatism: A Critique of Theory and Practice*, ed. E. Nell, Allen & Unwin, London.

Roberts, J. (1969a), 'A national development organisation', *New Zealand Journal of Public Administration*, 31:2, pp. 54–73.

Roberts, J. (1969b), 'A Note on the National Development Council', *New Zealand Journal of Public Administration*, 32:1, pp. 51–88.

Roberts, P. (1988), '"Supply-side" economics—theory and results', *Public Interest*, 93, Fall, pp. 16–36.

Robertson, J. (1994), *Children of Choice: Freedom and the New Reproductive Technologies*, Princeton University Press, Princeton.

Robinson, D. (1996), 'Where is the government going? Public sector strategic result areas can tell us', *Signpost*, March, pp. 3–4.

Roper, B. (1990a), The dynamics of capital in crisis: the political economy of New Zealand business 1974–1987, unpublished PhD thesis, Griffith University, Brisbane.

Roper, B. (1990b), 'Contested terrain', *New Zealand Monthly Review*, No. 325, pp. 6–12.

Roper, B. (1991a), 'From the welfare state to the free market: explaining the transition. Part I: The existing accounts', *New Zealand Sociology*, 6:1, pp. 38–64.

Roper, B. (1991b), 'From the welfare state to the free market: explaining the transition Part II: Crisis, class, ideology and the state', *New Zealand Sociology*, 6:2, pp. 135–76.

Roper, B. (1992), 'Business political activism and the emergence of the New Right in New Zealand, 1975 to 1987', *Political Science*, 44:2, pp. 1–23.

Roper, B. (1993a), 'A level playing field? Business political activism and state policy formation', in *State and Economy in New Zealand*, eds B. Roper and C. Rudd, Oxford University Press, Auckland.

Roper, B. (1993b), 'The end of the golden weather: New Zealand's economic crisis', in *State and Economy in New Zealand*, eds B. Roper and C. Rudd, Oxford University Press, Auckland.

Roper, B. (1995), 'Leading from the rear? A theoretical analysis of the contingent bureaucratic conservatism of the NZCTU leadership', in *Labour, Employment and Work in New Zealand 1994*, ed. P. Morrison, Proceedings of the Sixth Conference, Department of Geography, Victoria University, Wellington.

Roper, B. (1996), 'The collapse of Stalinism and the future of Marxism', *Access* 15:1, pp. 57–76.

Roper, J. (1995), Takeovers legislation: a Faircloughian discourse analysis, unpublished MA thesis, University of Waikato, Hamilton.

Roper, K. (1982), 'The impact of the Remuneration Act 1979–80', *New Zealand Journal of Industrial Relations*, 7:1, pp. 1–11.

Rosenberg, A. (1992), *Economics—Mathematical Politics or Science of Diminishing Returns?*, Chicago University Press, Chicago.

Rosenberg, W. (1986), *The Magic Square: What Every New Zealander Should Know About Rogernomics and the Alternatives*, Monthly Review Society, Christchurch.

Roseveare, D. and Millar, C. (1988), 'Testing the rationality of manufacturers' inflationary expectations', *New Zealand Economic Papers*, 22:1, pp. 3–13.

Rosier, P. (1986), 'Making a ministry' *Broadsheet*, May, pp. 17–22.

Roth, B. (1973), *Trade Unions in New Zealand: Past and Present*, Reed Education, Wellington.

Roth, B. (1978), 'The historical framework', in *Industrial Relations in New Zealand*, eds J. Deeks, B. Roth, J. Farmer, and G. Scott, Methuen, Wellington.

Roth, B. (1986), 'The New Zealand Trade Union Congress, 1950–51', in *Common Cause: Essays in Australian and New Zealand Labour History*, ed. E. Fry, Allen & Unwin, Wellington.

Roth, B. (1986), 'Legalised theft by deregistration', *New Zealand Journal of Industrial Relations*, 11:1, pp. 21–6.

Rowntree Foundation (1995), *Joseph Rowntree Foundation Inquiry into Income and Wealth, Volume 1*, The Joseph Rowntree Foundation, York.

Royal Commission of Inquiry on Social Security (1972), *Report on Social Security in New Zealand*, Government Printer, Wellington.

Royal Commission of Inquiry Upon Workers' Compensation (1967), *Compensation for Personal Injury in New Zealand*, Government Printer, Wellington.

Royal Commission on Social Policy (1988), *The April Report*, Government Printer, Wellington.

Rudman, R. (1974), 'Employer organisations: their development and role in industrial relations', in *Labour and Industrial Relations in New Zealand*, eds J. Howells, N. Woods, and F. Young, Pitman, Carlton.

Ryan, R. (1994), *A Survey of Labour Market Adjustments under the Employment Contracts Act 1991: Gender Analysis of the Employee Survey*, National Council on the Employment of Women, Wellington.

Sachs, J. (1994), *Russia's Struggle with Stabilization: Conceptual Issues and Evidence*, Proceedings of the World Bank Annual Conference on Development Economics, Washington DC.

Sassoon, A. Showstack (ed.) (1987), *Women and the State: The Shifting Boundaries of Public and Private*, Hutchinson, London.

Saunders, P. (1994), *Welfare and Inequality*, Cambridge University Press, Cambridge.

Savage, J. (1989), *Internal Labour Markets: Labour Adjustment Within Workplaces*, Research Monograph 45, New Zealand Institute of Economic Research, Wellington.

Savage, J. and Bollard, A. (eds) (1990), *Turning It Around : Closure and Revitalization in New Zealand Industry*, Oxford University Press, Auckland.

Saville-Smith, K. (1987), 'Women and the state', in *Public and Private Worlds*, ed. S. Cox, Allen & Unwin, Wellington.

Sayers, J. (1991), 'Women, the Employment Contracts Act and bargaining: a discussion paper', *New Zealand Journal of Industrial Relations*, 16:2, pp. 159–66.

Sayers, J. (1993), 'Women, the Employment Contracts Act, and labour flexibility', in *Employment Contracts: New Zealand Experiences*, ed. R. Harbridge, Victoria University Press, Wellington.

Sayers, J. and Tremaine, M. (1994), *The Vision and the Reality—Equal Employment Opportunities in the New Zealand Workplace*, Dunmore Press, Palmerston North.

Schroff, M. (1993), 'The Structure and Operation of the Cabinet in Relation to the Budget', in *Decision Making in New Zealand Government*, eds J. Nethercote, B. Galligan, and C. Walsh, Federalism Research Centre, Canberra.

Schwartz, H. (1994), 'Small states in big trouble: state reorganisation in Austria, Denmark, New Zealand, and Australia', *World Politics*, 46:4, pp. 527–55.

Segal, L. (1987), *Is the Future Female?: Troubled Thoughts on Contemporary Feminism*, Virago, London.

Self, P. (1993), *Government by the Market? The Politics of Public Choice*, Macmillan, Basingstoke.

Shaikh, A. (1980), 'Marxian competition versus perfect competition: further comments on the so-called choice of technique', *Cambridge Journal of Economics*, 4:1, pp. 75–83.

Shaikh, A. (1983), 'Falling rate of profit', in *A Dictionary of Marxist Thought*, eds T. Bottomore et al., Basil Blackwell, London.

Shaikh, A. (1987), 'Organic composition of capital', in *The New Palgrave: A Dictionary of Economics Volume 3*, eds J. Eatwell et al., Macmillan, London.

Shaikh, A. and Tonak, E. (1994), *Measuring the Wealth of Nations: The Political Economy of National Accounts*, Cambridge University Press, New York.

Shannon, P. (1991), *Social Policy*, Oxford University Press, Auckland.

Sharp, A. (1990), *Justice and the Maori*, Oxford University Press, Auckland.

Sharp, R. (1988), 'Old and new orthodoxies: the seductions of liberalism', in *Bowles and Gintis Revisited: Correspondence and Contradiction in Educational Theory*, ed. M. Cole, Falmer Press, Brighton.

Shaver, S. (1995), 'Women, employment and social security', in *Women in a Restructuring Australia: Work and Welfare*, eds A. Edwards and S. Magarey, Allen & Unwin, Sydney.

Shipley, J. (1991), *Social Assistance: Welfare that Works*, GP Print, Wellington.

Shirley, I., Easton, B., Briar, C. and Chatterjee, S. (1990), *Unemployment in New Zealand*, Dunmore Press, Palmerston North.

Simkin, C. (1951), *The Instability of a Dependent Economy*, Oxford University Press, London.

Singleton, G. (1990), *The Accord and the Australian Labour Movement*, Melbourne University Press, Melbourne.

Skocpol, T. (1985), 'Bringing the state back in: strategies of analysis in current research', in *Bringing the State Back In*, eds P. Evans, D. Rueschmeyer and T. Skocpol, Cambridge University Press, Cambridge.

Smith, A. (1981), *The Ethnic Revival*, Cambridge University Press, Cambridge.

Smith, A. (1986), *The Ethnic Origins of Nations*, Blackwell, Oxford.

Smith, L. (1992), *Achieving Excellence in a Competitive World*, speech notes.

Smith, M. (1993), *Pressure Power and Policy: State Autonomy and Policy Networks in Britain and the United States*, Harvester Wheatsheaf, London.

Smithin, J. (1990), *Macroeconomics after Thatcher and Reagan: The Conservative Policy Revolution in Retrospect*, Edward Elgar, Aldershot.

Smyth, A. (1996), 'A (political) postcard from a peripheral pre-postmodern state (of mind) or how alliteration and parentheses can knock you down dead in women's studies', in *Radically Speaking: Feminism Reclaimed*, eds D. Bell and R. Klein, Spinifex, Melbourne.

Spelman, E. (1990), *Inessential Woman: Problems of Exclusion in Feminist Thought*, The Women's Press, London.

Spoonley, P. (1993), *Racism and Ethnicity* (2nd ed.), Oxford University Press, Auckland.

St John, S. (1992), 'Superannuation policy', in *The Decent Society?*, eds J. Boston and P. Dalziel, Oxford University Press, Auckland.

Statistics New Zealand (1951–1981, 1991), *New Zealand Census of Population and Dwellings*, Wellington.

Statistics New Zealand (1993), *All About Women in New Zealand*, Social Policy Division, Publishing and Media Services Division, Statistics New Zealand, Wellington.

Statistics New Zealand (1993), *All About Women in New Zealand*, Wellington.

Statistics New Zealand (1994, 1995), *New Zealand Official Yearbook*, Wellington.

Statistics New Zealand (1996), *Key Statistics (March)*, Wellington.

Statistics New Zealand (1996), *Key Statistics*, January/February, June, Wellington.

Statistics New Zealand (various years), *Household Labour Force Survey*, Wellington.

Statistics New Zealand (various years), *Quarterly Employment Survey*, Wellington.

Statistics New Zealand, *Incomes*, (1992 and 1994).

Stephens, R. (1992), 'Budgeting with the benefit cuts', in *The Decent Society?*, eds J. Boston and P. Dalziel, Oxford University Press, Auckland.

Stephens, R., Waldegrave, C. and Frater, P. (1995), 'Measuring poverty in New Zealand', *Social Policy Journal of New Zealand*, 5, pp. 88–112.

Steven, R. (1978), 'Toward a class analysis of New Zealand', *Australian and New Zealand Journal of Sociology*, 14:2, pp. 113–29.

Steven, R. (1985), 'A glorious country for a labouring man', *Race Gender Class*, 1, pp. 38–56.

Steven, R. (1989), 'Land and white settler colonialism: the case of Aotearoa', in *Culture and Identity in New Zealand*, eds D. Novitz and W. Willmott, GP Books, Wellington.

Stocks, P., O'Dea, D. and Stephens, B. (1991), Who gets what now?, paper presented at the New Zealand Association of Economists' Annual Conference, Lincoln University.

Strassman, D. (1993), 'The stories of economics and the power of the storyteller', *History of Political Economy*, 25:1, pp. 147–65.

Sutch, W. (1966), *The Quest for Security in New Zealand, 1840 to 1966*, Oxford University Press, Wellington.

Sutton, F. (1985), Female-male pay differentials in the executive/clerical class of the public service, unpublished paper, Wellington.

Sweezy, P. (1942), *The Theory of Capitalist Development*, Monthly Review Press, New York.

Szaszy, M. et al. (1993), *Te Timatanga Tatau Tatau: Early Stories from Founding Members of the Maori Women's Welfare League*, Maori Women's Welfare League and Bridget Williams Books, Wellington.

Taylor, L. (1996), 'Sustainable development: an introduction', *World Development*, 24:2, pp. 215–25.

Taylor, L. (ed.) (1993), *The Rocky Road to Reform*, MIT Press, Cambridge, Massachusetts.

Te Puni Kokiri (Ministry of Maori Development) (1992), *Ka Awatea: A Report of the Ministerial Panning Group*, Government Printer, Wellington

Te Puni Kokiri (Ministry of Maori Development) (1993), *He Kakano: A Handbook of Maori Health Data*, Government Printer, Wellington.

Tennant, M. (1989), *Paupers and Providers: Charitable Aid in New Zealand*, Allen & Unwin, Wellington.

Tennant, M. (1993), 'Welfare organisations', in *Women Together: A History of Women's Organisations in New Zealand*, ed. A. Else, Daphne Brasell Associates Press, Wellington.

Thakur, R. and Gold, H. (1983), 'The politics of a new economic relationship; negotiating free trade between Australia and New Zealand', *Australian Outlook*, 37:2, pp. 82–8.

Therborn (1986), *Why Some Peoples are More Unemployed than Others*, Verso, London.

Thomson, D. (1991), 'Society and social welfare', in *The Future of the Past: Themes in New Zealand History*, eds C. Davis and P. Lineham, Department of History, Massey University, Palmerston North.

Thomson, J. (1992), *Personal Grievance Outcomes: Have there been any changes?*, Diploma in Industrial Relations Research Paper, Industrial Relations Centre, Victoria University, Wellington.

Thurow, L. (1975), *Generating Inequality: Mechanisms of Distribution in the U.S. Economy*, Basic Books, New York.

Treasury (1984), *Economic Management*, Government Printer, Wellington.

Treasury (1986) *Executive Summary of Communications Audit*, Government Printer, Wellington.

Treasury (1987), *Government Management*, Government Printer, Wellington.

Treasury (1990), *Briefing to the Incoming Government*, Government Printer, Wellington.

Treasury (1992), *The Treasury: A Profile*, Government Printer, Wellington.

Treasury (1993), *Briefing to the Incoming Government*, Government Printer, Wellington.

Tremaine, M. and McGregor, J. (1994), Negotiating the package: the managerial woman's experience in New Zealand's deregulated labour market, paper presented to the Third National Conference on Women in Leadership, Edith Cowan University, Perth.

Truman, D. (1951), *The Governmental Process*, Knopf, New York.

Urban Research Associates, Hyman, P. and Clark, A. (1987), *Equal Pay Study—Phase One Report*, Department of Labour, Wellington.

Van Mourik, A. Poot, J. and Siegers, J. (1989), 'Trends in occupational segregation of women and men in New Zealand: some new evidence', *New Zealand Economic Papers*, 23, pp. 29–50.

Vellekoop Baldock, C. (1971), *Vocational Choice and Opportunity*, University of Canterbury, Christchurch.

Venables, D. (1988), 'Our old boy network', *Listener*, 16 April.

Vowles, J. (1992), 'Business, unions, and the state: organizing economic interests in New Zealand, in *New Zealand Politics in Perspective* (3rd ed.), ed. H. Gold, Longman Paul, Auckland.

Vowles, J. (1993), 'New Zealand: capture the state?', in *First World Interest Groups*, ed. C. Thomas, Greenwood Press, Westport, Connecticut.

Vowles, J. and Aimer, P. (1994a), *Voters' Vengeance: The 1990 Election in New Zealand and the Fate of the Fourth Labour Government*, Auckland University Press, Auckland.

Vowles, J. and Aimer, P. (eds) (1994b), *Double Decision: The 1993 Election and Referendum in New Zealand*, Department of Politics, Victoria University, Wellington.

Vowles, J. et al. (1995), *Towards Consensus?: The 1993 General Election in New Zealand and the Transition to Proportional Representation*, Auckland University Press, Auckland.

Wade, R. (1990), *Governing the Market: Economic Theory and the Role of Government in East Asian Industrialization*, Princeton University Press, New Jersey.

Walby, S. (1986), *Patriarchy at Work: Patriarchal and Capitalist Relations in Employment*, Polity Press, Cambridge.

Walker, R. (1984), 'The genesis of Maori activism', *Journal of the Polynesian Society*, 93:3, pp. 267–81.

Walker, R. (1987), *Nga Tau Tohetohe: The Years of Anger*, Penguin Books, Auckland.

Walker, R. (1990), *Ka Whawhai Tonu Matou: Struggle Without End*, Penguin Books, Auckland.

Walker, R. (1992), 'The Maori people: their political development', in *New Zealand Politics in Perspective* (3rd ed), ed. H. Gold, Longman Paul, Auckland.

Walsh, P. (1984), The rejection of corporatism: trade unions, employers and the state in New Zealand, 1960–1977, unpublished PhD thesis, University of Minnesota.

Walsh, P. (1989), 'A family fight? Industrial relations reform under the fourth Labour government', in *The Making of Rogernomics*, ed. B. Easton, Auckland University Press, Auckland.

Walsh, P. (1991a), *Trade Unions in New Zealand and Economic Restructuring*,

Australian Centre for Industrial Relations Research and Teaching, Working Paper No. 17, Sydney University.

Walsh, P. (1991b), 'The State Sector Act 1988', in *Reshaping the State: New Zealand's Bureaucratic Revolution*, eds J. Boston, J. Martin, J. Pallots, and P. Walsh, Oxford University Press, Auckland.

Walsh, P. (1992), 'The Employment Contracts Act', in *The Decent Society?*, eds J. Boston and P. Dalziel, Oxford University Press, Auckland.

Walsh, P. (1994), 'An unholy alliance: the 1968 nil wage order', *New Zealand Journal of History*, 28:2, pp. 178–93.

Walsh, P. and Fougere, G. (1987), 'The unintended consequences of the arbitration system', *New Zealand Journal of Industrial Relations*, 12:3, pp. 187–98.

Walsh, P. and Ryan, R. (1993), 'The making of the Employment Contracts Act', in *Employment Contracts: New Zealand Experiences*, ed. R. Harbridge, Victoria University Press, Wellington.

Walsh, P. and Wetzel, K. (1993), 'Preparing for privatization: corporate strategy and industrial relations in New Zealand's state-owned enterprises', *British Journal of Industrial Relations*, 31:1, pp. 57–74.

Wanna, J. (1989), 'Centralisation without corporatism: the politics of New Zealand business in the recession', *New Zealand Journal of Industrial Relations*, 14:1, pp. 1–15.

Ward, A. (1974) *A Show of Justice: Racial 'Amalgamation' in Nineteenth Century New Zealand*, Auckland University Press, Auckland.

Ward, R. (1987), 'Foreign investment—a yen for something Kiwi', *Management*, 36:7, pp. 37–42.

Washington, S. (1988), 'Great expectations: the Ministry of Women's Affairs and public policy', *Race Gender Class*, 7, pp. 7–16.

Watson, S. (1995), 'Reclaiming social policy', in *Transitions: New Australian Feminisms*, eds B. Caine and R. Pringle, Allen & Unwin, St Leonards.

Watson, S. (ed.) (1990), *Playing the State: Australian Feminist Interventions*, Allen & Unwin, Sydney.

Weber, M. (1947a), *From Max Weber: Essays in Sociology*, Kegan, Paul, London.

Weber, M. (1947b), *The Theory of Economic Organisation*, Hodge, London.

Weeks, J. (1989), *A Critique of Neoclassical Macroeconomics*, Macmillan, London.

Wells, G. (1995), *Macroeconomics*, Nelson, Melbourne.

Whale, A. (1993), Voluntary welfare provision in a landscape of change, unpublished MA thesis, Department of Geography, University of Auckland.

Whitwell, J. (1990), 'The Rogernomics monetarist experiment', in *The Fourth Labour Government* (2nd ed.), eds M. Holland and J. Boston, Oxford University Press, Auckland.

Whitwell, J. (1992), 'Money and inflation: theories and evidence', in *The New Zealand Economy: Issues and Policies* (2nd ed.), eds S. Birks and S. Chatterjee, Dunmore Press, Palmerston North.

Wikander, U., Kessler-Harris, A. and Lewis, J. (eds) (1995), *Protecting Women: Labour Legislation in Europe, the United States and Australia, 1880–1920*, University of Illinois Press, Urvana and Chicago.

Wilkes, C. (1990), 'Class', in *New Zealand Society*, eds P. Spoonley, D. Pearson, and I. Shirley, Dunmore Press, Palmerston North.

Wilkes, C. (1993), 'The state as an historical subject: a periodization of state formation in New Zealand', in *State and Economy in New Zealand*, eds B. Roper and C. Rudd, Oxford University Press, Auckland.

Williams, F. (1989), *Social Policy: A Critical Introduction*, Polity Press, Cambridge.

Williams, J. (1985), 'Redefining institutional racism', *Ethnic and Racial Studies*, 8:3, pp. 323–48.

Williamson, O. (1970), *Corporate Control and Business Behaviour*, Prentice Hall, Englewood Cliffs, New Jersey.

Williamson, O. (1975), *Markets and Hierarchies: Analysis and Antitrust Implications*, Free Press, New York.

Williamson, O. (1985), *The Economic Institutions of Capitalism*, Free Press, New York.

Wilson, E. (1977), *Women and the Welfare State*, Tavistock Women's Studies, London.

Wilson, M. (1992), 'Employment Equity Act 1990: a case study in women's political influence 1984–90', in *Controlling Interests: Business, the State and Society in New Zealand*, eds J. Deeks and N. Perry, Auckland University Press, Auckland.

Wilson, M. and Enright, A. (1994), 'New Zealand's workforce policy: reflections on fairness in the 1990s', in *Leap Into the Dark*, ed. A. Sharp, Auckland University Press, Auckland.

Wolch, J. (1990), *The Shadow State*, Foundation Center, Los Angeles.

Wolfson, M. (1994), 'Eligo ergo sum: classical philosophies of the self in neoclassical economics', *History of Political Economy*, 26:2, pp. 287–25.

Wood, E. (1995), *Democracy Against Capitalism*, Cambridge University Press, Cambridge.

Wood, S. (1985), 'Work organisation', in *Work, Culture and Society*, eds R. Deem and G. Salaman, Open University Press, Milton Keynes/Philadelphia.

Wooding, P. (1992), *Macroeconomics: A New Zealand Introduction*, Prentice Hall, Sydney.

Woods, N. (1963), *Industrial Conciliation and Arbitration in New Zealand*, Government Printer, Wellington.

World Bank (1987), *World Development Report 1987*, Oxford University Press, New York.

World Economic Forum (1995), *World Competitiveness Report*, Geneva.

Wright, E. (1979), *Class Structure and Income Determination*, Academic Press, New York.

Yeatman, A. (1990), *Bureaucrats, Technocrats, Femocrats: Essays on the Contemporary Australian State*, Allen & Unwin, Sydney.

Yeatman, A. (1993), 'Voice and representation in the politics of difference', in *Feminism and the Politics of Difference*, eds S. Gunew and A. Yeatman, Bridget Williams Books, Wellington.

Yeatman, A. (1994), 'Women and the state', in *Contemporary Australian Feminism*, ed. K. Hughes, Longman Cheshire, Melbourne.

Yeatman, A. (1995), 'Justice and the sovereign self', in *Justice and Identity: Antipodean Practices*, eds M. Wilson and A. Yeatman, Bridget Williams Books, Wellington.

Zeitlin, J. (1989a), '"Rank and filism" in British labour history: a critique', *International Review of Social History*, 34, pp. 42–61.

Zeitlin, J. (1989b), '"Rank and filism" and labour history: a rejoinder to Price and Cronin', *International Review of Social History*, 34, pp. 89–102.

INDEX